Anatomy of a Short Story

Anatomy of a Short Story

NABOKOV'S PUZZLES, CODES, "SIGNS AND SYMBOLS"

Anatomy – from Latin *anatomia*, Greek *anatomē* (*ana*: separate, apart from, and *temnein*, to cut up, cut open)

Edited by Yuri Leving

continuum

Continuum International Publishing Group
80 Maiden Lane, Suite 704, New York, NY 10038
The Tower Building, 11 York Road, London SE1 7NX

www.continuumbooks.com

© Yuri Leving and contributors, 2012

All rights reserved. No part of this book may be reproduced, stored in a retrieval system, or transmitted, in any form or by any means, electronic, mechanical, photocopying, recording, or otherwise, without the permission of the publishers.

ISBN: HB: 978-1-4411-9606-4
PB: 978-1-4411-4263-4

Library of Congress Cataloging-in-Publication Data
Anatomy of a short story : Nabokov's puzzles, codes, "Signs and symbols" / edited by Yuri Leving.
p. cm.
Includes bibliographical references and index.
ISBN 978-1-4411-4263-4 (pbk. : alk. paper)-- ISBN 978-1-4411-9606-4 (hardcover : alk. paper) 1. Nabokov, Vladimir Vladimirovich, 1899-1977--Criticism and interpretation. 2. Short story. 3. Literature--Aesthetics. I. Leving, Yuri.

PS3527.A15Z56 2012
813'.54--dc23

2012016057

Typeset by Fakenham Prepress Solutions, Fakenham, Norfolk NR21 8NN
Printed and bound in the United States of America

In Memory of my Great-aunt Felya (Faina Grigorievna Pazovsky), who devoted 25 years of her life to a son diagnosed with schizophrenia

In Memory of Haim ben Mendel Deitshch, the veteran and fighter against the Nazis in World War II

CONTENTS

Part Four: Nervous System 157

Part Five: Dissection 202

CONTRIBUTORS

Hal Ackerman is an author, playwright, screenwriter, screenwriting teacher, and co-chairman of the UCLA screenwriting program. He is the author of *Write Screenplays That Sell: The Ackerman Way* (Beverley Hill, California: Tallfellow Press, 2003). His short story "Roof Garden" won the Warren Adler 2008 award for fiction. Ackerman has sold material to all of the networks and major studios. His 'soft-boiled' murder mystery, *Stein Stung*, will be out in March 2012. His play, "Testosterone: How Prostate Cancer Made a Man of Me," won the William Saroyan Centennial Award for drama and has been performed as a solo piece entitled PRICK at the 2011 United Solo Festival in New York City.

Larry Andrews is Professor Emeritus of English and Dean Emeritus of the Honors College at Kent State University. His B.A. in English from Ohio State and PhD in Comparative Literature from Rutgers led to a 41-year academic career that included teaching in Poland and Russia. His published research has ranged from Russian and French fiction to writing by African American women and honors education. His essays have appeared in Comparative *Literature, Neophilologus, Nineteenth-Century French Studies, Contemporary Literature, CLA Journal*, edited collections, and honors publications, along with Russian poetry translations in *Russian Literature Triquarterly*.

Gennady Barabtarlo, Professor of Russian at the University of Missouri, has written a number of books and articles on topics ranging from Pushkin and Tiutchev to Solzhenitsyn and especially Nabokov, concentrating mostly on his artistic means and ends. He also translated three of Nabokov's novels and all his English short stories into Russian. He has published original poetry and prose (collected, in part, in a 1998 book *In Every Place*). His most recent book came out in 2011 (St. Petersburg: Ivan Limbakh) under the title *Sochinenie Nabokova*, which can be translated, depending on the angle of view, as "Nabokov's Composition," "Nabokov's Syntax," and even "Fabricating Nabokov."

Murray Biggs is Adjunct Associate Professor of English and Theater Studies at Yale University. He is most interested in the interplay of text and performance, while teaching both dramatic literature and theater practice (acting and directing) in such courses as *"Shakespeare Acted," "The Actor and the Text," "The Foundations of Modern Drama,"* and *"The Drama of War."* Professor Biggs regularly directs undergraduate productions at Yale. Performance and dramatic criticism are the subjects of his published work.

Ruxanda Bontila is Associate Professor of British and American Literature at the University of Galati, Romania. She has published a number of books (*Vladimir Nabokov's English Novels: The Art of Defusing Subjectivism* [Bucharest: Editura Didactica si Pedagogica R.A., 2004], and articles including: "Our Nabokov: Romanian Appropriations" (*The Nabokovian*, 65 [2010]); "Updike's *Terrorist* Wayward World" (Editura Europlus, [2009]); "Problem Solving Policies and Fictional Power" (*The Nabokovian*, 62 [2009]); "Lolita's Take on History: A Romanian Perspective" (*EJES*, 12 (3) [2008], Routledge); "*Pnin*/Pnin's Search for Wholeness" (*The Nabokovian*, 57 [2006]), and "Vladimir Nabokov's 'Task of the Translator:' Identity in Need of Editing" (Cambridge Scholars Press, 2006).

William C. Carroll is Professor of English at Boston University. He has edited *The Two Gentlemen of Verona* (Arden Third Series), *Love's Labour's Lost* (New Cambridge Shakespeare Series) as well as Thomas Middleton's *Women Beware Women* (New Mermaid Series). He is also the author of *The Great Feast of Language in Love's Labour's Lost*, *The Metamorphoses of Shakespearean Comedy*, and *Fat King, Lean Beggar: Representations of Poverty in the Age of Shakespeare*. His first scholarly publication was "Nabokov's Signs and Symbols," and he has also published "The Cartesian Nightmare of *Despair*."

John N. Crossley is Emeritus Professor at Clayton School of Information Technology, Monash University, Australia. His early career was spent at Oxford, where he was the first university lecturer in mathematical logic. Crossley has written books on logic, mathematics, and computer science, in which he explores the field of logic in computer science, history of mathematics, and medieval history. He is the lead author of the book *What is Mathematical Logic?* (Oxford: Oxford University Press, 1972). He is also an avid photographer and his photographs were exhibited in Melbourne in 2005 under the title "Composition and Context."

Carol M. Dole is Chair of the English Department and Coordinator of Film Studies at Ursinus College in Pennsylvania. Most of her scholarly work focuses on film adaptations of British novels.

Alexander Dolinin is Professor of Slavic Languages at the University of Wisconsin-Madison, where he specializes in 19th- and 20th-century Russian literature, as well as Nabokov and Russian émigré literature. He is the author of books *True Life of the Writer Vladimir Sirin: Writings on Nabokov* [*Istinnaia zhizn' pisatelia Sirina: Raboty o Nabokove*] (St. Petersburg: 2004) and *Pushkin and England* (Moscow: 2009), as well as many articles on Nabokov in both Russian and English.

Alexander N. Drescher is a retired pediatrician and psychiatrist, living on a farm in the Berkshire Hills of Western Massachusetts.

David Field is Emeritus Professor of English at DePauw University, where he taught for 27 years. He received the Joan Westmen Battey Distinguished Teaching Award in 1996; In 2002–3, he was the recipient of DePauw's Exemplary Teacher award, and he also received the Mr and Mrs Fred Tucker Award for a Distinguished Career. He is a graduate of Washington and Lee University and received his PhD from the University of Virginia.

Wayne K. Goodman, M.D., is Chair of the Department of Psychiatry at Mount Sinai School of Medicine (New York) and is the Esther and Joseph Klingenstein Professor of Psychiatry. He is a pioneering researcher in the field of Obsessive-Compulsive Disorder (OCD), and served as the Director of the Division of Adult Translational Research and Treatment Development in the National Institute of Mental Health (NIMH). In addition, Dr Goodman is a professor of neuroscience and is a distinguished fellow of the American Psychiatric Association.

Geoffrey Green is Professor of English and Graduate Literature Advisor at San Francisco State University. His books of literary criticism include: *Novel vs. Fiction: The Contemporary Reformation; Literary Criticism and the Structures of History: Erich Auerbach and Leo*

Spitzer; Freud and Nabokov; The Vineland Papers: Critical Takes on Pynchon's Novel; Scholes Loves a Story: A Book for Bob. Professor Green recently published a short story cycles on themes of identity and disguise in music and drama, *Voices in a Mask.* He has published widely in journals of literary criticism, including many essays on Vladimir Nabokov. He is Executive Editor of the critical journal on contemporary fiction, *Critique* (Taylor & Francis).

John V. Hagopian taught at the Department of English, Binghamton University (SUNY), and lived in Binghamton. He published research on J. F. Powers, F. Scott Fitzgerald, Faulkner, and Ernest Hemingway, and his critical essays appeared in *The New York Review of Books, Harper's Magazine, Fitzgerald Newsletter,* and *Contemporary Literature* among others. He co-authored (with Slava Paperno) an essay "Official and Unofficial Responses to Nabokov in the Soviet Union" (*The Achievements of Vladimir Nabokov,* (eds). George Gibian, Stephen Jan Parker [Ithaca, New York: Cornell University Press, 1984]) as well as contributed an article, "Vladimir Nabokov," to *Dictionary of Literary Biography, 2: American Novelists Since World War II* (Detroit, Michigan: Gale Research/Bruccoli Clark, 1978).

John B. Lane is a professional cabinet maker. At the time of the writing his article, he was a mature student in the Honors English Program at Dalhousie University, Halifax, Nova Scotia.

Yuri Leving is Professor and Chair of Dalhousie University's Department of Russian Studies. He is the author of three books: *Train Station— Garage—Hangar: Vladimir Nabokov and the Poetics of Russian Urbanism* (2004, Short-listed for Andrey Bely Prize), *Upbringing by Optics: Book Illustration, Animation, and Text* (2010), *Keys to* The Gift: *A Guide to V. Nabokov's Novel* (2011), and has also edited and co-edited four volumes of articles: *Shades of Laura: Vladimir Nabokov's Last Novel* The Original of Laura (forthcoming), *The Goalkeeper: The Nabokov Almanac* (2010), *Eglantine: A Collection of Philological Essays to Honour the Sixtieth Anniversary of Roman Timenchik* (2005), and *Empire N. Nabokov and His Heirs* (2006). Leving has published over 70 scholarly articles on various aspects of Russian and comparative literature. He served as a commentator on the first authorized Russian edition of *The Collected Works of Vladimir Nabokov* in five volumes (1999–2001), and was the curator for the exhibition "Nabokov's *Lolita*: 1955–2005" in Washington,

D.C., which celebrated the 50th anniversary of the publication of *Lolita*. Leving is the founding editor of the *Nabokov Online Journal* (since 2007).

Irving Malin is an American literary critic (PhD, Stanford, 1958). He taught at the City College of New York from 1960 until his retirement in 1996. Malin wrote his dissertation on the fiction of William Faulkner and made his initial academic mark as a critic of American Jewish Literature, editing an early collection on the fiction of Saul Bellow, as well as a critical book and a general anthology on Jewish literature in the US. He subsequently became interested in writers who practiced innovative techniques, such as James Purdy and John Hawkes, as well as writers who broke down the boundaries between fiction and non-fiction, such as William Styron and Truman Capote. One of the pioneering academics to take an interest in metafiction and experimental writing, Malin was an early contributor to the *Review of Contemporary Fiction*, writing over 500 book reviews for this and other publications. Among his books are *William Faulkner: An Interpretation* (Stanford, California: Stanford University Press, 1957), *Saul Bellow and the Critics* (New York: New York University Press, 1967) and *Nathanael West's Novels* (Carbondale: Southern Illinois University Press, 1972).

Terry J. Martin (PhD, SUNY Buffalo, 1988) is a Professor of English at Baldwin–Wallace College. He is the author of *Rhetorical Deception in the Short Fiction of Hawthorne, Poe, and Melville* (Lewiston, New York: Mellen, 1999) and a translation of Anacristina Rossi's *La loca de Gandoca* (*The Madwoman of Gandoca* [Lewiston, New York: Mellen, 2006). He teaches Literary Theory and American Literature and is currently working on a book on beachcombing.

Charles William Mignon (1934–2009) was a scholar and editor of Early American literature. He taught at the University of Illinois (1963–7) and at the University of Nebraska, Lincoln (1967–2000), from which post he retired. In 1972–3 he was the Senior Fulbright Lecturer on American Literature at the University of Warsaw in Poland. In 1993 he received the Annis Chaikin Sorenson Award for distinguished university teaching. His scholarship concentrated primarily on the writings of Edward Taylor, and over the decades he provided early Americanists and historians astute readings of Taylor's *Preparatory Meditations* and other writings.

Álvaro Garrido Moreno holds a PhD from University of Zaragoza (Spain).

J. Morris has published fiction and poetry in many literary magazines in the U.S. and Great Britain, including *Missouri Review*, *Prairie Schooner*, *Subtropics*, *Five Points*, and *Fulcrum*. A critical essay, "The Gliding Eye: Nabokov's Marvelous Terror," first published in *The Southern Review*, was reprinted in *Twentieth-Century Literary Criticism*. He teaches at The Writer's Center in Bethesda, Maryland, outside of Washington, D.C. Morris's other career is as a songwriter and musician for *Mulberry Coach*, a collaboration with singer and lyricist Katie Fisher.

Vladimir Mylnikov (PhD, Volgograd Pedagogical University) teaches at The Defense Language Institute (Distance Learning Division, Russian Studies). He graduated from Kharkov University, Ukraine, with B.A. in English Translation and English Literature, and his dissertation was entitled "Autocommentary and its Function in Russian Literature." Dr Mylnikov taught Russian literature, drama, and the language in Russia, China (Xiamen University), Japan (International Language School, Kumagaya, Saitama), and the U.S. (Wesleyan University, CT; Monterey Institute of International Studies, CA.)

Brian Thomas Quinn is Associate Professor at the Department of Linguistic Environment of Kyushu University in Japan. His field of specialization is Russian and Slavic Languages and Literature, but he also teaches courses on American culture, inter-cultural communication, and medical English for undergraduate and graduate students. Among his articles are: "Aspects of Nabokov's Transition to English Prose in *The Real Life of Sebastian Knight*" in *Studies in English Language and Literature* 40 [1990]; "The Elusiveness of Superficial Reality in Nabokov's 'The Vane Sisters'" in *Studies in Languages and Cultures* (Faculty of Languages and Cultures, Kyushu University, 2005); "The Artist Surviving Exile in Nabokov's *Pnin*" in *Kyushu American Literature* 30 (1990); and "The Role of Ghostly Influences in Nabokov's *Transparent Things*" in *Studies in English Language and Literature* 43 (1993).

David H. Richter (PhD, University of Chicago) is Professor and Director of Graduate Studies in the English department at Queens College and professor of English at the Graduate Center of the City University of

New York. Richter publishes in the fields of narrative theory and 18th-century literature. His books include *Fable's End* (Chicago: University of Chicago Press, 1974), *The Progress of Romance* (Columbus: Ohio State University Press, 1996), *Ideology and Form in Eighteenth-Century Literature* (Lubbock, Texas: Texas Tech University Press, 1999) and *Falling into Theory* (Bedford/St. Martin's 2000). He is currently at work on two critical books: a cultural history of true crime fiction and an analysis of difficulty in biblical narrative.

Andrés Romero-Jódar holds a B.A. and an M.A. in English Philology, and a B.A. in Spanish Philology from the University of Zaragoza (Spain). He is a Research Fellow at the Department of English and German Philology of the University of Zaragoza, and forms part of the research group entitled "Contemporary Narrative in English." He is currently working on his doctoral thesis on narrative iconical genres and representation of trauma in graphic novels in English, and has published on these and related subjects in academic journals such as *Atlantis, Studies in Comics, Estudios Ingleses de la Universidad Complutense, Odisea, Revista Canaria de Estudios Ingleses, Journal of Popular Culture, Revista Alicantina de Estudios Ingleses, Revista de Literatura* (CSIC) and *Tropelías*.

Paul J. Rosenzweig was a Lecturer in the Department of English, University of Haifa, Israel. He published articles on Faulkner, Lawrence, and on James.

Pekka Tammi is Professor of Comparative Literature at the University of Tampere, Finland. He is the author of books and articles on narratology, intertextuality, and the interface of literary and linguistic text theories. He is currently mapping the tactics for representing consciousness in fiction and non-fiction from a pre-postnarratological angle.

Leona Toker is Professor in the English Department of the Hebrew University of Jerusalem. She is the author of *Nabokov: The Mystery of Literary Structures* (1989), *Eloquent Reticence: Withholding Information in Fictional Narrative* (1993), *Return from the Archipelago: Narratives of Gulag Survivors* (2000), *Towards the Ethics of Form in Fiction: Narratives of Cultural Remission* (2010), and articles on English, American, and Russian literature. She is the editor of *Commitment in Reflection: Essays in Literature and Moral Philosophy* (1994) and co-editor of *Rereading Texts/Rethinking*

Critical Presuppositions: Essays in Honour of H.M. Daleski (1996). She has founded and is editing *Partial Answers: A Journal of Literature and the History of Ideas*, a semiannual periodical currently published by the Johns Hopkins University Press.

Meghan Vicks holds her PhD in Comparative Literature from the University of Colorado in Boulder. Her dissertation, *Narratives of Nothing in Twentieth-Century Literature*, analyzes the relationship between nothingness and narrative in the works of Samuel Beckett, Nikolai Gogol, Herman Melville, Vladimir Nabokov, and Victor Pelevin.

Olga Voronina is Assistant Professor of Russian at Bard College. Formerly deputy director of the Nabokov Museum in St. Petersburg, she received PhD in Slavic Literature from Harvard University. Dr Voronina is currently co-editing and co-translating Vladimir Nabokov's *Letters to Véra*, previously unpublished.

Frederick H. White is Associate Dean of the College of Humanities and Social Sciences at *Utah Valley University and Associate Professor in the Department of Languages*. He is the author of *Memoirs and Madness: Leonid Andreev Through the Prism of the Literary Portrait* (Montreal: McGill-Queen's University Press, 2006), and has recently completed a second monograph, *Neurasthenia in the Life and Works of Leonid Andreev*. Much of White's scholarly research is concerned with the scientific discourse concerning mental illness at the beginning of the 20th century.

Michael Wood is Charles Barnwell Straut Class of 1923 Professor of English and Comparative Literature at Princeton University. He studied French and German at Cambridge University, and has taught at Columbia University and at the University of Exeter in the U.K. He has written books on Vladimir Nabokov, Luis Buñuel, Franz Kafka, and Gabriel García Márquez, as well as *The Road to Delphi*, a study of the ancient and continuing allure of oracles. Among his other books are *America in the Movies and Children of Silence*. A member of the American Philosophical Society and of the American Academy of Arts and Sciences, he is a regular contributor to the *London Review of Books* and the *New York Review of Books*. Dr Wood also frequently writes for other journals. At Princeton, he teaches mainly contemporary fiction, modern poetry, and the theory and history of criticism. His most recent book are *Literature and the Taste of Knowledge* (Cambridge: Cambridge University Press, 2005) and *Yeats and Violence* (Oxford: Oxford University Press, 2010).

ACKNOWLEDGMENTS

I wish to express my gratitude to Keith Blasing, Alexander Drescher, Cheryl Hann, and Miriam Breslow. I am indebted to Ellen Pifer for introducing me to the Continuum International Publishing Group, which has accepted this project with enthusiasm. It has been a constant pleasure to work with Haaris Naqvi, my editor at Continuum, who has assisted me in the preparation of this volume at all its stages. I also extend grateful thanks to the authors themselves, their families, appointed literary agents, and publishing companies for the permission to reprint the articles listed in the "Credits" section. The entries appear under their original titles, which, in some cases, have been amended for the purposes of the present volume.

The text of the short story "Signs and Symbols," first printed in *The New Yorker* (1948), appears in this anthology with the permission of the Vladimir Nabokov Estate and by special arrangement with the Random House and the Andrew Wylie Agency. It is reprinted from *The Stories of Vladimir Nabokov* (New York: Random House, 2007, pp. 598–603).

Vladimir Nabokov's correspondence with *The New Yorker* regarding "Signs and Symbols" (1946–8) is reproduced with the kind permission of Dmitri Nabokov and the Andrew Wylie Agency; Katharine White's correspondence is published courtesy of Roger Angell (*The New Yorker*).

Lastly, and most importantly, I wish to thank my own family: my wife, Ella, who helped me make the decision with this edition's cover; my daughter Lola, for whom "Signs and Symbols" was the first short story by Nabokov she has ever read; and my son Leva, who is still only learning the signs and symbols around him.

INTRODUCTION

Breaking the code: Nabokov and the art of short fiction

Anatomy of a Short Story is a unique anthology devoted to a single short story—"Signs and Symbols" by Vladimir Nabokov, an open-ended *tour de force* in prose which challenges readers to break its mysterious code.

Since its first publication in 1948, the story has generated a plethora of critical responses. One of Nabokov's *shortest* short stories, "Signs and Symbols" has been called "one of the greatest short stories ever written" and "a triumph of economy and force, minute realism and shimmering mystery."[1] The body of critical essays and scholarly articles devoted to this text that is only 5 pages long (2,160 words) continues to grow. Part of the classical short fiction genre, Nabokov's "Signs and Symbols" (one of his last experiments in short prose) is striking for its lexical density and contains a surprising structural element: what the writer described in his letter to Katharine White, editor of *The New Yorker*, as an "inside," "inner scheme," and "a system of mute responses."[2]

The goal of the present collection of articles is to provide an approach to the narrative "riddles" of "Signs and Symbols." Several pieces have been written specially for this edition, while others have appeared earlier in scholarly journals or have been printed as book chapters. Many of these publications, however, have been shortened (for example, recapitulations of the plot and other obvious repetitions have been omitted); these scattered sources are now gathered under one cover, with a unified scholarly apparatus, an introduction, bibliography, and index. *Anatomy of a Short Story* is far from a simple recycled product: it should serve as an invaluable resource for all those interested in a comprehensive analysis of this challenging short story; it will also prove handy for teachers of modernist fiction in general and of Vladimir Nabokov's writings in particular, since the work is regularly included in the syllabi of the American, English, Russian, and comparative literature courses at universities and colleges worldwide.

Nabokov's "Signs and Symbols" itself opens the volume. The sentences in the text of the story are numbered, and hence the citations throughout the volume include both a page number and a line number. The original story is followed by an interdisciplinary roundtable discussion of Nabokov's story, also specially produced for this edition, with the participation of readers representing five different disciplines: a doctor specializing in obsessive-compulsive and anxiety disorders; a mathematician; a literary critic; a theater director; and a screenwriter. The archival correspondence between Vladimir Nabokov and Katharine White concerns the history of publication of "Signs and Symbols" in the magazine and appears here for the first time, revealing the peculiar relationship between the reputable publisher and the literary genius.

The scholarly debate over the text itself is presented in 30 articles written between 1974 and 2011. The youngest contributor to this collection, Meghan Vicks, has just completed writing her PhD dissertation, which explores narratives of zero in modern and postmodern literature (Nabokov is analyzed along with Pelevin, Beckett, Melville, and Gogol). William C. Carroll, the author of the earliest critical essay on "Signs and Symbols" (published in 1974), is still very fond of his essay—it was, in fact, the first thing he had published as a scholar ("It was the result of teaching the story in a Nabokov seminar at Boston University and not being able to figure it out at the time").[3] Carroll became interested in Nabokov in his senior high school English class, when a daring (for 1962) teacher pretended "not" to recommend *Lolita* to his honors students. Of course, several of the students became huge fans of the writer, and among them was Carroll, who continued reading and collecting Nabokoviana through college and graduate school. When he submitted his essay to *Russian Literature Triquarterly*, the editor, Carl Proffer, said he would instead use it for the *Book of Things* collection, which Nabokov himself took the time to read and enjoy.[4]

These and other interlocking echoes are deliberately preserved in our collection, including the three cross-referenced tables of contents: the main one at the beginning is structured thematically; the other two, placed at the end, are arranged in chronological order (by the date of publication), and alphabetically (by the author's last name). As one of the anonymous peer-reviewers of this book at the manuscript stage neatly observed, "I leave it to Nabokovians to relish the appearance in a single volume of the authors Green, Field, and Wood; of Dole and Dolinin; and of the marvelously paired William Carroll and Carol Williams (*cf.* Campbell and Beauchamp in *Pale Fire*)."

The collection introduces both the complexity and the intellectual beauty of Vladimir Nabokov's writing style, as well as some of the moral dimensions of his oeuvre (the story covertly deals with the Holocaust). Though he strongly disapproved of Nabokov's last fragmentary novel, *The Original of Laura*, Martin Amis has called "Signs and Symbols" an "insanely inspired" text. Such an admission articulated by a leading contemporary English-language writer is notable because it demonstrates that Nabokov's miniature masterpiece still plays an active role in modern literary discourse.[5] (One of the present collection's contributors, an author himself, exclaimed after rereading the story: "As a writer it makes me want to take my typewriter and throw it out the window"). Mary Gaitskill has recently recorded her reading of Nabokov's story (still stubbornly referred to by the journal as "Symbols and Signs" instead of "Signs and Symbols") and discussed it with *The New Yorker*'s fiction editor, Deborah Treisman.[6]

What is so special about the story itself—apart from its economy of style and the missing resolution at the end—that it continues to bother readers and scholars alike? If perused closely, it turns out that the narrative strategies that Nabokov employs in his short fiction are not necessarily those that normally define the genre's parameters. In a brief guide on how to write a perfect piece of short fiction (appropriately entitled "Anatomy of a Short Story"), T. N. Tobias offers nine rules of thumb.[7] In the order of appearance, they are:

1. Know Your Ending
2. Introduce Conflict Early

3. Stick to the Premise
4. Use Structure
5. Image is Everything
6. Simplify
7. Limit Point of View
8. No History Lessons
9. Experiment

Any systematic application of each of these pieces of advice to Nabokov's short story will turn out to be challenging, but let us try. Know Your Ending: well, *Nabokov* knows his finale. But do we? This is exactly the shtick. Introduce Conflict Early: it is right there, in the very first sentence, which contains the word "problem," a victim, and not just some unfortunate illness but an unequivocal madness. Stick to the Premise: the author does, to the extent that a reader becomes dizzy. We want some development, but Nabokov's text, like a broken record, circles around and replays the same theme of human suffering ad infinitum. Use Structure: the story is divided into three parts, but one should not expect a typical three-act drama, where each act has a different tone to it. Here the major incidents occur beyond the story's frame: the main character is missing, and those who care about him encounter scores of obstacles; the climax is continually postponed; a state of equilibrium will never be achieved. Image is Everything: hard to disagree—just symbols and signs, and signs and symbols. Simplify: one of Nabokov's most calculated stories in terms of precision, it is also one of his densest. The language is plain, the imagery is convoluted. Contradictory, isn't it? Limit Point of View: the story is mostly filtered through the young man's mother's perception, but there are also Herman Brink (or his diagnosis) and the patient's own phobias, with snippets being carefully reproduced in the narrative. No History Lessons: there is no direct moralizing, indeed, but "the image of our sorrow"[8] against the ominous backdrop of the Holocaust is hard to miss. Experiment: the whole story can be seen as a teasing foray into the art of fiction and a precursor of the reader-response criticism advocated in theoretical works of Stanley Fish, Wolfgang Iser, Hans-Robert Jauss, Roland Barthes, and others.

According to Wolfgang Iser, the literary work is not an object in itself, but an effect to be explained. What is more, Iser has asserted that the reader's response is controlled by the text itself.[9] Nabokov's short story obviously creates an "implied" reader who develops expectations and produces meanings (in his model the text controls its audience); on the other hand, there are also readers who resist compliance with the text's almost totalitarian imposition of narrative mode and psychological prefiguring. I will illustrate the point by describing the two polarized camps that have transpired in the scholarly debate over "Signs and Symbols" just in the last decade. The argument was reignited in 1995, when Donald Barton Johnson, the editor and founder of NABOKV-L (an electronic forum dedicated to Nabokov's life and art), proposed to take an informal poll among the listserv subscribers, who were invited to contribute to the analysis of the meaning of the third phone call along with any rationale.[10] By the mid 1990s the piece had already been subjected to numerous critical treatments—as Johnson himself suspected, largely thanks to its inclusion in a Norton anthology widely used in English courses.[11] Nine years later, the same electronic forum witnessed another intense exploration of "Signs and Symbols." This time it was from Dr Anthony Stadlen, a prominent psychoanalyst, who proffered the discussion of Nabokov's short story by posing a series of questions that were fresh and skeptical. The quote is lengthy, but worth reproducing in full:

> Why should we believe even the first sentence of this story? What does it mean for someone to be "incurably deranged in his mind"? I ask this in all seriousness as a psychotherapist, so-called. Someone like Nabokov who writes about, and even impersonates, as narrator, what we may loosely, or not so loosely, call madmen, has to decide, or at least decide not to decide, whether these persons are responsible agents subject to the moral law, or some kind of subhuman whose actions are not, in a true sense, actions at all, but merely the outcome of some process gone wrong in the human-looking entity that still bears a human name. Nabokov meets this challenge magnificently, by making it crystal clear, both within his fiction (for example, in *Despair*, *Lolita* and *Pale Fire*) and outside it (for example, in his preface to *Despair* and in *Strong Opinions*),

that he sees his madmen as moral agents. It is true that, at times, Nabokov seems less certain of this position, as when he says that Raskolnikov [from Dostoyevsky's *Crime and Punishment*] should be medically examined. But Hermann, Humbert and Kinbote would be of no interest if they were mere automatons, lacking human autonomy and responsibility.

So who is this narrator who tells us at the outset that the son in "Signs and Symbols" is "incurably deranged"? I would not believe this if told it by a psychiatrist or psychotherapist about a real person. Why should I believe it here?

All we can say from the narrator's account is that the young man has been deposited in the "sanatorium" —though why, if he is "incurable"? Presumably because he is an embarrassment (evidently "the Prince" wants him to be there and is paying). But evidently Aunt Rosa didn't worry about him (although admittedly this "inaccessib[ility]" is a later development, in the United States), because all those she worried about were put to death by the Germans. She worried about real things: train accidents, bankruptcies, cancer.[12]

According to Stadlen, the untrustworthiness of Nabokov's narrator is apparent from the contradictory sentences ("He had no desires" and "What he really wanted to do was to tear a hole in his world and escape"). "Who is making these contradictory attributions?" he inquires, suggesting that the first appears to be the narrator's endorsement of an attribution by both parents; the second apparently constitutes "the narrator's endorsement of an attribution by the mother, or perhaps the endorsement of the mother's endorsement of an attribution by the doctor."[13] Questioning the reasons for "the spell" of the mere unsubstantiated assertions about the young man's inaccessibility and incurability, as well as refusing to accept the (unattributed) assertion that the protagonist wants to escape from the "world" rather than from incarceration in a sanatorium, Stadlen proposes a possible explanation of the third telephone call, as made by the young man himself, while still alive.

Andrew Brown responded to Stadlen's comments, particularly those marking the distinctions between different styles of narrative voice. Responding to the question, "Why believe even the first sentence ...?" Brown argues that "in the case of an omniscient narrator, the reader has little choice." We must listen closely and skeptically to a Humbert or a Kinbote. They both have agendas of their own. An omniscient narrator does not. In authorial terms, an untrustworthy narrator is only possible if there is an alternative narrator available. What one would be asking for, in essence, would simply be an entirely different story. An omniscient narrator requires the writer to count on the reader's coming through with the old "willing suspension of disbelief" stuff.[14]

Thus, according to Brown, the "incurable madness" of the young man is a condition that Nabokov's readers are obliged to accept at face value, just as the statement that the father's dentures are "hopelessly uncomfortable." Essentially, Brown believes that "we can't let a rampant literal-mindedness dog us through every such statement." In sharp contrast to many critics, Brown also claims that Dr Brink is "a professional (the story gives us no reason to suppose otherwise) and the young man's parents have 'puzzled out' his condition. To others, though, the young man's delusions are beyond the comprehension of lay people not familiar with psychosis."[15]

Similarly, Brown disputes another of Stadlen's remarks concerning the young man's allegedly being "inaccessible to normal minds." If this were true, Stadlen had maintained, "how could the self-styled 'normal minds' know, for instance, that the 'inaccessible' one has 'no desires'? Indeed, how could the learned Dr Brink write his paper about him?" Nevertheless, Brown refutes:

> To the narrative challenge of "Signs and Symbols," it would seem to strain a point to say a contradiction exists between the young man's parents' difficulty in selecting a gift for him because he "has no desires," and the statement five paragraphs later that what the young man "really wanted" was to tear a hole in his world and escape. The second statement is clearly in response to a fellow patient's thought that the young man was learning to fly. This is not a contradiction between having no desire that a birthday gift would satisfy, and an apparent desire to die.[16]

The difference of opinions is likely irresolvable, but it is the poetic nature and the richness of "Signs and Symbols" that encourage and allow such seemingly contradictory approaches to its riddles. By the same token, there is also something inherent to human nature that makes us respond to Nabokov's signs and symbols as we do— that dangerous proximity of poet's imagination and "madness," which once was compared to the "forests of symbols" in Charles Baudelaire's "Correspondences":

> Nature is a temple where living pillars
> Let sometimes emerge confused words;
> Man crosses it through forests of symbols
> Which watch him with intimate eyes.[17]

In the spring of 2008, four years after the initial dispute, Anthony Stadlen conducted his "Inner Circle Seminar" on "Signs and Symbols" in London.[18] At the same time there occurred yet another attempt to subject Nabokov's short story to a collective close reading on the same listserv (D. B. Johnson had left his editorial post by that time). The new moderator, Susan Elizabeth Sweeney, was hoping to engage the subscribers in discussing the story, but the conversation died soon after the first three paragraphs were analyzed. It so happened that this was around the same week as Dmitri Nabokov announced the controversial decision to publish his father's incomplete novel *The Original of Laura*, which caused scholarly attention to be diverted to a new and intriguing subject.

Anatomy of a Short Story once again puts Nabokov's tantalizingly cryptic text under the microscope.

A PRIMARY TEXT
Heart

"Signs and Symbols"
Vladimir Nabokov

I

1 For the fourth time in as many years they were confronted with the problem of what birthday present to bring a young man who was incurably deranged in his mind. He had no desires. Man-made objects were to him either hives of evil, vibrant with a malignant activity that he alone could perceive, or gross comforts for which no use could be found in his abstract world. After eliminating a number of articles that might offend him or frighten him (anything in the gadget line for instance was taboo), his parents chose a dainty and innocent trifle: a basket with ten different fruit jellies in
10 ten little jars.

At the time of his birth they had been married already for a long time; a score of years had elapsed, and now they were quite old. Her drab gray hair was done anyhow. She wore cheap black dresses. Unlike other women of her age (such as Mrs Sol, their next-door neighbor, whose face was all pink and mauve with paint and whose hat was a cluster of brookside flowers), she presented a naked white countenance to the fault-finding light of spring days.

Her husband, who in the old country had been a fairly successful
businessman, was now wholly dependent on his brother Isaac, a
20 real American of almost forty years standing. They seldom saw him
and had nicknamed him "the Prince."

That Friday everything went wrong. The underground train lost
its life current between two stations, and for a quarter of an hour
one could hear nothing but the dutiful beating of one's heart and
the rustling of newspapers. The bus they had to take next kept
them waiting for ages; and when it did come, it was crammed
with garrulous high-school children. It was raining hard as they
walked up the brown path leading to the sanatorium. There they
waited again; and instead of their boy shuffling into the room as
30 he usually did (his poor face blotched with acne, ill-shaven, sullen,
and confused), a nurse they knew, and did not care for, appeared
at last and brightly explained that he had again attempted to take
his life. He was all right, she said, but a visit might disturb him.
The place was so miserably understaffed, and things got mislaid or
mixed up so easily, that they decided not to leave their present in
the office but to bring it to him next time they came.

She waited for her husband to open his umbrella and then took
his arm. He kept clearing his throat in a special resonant way he
had when he was upset. They reached the bus-stop shelter on the
40 other side of the street and he closed his umbrella. A few feet away,
under a swaying and dripping tree, a tiny half-dead unfledged bird
was helplessly twitching in a puddle.

During the long ride to the subway station, she and her
husband did not exchange a word; and every time she glanced at
his old hands (swollen veins, brown-spotted skin), clasped and
twitching upon the handle of his umbrella, she felt the mounting
pressure of tears. As she looked around trying to hook her mind
onto something, it gave her a kind of soft shock, a mixture of
compassion and wonder, to notice that one of the passengers, a
50 girl with dark hair and grubby red toenails, was weeping on the
shoulder of an older woman. Whom did that woman resemble? She
resembled Rebecca Borisovna, whose daughter had married one of
the Soloveichik—in Minsk, years ago.

The last time he had tried to do it, his method had been, in
the doctor's words, a masterpiece of inventiveness; he would have
succeeded, had not an envious fellow patient thought he was

learning to fly—and stopped him. What he really wanted to do was to tear a hole in his world and escape.

60 The system of his delusions had been the subject of an elaborate paper in a scientific monthly, but long before that she and her husband had puzzled it out for themselves. "Referential mania," Herman Brink had called it. In these very rare cases the patient imagines that everything happening around him is a veiled reference to his personality and existence. He excludes real people from the conspiracy—because he considers himself to be so much more intelligent than other men. Phenomenal nature shadows him wherever he goes. Clouds in the staring sky transmit to one another, by means of slow signs, incredibly detailed information regarding him. His inmost thoughts are discussed at nightfall, in 70 manual alphabet, by darkly gesticulating trees. Pebbles or stains or sun flecks form patterns representing in some awful way messages which he must intercept. Everything is a cipher and of everything he is the theme. Some of the spies are detached observers, such are glass surfaces and still pools; others, such as coats in store windows, are prejudiced witnesses, lynchers at heart; others again (running water, storms) are hysterical to the point of insanity, have a distorted opinion of him and grotesquely misinterpret his actions. He must be always on his guard and devote every minute and module of life to the decoding of the undulation of things. The 80 very air he exhales is indexed and filed away. If only the interest he provokes were limited to his immediate surroundings—but alas it is not! With distance the torrents of wild scandal increase in volume and volubility. The silhouettes of his blood corpuscles, magnified a million times, flit over vast plains; and still farther, great mountains of unbearable solidity and height sum up in terms of granite and groaning firs the ultimate truth of his being.

II

When they emerged from the thunder and foul air of the subway, the last dregs of the day were mixed with the street lights. She wanted to buy some fish for supper, so she handed him the basket 90 of jelly jars, telling him to go home. He walked up to the third landing and then remembered he had given her his keys earlier in the day.

In silence he sat down on the steps and in silence rose when some ten minutes later she came, heavily trudging upstairs, wanly smiling, shaking her head in deprecation of her silliness. They entered their two-room flat and he at once went to the mirror. Straining the corners of his mouth apart by means of his thumbs, with a horrible masklike grimace, he removed his new hopelessly uncomfortable dental plate and severed the long tusks of saliva
100 connecting him to it. He read his Russian-language newspaper while she laid the table. Still reading, he ate the pale victuals that needed no teeth. She knew his moods and was also silent.

When he had gone to bed, she remained in the living room with her pack of soiled cards and her old albums. Across the narrow yard where the rain tinkled in the dark against some battered ash cans, windows were blandly alight and in one of them a black-trousered man with his bare elbows raised could be seen lying supine on an untidy bed. She pulled the blind down and examined the photographs. As a baby he looked more surprised than most babies. From a fold in the album, a German maid they had had in
110 Leipzig and her fat-faced fiancé fell out. Minsk, the Revolution, Leipzig, Berlin, Leipzig, a slanting housefront badly out of focus. Four years old, in a park: moodily, shyly, with puckered forehead, looking away from an eager squirrel as he would from any other stranger. Aunt Rosa, a fussy, angular, wild-eyed old lady, who had lived in a tremulous world of bad news, bankruptcies, train accidents, cancerous growths—until the Germans put her to death, together with all the people she had worried about. Age six—that was when he drew wonderful birds with human hands and feet,
120 and suffered from insomnia like a grown-up man. His cousin, now a famous chess player. He again, aged about eight, already difficult to understand, afraid of the wallpaper in the passage, afraid of a certain picture in a book which merely showed an idyllic landscape with rocks on a hillside and an old cart wheel hanging from the branch of a leafless tree. Aged ten: the year they left Europe. The shame, the pity, the humiliating difficulties, the ugly, vicious, backward children he was with in that special school. And then came a time in his life, coinciding with a long convalescence after pneumonia, when those little phobias of his which his parents had
130 stubbornly regarded as the eccentricities of a prodigiously gifted child hardened as it were into a dense tangle of logically interacting illusions, making him totally inaccessible to normal minds.

This, and much more, she accepted—for after all living did mean accepting the loss of one joy after another, not even joys in her case—mere possibilities of improvement. She thought of the endless waves of pain that for some reason or other she and her husband had to endure; of the invisible giants hurting her boy in some unimaginable fashion; of the incalculable amount of tenderness contained in the world; of the fate of this tenderness, 140 which is either crushed, or wasted, or transformed into madness; of neglected children humming to themselves in unswept corners; of beautiful weeds that cannot hide from the farmer and helplessly have to watch the shadow of his simian stoop leave mangled flowers in its wake, as the monstrous darkness approaches.

III

It was past midnight when from the living room she heard her husband moan; and presently he staggered in, wearing over his nightgown the old overcoat with astrakhan collar which he much preferred to the nice blue bathrobe he had.

"I can't sleep," he cried.

150 "Why," she asked, "why can't you sleep? You were so tired."

"I can't sleep because I am dying," he said and lay down on the couch.

"Is it your stomach? Do you want me to call Dr Solov?"

"No doctors, no doctors," he moaned, "To the devil with doctors! We must get him out of there quick. Otherwise we'll be responsible. Responsible!" he repeated and hurled himself into a sitting position, both feet on the floor, thumping his forehead with his clenched fist.

"All right," she said quietly, "we shall bring him home tomorrow 160 morning."

"I would like some tea," said her husband and retired to the bathroom.

Bending with difficulty, she retrieved some playing cards and a photograph or two that had slipped from the couch to the floor: knave of hearts, nine of spades, ace of spades, Elsa and her bestial beau.

He returned in high spirits, saying in a loud voice: "I have it all figured out. We will give him the bedroom. Each of us will spend

part of the night near him and the other part on this couch. By
turns. We will have the doctor see him at least twice a week. It
170 does not matter what the Prince says. He won't have to say much
anyway because it will come out cheaper."

The telephone rang. It was an unusual hour for their telephone
to ring. His left slipper had come off and he groped for it with his
heel and toe as he stood in the middle of the room, and childishly,
toothlessly, gaped at his wife. Having more English than he did, it
was she who attended to calls.

"Can I speak to Charlie," said a girl's dull little voice.

"What number you want? No. That is not the right number."

The receiver was gently cradled. Her hand went to her old tired
180 heart.

"It frightened me," she said.

He smiled a quick smile and immediately resumed his excited
monologue. They would fetch him as soon as it was day. Knives
would have to be kept in a locked drawer. Even at his worst he
presented no danger to other people.

The telephone rang a second time. The same toneless anxious
young voice asked for Charlie.

"You have the incorrect number. I will tell you what you are
doing: you are turning the letter O instead of the zero."

190 They sat down to their unexpected festive midnight tea. The
birthday present stood on the table. He sipped noisily; his face was
flushed; every now and then he imparted a circular motion to his
raised glass so as to make the sugar dissolve more thoroughly. The
vein on the side of his bald head where there was a large birthmark
stood out conspicuously and, although he had shaved that morning,
a silvery bristle showed on his chin. While she poured him another
glass of tea, he put on his spectacles and reexamined with pleasure
the luminous yellow, green, red little jars. His clumsy moist lips
spelled out their eloquent labels: apricot, grape, beech plum,
200 quince. He had got to crab apple, when the telephone rang again.

FORUM
High Pressure

Psychosis, performance, schizophrenia, literature

An interdisciplinary roundtable discussion on Nabokov's "Signs and Symbols"

Hal Ackerman, Screenwriter (*UCLA*)
Murray Biggs, Theater scholar (*Yale University*)
John N. Crossley, Mathematician (*Monash University*)
Wayne Goodman, Psychiatrist (*Mount Sinai School of Medicine*)
Yuri Leving, Moderator (*Dalhousie University*)
Frederick White, Literary scholar (*Utah Valley University*)

Approaching the story through film

Yuri Leving: *Could you imagine a screen adaptation of Nabokov's short story "Signs and Symbols"?*

Hal Ackerman: My first glib kneejerk answer is that "Signs and Symbols" would never be made as a feature film, certainly not an American feature film. I knew there'd been a few successful screen adaptations of short fiction like *Brokeback Mountain* and

Million Dollar Baby. To my great surprise though I discovered an impressive list of others, hundreds of them, including *Rear Window*, *2001: A Space Odyssey*, *It's A Wonderful Life*, *Memento*, *The Fly*.

Yuri Leving: *If the aforementioned movies were so successful in turning fascinating texts into rich visual narratives, what is the secret, then?*

Hal Ackerman: Let's look at what a movie can do. It gives an audience access through two senses, sight and sound. What we can see and what we can hear. Most successful film adaptations from other media begin with material that is rich in these external stimuli. This is why plot-driven stories (crime, action) are the most easily adaptable, and why novels that delve into the inner lives of characters—thoughts, feelings, philosophies—are the most challenging and least successful in both commercial and artistic terms.

Yuri Leving: *What would be the hardest part in making a film based on "Signs and Symbols"?*

Hal Ackerman: What do we actually *see* and *hear* in this story? A couple goes quietly on bus and train to a sanatorium where a brief scene takes place with a nurse, after which they return home and eat, have some tea, decide to go again tomorrow and the phone rings. All of the power and intensity of the story is laid in under the surface, in the back-story, in repressed and fractured and delusional hopes, in off-screen implied events. The compression with which Nabokov expresses all of this in spare prose is his genius. A screenwriter would have to deftly and with a light hand recreate the family's past, the boy's present life, and the psychological atmosphere that pervades all of their lives.

Yuri Leving: *Do you think there is any real chance that Nabokov's short story might be translated into a visual language?*

Hal Ackerman: The likelihood of sustaining this delicate web for the duration of a feature film is slim. A more probable film life for this story would be a 15–20-minute short (for which there would be no commercial market) made by a film student and shown in festivals. A festival audience would be far more willing and receptive to the quiet tone, the lack of overt larger-than-life action, and the pulled-punch ambiguous ending, all of which inform the essential truth of this story. The cinematic "opening up" would not need to be a gaping yaw, but well-chosen glimpses into the current and past lives of parents and child.

Yuri Leving: *What would be your perfect cast (all the stars' costs, of course, would be covered)?*

Hal Ackerman: A few possible pairings might be: Helen Mirren/Tom Wilkinson; John Lithgow/Meryl Streep; Paul Giamatti/Laura Linney. Probably not Brad Pitt and Angelina Jolie.

Yuri Leving: *If you were asked to write the screenplay, how might you approach it? Would you feel the need to add a great deal of "background material"? Would you count on any special montage techniques or computer-generated imagery (CGI)?*

Hal Ackerman: This is definitely not a CGI movie. Paraphrasing Billy Wilder when asked about special effects, he said, '"Yeah, we have special effects. We call it dialogue." To the larger question of creative approach and use of background material, it would depend upon whether an attempt would be made to open the story up to a feature-length film, or stay close to its own time frame and write it as a short. In the latter case not a lot would need to be added, though the time taken for the protagonists' trip to the institution could certainly be used as a hinge for flashbacks into the recent and deeper past. Expanding the project to feature length would be fraught with danger. Even with the lovely hypothetical you propose, that the salaries of the stars are paid, movies cost a bundle to make. Financing and recouping cannot be completely ignored. But on purely creative considerations, expanding the story, "opening it up" as they like to say, requires that a screenwriter invent material that in the story is only implied. While there are notable exceptions (David Seidler, Aaron Sorkin, Steve Zaillian, Nicole Holofcener to name a few), screenwriters are not generally thought of (or hired) for their literary chops. You'd want to find a writer and director with the sensitivity and ability to digest the story and transliterate it to the larger narrative canvas. The intense understated intimacy cannot be lost. Whatever back-story was dramatized would have to stand on its own dramatically, and at the same time enhance and blend seamlessly into the original material. The boy's life would inevitably become a tangible onscreen part of a feature film. This was done with great success in *Ordinary People*.

Approaching the story through theater

Yuri Leving: *If you were asked to stage Nabokov's short story, what would be your possible course of action? Would you need to make any amendments or revisions to the storyline? What would you want to highlight and what, possibly, would you want to diminish? Would you keep the open end? Would you create an alternative climax in the story?*

Murray Biggs: Since the story itself hardly needs improving, a theater adaptation could and should hew closely to Nabokov's narrative line. The original highlights the mother's character and situation and her relationship with her husband, especially as conditioned by their son's ailment. This should provide the core of the drama. The story's Pinteresque open end lends itself to reproduction on stage, especially in the modern theater, whose audiences are used to, and enjoy, being left with an ambiguous future for the action and its players.

Yuri Leving: *What would be the most obvious challenges in adapting "Signs and Symbols" for a theatrical performance?*

Murray Biggs: Given that this theater piece would work best as a one-act rather than a longer play, the main challenge would be reducing the cinematic sequence of several locations to, at most, two. My choice would be to start the play in the waiting-room of the sanatorium, where the couple's conversation could establish whatever "back-story" is necessary before the entrance of the nurse (the only other character in the adaptation) and her account of the son's present condition. A significant challenge here, as throughout the drama, would be to create the spoken dialogue that Nabokov mostly omits. His clues, however, are sufficiently specific to make this a manageable task.

The waiting room being sparsely furnished, it would not take long to switch to the second set, the couple's living room. Ideally the stage would simply swivel to reveal it. The second scene would start with the husband inside the room, rather than on the steps outside, waiting for his wife's arrival with the fish. He could here accomplish some of the solo business described in the story, perhaps adding a monologue (to the mirror) reflecting on his and the family's latest situation.

It would be possible, during the scene change, to add back-projections of the couple's weary journey home by bus and subway, although it's not obvious to me at this early stage that that would be necessary. Rather it might diminish the concentrated impact that a *short* play needs.

An important element of the story is the wife/mother's collection of memorabilia. Although this would be better represented on film (in close-up), it should be given a central place in the action of the play, accompanied by such text as is necessary, perhaps in monologue, although more credibly in the theater—in a perhaps necessary departure from the story—in dialogue with the man. The couple's souvenirs both mirror the loss of their son and compensate for it.

Yuri Leving: *Imagine directing a play based on "Signs and Symbols": What would be your genre choice? Would you resort to any special effects? Costume designs? Preferable setting? Your type of a music score? (Give free rein to your fantasy!)*

Murray Biggs: If I *had* to name a genre, I suppose it would be "situation drama". Apart from the possibility of back-projections, there would be no special effects. The story is driven, after all, by the two older people with their shared history and psychology; it's principally a study of character in a particular series of distressed situations. Their drab costumes should express all of that as realistically as possible, indeed as prescribed in the story. Any musical accompaniment (say for beginning, scene-change, and end) should quietly underscore the sadly plausible distortions of their lives: a piano piece by Russia's own Scriabin, perhaps?

A theatrical version of Nabokov's story would also need, and gain by, several gaping silences, in which what we in theater call "subtext" would speak up loud and clear.

Yuri Leving: *Could you list an ideal cast for such a play and briefly defend your selection in each specific case (appearance, psychological characteristics, previous roles, etc)?*

Murray Biggs: I could imagine an experienced international cast, with Judi Dench and Michael Gambon, and Fiona Shaw as the nurse. The faces of these two principals, neither conventionally romantic, speak for themselves. Each can convey hidden abysses of nuance and emotion. Fiona Shaw comes to mind as the strong, even stern, woman of authority, as in the film *The Last September* (also featuring Michael Gambon as a put-upon husband). An alternative to Dench would be the Irish actress Cathleen Delaney, whose face (as in John Huston's film of *The Dead* or Neil Jordan's *The Miracle*) perfectly expresses Shakespeare's "ravel'd sleeve of care."

But why not an all-Canadian cast drawn from the two notable Ontario theater festivals: Michael Ball and Mary Haney from the Shaw Festival in Niagara-on-the-Lake, and Seana McKenna from Stratford as the nurse?

Yuri Leving: *The central thematic question of "Signs and Symbols" (as formulated by J. Hagopian) is whether the boy and his parents are deluded in thinking that nature and the universe are hostile to them. Is the boy's paranoid interpretation, in fact, a delusion? How should one tackle this dichotomy, which is easily accomplished in fiction, but becomes another matter when transferred to the visual or performative medium?*

Murray Biggs: I would distinguish sharply between the parents' and the boy's perceptions of reality. The boy seems to be genuinely and totally deluded, whether or not the given medical description of his state is authentic. Some of the pathos of the writing comes from the parents' empathy with their son's mental world but at the same time their divorce from it.

Approaching the story through mathematics

Yuri Leving: *Prose and, especially, poetry, like mathematics, have developed rules for working with strings of symbols. Akin to mathematicians, the readers of fiction are looking for meanings behind the signs and symbols. By analyzing the writer's syntax (the study of the way that language is put together from symbols), how might this influence our understanding of the general semantics of art?*

John N. Crossley: Many mathematicians, including this one, are obsessed with the notion of (abstract) structure. There are two levels (at least) at which we may look at the syntax. For this short story there is the overall structure and then the structure at sentence level. Nabokov's overall structure is almost conventional, but not quite. The scene is set. A disturbing element is introduced (the son's illness). The parents go away to try to resolve the situation. A solution is proposed. Then there is an unexpected element—the phone calls. But then, instead of resolving the situation, Nabokov leaves the reader hanging. There is one obvious ending, but isn't Nabokov smarter than that? So you look for other possibilities.[1]

When we look at the sentence structure we find that Nabokov's approach is Orwellian: he uses simple words. This conveys a sense of mundanity and the drabness of the parents' existence. It also builds up an oppressive feeling. In addition, Nabokov has provoked the reader by titling his story "Signs and Symbols," so the reader is on the lookout for them. Numbers and playing cards are the most obvious items with symbolic power. Let me consider the cards first.

Turning up the ace of spades even in an innocent card game always struck fear into my superstitious mother. To her, and to many others, it symbolized death, though the card is also interpreted simply as calamity of some sort of other. The knave of hearts in turn symbolizes some young man. The reference here, at least in the reader's and the mother's mind, is virtually unambiguous—it is to the son. The nine of spades is more ambiguous. In the *Arcana Arcanorum* it is interpreted as "Taking one's position too seriously; overconfidence."[2] In the Tarot, the nine of spades does not occur, but the nine of swords has the meaning of sorrow and anguish.[3]

It is perhaps worth recalling that one of the secrets of success of (some) astrologers is their making the appropriate interpretation of such an ambiguous turn of cards.

Now let me turn to numbers. In the space of just over two thousand words or about four pages, I counted ten mentions of specific (whole) numbers plus another three implicit ones and, on top of those, the reference to calculation: "the incalculable amount of tenderness contained in the world." This density of number words is greater than my use of specific numbers in a recent book on mathematical ideas of number![4] Nabokov's explicit numbers are all even ones: 0, 2, 4, 6, 10, and 40. These are feminine numbers according to Pythagoras (and Plato) and this corresponds to the dominance of the mother in the story. Was this Nabokov's intention? We do not know.

From ancient Greek times, six has been called the first perfect number.[5] For Jung, the number four indicates completion or perfection. The received wisdom is typified by the statement that Jung "found the quaternity to be the archetypal foundation of the human psyche."[6] There is a strong correspondence between numerical aspects of Jung's psychology and Pythagorean number symbolism.[7]

Does ten signify what Pythagoreans called the *tetraktys*? If so, it signifies completion, for the *tetraktys* is comprised of a triangular array of ten dots or pebbles arranged in four rows to form a triangle, thus:

It contains $1 + 2 + 3 + 4 = 10$ pebbles. Forty, perhaps reinforcing this, combines both four and ten.

Now the dangers of interpreting such numbers, or sequences of numbers, are great. Unless the author explicitly explains their significance, each number can have many different interpretations. So to say that a text encodes a message it is necessary to have a consistent interpretation throughout the work. An author may provide such. In rare cases, such as an acrostic, the message may be visible. By employing codes, the opportunities given to the reader to interpret them are multiplied, and this can be a large part of what makes the story interesting. While it is clear that possible codes can be profitable is, on the one hand, clear in the commercial sense from books such as Dan Brown's *Da Vinci Code*, but in an intellectual sense the value is much less obvious.

Yuri Leving: *In his "Signs and Symbols" Nabokov mixes two domains, e.g. people and natural numbers. Could you offer a mathematical model for this particular short story?*

John N. Crossley: "Silence is one of the most important parts of music." This was the opinion of John Cage a long time ago, and many other composers have expressed similar sentiments. Nabokov's short story has many silences, though on first reading one is suddenly catapulted headlong into the abyss of the soliloquy on the madness of the son. On second reading, or when reading the story aloud, a long pause is called for at this juncture. The silences are the holes in the dark, even dull, tapestry of the lives of the protagonists—a tapestry that is vermiculated with the harsh, startling thread of the son's madness. The holes do not let in light but darkness. But they also allow the reader to participate in the story in the same way that a good painting involves the viewer and makes him or her construct a picture that is, at least partially, their own.

So in looking at the structure of the story I see a tapestry with lots of holes in it. The holes are traps for the reader, who is forced to make decisions at each void. In some places the choice seems predetermined—for example, at the beginning of the soliloquy one feels compelled to go on reading to find out what is happening. At the very end, on the other hand, there is a void that can be filled in one obvious way: the suicide of the son. But Nabokov is cleverer than that. He draws you in so that you feel involved and care about the son, and the parents. Partway through the story the mother thinks of "the endless waves of pain ... she and her husband had to endure." What pains? Surely not just of the son's illness: from Minsk they had gone back and forth trekking across Germany. Were they fleeing the Nazis? They had ended up in America, so this seems very likely, but they were not strict Jews, for they had been riding public transport after dark on the eve of Shabbat. The pains filled their lives, especially the living death of their son. If the son committed suicide, what would fill the void in their lives? Their whole days circled around the son, even if they did not see him.

Later you think about the end, and whether there is a less-obvious ending. Then you go back to look at other signs and symbols in the story, trying to find clues to what is "really" going on. Are the numbers significant? What do the photographs tell us? Are the playing cards clues for us, or for the mother?

Yuri Leving: *John Nash, a mathematical genius struggling with paranoid schizophrenia, who lent his story to the main character of* A Beautiful Mind *(Dir. Ron Howard, 2001), exclaims in the Hollywood movie: "What truly is logic? Who decides reason? My quest has taken me to the physical, the metaphysical, the delusional, and back. I have made the most important discovery of my career—the most important discovery of my life. It is only in the mysterious equations of love that any logic or reason can be found." To what extent can this formula be applied to the problems raised by Nabokov's short story (parental love, loss of loved ones, the inability to control the physical laws of nature, and the very notion of "reason in fiction")?*

John N. Crossley: In extreme states of mind the sufferer often makes interpretations that a more ordinary person would not. This can be both a boon and a bane. On the one hand it can reveal unsuspected connections and on the other it may lead to nonsense. The problem is deciding which is which, something the sufferer may not be able to do. So although I display enthusiasm, even passion, for some results in mathematics, I do not describe these in terms of the usual affective emotions, such as love, hate, fear, etc. Instead they are emotions such as excitement, surprise, and delight. In the case of the Nabokov story I am drawn in by compassion for the parents and concern for the son. I have known people in circumstances akin to those in the text and the story rings true; it evokes memories that are disturbing and confronting. It reveals the way that one reacts to these overwhelming difficulties.

There is a logic to our feelings, but at present, and for the foreseeable future, it is not explained in a neat formal language such as mathematics uses. Even Jung, who started investigating the connections between the psyche and number, made little progress.[8] Psychologists and philosophers still have a long way to go before we shall have such languages.

Yuri Leving: *In the essay "Narrative Entrapment in* Pnin *and 'Signs and Symbols,'" David Richter states that the author "makes the reader his ironic victim by seeming to license a response, then turning and attacking him for this presumptuous collusion" (A224: 10). What will be the likely results if one is to apply ideas of mathematical logic to deciphering Nabokov's "Signs and Symbols"? Will we be able to solve the riddle of this short story?*

John N. Crossley: Mathematical logic utilizes formal languages that are context free. That is to say, the meanings of the symbols are the same, independent of their surrounding words. Ordinary language writing and storytelling in particular are highly context sensitive. The very word "it" clearly has different interpretations depending on its context. So, at the present time, we have no way of formalizing stories.

As an example of the difficulty, consider the following paragraph of the story:

> It was past midnight when from the living room she heard her husband moan; and presently he staggered in, wearing over his nightgown the old overcoat with astrakhan collar which he much preferred to the nice blue bathrobe he had. (A13: 145)

Google Translate, after a few iterations, rendered this as:

> It was after midnight when he heard groans from the living room with her husband, and now wrapped up, wearing her nightgown in the old Persian coat with collar, he preferred the blue dress was beautiful.

Such translation was achieved by formally translating words, and sometimes phrases, without an overall contextual viewpoint. Of course, mechanical translation will improve, indeed it has dramatically improved over the last 50 years, but there is still a long way to go.

There is another difficulty. At each important point in the story there is a choice, sometimes for the writer, sometimes—as mentioned above when talking about holes—for the reader. Even if there are only 2 choices at each point, if there are 10 points there will be 1,024 possibilities. When we are presented with a finished story, then this represents just one of such possibilities. Trying to work out what went on in the writer's mind is therefore a huge task—we need to see which choice the writer made at each point. A skilful writer such as Nabokov does not even present us with a simple choice: he leaves many choices up to us. This is one of the ways he draws us in. So I agree with David Richter that the writer "makes the reader his ironic victim." Nabokov makes us care about what happens to the son and his parents.

Yuri Leving: *Is it possible that Nabokov's story has no definite solution at all, or poses limits to interpretation in terms of mathematics?*

John N. Crossley: Why should Nabokov's story have a "solution"? In mathematics in general there is usually a solution even if, in some cases, the (meta-)solution is that it is not possible to calculate a solution. In a story, however, if a question is posed without an answer then there is a real question as to whether the author implies a solution, or whether, as in the case of the present story, Nabokov wants the story to haunt the reader and make him, or her, live with the continuing problem and engage in a debate over several possible solutions.

Perhaps we want a "solution" because we want a neat ending, we long for the phrase "and they lived happily ever after." Then we can go our way in peace and do something else. But Nabokov puts us in a situation the like of which we may encounter in real life, and in real life there are dilemmas about what course of action one should take. And then, if someone does commit suicide, there are the recriminations about what would have been the best course of action and whether we could have prevented the suicide. "Surely something *more* could have been done" is an ever-present thought.

There are virtually no limits to interpretation of Nabokov's story—the holes in the story guarantee that—but Nabokov corrals the reader into thinking of a quite limited range of possibilities. The same is true of great paintings where the particular lie of an arm, or presence of an object, may invoke different feelings on the part of the viewer. Sustained, as opposed to passing interest, depends on the many-layered nature of the work of art or, in this case, the story.

Approaching the story through psychiatry

Yuri Leving: *If you were asked to diagnose a patient based on the symptoms as ascribed to the young hero of Nabokov's "Signs and Symbols," what would your likeliest expert clinical diagnosis be?*

Wayne Goodman: Schizophrenia is the most likely diagnosis of the young man in the story. He presents with a chronic history (at least four years) of delusional thinking. The delusions of schizophrenia are fixed, unshakeable, false beliefs that can be both complex and bizarre. Paranoid delusions, in which the person feels persecuted, are most common. The character of the delusions can oscillate between paranoia and grandiose. An example would be someone who fears his special powers evoke jealousy in others that threatens him. The content of the delusions of the young man seem both a blessing and a curse.

The typical clinical course of schizophrenia is onset of psychotic symptoms such as delusions and hallucinations in early adulthood. Frank psychosis is usually preceded by the emergence in childhood of odd behavior or thinking. This pattern fits that of the young man in the story.

Besides schizophrenia, the differential diagnosis includes delusional disorder and bipolar disorder. Grandiose delusions, like those of the young man, are common in the uncommon condition called delusional disorder. However, the bizarre nature of his delusions is at odds with this diagnosis. Patients with bipolar disorder can experience grandiose delusions during a manic episode. And they certainly can be suicidal. Whereas bipolar disorder is characterized by prominent alterations in mood, the young man's most striking feature is a thought disorder.

Yuri Leving: *This is purely hypothetical: Is the patient's mental condition, as described by the writer in this story, curable? What would be the possible methods of treatment for such a patient? What sorts of psychopharmacology and/or behavior modification might you recommend?*

Wayne Goodman: Some symptoms of schizophrenia show a good response to medication treatment. These include delusions and hallucinations. Depression, a common complication of schizophrenia, can also be effectively treated with medications. Unfortunately, no cure has been discovered for schizophrenia. With modern treatment, the young man should be well enough to leave the hospital and be treated as an outpatient.

Yuri Leving: *In his letter to Katharine White, the editor of The New Yorker, Nabokov emphasized: "'Referential mania' (mihi) is a special form of persecution mania. I am the first to describe it and give it a name" (July 6, 1947). Do you see any similarities between this and other existing scientific diagnoses (known or described by clinical specialists)?*

Wayne Goodman: This term, "referential mania," is not in use today. The most similar terms in use are "ideas of reference" and "delusions of reference." The former commonly refers to a negative emotional bias in which innocuous or irrelevant comments are misperceived as criticisms. The latter refers to flagrantly false and persistent conspiracy theories. As mentioned earlier, delusional thinking can blend paranoid and grandiose dispositions to the outer world. Nabokov was not the first to describe persecutory delusions laced with ideas of grandeur. He was preceded by Emil Kraepelin, Eugen Bleuler, and others.

Yuri Leving: *Despite Nabokov's assurances, Katharine White continued pressing and asked Nabokov: "Do you mean [the story] to be straight fiction, or do you mean it to be a parody or satire on the gloomy new school of psychiatric fiction? I believe that it is the latter—and if I am wrong you'll be very annoyed with me" (July 10, 1947). Are you aware of the impact of a "new school of psychiatric fiction" on either medical science or literature in the 1960–70s and whether there is any correlation between it and a real state of contemporary psychiatry? Can you see any implied satire aimed at psychiatry or medical professionals in Nabokov's short story?*

Wayne Goodman: I am not familiar with the literary school of psychiatric fiction, but, like other fans of Alfred Hitchcock, I can think of films from the mid 20th century that were influenced by psychoanalytic thinking. *Spellbound* is a prime example with its own share of signs and symbols. This 1945 mystery features an imposter heading a mental asylum and a dream sequence designed by Salvador Dali that provides clues to a murder.

Nabokov expresses disdain for the institution of psychiatry in his description of a calloused nurse who "brightly" reports the young man's latest suicide attempt. The ineptitude of the hospital is illustrated by relating that a fellow deluded patient and not a staff member prevented the young man from falling to his death.

Movie stills from Alfred Hitchcock's Spellbound *(1945), combining Freudian symbolism and Salvador Dali's surrealism.*

Yuri Leving: *All the interpretations of "Signs and Symbols," as suggested by scholar David Field, move from the question of whether or not the boy commits suicide to a consideration of the very foundation of knowledge: Can anyone know anything definitely? Are there any principles for determining reality? Are we not in fact all insane as we try to make some relative order of the world?*

Wayne Goodman: What's Normal?: Whether defined statistically (as deviation from a normal distribution), or according to the psychiatrist's schema for making a diagnosis, the young man in the story is living in a world of his mind's own creation that has little bearing to reality.

Approaching the story through literary studies

Yuri Leving: *In Michel Foucault's understanding of madness and institutional spaces, there is a deep suspicion about the "treatment" of the insane. What was the situation with asylums in Russia prior to Nabokov's departure? Although Nabokov's "Signs and Symbols" was published two decades earlier, do you note any similarities between Foucault's and Nabokov's treatment of institutional spaces?*

Frederick White: Psychiatry emerged as a distinct specialization in Russia only during the 19th century. In 1857 the first department of psychiatry was established at the Medical Surgical Academy in St. Petersburg. Students received both clinical and theoretical training and many studied or had contacts with leading European psychiatrists and neurologists. In 1900, Pavel Iakobii published a book entitled *The Principles of Administrative Psychiatry*. Iakobii, who had spent many years as a physician in Europe and practiced psychiatry in Moscow, presented a radical argument that class fears were to blame for the mistreatment of the insane in Russia. The ruling social classes built asylums to remove from society perceived enemies and competitors as well as anyone who displayed uncontrolled passions or incomprehensible behavior. Therefore asylums and hospitals were not designed to treat the ill, but to detain them, thereby turning psychiatrists into wardens in charge of a captive population.

In *Madness and Civilization*, Michel Foucault concentrates on the 1657 establishment of the *Hôpital Général* in Paris, which he understands to be a semi-judicial and administrative structure, rather than a medical institution to help the sick and poor. Almost 20 years later, an edict was passed by the king to enlarge the *hôpital général* to each city in the kingdom, thereby expanding the reach of bourgeois and monarchical control. Foucault argues that this network began a period of confinement in which those who had once been driven from city limits (beggars, indigents, and the insane) were now contained and housed apart from the general population. In these hospitals, labor was instituted as exercise and combined with moral rehabilitation to justify the site constraints and administrative enforcement. In this equation, there are both economic (putting the idle to work) and moral (maintaining the city for the virtuous) factors at play in herding undesirables into institutional spaces. The insane were grouped together with other unfortunates and little was done to treat, much less cure, their ills.

In "Signs and Symbols," a young man is incarcerated in a mental institution in Boston or New York because he is "incurably deranged." He is a danger to himself as he has tried to commit suicide at least twice. When his parents arrive, they are not allowed to see their son, but are confronted instead by the administrative face of the institution in the form of a nurse who "they did not care for." There is some doubt about the type of care their son is getting, since the first time he tried to commit suicide, it was unsuccessful only due to an "envious fellow-patient." The doctors marvel at the son's "inventiveness" and write academic papers about his condition, but there is no mention of treatment. The mother herself doubts the curative possibilities of the institution as "neglected children" are left "humming to themselves in unswept corners." (A13: 141) The boy's father believes that they should bring their son home or they will be responsible for his death.

Although much must be extrapolated from Nabokov's short story, it is clear that, like with Iakobii and much later with Foucault, the institution's main aim is to segregate the ill from the well. The parents' desire to bring their son home will most certainly be met with refusals from the institution, doctors, and even family members ("It does not matter what the Prince says": A11: 62–73). As Foucault would later argue, the establishment of mental asylums is for the sane, not the insane. Treatment is not the issue, rather the incarceration of the ill. In Nabokov's story, we find a similar dilemma in which the parents must either go against the norms of society (allow the insane to live within society), or take moral responsibility for the certain death of their son (through institutional neglect he will eventually be successful in killing himself).

Yuri Leving: *Is there any particular tradition of madness in Russian or European literature and culture that Nabokov alludes to here?*

Frederick White: Russia's cultural and scientific understanding of madness was originally influenced by German writers such as Joseph Eichendorff, Ludwig Tieck, Novalis, and E. T .A. Hoffmann; philosophers such as Arthur Schopenhauer and Friedrich Nietzsche; and psychiatrists such as Emil Kraepelin and Sigmund Freud. By 1875, the vast majority of professors in Russia had received their first degrees in Germany. A fundamental shift in medicine occurred around this time, altering the way in which madness (and all other illnesses) would be conceptualized and discussed. German medicine suggested that illnesses have a pathology—medicine was no longer about symptoms as much as about causal agents and organic forms. In psychiatry, this shift resulted in an evolution of thought on madness—there would now be one conceptual norm with deviations or variations from that norm.

This evolution of thought is reflected in Russian artistic depictions of madness. We might start in the Romantic period with Aleksandr Pushkin and Vladimir Odoevskii in which we find fantastical stories about characters being driven mad by fear or supernatural forces. Nabokov seems to draw especially from Pushkin's "The Bronze Horseman" and "The Queen of Spades." With Nikolai Gogol we find the last remnants of a Romantic Realism, in which fantastical madness is now brought on by real-world pressures—poverty, drug abuse, depression. These socio-economic factors are then fully exploited by Fyodor Dostoevsky, whose characters habitually struggle to maintain their sanity despite the outward pressures driving them towards madness. The underground man, Goliadkin, and Raskolnikov are examples of characters who attempt to maintain sanity through excessive reason. Nabokov's *Despair*, as an example, seems to rethink Dostoevsky's "The Double."

With the beginning of the 20th century, Russia (as with Europe) begins to interpret metal illness in a new and different way. In an attempt to carve out a place for psychiatry within medicine, madness would now be dealt with as a disease. In response, artists at first rejected scientific medicine in favor of the irrational, championing madness over reason, yet they too eventually began to reflect in their works the contemporary medical discourse of the time. Gone was the German Romantic notion of *irrational inspiration*, replaced by a growing suspicion that civilization was under threat of moral and mental devolution. As a result, the aim of psychiatry was to depict a disease that had no uniform symptomatology. Identification and then isolation of the insane individual as a possible dangerous menace to society replaced the Romantic notion of the mad genius. This medical discourse of identification and incarceration can be found in works by Vsevolod Garshin ("The Red Poppy"), Anton Chekhov ("The Black Monk"; "Ward No. 6") and Leonid Andreev ("The Thought"; "My Notes").

Later, Freud had an *indirect* impact on the Soviet Union (many of his ideas were reconfigured without direct attribution), but was recognized and quite influential in European intellectual and popular thought. His theories on psychoanalysis and the treatment of the mentally ill became ubiquitous in intellectual discourse of the 20th century. Although Nabokov referred to Freud dismissively as the "Viennese witchdoctor," the author's references to and parodies of Freudian psychology suggest that he had more than a passing knowledge of this medical discourse.

Yuri Leving: *Stephen Parker curiously suggests that the disease of "referential mania" might also be some type of literary sickness that readers can suffer from if they get too involved in a text and begin to over focus on it at the expense of the real world around them. Is it possible that Nabokov exposes or even derides here not only the medical discourse but also literature itself (and in direct reference: literary criticism as well)?*

Frederick White: Parker's suggestion is a little disconcerting as it smacks of Max Nordau's theories on degeneration at the beginning of the 20th century. The physician Bénédict Augustin Morel developed the idea of mental degeneration during the second half of the nineteenth century. Morel successfully argued certain elements of society were devolving, becoming genetically weaker with each generation, which would result in imbecility and sterility. Nordau expanded the concept beyond psychiatry, recognizing degeneration in the decadence and willful rejection of moral boundaries in *fin de siècle* Europe. In essence, Nordau transferred Morel's scientific theory of mental degeneration from the insane asylum to the literary *avant-garde*. His book, *Degeneration* (1892; Russian translation 1893), was concerned with the pathology of artistic production, whereby the very act of creation results in the release of vapors that are both the source of creative fantasy and the result of physical illness. Henrik Ibsen, Oscar Wilde, Paul-Marie Verlaine, Charles Baudelaire, Richard Wagner, and many others fell into his purview. Nordau's goal was to stigmatize these cultural figures as perverted and sick. The key assertion was that not only the art, but also the artist, was degenerate, depicted as a dangerous spokesmen for the world of the debauched *fin de siècle*, nourishing a neurotic audience with artistic delusions. Nordau and his pseudo-scientific methods were used extensively by Russian critics to stigmatize their own literary competitors until as late as the 1930s. As such, I am resistant to the notion that "Signs and Symbols" can spread "referential mania" to its readers, thereby perpetuating Nordau's dubious assertions.

I think that Nabokov himself would find Parker's suggestion appetizing for derision. After all, he enjoyed poking a stick at Freud and his followers during his lifetime. For example, in his 1963 introduction to *The Defense*, Nabokov states:

> I have made it a rule to address a few words of encouragement to the Viennese delegation. The present foreword shall not be an exception. Analysts and analyzed will enjoy, I hope, certain details of the treatment Luzhin is subjected to after his breakdown (such as the curative insinuation that a chess player sees Mom in his Queen and Pop in his opponent's King), and the little Freudian who mistakes a Pixlok set for the key to a novel will no doubt continue to identify my characters with his comic-book notion of my parents, sweethearts and serial selves. For the benefit of such sleuths I may as well confess that I gave Luzhin my French governess, my pocket chess set, my sweet temper, and the stone of the peach I plucked in my own walled garden.

Here, Nabokov is able to chastise both psychoanalysts and the would-be Freudian literary critic. Similarly, I think that Nabokov would relish the notion that a bunch of educated individuals would read too much into his diagnosis of "referential mania." The bait seems to have been provided for us to drive ourselves into some sort of mania while looking for all of the possible references that Nabokov has or has not planted in his works for us to find (or not).

Yuri Leving: *Given that "Signs and Symbols" has a rather brief explanation of the character's mental illness, can you draw any inferences from Nabokov's other works about his depiction of madness?*

Frederick White: Earlier in Nabokov's literary career, he concentrated on the issue of mental illness in both *Despair* and *The Defense*. In both of these works, Nabokov draws from a rich tradition, as noted above, of literary texts that depict madness. A brief discussion of these texts opens to us a few seemingly random details in "Signs and Symbols" that, not surprisingly, augment Nabokov's treatment of the son's illness.

The Defense was first published in 1930 and tells the story of a Russian émigré chess champion, Luzhin, who eventually goes mad and commits suicide. Although Luzhin suffers several break-downs prior to his suicide, no medical diagnosis is offered, other than the suggestion that he has exhausted himself from too much mental activity (some version of neurasthenic mania). Even so, it is quite clear that Nabokov wished to create a character who from early childhood finds refuge from an overactive mind in the logical and rational moves of the chess game. Unfortunately, Luzhin's obsessive compulsion to find patterns in daily life, which made him so successful at chess, also causes his ultimate demise. Although we have less detail about the son in "Signs and Symbols," Nabokov's reference to "referential mania" suggests a similar malady in both the son and in Grand Master Luzhin. Some credence is given to this comparison by Nabokov's own allusions to *The Defense* in this short story. For example, there is mention that the son's "cousin [is] a famous chess player." Also, both Luzhin and the son displayed "eccentricities of a prodigiously gifted child." Given the inter-connectedness of Nabokov's literary world, I do not think that it is too preposterous to look to the symptomatology of Luzhin to better understand what Nabokov means by "referential mania."

Despair was first published in Russian in 1934. In this work, Nabokov tells the tale of Hermann, who believes that he has met his double, and, as a result, decides to kill the double in order to collect on his own life-insurance policy. The problem is that Hermann is deranged and the double, as it turns out, is not actually a double, only perceived to be such by Hermann. After the murder, it is revealed in the newspapers that the victim looks nothing like the murderer, although the dead man is dressed in Hermann's clothes. This story shares similarities with Dostoevsky's "The Double," in which the character Goliadkin perceives of his own double in the work place, a man who is significantly more successful than Goliadkin himself. Nabokov also makes references to *Crime and Punishment* and Raskolnikov, who commits murder for personal gain and then is haunted to near madness for this decision.

In *Despair*, Nabokov also makes passing references to Pushkin's "The Bronze Horseman" and "The Queen of Spades." The hero of both Pushkin's and Nabokov's stories is Hermann. In "The Queen of Spades," Hermann commits murder to learn the secret card combination that will make him rich. Just as he seems to play this winning hand, one of the cards changes to the queen of spades, and he sees the face of the woman whom he has killed for the card combination, while also losing his fortune to this misplay. Hermann then spends the rest of his life in an insane asylum going over this three-card combination. We see this reference once again in "Sign and Symbols": "the knave of hearts, the nine of spades, the ace of spades, the maid Elsa and her bestial beau." (A13: 165) The bestial beau would be Pushkin's and Nabokov's Hermann.

Finally, Nabokov makes several momentary allusions to the medical science of the beginning of the twentieth century with references to phrenology, dangerous lunatics, and those who have morally perished. Degeneration theory suggested that mental illness was related to both the moral and mental decline of the individual, which would result in criminal behavior. Clearly, Hermann's mental illness is a factor in his criminal behavior. Nabokov also takes a funny swipe, for good measure, at psychoanalysis and their proponents: "those irresponsible scribblers, those purveyors of thrills, those villainous quacks." In this work, then, Nabokov seems to have little faith in the medical profession and even creates a character who parodies many of their medical theories.

It is often dangerous in literary studies to make associations between literary works without substantiation by the author himself, whether a reference in a letter to a colleague or a note in a diary. In the case of Nabokov, however, the referential *game* is one established by the author himself and invites just the type of associations that are normally taboo with other authors. As such, I think that we can gain insights into the madness of the son in "Signs and Symbols" by following Nabokov's literary allusions, especially in this case, as there is so little actual information about the real diagnostic details of the son's illness.

An attempt at synthesis

Yuri Leving: *This is a general question to everyone. Please contemplate the following question based on your personal reading of the short story: The third phone call is an open ending for "Signs and Symbols" which Nabokov might have utilized to create an atmosphere of mystery and suspense. Is the third call from the hospital, reporting that the son has finally succeeded in committing suicide? Is it the unknown girl dialing a wrong number again? Could it be the couple's son himself calling? How do you interpret the ending, given the events that have preceded it?*

John N. Crossley: The obvious response is to feel that when the phone rings for the third time it is the hospital calling to say that the son's most recent attempt at suicide has succeeded, though there is clearly the possibility of a third call for "Charlie." In the former case one may take comfort from the belief that this will bring closure for the parents, but anyone who has been close to a young person who has committed suicide knows that there are all sort of emotions that erupt. Further, there is always a void left. For the parents here, their life has been largely filled by their son. What life will they have if he is gone?

There is at least one further possibility, one other ending. The parents, or perhaps, rather, the mother, could just let the ringing of the phone lapse. If answering it would bring the expected bad news, then there is nothing that they can do at this hour of night, since they are dependent on public transport. In any case, they were already proposing to go to the hospital in the morning. If it is not the hospital, it could be the girl again, and again there is nothing more they can do. They do not seem to have many friends, so it is unlikely that one would be calling at this time. So there is nothing to be done now. There is no peace, and yet, the rest is silence.[9]

Murray Biggs: Since I've already expressed a preference for the story's open end, I refrain from answering this question. The theater audience should be left to pose such questions for and to themselves, answering them (if at all) as they please. For me, the whole impact of Nabokov's ending resides in this unknowable.

Frederick White: "Signs and Symbols" is very reminiscent of Gothic horror literature, in particular "The Monkey's Paw" (1902) by W. W. Jacobs. I cannot be certain that Nabokov was paying homage to Jacob's short story, but there are too many similarities to ignore. More importantly, an examination of Jacob's story gets to the heart of your question. "The Monkey's Paw" begins with a father and son playing chess (a favorite of Nabokov), which is interrupted with the arrival of the Sergeant-Major. The father, Mr White, eventually prods the Sergeant-Major into telling the story of his mummified monkey's paw. It seems that an old Fakir wanted to show that fate ruled people's lives and that those who interfered were punished. The old Fakir put a spell on the paw so that three different men could each have three wishes from it. I might note the repetition of threes, which is also essential to Nabokov's story. Upon questioning, it is learned that the Sergeant-Major has received his three wishes, and rather than selling the paw or passing it on to someone else, he decides to toss it on the fire. Mr White pulls the paw out of the fire, but the visitor warns that he cannot be held accountable for the talisman, believing that it should be destroyed.

Later, Mr White takes the paw, and, after admitting that he already has all that he wants from life, wishes for £200. The money does not suddenly appear, but Mr White is sure something occurred, as the paw twisted in his hand as he was making the wish. The next day, the couple's son leaves for work, and the wish is almost forgotten until later in the day, when a representative from the mill arrives at the White's home to say that their son has been caught in the factory's machinery and killed. The company offers the couple £200 as compensation.

The couple is devastated by their loss, but one day Mrs White remembers the monkey's paw and she asks her husband to use the second wish to bring their son back from the dead. The father is reluctant because not only has his son been dead for ten days, but the young man was mangled by the machinery, and could hardly return from this experience whole. The couple argues, but the wife is insistent. Mr White concedes and wishes that their son were alive once again. As the evening approaches, there is a knock at the door. Mr White is afraid to open the door, but his wife is certain that it is their son returned. Mrs White runs downstairs to open the door, but cannot reach the bolt. The faint knocking continues and Mr White fumbles for the monkey's paw and makes his final wish. The knocking ceases. When his wife finally opens the door, there is nothing there. The reader is left to wonder whether this was really their son or if all of this was simply a series of coincidences: the death of their son, the £200, and the faint knocking at their door.

Whether Nabokov had this particular tale in mind is unclear, but a similar narrative arc results in an analogous mystery. In "Signs and Symbols" we again have a husband and wife who have lost their son, this time to madness. They too feel guilty, this time due to his institutionalization and, in their minds, his abandonment. They too contemplate changing the fate of their son by caring for him themselves (can we suggest bringing him back to life?) in their own home. Yet, before this can happen, the couple is confronted with two misplaced telephone calls to an unknown Charlie. The story ends with a third call, late at night, that may again be for Charlie, or may be the hospital calling to say that their son has committed suicide. Is it their son? Is it a bad omen? We will never know. Just with Jacobs' story, there is no correct answer. The reader cannot figure out who is calling or if the mangled corpse is actually knocking at the door. Horror and terror, the main components of the Gothic story, are effectively created because we do not know and never will. Therefore, I suggest that Nabokov has established several possibilities for the third call on purpose, and has intentionally given no concrete clues to a *correct* answer because the story would lose all of its suspense once deciphered, if that was possible.

Wayne Goodman: I interpreted the third phone call as a call from the hospital informing his parents that their son has escaped. By that I mean either through suicide or leaving the grounds. The son was determined to "tear a hole in his world" and the hospital staff was incapable of stopping him. But I do not envision a happy reunion with his family. There is no room in their world for him.

Hal Ackerman: It is tempting, of course, to supply an answer to the story's final question. Given Nabokov's sense of humor, if there were an answer, it might be a wrong number or a Canadian pharmacy spam calling to sell Viagra. The decision of how to end the film speaks to the differing expectations that audiences bring with them. Contemporary feature film audiences, sadly, do not relish ambiguity. (Certainly the executives who pre-decide these questions believe that to be true. I once had an executive tell me "We have a C-List audience. Write down to them."). Purveyors of literary fiction are far more open to challenge. Think of "The Lady or the Tiger." There's no answer given. Movies (famously, *Casablanca*) have had several endings shot, the director ultimately settling on one. With today's interactive technology, audiences might be given the choice of several answers.

CRITICISM

PART ONE
Bone Structure

Frameworks

Vladimir Nabokov's correspondence with *The New Yorker* regarding "Signs and Symbols," 1946–8

Olga Voronina

Vladimir Nabokov first met Katharine Sergeant Angell White, the editor at *The New Yorker* and one of its founders, through Edmund Wilson. Mrs White, who had taken a leave of absence from the magazine to spend time in Maine with her husband, writer E. B. White, admired Nabokov's stories, published in *The Atlantic*. In January, 1944, after returning to New York and resuming her job, she told Wilson her dream—to have Nabokov shift allegiances and start publishing for them. Wilson introduced this idea to his Russian friend, mentioning, among other things, *The New Yorker* rates (they were much higher than those at *The Atlantic*). In a letter to Wilson on January 11, Katharine White mentioned her being "anxious to have Mr Nabokov send us prose as well as poetry." In June, the money-conscious Nabokovs received the first advance from *The New Yorker*. "Time and Ebb," however, the short story Nabokov submitted in September, failed to launch the relationship with perfect mutual understanding and good will. Referring to her colleagues ("we all feel"), Mrs White rejected Nabokov's "mocked learned style" and regretted that, "sometimes, in spite of its being parody, [the story] becomes rather heavy reading" (September 28, 1944).[1] Nabokov retorted in a similarly blunt manner: "I was a little shocked by your readers' having so completely missed the point of my story" (October 26, 1944).

The sharpness of this early exchange is emblematic of what followed. By and large, the relationship between a writer and an editor progresses towards greater mutual understanding. Professional sympathies may or may not lead to a friendship, but the evolution of reciprocal tolerance is typically expected. Nabokov took an immediate liking to the impeccably polite, knowledgeable, ironic, and responsive Mrs White as well as to her talented husband, whose love of the outdoors and a life-long fondness for dachshunds he found most endearing. But no matter how affable their letters were regarding all matters personal, their arguments of technique never ceased. Neither Nabokov's increasing fame nor his firmness in resisting editorial interference would stop Mrs White from unfailingly criticizing chapters from what was to become *Conclusive Evidence* and *Pnin*. She insisted that "Curtain Raiser," an autobiographical story, was written "more hastily" than Nabokov's other work (July 28, 1948). She demanded that he take scientific words out of "Portrait of My Mother," and complained that the famous synaesthesia passage was too long ("Once the reader gets the idea we believe that he may find the color description of your mental images of the letters a bit prolonged and we do honestly feel that, coming so near the start of the story, it might make him think the piece to be of a very different nature from what it turns out to be" [March 1, 1949]). Finally, she would become alarmed at Nabokov's "political passages," asking him to shorten them as well as to change the tone of "Student Days," which seemed to her "a little harsh and hysterical" (November 8, 1949). To these comments, expressed in a patient and often apologetic tone, Nabokov responded curtly and without remorse. "Do please, please say you will rework ["Student Days"] for us," pleaded Mrs White. "I am terribly sorry but what you suggest is quite impossible" was the typical reply she would get (November 9, 1949).

This was not a battle of wills, as it may seem at first glance. Nabokov appreciated every correction from his editor that might help him avoid embarrassment. Though he was a master like no other, he was still grappling in the 1940s with the intricacies of English, some of them semi-hidden, like tree roots on a wanderer's path, others lying in plain view. The correspondence about "Signs and Symbols," which yielded the greatest number of letters per one Nabokov story published in *The New Yorker*, ended with

Nabokov's request that Mrs White alter the line "with his elbows raised" to "with his bare arms clasped under his head" (March 29, 1948). The change was impossible, she said: "Arms can't be clasped—only hands" (April 1, 1948).

Nabokov was mortified even more to find out that his reference to "broken blossoms" in the same story harbored sexual connotations. "You are absolutely right about the broken blossoms affair," he wrote back in haste. "I did not mean it to come through the mother's mental screen but I confess I did not realize the whole effect of the platitude" (March 29, 1948).

Authorial ambition also had little to do with Nabokov's resistance. After a few short stories and poems edited by Katharine White, the writer began to value her judgment and anticipate her disapproval even before it was expressed. On July 5, 1945, for example, he began his letter of submission with self-criticism, saying that not only the title of "Curtain Raiser" was "optional," but that one of the passages in the story might "be not quite seemly on the pages of a magazine." Calling himself a "self-centered author," Nabokov thanked Mrs White for her "readiness to see [his] point of view" (March 29, 1948).

The real crux of whatever misunderstanding there existed between Nabokov and Katharine White was the difference in their picturing the audience for Nabokov's work. *The New Yorker* catered to the "average" reader, characterized by his or her affiliation with the middle class, some academic background, and whole range of interest in literature, from ardent to none. For Nabokov, such a reader was nonexistent. He kept telling his editor to stop imagining bubbleheads and philistines lurking behind *The New Yorker* pages. She could not. In a letter of November 8, 1949, the phantom reader re-emerged:

[A]gain, this is the matter of tone, into which the reader reads so much more than the author sometimes intends. Understatement, we think, usually conveys the point more convincingly than overstatement, and you do not want your readers to take sides, in their emotion, against your point of view just because you have expressed it too strongly. Do you see what I mean?

Nabokov responded without hesitation. He withdrew the story,[2] commenting on his decision in a mockingly regretful voice: "It is quite staggering to think that those immortal dumpy club women will not foregather any more on your pages" (November 9, 1949).

His disapproval of the imagined community of *The New Yorker* readers notwithstanding, Nabokov remained with the magazine for 30 years. During five of them, Katharine White nursed his English and nurtured it to perfection. Distrustful of others who might misinterpret Nabokov's intentions, she was one of his most attentive and caring readers. She left the magazine in 1949, passing Nabokov on to William Maxwell and other editors. Their correspondence about "Signs and Symbols" reveals her exactness and an almost maternal circumspection. It also speaks of Nabokov's unfailing gratitude to his editor.

January 1, 1946

Dear Mrs White,

Thanks for your charming letter. I do have a story for you—but it is still in my head; quite complete, however; ready to emerge; the pattern showing through the wingcases of the pupa. I shall write it as soon as I get rid of my novel,[3] i.e. in a couple of months. [...]

Very sincerely yours,
V. Nabokov

I (and my son) enjoyed hugely your husband's last book.[4] I have admired his art since his red barn cast that blue shadow (in Harper's?)[5]

January 30, 1946

Dear Mr Nabokov,

[…] Bunny[6] says you are very much involved in your novel, but, even so, here I am nagging you again with the wild hope you may have a poem or a story to send us. I know that sometimes authors who are doing a book like to take a breather and write something short, and I'm hoping this might be true of you. So many of our current contributors seem to be in a slough of bad writing that we badly need your touch. […]

Sincerely Yours,
K. White

April 9, 1946

Dear Mrs White,

[…] I have a story kicking in my womb, but it will have to stay there until I am through with the novel. […]

Sincerely yours,
V. Nabokov

April 11, 1946

Dear Mr Nabokov,

[…] I am anxious to have your novel go well and quickly so that you can give birth to the story which is kicking around so actively. Remember, it is very dangerous for the child to be delayed! […]

Sincerely yours,
Katharine S. White

January 2, 1947

Dear Mr Nabokov,

This note is to wish you Happy New Year and to ask whether there's a chance that you may be able to send us some poetry or a story before long. I'm afraid that there notes from me sound like the buzzings of a gadfly. Please don't read them that way for I only write because it's such a pleasure to all of us here when one of your manuscripts comes in that we miss them when they don't. A Nabokov story or poem would start the new year off well in these offices. [...]

Sincerely yours,
Katharine S. White

July 3, 1947

Dear Mr Nabokov:

This is just a note, typed by myself as my country secretary comes only every other day, to tell you that the answer is "yes" on "Symbols and Signs," which we think a most unusual and effective story. A check will go to you when it is edited and in proof and I'm assuming that we have your usual permission to edit. I don't foresee any very drastic changes—just routine. Ross seems to feel that the severing of the tusks of saliva from the dental plate is just too disagreeable—or anyway that he'd prefer not to have them there. Is that okay? One thing we need to know is whether Herman Brink is a real name or not and whether "referential mania" is a real disease or one you invented. If the name is that of a real doctor we might have to change it or reword to show he was not in charge of this boy's case. If the term "referential mania" is invented, that presents more of a problem. Possibly you'd write me an airmail note about these small points. In any case I'll go ahead to put the piece through and we can thrash the details out in proof.

It's a pleasure to be buying one of your stories again. I hope that you'll soon have the Russian memories for us again, in new form. Colorado must be good to be in—so is Maine. I was awfully disappointed not to be able to come to Cambridge that night or to see you and Mrs Nabokov. The journey really had put me to bed. I have a miserable trouble in my spine that gets stirred up to be seriously painful when I motor, go on trains, or do things like packing trunks. That Friday night was the end of a frightful two weeks. I ought to have known better than even to have planned to see you and I hope that I did not upset your plans too badly.

Sincerely yours,
Katharine S. White

July 6, 1947

Dear Mrs White,

Thank you for your note. I am very glad you like the story.

The doctor is purely fictional. Should you discover that one of that name exists—which would be an odd coincidence—I would not object to a re-christening.

The saliva is another matter. I would hate to see it go. I would agree to part with it, if you insist, but the parting would be quite a wrench.

"Referential mania" (mihi) is a special form of persecution mania. I am the first to describe it and give it a name.

We both regretted very much that you were so sick when you came to Boston. We hope that you will be well again after your summer rest.

Sincerely yours,
V. Nabokov[7]

July 10, 1947

Dear Mr Nabokov:

I hope that the first check for "Symbols and Signs" has reached you now—it should have.

About the story, I've decided to ask you what your intention is in it, since there are differing interpretations on that point in the office. Do you mean it to be straight fiction, or do you mean it to be a parody or satire on the gloomy new school of psychiatric fiction? I believe that it is the latter—and if I am wrong you'll be very annoyed with me. On the other hand, Mr Ross and Mr Lobrano, unless I misinterpret their opinion sheets, think it is a straight-forward and moving short story, (and as for its being moving, I agree on that, satire or no satire, and I admit that on first reading I took it to be straight. The point is that if it *is* satire, we ought not to remove the tucks of saliva and your other particularly gruesome, realistic details, and we probably should give it a subtitle of some sort, to give the reader a steer. Some such thing as "After a Holiday Excursion into the Gloomy Precincts of the Modern Psychiatric Novel" might do it, or any thing you can think of that is better. Then every touch you give of what might be considered over-writing in a straight realistic story ought to be retained and even heightened. If, however, it is pure realism, then we ask your permission to tone down the realism, just for fear the story might be considered overwritten and overwrought, and seem like a parody without your intending it to be one.

I have been at a disadvantage on this piece because of your being at a distance and because of my working at long distance from the office. It is always more difficult to discuss details of any manuscript with my colleagues by letter instead of in conversation, and one long distance telephone call, when I might have been able to clarify matters, proved almost entirely inaudible.

I'll go as far as to say that I believe this story, whatever your intention, will be better as satire than as realism and hope that you'll be willing to let it read that way, and to add a clarifying subtitle and possibly some additional touches of grimness that you could add in proof. (I don't of course yet know whether the other

editors will agree with me on this, but I rather think they will.)
For one thing, your invention of a new mania, which, by the way,
seems to be wonderfully ingenious, seems to me to throw the whole
thing out as straight fiction. That section would be very funny if the
reader were really on it.

I hope you'll be willing to admit that the two differing interpretations show that you have not quite put the story over, either as
one thing or the other. But this doesn't mean that it can't be made
to go either way you intend, with a bit of fussing. Whatever your
answer, I hope you'll find the situation in the New Yorker office
rather comic, and trust you'll be more amused than annoyed by it.

Let me hear. Referential mania (mihi)!

K. S. White

July 15, 1947

Dear Mrs White,

I have tried to look at my story from every possible point of
view, and this is the result of my re-examination.

Not withstanding all my efforts, I fail to see your point. I do not
see it as a parody, and I do not see why it matters whether it is or
is not one. It is a good sample of my usual style and outlook and I
do not find it either overwrought or overwritten.

If you insist on having a subtitle (which I do not think
necessary), have one by all means. I should prefer it to be as short
as possible, —I am afraid, I do not understand to what 'Modern
Psychoanalytic Novels' you refer (unless they are my own) for I
don't read much fiction.

Very sincerely yours,
V. Nabokov

July 19, 1947

Dear Mr Nabokov:

Thank you for your letter of the fifteenth. It's exactly the definitive sort of answer that clarifies the whole business, and you'll be glad to know that most of the other editors read the story as you intended it to be read. I was the one who was nagged by the suspicion that there might be more than met the eye in your piece. It was when I came to edit it that the grim details began to accumulate in my mind and that these (together with your having wrote that you had invented "referential mania," on top of a year or two of novels and plays dealing with psychotics) suggested to me that you might have a satiric invention as well as a purely fictional one. I was wrong and it makes it really much simpler that I was. There will be no subtitle. I stick to my guns that unless the story was satirical, you may have overwritten it at a few points and a preliminary proof from the office (which is still somewhat unexplained until the final queries come in) makes me suspect that Mr Ross and the others also thought that you had overemphasized the grimness occasionally. I reported him and Mr Lobrano wrong, I am told, when I said that they interpreted the story as pure realism. What Mr Lobrano wrote about it was that it was a "brilliant oddity." At any rate, we are all in agreement that the story is outstanding, however one looks at it.

If my letter annoyed you, you must blame only me and not the magazine. I've never known, though, how to act as an editor conducting business by mail, except to speak with the same frankness and forthrightness that I would if I were talking to an author. If I could have seen you, I could just have asked your intentions before the piece was edited, or if there had not been the rush to get a check to you, I could have inquired by letter. And now I apologize for bothering you thus. I am not apologetic, though, for telling you my honest doubts, and I can't help hoping that you would rather have had me do so. Am I forgiven?

Because of the difficulties of editing at long distance when one is not able to discuss details face to face with one's colleagues, I'm going to ask Mr Lobrano to send you your author's proof, for your approval, edited as he and Mr Ross decide. My initial editing to get the story into proof embodied few changes because the story was written in excellent English. I doubt that any further editing will be anything very drastic.

<...> Please forgive this messy and ill-typed letter which is written in haste to catch the last mail before Sunday.

Faithfully yours,
K. S. White

––––––––––––––––––––

July 22, 1947

Dear Mrs White,

Do not give another thought to the little misunderstanding about the story: I know your kind interest in my work and, if only for this reason, was certainly not annoyed by your letters.

Sincerely yours,
V. Nabokov

––––––––––––––––––––

January 26, 1948

Dear Mr Nabokov:

<...> I am enclosing a vari-type copy of "Butterflies." This is not an author's proof. <...>

I hope you will have time to work on this soon because we are threatened with a printers' strike and I would like to get it set up as fast as possible. This strike and various other matters are why we have been so slow. We are standing on our heads, so to speak. This is another reason why you have not yet had a proof on "Symbols and Signs." That went out of my hands last summer but I am getting it taken up this week, and hope to have a proof for you soon.

Faithfully yours,
K. S. White

March 8, 1948

Dear Mr Nabokov:

<...> I enclose at last the author's proof on "Symbols and Signs." As you will remember, I wrote you when we bought it that there were a few things we all felt the story would be better without, but there are not many and I think you will find the story substantially as you wrote it. Mr Ross writes on his notes "Think this very good story and hope that Mr Nabokov will do more third person current stories. This is a very good picture of hopeless misery to me." But he did ask that the tusks of saliva, the birth mark, and a few other things be taken out, and I hope you will agree that the story is improved thereby, or at least not injured. I will put the notes on a separate sheet.

Did I tell you—I guess not—that in April I have to go to the hospital for an operation on my spine? It will be one of those prolonged affairs, I am afraid, but William Maxwell is returning to take my place for two or three months and you will be hearing from him probably. He is a first rate writer himself and one of our oldest editorial hands and I'm sure you will like working with him. I am trying to finish up all the proofs now available before I go and I very much hope you will have a story or two in before I leave which won't be until the end of the first week in April. I shall be reading manuscripts again by the first of July I hope, though I won't get out of a brace until fall. This business probably comes from an old injury to my spine that I got from falling on the ice when in Maine five or six years ago.

Sincerely yours,
K. S. White[8]

March 13, 1948

Dear Mrs White

I am very sorry to hear that you will have to undergo an operation. I do hope that it will definitely relieve you of those pains you have been suffering for so long.

In regard to the proofs of "Signs and Symbols," I am afraid I cannot accept most of the alterations and omissions. Frankly, I would prefer you not to publish the story at all if it had to be so carefully mutilated. In fact I am completely against the whole idea of my stories being edited. Among the alterations inflicted upon this story, there is not a single really necessary one and many are murderous. I add a list of the things I really want restored (from my script). There are some additional things noted on the galleys. Other changes (transposition of words, etc.) are also unwarranted though less important. All this has distressed me to such a degree that I have had to interrupt for a time my work on a new story.

If you accept my restitutions, please send me the proofs again.

Very sincerely yours,
V. Nabokov[9]

March 22, 1948

Dear Mr Nabokov:

I am exceedingly sorry that the proof of "Symbols and Signs" upset you and interrupted your work on a new story. Let me say at once that we are willing to make almost all the changes or stets that you ask for but we do ask your reconsideration and rewording of two or three places for reasons I will explain. I certainly hope that by cooperation we can work out the matter to our mutual satisfaction. But before I go into details, will you bear with me while I go back over the history of this manuscript since I think it will give some light on why we got into such difficulties over it?

As you know, I have made a habit of sending you, on every manuscript of yours we buy, a typescript or vari-type copy showing our suggested editing and queries, and asking your help or approval of every word changed from your original—all this before we put the piece into type or buy it. After we have your consent on changes, we then buy the manuscript, set it in type, and send you the usual author's proof. With most writers the first step is omitted and we send them only an author's proof, unless there is some special reason to consult them. (Of course if the author is in New York we talk over the editing.) We are glad to put in this extra step in your case because your writing is particularly complex and subtle, your subject matter is apt to be exotic and special, and your idiom and style is particularly personal and, too, it often includes foreign words, matters of English usage, etc. Only in the case of "Symbols and Signs" was this first step of submitting to you the edited piece in typescript form omitted, and the story set in type at once. The reason this happened was that you were in Colorado and wrote that you were short of cash and asked me to wire you whether we were buying the story. I was in Maine by that time and the whole office was on vacation schedules but I got on the long distance phone and arranged a small immediate advance, and also, in order that you should not be delayed in receiving the rest of your check for the story, since I had no way of knowing whether the advance would be enough for your needs, I omitted the first step of sending you the story edited in typescript, and had the story set in type after the usual editing. Because we pay by measurement of type, there would have been no way of getting you a check without considerable delay—perhaps two weeks or more of correspondence back and forth to Colorado would have been involved if I'd sent you a typescript of it. Also I had written you earlier telling you that Mr Ross had asked for some modifications of your unpleasant details and I also asked for permission to give the story the usual routine editing. Your letter had made me think it was safe to go ahead. Well, that is water over the dam, but I now realize that you would have not suffered so over the author's proof if I had not tried to speed the payment up for you, and it never occurred to me then that we would have difficulties on the changes since they seemed to us not very considerable. Also, I want to remind you that author's proofs are sent just so that the author may receive explanations for changes, if they need explanation, and so that he may reword the editing in his own way. All rewordings on proofs must be always considered dummy wordings and we *want* authors to reword such changes in their own way. Changes involved in editing are usually merely suggestions. I know from personal experience that our author's proofs are annoying to get (I mean I know it on things I have written myself) but in the end I've found, and so have most writers, that at least *some* of the points are well taken and improve the piece. Those that are not, can usually be eliminated. Of course Mr Ross, as editor-in-chief, reserves the right not to print anything he really disapproves of or finds he does not care to print. But he is a great admirer of your writing, particularly likes "Symbols and Signs," and is willing to accept almost all your stets. I am one of those here who think we over-edit, and I half think that some of us in the fiction department are making some headway toward getting the editing reduced. It's a case I shall press for as long as I work here. I know that Mr Lobrano feels much the way I do. But I am only a middleman in some ways—I argue the cause of the writer with the editor-in-chief with whom I sometimes agree and sometimes do not.

Now, to turn to the proof. I have made a new proof showing that we accept your stets on everything except at (A), (B), and (C), and these we ask you to reconsider, if you will be so very kind. I'll take up B) first, as it is the most important. When I sent the proof, I forgot to explain to you the magazine's reason for the cut of this passage, and failed to tell you that if you did not want it cut we hoped you would reword for the following reasons: First of all, your stet of this passage meets with our approval up though 'humming to themselves in unswept corners.' It is only the passage about the weeds that we do not think we want to print and hope you may be willing either to cut it or reword. First of all it includes two clichés—1) the farmer's 'simian stoop' which phrase has become a sort of literary cliché, and 2) the 'broken blossoms' which are words that are apt to make Americans laugh. You could probably not know why and I should have explained. There was in the early days of "big" motion pictures, a ghastly and flamboyant and sentimental Cecil B. de Mille picture called "Broken Blossoms" with Lillian Gish, if I remember—that has rather ruined that phrase for good I am afraid. It is of course also used in sentimental fiction. This part of the sentence also uses the 'pathetic fallacy,' i.e. the weeds shrink, etc., and are given human attributes. Perhaps this is intentional on your part since you are putting thoughts as the mother would think them, and this could undoubtedly be, too, your argument for use of the clichés. But if so, we don't really think that the device works. Most people's literary taste has been conditioned against the use of the pathetic fallacy, especially in prose. We feel that the story suffers artistically in that readers will think this merely a case of overwriting and overwrought prose. Couldn't you make your effect and get over your idea by rewording this sentence, to make the farmer crush the weeds rather than their shrinking from him and to simplify this clause that leads up to "as the monstrous darkness approaches?"

At A) the phrase "with his elbows raised" was cut merely because it was confusing and gave us no picture since it could mean so many positions. Would you please reword to make it clear? Do you mean that he lay on his back, propped up on his elbows? If this is what you meant I suspect that he would not be "supine." Or do you mean "with his hands clasped behind his head and his elbows raised?" This would make a clear picture. But as the sentence now reads he seems to be lying absolutely flat and then lifting his elbows, though one can't be sure, which a thing a relaxed and supine person isn't apt to do. We're glad to have the elbows but just want the wording to give the reader a clear picture.

On the last galley at C), your restoration if the birthmark is our final problem. This was one of your touches that Mr Ross felt overdid your unpleasant detail and he and all of us were bothered from the literary point of view by the fact that the reader had early been given a picture of the old man—his swollen veins, his toothless mouth, his brown-stained hands, his clothes—everything in fact except the birthmark which was, presumably, the most striking note in his whole appearance. Then this pops up in the very last paragraph and the reader must entirely revise a mind's eye picture that by then is pretty well fixed. With old people the vein on the side of the forehead does often stand out conspicuously, whether there is a birthmark or not—it is in fact one of the signs of an incurable form of heart disease. This I know because we ran a John McNulty story called "The Snake Is Out" —the snake being that vein. His description was considered so accurate that a heart specialist asked permission to reprint his story in a medical journal. Therefore the birthmark is not "essential" from the physical point of view. If you want it for literary reasons I can only plead that you reconsider. Not only is there this problem of its appearing so late but also we are all with Mr Ross in this case in thinking that it perhaps is so unpleasant as to make the reader less sympathetic to the old man, who up till then has been pathetic and appealing as an example of the tragedy of old age, but who has not been physically repellant. Let me know what you think.

Anyway I do hope that you will not want the story *not* to be published. We very much want to use it this spring and I would have to have to ask you to buy it back from us. If you think these three points make no sense, please let me know. If you are willing to reword it at A) and B), we'll be grateful. And I also hope you'll be willing to omit the birthmark. I should make it plain that in all three places every editor who has read the story is in agreement with Mr Ross. I enclose your author's proof and a fresh proof showing all the places we accept your stets and leaving open only these three passages. Time is getting short for me here and also we need to know whether we may schedule this story, so I hope to hear from you soon. I shall send you an author's proof on 'Butterflies' in a day or two. Forgive my long-windedness—the letter is so long only because I wanted to be absolutely clear and because I could not talk to you. Distance has been our greatest enemy on this story—indeed in all our dealings.

Faithfully,
K. S. White

March 29, 1948

Dear Mrs White,

I have been ill with the flu and could not attend to this letter. I asked my wife to call up the New Yorker office regarding a request by the BBC for broadcasting rights of "The Portrait of My Uncle" and, using this opportunity, to let you know that I accepted the A, B and C suggestions you made in your last letter.

Many thanks for your great kindness and care in regard to the story. Here are the final alterations:

A. "With his bare arms clasped under his head" instead of "with his elbows raised".
B. Stop at "farmer".
C. Delete "where there was a large birthmark".

I hope you will publish the "Butterflies" soon (and please do have them printed before the lepidopterist Avinov's "Profile" which, he tells me, is being done by Hellman). I am sending you a new story in a couple of days. If possible, I would like both "Butterflies" and the new story to precede "Signs and Symbols." I would then have a sixth story in a somewhat different vein from my childhood recollections.

I want to tell you how much I appreciate your readiness to see the point of view of self-centered authors. You are absolutely right about the broken blossoms affair. I did mean it to come through the mother's mental screen but I confess I did not realize the whole effect of the platitude.

I do hope you will be quite well again soon. I shall miss our correspondence in the meanwhile.

Sincerely yours,
V. Nabokov

April 1, 1948

Dear Mr Nabokov:

[A]rms can't be clasped—only hands.

Faithfully yours,
K. S. White

May 2, 1948
From: V. Nabokov
To: W. Maxwell

[VN agrees to "Colette's" coming after "Signs and Symbols."]

May 4, 1948
From: W. Maxwell
To: V. Nabokov

Maxwell says that "Signs and Symbols" are coming in "the next week's issue" and that "judging by the universal delight I would say that more pieces you do in the autobiographical series, the happier *The New Yorker* will be. There is really no one that we would rather have in the magazine."

Lost in revision: The editing of "Signs and Symbols" for *The New Yorker*

J. Morris

Was Vladimir Nabokov successful in resisting major editorial changes to his stories by the *New Yorker* magazine? Such is the impression Brian Boyd creates in his biography. But the evidence argues otherwise. Let us consider an example.

Nabokov's "Signs and Symbols" —Boyd rightfully calls it "one of the greatest short stories ever written"[1] —was first published in the May 15, 1948, issue of the *New Yorker*. From Boyd we learn that Nabokov was often at odds with its editors over their attempts to homogenize his style. "Signs and Symbols" was no exception. Nabokov wrote to Katharine White,

> Frankly, I would prefer you not to publish the story at all if it is to be so carefully mutilated. In fact I am completely against the whole idea of my stories being edited. Among the alterations inflicted on this story there is not a single really necessary one and many are murderous" [March 13, 1948].[2]

Boyd goes on to say, unequivocally, "fortunately his rights as author prevailed," leaving the impression that Nabokov successfully resisted "the whole idea" of editing the story. This impression is supported by a quoted statement from a letter by Edmund Wilson to White: "I have read the Nabokov stories ["Signs and Symbols" and "My English Education"], and I think they are both perfect. *Not a word should be changed.*"[3] Boyd says nothing of White's reaction, and the matter is dropped, again with the obvious implication that Nabokov had his way.

But did he? A comparison of the *New Yorker* version of "one of the greatest short stories ever written" with the text eventually included in *Nabokov's Dozen*[4] reveals at least three startling discrepancies, along with dozens of minor but dismaying word-shufflings, abridgements, and paraphrases. The cumulative result is a major transformation for the worse. This makes "Signs and Symbols" of particular interest as a test case for Boyd's more general implication that Nabokov always rejected editing on this level from the *New Yorker*.[5]

To begin with, the title itself is altered. "Signs and Symbols" appeared in *The New Yorker* as "Symbols and Signs." It is hard to imagine the point of this inversion, but it does not, at any rate, offend.

Then we find that two of the most memorable descriptions in the Doubleday version—both of them dear to Nabokov admirers, I believe, and presumably to Nabokov himself—are missing from the magazine version. "He kept clearing his throat in a special resonant way he had when he was upset" appears in *The New Yorker* simply as "He kept clearing his throat, as he always did when he was upset." And "he removed his new hopelessly uncomfortable dental plate and severed the long tusks of saliva connecting him to it" is truncated into "he removed his new, hopelessly uncomfortable dental plate."

These are the most startling and misguided changes, but no paragraph escapes emendation. The general tenor of *The New Yorker*'s editing can be suggested by the following typical comparison. Book version:

> The telephone rang. It was an unusual hour for their telephone to ring. His left slipper had come off and he groped for it with his heel and toe as he stood in the middle of the room and child-ishly, toothlessly, gaped at his wife. Having more English than he did, it was she who attended to calls. (A14: 172)

Magazine version:

> The telephone rang. It was an unusual hour for it to ring. He stood in the middle of the room, groping with his foot for one slipper that had come off, and childishly, toothlessly, gaped at his wife. Since she knew more English than he, she always attended to the calls. (A14: 172)

What has been lost? Nabokovian precision, obviously. It was the *left* slipper, and he groped with his *heel and toe*, but *The New Yorker* won't allow us to know this. Likewise, *having more English* is more accurate, more pertinent: she might *know* a great deal of

English, but one needs to *have* it at one's disposal to answer a phone call. Also gone is the nice pairing of *groped* and *gaped*.

What has been gained, if anything? A closer approximation to *The New Yorker* guru E. B. White's *Elements of Style*, with its monomaniacal emphasis on "economy," "simplicity," and other alleged features of "good writing," and, to be fair, the slight redundancy removed by substituting *it* for the second *telephone* is perhaps felicitous. But the overall score is very bad indeed, not only here but in virtually every line of the story.

What to make of all this? The endless and usually deleterious tinkering, the title change, the removal of those two marvelous descriptions? Allowing for disagreement over whether this is bad editing—clearly, I believe it is—there can be no doubt that it is *heavy* editing; editing aimed not at clarifying the author's style but at altering it. Surely, then, the evidence just examined argues against Boyd's claim that Nabokov was able to veto major changes in his stories by *The New Yorker*. More probably, he was forced to compromise. In this case one can only speculate about the "mutilations" Nabokov must have refused, while agreeing to those that remain. That he was willing to compromise with *The New Yorker* is apparent from the *Selected Letters*. A 1955 note to White finds him "cheerfully" agreeing "to accept some thirty minor alterations" in an excerpt from *Pnin*, though he goes on to object to several others which "it would be agony to even contemplate replacing [with] mere inorganic links when I have taken such pains with the inner linkage and balance."[6] Also apparent from the *Selected Letters* is the reason for Nabokov's tractability: an overall feeling of deep gratitude and admiration for *The New Yorker*, which he frequently praises for its generosity and excellent content.

It is of course possible that Nabokov compromised not at all on "Signs and Symbols," and that the Doubleday version is a revised and improved story, reworked by Nabokov 10 years after its *New Yorker* publication. But given *The New Yorker*'s penchant for the very sort of editorial homogeneity displayed in the variances under discussion, and given the cited instance of Nabokov's "cheerful" (one wonders) agreement to "minor" (one wonders) alterations, it seems more likely that *The New Yorker*'s "Symbols and Signs" is a Whitened version of the story, which Nabokov restored to its original form for *Nabokov's Dozen*.

I think, in closing, that this little investigation helps us better understand Nabokov's situation in the 1940s: an émigré author quite unknown in America, financially strapped, delighted to have found a home in *The New Yorker*, and willing (to a degree unacknowledged by Boyd) to accept even the miserable editing he was offered in "Signs and Symbols."[7]

Consulting the oracle

Michael Wood

"Ambiguous gifts, as what gods give must be"
Empson, "This Last Pain"

"For a train of thought is never false"
Conrad, *Under Western Eyes*

I want to talk about oracles—literal and metaphorical ones.[1] Oracles offer not only interesting problems in interpretation, but also complicated models of interpretation, and what engages me most in them is the mixture of their supposed infallibility and their actual uncertainty; or to put that from the point of view of those consulting the oracle, the hunger for infallibility combined with an almost stoic acceptance of the deepest doubt. The oracle is the surest thing in the world, and also the most ambiguous. This is not perhaps the most characteristic of our critical dilemmas—we live in less lurid territories—but it is, I think, an exemplary one because it is so extreme; a drastic fiction, if you like, for many of our critical quandaries, in literature and elsewhere.

The first part of the lecture explores some of the implications of oracles for the practice of interpretation. In this part we can, I think, be as skeptical as we like; the more skeptical the better, perhaps. In the second part I look closely at a story in which something like belief in an oracle becomes almost irresistible; and my question, to sound a bit like an oracle myself, would be what the faith of skeptics might look like, or what the meaning of faith, their own or anyone else's, might be for skeptics. This is an argument, I hasten to add, in favor of skepticism rather than against it.

"They were given the choice," a brief parable by Kafka runs,

> between becoming kings or the couriers of kings. The way children do [*nach Art der Kinder*], they all wanted to be couriers. And so there are only couriers chasing about the world and, since there are no kings, shouting to each other their now meaningless messages [*die sinnlos gewordenen Meldungen*].

They would like to put an end to their miserable life but they dare not because of their oath of service.

A courier without a king is like an oracle without a god; and we recognize the condition of much modern literature and almost all modern criticism. But what are we to do? We could abandon our oaths of service and end our miserable literary lives. We could rectify the initial, childish error, and crown ourselves or others as kings. Ourselves: the reader. Others: Marx, Freud, Foucault, history, language, the tradition, the culture, the text, the mother, the body, the Other. And of course people are doing these things, and have been doing them for some time—indeed forever, if we take Kafka's view of kingship and meaning. What I should like to do is to resist the elegant darkness of Kafka's parable, and ask what happens if we keep our oaths of service and think again about the messages. We need to note, for example, the touch of pathos Kafka has smuggled into the phrase about the "*now* meaningless messages," the messages which have *become* meaningless. There were kings once, apparently; before the choice, before the fall. Or there was meaning. This slight smudging of the issue helps us to think our way out of what seems to be a trap. We can ask: if there were kings, how would the messages be different? When there were (thought to be) kings, how were the messages (thought to be) different? It is part of my argument that the differences may not be as great as they seem.

There were oracles in ancient Greece as early as the 8th century BC—the high point of their activity seems to have been between the 7th century and the mid 4th. Greek peace treaties regularly included free access to the oracles as one of their first clauses. Many of the oracles were associated with Apollo, the most famous being the one at Delphi, where the god communicated his views through a priestess, known as the Pythia; but Zeus had oracles too, notably at Dodona, where he spoke through the rustling of the leaves of a great oak. In their later life, the oracles were chiefly consulted by individuals rather than cities or states, and their authority waned. But they were still lively enough in AD 391 for Theodosius to issue an edict against them.

Contrary to popular belief, ancient and modern, and contrary to most meanings of the word, oracles were not always ambiguous. An American scholar, Joseph Fontenrose, has argued that they were not ambiguous at all, that the belief in the ambiguity of oracles, or at least of the Delphic oracle, is "wholly modern." Apollo simply speaks the truth when asked for it.[2] Nice of him. This is going a bit far, since the ambiguity of the oracle was already legendary, and amply illustrated, in Herodotus, writing around the middle of the 5th century BC. What Fontenrose means, I think, is that the god could be helpful; that the object of so intense and so long-lasting a worship was not a mere mischief-maker. Plutarch, who was the priest of Apollo at Delphi from around AD 85 to his death in around AD 126, makes an interesting distinction along these lines. In one dialogue he writes of the "God who is dear to us," and who helps us in the conduct of life, bringing "remedies" and "solutions" to our problems through his oracles; "on the other hand, when it is matter of intellectual difficulties, it is rather the god himself who raises them, and proposes them to naturally philosophical minds ..."[3]

This seems a neat and perhaps too kindly division of practical life from the intellect, a priest's apology for the god, but it does correspond to what modern scholars make of the archeological evidence. Ancient inscriptions, as distinct from literary or historical texts, suggest that the god could speak quite unambiguously, that his instructions, for building a city say, or accomplishing certain religious rites, were perfectly clear, "d'une clarté parfaite"; "toujours directes et parfaitement claires."[4]

Popular belief was not wrong, though, and scholars get into terrible tangles on this score. Here, for example, are Parke and Wormell, in their splendid standard work on the Delphic oracle:

> the Delphic oracular style was not developed with the conscious purpose of baffling and bewildering the enquirer. It is truer to say that obscurity was an essential element in this literary genre ... This does not mean, however, that the Pythia had any scruples about misleading and bamboozling the enquirer if it suited her purpose.[5]

Conscious purpose, essential element, suited her purpose. This takes some unraveling, but seems to mean that the main (religious) purpose of the oracle was not to mislead, although (politically) it could and it often did. French scholars say the same thing: clarté parfaite on the one hand; recondite and often-cruel riddles on the other.

Out of this welter of fascinating material—life is short and so, relatively, are lectures—I want to point to three considerations, one very broad and simple, the other two large enough but a little more intricate.

a) The god never speaks directly, he always uses a human agent; Pythia or priest, someone interprets even the rustling of the leaves. The god uses human language, that is, enters and communicates through a historical culture. He says in effect, like Eliot's Sweeney, "I gotta use words when I talk to you." Even a king's message requires interpretation, and even the simplest oracle requires a human conduit. The truth of an oracle is decided not only by its human outcome, but an act of collation, a matching of the god's words to human deeds. "Ambiguous gifts, as what gods give must be." This not just Empson using an Empsonian word, it is Empson reminding us what the gifts of gods are like, how much they depend also on the receiver.

There is no equivalent here for the direct revelation given to Old Testament prophets or Christian mystics. I should guess there are elements of indirection there too, but that is another story. The place of language in the god's relation with us seems to be the enduring and central meaning of Heraclitus' famous saying: "The Lord whose oracle is at Delphi neither tells nor conceals, but gives signs." ("Tells" is *legei*, related to logos and legislation; "conceals" is *kryptei*, related to cryptic; and "gives signs" is *semainei*, related to semantics and semiotics.) There are other translations, but the variants are small, and the sense is pretty clear. In all versions there are two things the god doesn't do and one he does do. What he does do, we might say, is *mean* something. He doesn't speak and he doesn't hide, but he means. The meaning, however, is not simply given to us. It has to be taken, as Lionel Trilling said in another context.

b) Not all oracles are ambiguous, far from it; but any of them could be, and this, it seems to me, transforms the whole question of their interpretation. The people of Cnidos, for example, lived on a peninsula they thought they would like to turn into an island, and so they started to dig through the isthmus that connected them to the mainland. There were various mishaps during the digging, "workmen got hurt by splinters of stone in various places about the body, especially the eyes, more often than might have been expected. Indeed, there was something so unnatural about it, that they sent to Delphi to ask what it was that was hindering their work."⁶ The Pythia answered iambically:⁷

Do not fence off the isthmus; do not dig.
Zeus would have made an island, had he willed it.⁸

Do not dig. Can't say plainer than that. But the examples of other, riddling oracles suggest that the plainest talk can be reinterpreted, reinvested. Even something as straight as "Do not dig" could have other meanings. So it is with all texts, we might say, and this, I think, is what Paul de Man was trying to tell us in his tortured way: confusing the fact that all texts could be ambiguous with the proposition that all texts are. It is important that we know, in context, that some texts are not ambiguous; that stop at a level-crossing means stop, and is not a bit of railway irony. But it is also important to remember that no text, however simple, is permanently, perfectly, preternaturally safe from ambiguity.

And of course, the famous oracles are luridly ambiguous. Or are they? The Spartans, for example, consulted the oracle at Delphi to see how they were likely to do in their attempt to conquer the Arcadians. This was the answer they got—"the most brilliant of ambiguous oracles," Parke and Wormell say.

Arcady? Great is the thing you ask, I will not grant it.
In Arcady are many men, acorn-eaters,
And they will keep you out. Yet, for I am not grudging,
I will give you Tegea to dance in with stamping feet
And her fair plain to measure out with the line.⁹

The Spartans "failed to perceive the ambiguity of this oracle," Herodotus says; that is, they read it, quite plausibly, as meaning they couldn't have the whole of Arcady, but they could have Tegea. In fact, they lost the battle even for Tegea, and Apollo's oracle was fulfilled by those who were taken prisoner; they had to dance on Tegean soil with stamping feet, and to measure out the Tegean plain with the chains they themselves had made for the Tegeans they hoped to conquer. This looks like a moral fable, not only about hubris and the desire for power, but about close reading, or the failure to attend to verbal and other clues. The god says "I will not grant it," and that the Arcadians "will keep you out." The

Spartans hear this, but miss the mischief, the irony, in "for I am not grudging"; and the possibilities of double meaning which any questioner of an oracle ought to be on the lookout for.

If that is the most brilliant of ambiguous ancient oracles, the most "notorious" (Parke and Wormell) is one given to Croesus. And indeed the whole story of Croesus' relation to oracles is of great interest.

Croesus, king of Lydia, was a careful man, and didn't consult authorities without testing them. He sent messengers to half a dozen Greek oracles and to one in Libya, instructing them to inquire, exactly one hundred days after their departure from Sardis, what the king was doing at exactly that moment. The answers of the other places aren't recorded, Herodotus says, but the Pythia at Delphi scarcely waited for the question before producing some wonderfully opaque stuff, in hexameters, about a tortoise and a lamb being cooked in a bronze pot with a bronze lid. This, of course, is just what Croesus was doing: his idea of a wildly improbable event, "something which no one would be likely to guess," as Herodotus puts it. Croesus is impressed with the answer when it reaches him, showers gifts on the temple at Delphi, and consults the oracle several times, putting great faith in its answers, with disastrous consequences. He is told that if he attacks the Persians he will "destroy a great empire" —his own, as it happens. He is (apparently) told that his reign will last until "the day that a mule shall sit on the Median throne," and Herodotus sets him up charmingly as the fall guy, the naïve reader—strangely so, for such an intelligent and cautious man. Proof, perhaps, as Macbeth and the Spartans also knew, that the interpretation of oracles has much to do with what we want to hear.

"This reply," Herodotus says, "gave Croesus more pleasure than anything he had yet heard; for he did not suppose that a mule was likely to become king of the Medes, and that meant that he and his line would remain in power for ever." He did not suppose that a mule was likely to become king of the Medes. Alarm bells are ringing everywhere; but not for Croesus. Even if we have no idea what this line means, we are pretty sure it can't be taken literally. Croesus' last consultation of the oracle is also an unhappy one. He asks what he can do about his son's lifelong dumbness, and is told he doesn't want to know, that it would be better for him not to hear his son's voice, that his son will speak his first words on a day of sorrow. In effect, when Croesus is defeated by the Persians, about to be killed by a Persian soldier, the son calls out "Do not kill Croesus!" "Those were the first words he ever uttered," Herodotus says, "—and he retained the power of speech for the rest of his life." Croesus is not killed, however, and his conqueror, Cyrus, is grateful to him for being such a gracious loser, and would like to do something for him. This is the most intricate and interesting part of the story, I think. Croesus says he would like the chance to "reproach Apollo for his deceit." Cyrus agrees, and allows Croesus to send messengers to Delphi to ask the god if he is not "ashamed to have encouraged Croesus by his oracles to invade Persia ... And they were also to ask if it was the habit of Greek gods to be ungrateful."

The Pythia's answers are exemplary. First she says, correctly enough, that the way things are is the way things are, or more precisely, "that not God himself could escape destiny." Then she points out that Croesus was not inquisitive enough, too much of a New Critic, perhaps, intent on what he thought the text itself meant, not attentive enough to context or the referent. "After an answer like that," the Pythia said (being told he would destroy a great empire), "the wise thing would have been to send again to inquire which empire was meant, Cyrus' or his own." We may wonder, skeptically, what the answer would have been if he had made this second enquiry. As for the mule, poor Croesus was just too much of a literalist, unable to see the metaphor that was staring him in the face. Cyrus was the mule, because his mother was a Mede and his father was a Persian. Easy. The saddest part of this story is its ending. When these answers are reported to Croesus, he agrees that the god is innocent and that he has "only himself to blame." Macbeth's rage is not for him, and he doesn't have the Christian option of attributing oracles to the devil.[10]

This is a story, I think, or a set of stories, about the dangers of interpretation. Interpretation makes for vast, calamitous differences. We are not in a world of easy pluralism, where all interpretations are tolerated because none of them matters.

It is also a story about reinterpretation. There are two modes of time here, as in a story by Borges. In one of them, the Pythia knows the outcome of the prophecy as she makes it; her knowledge includes a knowledge of Croesus' misreading. In the other, Croesus has not misread the prophecy, he has simply read it, and its 'true' meaning is not yet available.

The prophecy is then revised or at least finalized after its fulfillment. The oracle about the great empire was neither ambiguous nor vague; it was specific but unattached, it spoke, like Macbeth's witches, about the battle being lost *and* won, as all battles are if they are not drawn. After the battle, it can name names. The corollary of the suggestion that all oracles could be ambiguous is that there is no oracle that cannot be reinterpreted, one way or another. The difference is not in the event but in the story that surrounds the event. It is the difference between reinterpreting a broken promise to make it look as if you had kept it, and just admitting that you have broken it.

There is in such adjustments a touching fidelity to the ideas of coherence and authority: the oracle can't be wrong; the promise can't have been broken. But there is also a huge space for confusion and hypocrisy and worse. When one Philomelos attacked Delphi in 356 BC, he tried to force the Pythia to prophesy for him. She refused. He insisted. She kept refusing, and finally said "You can do what you want." Philomelos took this as his oracle. There is a similar story about Alexander, arriving in Delphi some 20 years later. The Pythia, threatened, says "You are invincible," and Alexander takes this as the official response he needs. The idea of these, and less brutal acts of reinterpretation, leads me to my next point.

(c) Roland Crahay suggests that it is a sort of law of literary composition in Greece that the oracle should appear in history after the event.[11] This might seem an obvious point, but there is no historical reason why a writer from, say, the 5th century BC onwards could not have written of an oracle whose outcome was not yet known. No one is suggesting, of course, that oracles did not, historically, prophesy, and even prophesy correctly on occasion. As Parke and Wormell dryly say, "Apollo must have had his genuine successes." But our accounts of complex oracles do come after the event, and this fact of lateness has important literary and political implications.

You tell the story of these oracles only after they have come out; rather as news is news only after it has happened. Such predictions not only necessarily come true but offer strong narrative metaphors of necessity. As a student of mine once said about the effect of prophecy in García Márquez's *One Hundred Years of Solitude*, "all is predetermined, not because it has been predicted, but because it has already happened."

Hindsight rewrites. It doesn't, in these cases, falsify or forget in any Orwellian sense; it revises meanings rather than facts. Creeping into past events, it becomes its own future, as in the idiom "was to," found everywhere in García Márquez's novel, but also in everyday life and in most languages, I believe, a sort of oracle woven into ordinary discourse. It is perhaps worth pausing over this usage, since it so unobtrusive and so frequent. "Was to" may simply indicate a plan, as in "We were to have lunch yesterday, but she couldn't make it." Often it indicates a destiny, as in "It was, or was not, to be." It almost never changes the narrative sense of a proposition, the content of what happened. But it changes the whole sense of the narrative. *One Hundred Years of Solitude* begins: "Many years later, as he faced the firing squad, Colonel Aureliano Buendia was to remember that distant afternoon when his father took him to see the ice." In order to write the sentence in a simple past tense ("Colonel Aureliano Buendia remembered ..."), the narrator would need to be situated in a time later than the firing squad, later than many years later. The sense would be the same, but there would be no idea of destiny or compulsion: what happened, happened. If you write "was to" you are not only situated at the later date, you are claiming that later date as the site of fulfilled knowledge, and you have made the intervening events seem necessary, not only a story but a destiny. This, I should like to suggest, is what a destiny is, even in the hardest cases: a life become a story, which in turn has become inevitable in its movements and outcome. Frank Kermode speaks of the witches in Macbeth as dressing the present in the borrowed robes of the future. What happens with destiny is that the present offers itself as yesterday's future, as the only future the past could have. As indeed it is-now.

There is a wonderful example of the incursion of destiny in *Paradise Lost* where, in the argument to Book V, Raphael is said to have been sent to talk to Adam "to render [him] inexcusable"— "God to render Man inexcusable sends Raphael to admonish him of his obedience, of his free estate, of his enemy near at hand; who he is, and why his enemy, and whatever else may avail Adam to know." The sense is clear.

God wishes to give Man a comprehensive warning, to afford him every opportunity to reject Satan. If this generous, encompassing gesture fails, Man will be inexcusable. But the language actually says something else, almost the reverse: God is making every effort to render Man inexcusable. In this phrasing, God's foreknowledge looks like an intention; the final result, the freely chosen and therefore inexcusable fall, has got tangled in the earlier movement of events.

The oracle is an infallible authority who talks to us fallibly.

A dark and comic version of this structure is found in Kafka's response to his friend Max Brod's question about hope. Kafka said he thought that God had created the world on one of his bad days, that we were one of God's bad moods. So you think there is no hope, Brod asked. Kafka smiled, and said, "Oh plenty of hope. But not for us."[12]

Even the darkest version of the story retains the idea of authority, although there may be torture in the very idea. The god's word is sure and (in theory) available; access to it is uncertain, subject to interpretation. Derrida's famous slogan *Il n'y a pas de hors-texte* expresses half, and perhaps more than half, of this perception. *Hors-texte* looks like a formation along the lines of *hors-la-loi*, an outlaw. The suggestion would be not that there are no outlaws—even theorists are susceptible to some empirical evidence, and one of the things theory can't do is make muggers go away—but that even outlaws have their laws, or, possibly, that even outlaws are defined by the very laws they reject. But an *hors-texte* in French (this is, I think, its only meaning in ordinary usage) is a plate or illustration in a book. It doesn't count in the numbering of the pages. It's in the book but it's not the text. So the aphorism says that even the pictures are a text, have to be read; and more dramatically, that all the pages count, even the unnumbered ones, that there is nothing in the book which is not the book. It doesn't say, I think, or it doesn't say except as a means of making mischief, that the book is all there is. It says something more like Wittgenstein's "Whereof we cannot speak thereof we must remain silent." The book may not be all there is but it's what we've got. We're not going to get any closer to the god than this.

This is quite different from believing that instruction or authority, or whatever we seek at the oracle, is not available to us in any form, or is entirely relative, or doesn't exist. And it is quite different from believing the god is easy of access or ours alone or the possession of any particular group. It is also different from believing in a reasonable plurality of modest portions of knowledge and principle, something like Richard Rorty's pragmatism. The oracle tells us a wild story, and good sense (and much modern philosophy) suggests we should give up such extreme old games, and settle for the certainties that are to be had; and this, of course, is what we do most of the time. There are certainties, and we should not squander them in doubts we don't need to indulge. J. L. Austin has a very funny passage about verifying that a telephone is a telephone:

> If, for instance, you tell me there's a telephone in the next room, and (feeling mistrustful) I decided to verify this, how could it be thought *impossible* for me to do this conclusively? I go into the next room, and certainly there's something there that looks exactly like a telephone. But is it a case perhaps of *trompe l'oeil* painting? I can soon settle that. Is it just a dummy perhaps, not really connected up and with no proper works? Well, I can take it to pieces a bit and find out, or actually use it for ringing somebody up—and perhaps get them to ring me up too, just to make sure. And of course, if I do all these things, I *do* make sure; what more could possibly be required? This object has already stood up to amply enough tests to establish that it really is a telephone; and it isn't just that, for everyday or practical or ordinary purposes, enough is *as good as* a telephone; what meets all these tests just *is* a telephone, no doubt about it.[13]

However, there are limits to what good sense can do for us; there are areas of need it scarcely touches. The story of the oracle dramatizes what we continue to want, in spite of good sense, and it dramatizes our continuing failure to get it. It offers us, we might say, crazy wisdom rather than right reason, the compacted, quirky wisdom of an old story; counsel, as Walter Benjamin defined it. A storyteller "has counsel" for us, Benjamin said, conscious that the idea of having counsel was "beginning to have an old-fashioned ring," even in 1936. He thought this was because experience was becoming less and less communicable, and he was probably right. I should want to think of the story, rather than the storyteller, as having counsel for us, but Benjamin's next formulation is wonderfully subtle, and suggestive. "After all, counsel is less an answer to a question than a proposal concerning the continuation of a story which is just unfolding."[14]

I should like to turn now to a story which I think has counsel for us, although the counsel may be distressing, and the oracle in question scarcely even gives signs: it makes obscure gestures. The story, however, is called "Signs and Symbols."

It is by Vladimir Nabokov, and it was published in *The New Yorker* in 1948. Nabokov referred to it as his story about the old Jewish couple, although we don't learn directly from the work itself that the people are Jewish. We know the couple are immigrants in America, that they have left behind a dark and turbulent European history; that the husband's brother, Isaac, nicknamed "the Prince," has done well in the new world; that they speak Russian, that their English is not good. They live in a big, unnamed American city. Their son, born late in the marriage and now about 20, is in a mental hospital, "incurably deranged in his mind." The couple set out to visit him, taking a birthday present, a basket of ten assorted jams in little jars. They are not allowed to see him, because, they are told, he has "again attempted to take his life." The couple return home with their present and consider the possibility of removing their son from the hospital, having him to live with them. This is all that happens in the story ... Or all but one haunting thing, which gives the work its eerie resonance, picks up and prolongs its implications, carries it beyond observation and tenderness into the territory of the oracle.

The old couple's son has been diagnosed as suffering from something called "referential mania," which sounds like a literary disease, even like a lot of literature. Reference become mania: an unsympathetic definition of realism. But the young man's case is more complicated, more clinical. And his affliction is virtually all we know of him in the story. Apart from a face blotched with acne and a shuffling walk, he is his mania:

In these very rare cases the patient imagines that everything around him is a veiled reference to his personality and existence. He excludes real people from the conspiracy—because he considers himself to be so much more intelligent than other men. Phenomenal nature shadows him wherever he goes. Clouds in the staring sky transmit to one another, by means of slow signs, incredibly detailed information regarding him. His inmost thoughts are discussed at nightfall, in manual alphabet, by darkly gesticulating trees. Pebbles or stains or sun flecks form patterns representing in some awful way messages he must intercept. Everything is a cipher and of everything he is the theme

... He must always be on his guard and devote every minute and module of his life to the decoding of the undulation of things. The very air he exhales is indexed and filed away. (A11: 62)

We recognize the scenery, if not the condition. This is the animated landscape of Romantic poetry, but experienced as paranoia. Clouds, trees, air (the passage continues with mentions of plains, mountains and firs) all speak, as in so many poems, but don't speak *to the person*. It's as if a whole region were whispering behind Wordsworth's back, and whispering about him. The absence of other people makes this seem rather different from other types of paranoia; but paranoia is what it is, since it deals in secrecy and conspiracy, and humankind finds them absolutely everywhere.

Etymologically (I learn from the *Oxford Companion to the Mind*—a splendid book, even if the title sounds as if it might have been invented by Nabokov), paranoia means "being out of one's mind," and apart from its clinical definition, "has slipped into general use to refer to enhanced suspiciousness." Only "slipped"? A paranoid question. "Enhanced" is a little odd, since it (sadly) seems to assume a going rate of suspicion, a steady state prior to enhancement. Clinically, paranoia is:

the name given to one type of functional psychosis ... in which the patient holds a coherent, internally consistent, delusional system of beliefs, centering round the conviction that he (or, more rarely, she) is a person of great importance and is on that account being persecuted, despised, and rejected.

"More rarely, she." A great deal of history is crowded into that bracket: perhaps you have to be pretty important to have delusions of importance? The *Companion* goes on to point out that people who are not mentally ill may also have traits associated with paranoia (if they are, for example, "opinionated, touchy, and have an idea of their own importance which the rest of the world does not endorse") and that "paranoiac delusions bear a disconcerting, embarrassing resemblance to the beliefs held and propagated by founders of religions, by political leaders, and by some artists ..."

What sort of idea of our own importance would be delusional? The test can only be empirical and local, external to the person, since the (coherent, consistent) delusion will be ingenious and entirely plausible in its specialized rationality, ready to bend any evidence at all to its own purpose; rather like a willful, mysterious reading of an oracle that seemed perfectly clear to everyone else. But then, what sort of empirical test do we apply? The famous crazy cases are easy enough to spot. If I think I am Napoleon, or that my actions have the consequences of those of Napoleon, the delusion is clear: almost any piece of my life will serve as a test. But suppose I get the sense of my own importance slightly but disastrously wrong, find myself only just but unmistakably over the edge into paranoia. Where was the edge, what marked it? I'm not suggesting there isn't an edge, or that we couldn't recognize it practically; only that seeing the edge could be a delicate affair, and that we live, perhaps necessarily, among relatively unquestioned hierarchies and pools of opinion: agreements about what matters, what is reasonable, what is sane. Communities work in this way, but a community will feel like a conspiracy if it's against you.

And it may be against you. These matters are historical as well as psychological. Whole social groups, even whole nations, have gone *crazy*, taking their craziness as a norm; and to point to this craziness has been to become abnormally suspicious and mistrustful, as when one might imagine, at the time of Dreyfus, that the French army could forge evidence, or, more recently, that the British police could possibly do the same. The point is that enhanced suspiciousness may be horribly wrong, an isolating, suicidal mania; and it may be horribly right, a desperate diagnosis of a culturally improbable truth. There is no mistaking which is the case of the young man in Nabokov's story. But the possibility of the other case connects him to us, and to his parents and their history. The young man is said to be "totally inaccessible to normal minds" (A12: 132), but there are doubts lurking even in the terrible security of that exclusion. He is painfully separate from us, but also painfully like us; inaccessible but not beyond our imagination; other but not an alien.

And what happens when otherness speaks to us, when a communication seems to reach us from a different world, the world of difference? When referential mania joins the real, like an oracle inviting us to recognize our history in a riddle? This is where "Signs and Symbols" ends, and I need now to mention the one other thing that happens in Nabokov's story. It is quite simple. The telephone rings. The time is past midnight, "an unusual hour" for a telephone call to this flat.

It is a wrong number: the girl on the line wants to speak to some unknown person called Charlie. The old woman, whose English is better than the old man's, explains the mistake. The telephone rings again. It is the same girl, and the old woman explains again, in great detail: "You have the incorrect number. I will tell you what you are doing: you are turning the letter O instead of the zero." (A14: 188) The couple were awake anyway, drinking tea, discussing the future of their son. The old man rather childishly concentrates on the jam jars, the present they have taken to the hospital and brought back. He reads off the names of the different varieties. These are the last two sentences of the story. "His clumsy moist lips spelled out their eloquent labels: apricot, grape, beech plum, quince. He had got to crab apple, when the telephone rang again." (A14: 198)

What do we hear in this room, in these minds, when the telephone rings for the third time? I hear common sense (the old couple's, mine, no doubt Nabokov's) telling me that it is the same wrong number again, the girl who wants Charlie. I can't know this for sure, though, unless someone picks up the telephone, and no one ever will. This fictional telephone can no more be picked up than Ophelia can be resurrected. Equally, of course, it will keep ringing for as long as anyone reads the story. What other voices say to me is: this time it's the hospital, it's bad news, something has happened to the son. Or: it is the wrong number, but it's meant for the old couple all the same, some malign force is using this mistaken girl to torture them. It is because the call might be from the hospital that the very wrongness of the number seems cruel. Could the old couple *not* think this, *not* feel persecuted at their midnight tea? Can we *not* feel this on their behalf? In this context, even the slight suspicion of a conspiracy, ordinary unenhanced suspicion, becomes a form of pain. Do we, perhaps for the first time, wonder whether there is something hereditary about referential mania, dormant but always possible in this generation? Or do we think referential mania must be intuitively correct after all, the only way we can possibly account for the brutal, ingenious, so-called accidents of the world? The strength of this story, I think, is that what seems to be the "right" reading, the banal, accidental wrong number, is simultaneously the sanest and the hardest to settle for. We have been set up, by the account of the young man's mania and the hints of his parents' history, to believe in pain, but not in accidents. This belief is reinforced, of course, by the fact that the endlessly ringing telephone is not, cannot be, a textual accident, since it is where Nabokov deliberately ends his story.

At the level of represented life in the fiction there is a question which pits, let us say, the possible craziness of a person against the possible craziness of the world, and pits against both the merely random, the realm of chance. We are suspended here, with the characters. On the level of the writing, however, the question is answered, chance is abolished. The doubt *in* the story, so to speak, is cancelled *by* the story. If the couple could know they were figures in a fiction, they would know they were being tormented by Nabokov, author of the ominous third telephone call, and indeed of the other calls, and of the couple and their unhappy son. Other characters in Nabokov do possess just this kind of knowledge, and one (Adam Krug in *Bend Sinister*) goes mad because of it. Here, the two levels are quite separate, the second easily forgotten; but they can be seen to comment on each other. In the story, there is the frightened interpretation of chance, the difficulty of believing that chance is what it is; in the writing both an absence of chance and a carefully orchestrated interest in chance, a confirmation of our difficulty. This world *is* organized by a malign or at least mischievous agency, someone *is* whispering about these people behind their backs. A text like "Signs and Symbols" is a metaphor for a world which is ordered but unsympathetic, run by a heavy-handed deity whom paranoia would rightly suspect of wanting to trash what is most precious to us, or at least wanting to tease us with that very suspicion. To compare the slight with the sacred, it is like the world of *Oedipus Rex* seen from the point of view of the protagonists, and without the context of piety Sophocles' play also possesses. Or it is the world of Croesus in intricate defeat. This is not the way the world is, I hope, or not all the time; but it is the way it may feel, and must feel to many.

Brilliant and malign designs, imitations of paranoia, are means by which skeptical writers meet some of the needs of belief. A vision of order and a sense of the world's actual disorder go together, at least in an image or a story; like reality and justice in Yeats's magical system. There is a plot, but it may be against you; it may be against you, but there is a plot. Even friendly designs, like those of Fielding and Joyce, seem to meet the same need: the disbeliever in the world's order makes extravagant order in a novel.

In Nabokov, I think, there is an accent or inflection which changes, even reverses the direction of the strategy. We see not the fictional belief of a skeptic, but the ingeniously articulated doubts of some sort of believer. Design in Nabokov's fiction is far too intricate to be ignored, far too fragile and arbitrary to offer a consoling image of providence or a beneficent creation. We can't see the king, but the couriers are working for someone. The oracle is far from uncertain, but it certainly is an oracle.

Oracles, ancient or modern, with or without gods, meet our need to believe in die infallible, in what the *OED* calls undeniable truth; and at the same time they make room for our regular experience of fallibility, our awareness that all truths, even the most precious or the most sacred, can be and are denied. It's not that there is no certainty, only that there isn't as much as we want, or it isn't placed where we want it.

Austin once spoke of particular, rather loosely behaved words which help us to "meet the innumerable and unforeseeable demands of the world upon language",[15] and I think that a willingness to want certainty and to put up with not getting it, an agility in interpretation combined with our oath of service, may do something similar for the demands of the world upon our faith. I am thinking of faith in a secular sense as well as in an appropriately religious one. Our faith might be in friendship or affection or our politics, or in just being able to get through the day, and the world is full of assaults upon such faith. That's when we turn to the astrology columns, those daily oracles, not because we believe them, but because, as Sydney Greenstreet used to say to Humphrey Bogart, we like their style; because we need the wisdom they do not have, the stories they are not quite able to tell. "He speaks like the oracles to puzzle the world," Dryden said. But oracles don't puzzle the world, they mime the world's puzzles, and they are likely to appear wherever and whenever the world feels like a puzzle to us.

PART TWO
Vascular System

Signs

Arbitrary signs and symbols

Alexander N. Drescher

> And the LORD said unto him, This the land which I swore unto
> Abraham, unto Isaac, and unto Jacob, saying, I will give it unto
> thy seed: I have caused thee to see with thine eyes, but thou shalt
> not go over thither. So Moses the servant of the LORD died
> there in the land of Moab, according to the word of the LORD.
>
> Deuteronomy 34.4–5, King James Version

Introduction

The data for this reading of Nabokov's "Signs and Symbols" are
drawn from three sources: evidence internal to the story; correc-
tions made to *The New Yorker* version[1] when Nabokov regained
control of the text from his editors; and, as a result of Nabokov's
concern that the story was not well understood, helpful hints he
imbedded in the novel *Pnin*.[2] Assuming the reader's familiarity with
the text, the sequence of the story is not retained so as to unite
elements of the argument.

For Nabokov, acclaim for this story's "human interest"[3] and
argument over its indeterminate ending missed an essential aspect of
the story.[4] While Toker has suggested that the continuing search for
missing elements has detracted from Nabokov's profound concern
with man's inhumanity to man (A203),[5] the intent here is to the
contrary, to propose a reading which extends the tragic content.[6]

Despite professed indifference to his readership,[7] Nabokov probably made this story more difficult than he intended. Counter-intuitive meanings are one problem: literal when metaphor or allusion are implied, and vice versa. Another is the absence of a reliably objective narrator, for almost every declaration may be in some form of indirect discourse, and probably is. Nabokov expected his readers to ponder over the meanings they would attribute to this text and, for this purpose, several definitions from the Webster Second Edition are displayed in the Appendix.[8] In reading Nabokov, I assume that there are no extraneous details, nothing is accidental, odd usages and repetitions require particular attention, and some misleading gambits are best refused. As the two main characters lack names, their status as Wife and Husband are capitalized for easier reference.

Nabokov opposed vigorously but without effect *The New Yorker*'s decision to reverse his title to "Symbols and Signs."[9] This revision lost resonance with the medical phrase *signs and symptoms*; an invitation to question the diagnosis of the disturbed young man at the center of this story. Also gone was the division of the story into the numbered sections that underscore its many sequences of three.[10]

Past history: time

Although a relative timeframe is outlined for the young man's 20 years of life, Nabokov presents a problem in calculation by withholding any fixed point of reference. Stadlen has noted that the first section of the story contains 7 paragraphs, the second 4, and the third 19, which reversed yield 19–4–7.[11] For the reasonable reader who finds this a contrived basis for dating the story to 1947, there is amusing confirmation.

In the third section of "Signs and Symbols" as it appears in the Vintage edition of *The Stories of Vladimir Nabokov*, the *19* paragraphs include:

> [3-12] "Can I speak to Charlie," said a girl's dull little voice.
> [3-13] "What number you want? No. That is not the right number."

[3-14] The receiver was gently cradled. Her hand went to her old tired heart.
[3-15] "It frightened me," she said.
[3-16] He smiled ...

But, there were only *18* paragraphs in this same passage in *The New Yorker*:

[3-12] "Can I speak to Charlie," a girl's dull little voice said to her now
[3-13] "What number do you want? ... No. You have the wrong number."
[3-14] She put the receiver down gently and her hand went to her heart. "It frightened me," she said.
[3-15] He smiled ...

In the service of consistent style, Nabokov's editor Katharine A. White had condensed paragraphs 14 and 15 in the original manuscript. Not only did Nabokov restore these paragraphs to their original state in further publications, but five years later—to prod his readers and perhaps have the last word—he placed in "Pnin's Day"[12] the incident in which Pnin requests a volume from the library which he has already withdrawn:

"It can't be!" cried Pnin. "I requested on **Friday Volume 19, year 1947, not 18**, year 1940" ... "Eighteen, 19," muttered Pnin. "There is not great difference! **I put the year correctly,** *that* **is important! ... They can't read, these women. The year was plainly inscribed** [emphasis added].

For further emphasis, the library visit occurs on Pnin's own birthday, May 15, by no coincidence the publication date of "Symbols and Signs."[13]

Past history: place

Although not the principal significance of 1947, the fixed point allows the reader to place the family's travels and their son's illness in the historical context of Germany.[14] Unlike his brother, Isaac, who chose to emigrate circa 1909, the Husband was forced to leave Byelorussia after the 1917 Revolution. In 1927 Berlin, the couple, in their 40s *already*,[15] had their only child. Unusually aware of his surroundings as an infant, the boy develops into a wary and avoidant four year old. Nabokov introduces a squirrel and later wallpaper, as he will do in *Pnin*, as signs of potential danger. With Nazi power increasingly evident in 1933, the child has insomnia, but is seen by his parents as artistically sensitive. He draws *wonderful* pictures of sirins, creatures in some traditions lethal on sight, but which also allude to Nabokov's own German experience. The character Luzhin, ominously associated with windows and death,[16] is a cousin of the family. Even in 1935, the parents minimized the impending danger but also their son's odd behaviors. The Wife, blind to irony, recalls a frightening picture as *merely ... show[ing] an idyllic landscape with rocks on a hillside and an old cart wheel hanging from the branch of a leafless tree.* The allusion is to "The Triumph of Death" by Peter Breughel the Elder. The cart wheel is an instrument of torture.[17]

"The Triumph of Death" (detail), Peter Breughel the Elder

"The Triumph of Death," Peter Breughel the Elder

How the family obtained papers to leave Germany for the United States in 1937 goes unsaid, but they avoided thereby "concentration" at the newly opened camp at Ettersdorf. This extraordinarily unlikely event[18] can account for the couple's resentment of Isaac, the *real American*.[19] Even though his generosity is sparing— Isaac supports the couple (albeit in a walk-up), provides the Husband's false teeth (albeit ill-fitting), and pays (complainingly) the considerable fees for their son's long hospitalization[20] —his penny-pinching fails to explain their intense ingratitude. Mocking him as *the Prince* for his pre-occupation with money, in analogy to a "Jewish–American Princess," they suppress that Isaac negotiated and purchased their flight from the Holocaust. *The Prince* had worked a Machiavellian favor too great to repay or to forgive.

After 4 years in America, the 16-year-old is hospitalized; the family suffering continues; in Germany, unthinkable atrocities. Summarizing, the Yiddish-inflected syntax with which the Wife partakes in the narrative gives way to Nabokov's rhythmic, alliterative prose as the sensibilities of author and his character merge:[21]

She thought of the endless waves of pain that for some reason or other she and her husband had to endure; of the invisible giants hurting her boy in some unimaginable fashion; of the incalculable amount of tenderness contained in the world; of the fate of this tenderness, which is either crushed, or wasted, or transformed into madness; of neglected children humming to themselves in unswept corners; of beautiful weeds that cannot hide from the farmer and helplessly have to watch the shadow of his simian stoop leave mangled flowers in its wake, as the monstrous darkness approaches. (A13: 135)

Examination and diagnosis

The story begins with a conclusion: the *young man ... [is] incurably deranged in his mind*. However, since this text challenges the convention of objective narration, Nabokov's "good reader" needs ask "says who?" For *poorly shaved, acne, shuffling, uncommunicative* might indicate no more than unhappy adolescence, although disinterest and wariness of *gadgets* are more worrisome. The narrative tone is uncomfortably judgmental and the gift is described in fairytale language, as for a child in need of coddling: *... dainty and innocent trifle: a basket with ten different fruit jellies in ten little jars*. The patient is not taken very seriously, despite two attempts to jump from a window. Additionally, Nabokov wished to mark the word *ten*, which occurs six times in the story.[22]

His parents accept the doctor's conclusion: the boy's thoughts may be dismissed as delusional. *A priori*, it is unlikely that Nabokov is equally confident. Even the reader favorably inclined toward psychiatry may wonder if Dr Herman Brink in his paper projects some of his own foibles on to his patient: grandiosity, self-reference, impersonality, superiority.

But then a transition occurs in the text from the language of clinical studies to the subjective voice of the young man. In parallel with the poetic passage joining the Wife and author, Nabokov's prose inhabits the internal confusion and external incomprehensibility of the boy's thinking:

Phenomenal nature shadows him wherever he goes. Clouds in the staring sky transmit to one another, by means of slow signs, incredibly detailed information regarding him. His inmost thoughts are discussed at nightfall, in manual alphabet, by darkly gesticulating trees. Pebbles or stains or sun flecks form patterns representing in some awful way messages which he must intercept. Everything is a cipher and of everything he is the theme. Some of the spies are detached observers, such are glass surfaces and still pools; others, such as coats in store windows, are prejudiced witnesses, lynchers at heart; others again (running water, storms) are hysterical to the point of insanity, have a distorted opinion of him and grotesquely misinterpret his actions. He must be always on his guard and devote every minute and module of life to the decoding of the undulation of things. The very air he exhales is indexed and filed away. If only the interest he provokes were limited to his immediate surroundings—but alas it is not! With distance the torrents of wild scandal increase in volume and volubility. The silhouettes of his blood corpuscles, magnified a million times, flit over vast plains; and still farther, great mountains of unbearable solidity and height sum up in terms of granite and groaning firs the ultimate truth of his being. (A11: 66)

Durantaye reviews and extends the literature on the everyday details by which the author or his favored characters discern patterns of benevolent openings from the present world to something beyond.[23] Following this formulation, the boy's thinking can be interpreted as the result of extreme hyper-attunement, a matured version of the "surprise" he experienced as an infant. He is uncontrollably flooded by distant, horribly malignant images of the Holocaust. Those patterns, which otherwise would have given him artistic entry beyond himself, are entirely blocked out or distorted; for example, one of Nabokov's "signature" details, the standing, reflective puddle becomes *hysterical ... running water*. Lacking protective moral dullness, he is overwhelmed by the distant reality, and can blunt his vicarious suffering only through the bizarre substitutions of madness. As measure, mirror and amplifier of an unbearable world (*his blood corpuscles, magnified a million times*), deciphering the images he protectively encodes would be fatal.

Laboratory data

Yet, an existential illness should improve along with the world it mirrors. It is 1947. Even the cynical narrator of *Pnin* allows that things can go well:

Some people—and I am one of them—hate happy ends. We feel cheated. Harm is the norm. Doom should not jam. The avalanche stopping in its tracks a few feet above the cowering village behaves not only unnaturally but unethically. Had I been reading about this mild old man, instead of writing about him, I would have preferred him to discover, upon his arrival to Cremona, that his lecture was not this Friday but the next. [25]

On close examination, Nabokov provides a number of veiled counter-signs that doom will be cheated.

1) The principal importance of 1947 to Nabokov: It is springtime, *Mrs Sol's hat, the fault-finding light*, and a Friday holiday, *school children on the bus*, and *the underground train lost its life current between two stations* but continued on. This particular Friday, when everything went wrong (known by its antonym: Good Friday), was April 4.[24] That Friday evening the couple did not celebrate the Sabbath after sundown. Moreover, they were unaware of an historical/solar/lunar convergence: this Good Friday was also Nissan 14 in the year 5707, the evening before the Passover.

2) The sanatorium is suspect,; the nurse's report of a second suicide attempt so unfeeling as to be possibly false or even vindictive. The doctor's report of the first no better, glibly offensive, *a masterpiece of inventiveness*. Even that of a witnessing patient is questionable: *he was learning to fly*, if like a bird, hallucinatory but possibly only *envious* of a flight towards freedom. *What he really wanted to do was to tear a hole in his world and escape* is equally ambiguous, *escape* life or the sanitarium; the self-important *really* can belong to no one but Dr Brink.

3) The Wife's old, worried, wild-eyed Aunt Rosa and friend Rebecca Borisovna have been killed by the Germans:[25] "some playing cards and a photograph or two ... had slipped from the couch to the floor: knave of hearts, nine of spades, ace of spades, Elsa and her bestial beau" (A13: 163).

Given that Nabokov would not write the impossible cliché *a photograph or two*, the phrase must denote simultaneously two distinct entities. Excluding one photograph as the servant and her Nazi boyfriend, the three playing cards must be just that, and also metaphorically a second photograph: Rebecca's two dead grandchildren, aged nine and one, and her "knave of hearts" son-in-law. The Wife unjustly holds him a guilty rogue for retaining his family in Byelorussia.

But despite the sad memories evoked, the three cards are auspicious. Dolinin alludes to the magical three card sequence in

Pushkin's "The Queen of Spades," given to the scoundrel protagonist by the ghost of the old noblewoman whose death he caused. Their play (3–7–Ace) wins the first two hands, but loses the third; the winning ace turning into the image of the dead Countess, the queen of spades. Hermann, his fortune gone, goes over the edge into madness.[26] However, played in the same three games, the series of cards that fall to the Wife (J–9–Ace) result in two near losses and a final win.[27] Consistent with Nabokovian fate, this favorable omen has been influenced by Aunt Rosa and Rebecca, meddling with chance from the beyond.

4) The husband is fragile and upset; distinct from his son's adolescent disarray, he shows signs of wear: *his old hands (swollen veins, brown-spotted skin), clasped and twitching.* Readers have taken the image of a *tiny half-dead unfledged bird ... helplessly twitching in a puddle* to foretell the *unfledged* son's death, but *twitching* connects to the father. Although it may be hyperbole, he says as much: *I can't sleep because I am dying.* The stated cause of his anguish is believing himself accountable for his son's suffering: *Otherwise we'll be responsible. Responsible!*, but his history suggests another equally irrational idea—that he is guilty of his own survival.

Prognosis

Section 3 presents the three potentially ominous phone calls. In response to the second, a reminder of two unsuccessful suicide attempts, the Wife explains: "You have the incorrect number. I will tell you what you are doing: you are turning the letter O instead of the zero" (A14: 188).

I read this as Nabokov's caution to the reader—in the next paragraph, avoid making the same error as this unsophisticated caller, mistaking one arbitrary sign for another:

> They sat down to their unexpected **festive** midnight tea. ... he put on his spectacles and re-examined **with pleasure** the **luminous** yellow, green, red little jars. His clumsy moist lips **spelled out** their **eloquent** labels: apricot, grape, **beech** plum, quince. He had got to crab apple, when the telephone rang again. [(A14: 190); emphasis added]

Festive is not a cruel irony, even unrecognized it is Passover. The Husband re-examines the jars *with pleasure*, perhaps expecting an il*lumin*ation or something that will speak out to him (and the reader) through their *eloquent* labels, which he (and the reader) must not read, but *spell out*. Doing so, the careful reader finds that the old man misreads the third label, beach plum as *beech plum*, an example of typographic free indirect discourse.[28] For the poor linguist with enough German for business, under the pressure of memory, *beach* becomes *beech*, which recalls *Buchen*, beech trees.[29] Likewise, *plum* associates to *Pflaume* and *Pflaumenbaum*, literally *flame* and *burning tree*. Unable to free his thoughts from the past, beach plum jelly returns him to thoughts of Buchenwald, the beech forest site of the Ettersdorf camp. Nabokov repeats this hidden allusion, almost metonymic for the Holocaust, in *Pnin*:

> ... because, if one were quite sincere with oneself, no conscience, and hence no consciousness, could be expected to subsist in a world where such things as Mira's death were possible. One had to forget—because one could not live with the thought that this graceful, fragile, tender young woman with those eyes, that smile, those gardens and snows in the background, had been brought in a cattle car to an extermination camp and killed ... burned alive in a pit on a gasoline-soaked pile of beechwood ... she was selected to die and was cremated only a few days after her arrival in Buchenwald ... [135]

However, this quietly righteous Husband cannot forget. The history of his escape and flight approaches Pisgah.

* * *

The third phone call is not the dim girl again, not the hospital reporting a suicide, not an indeterminate ending focused on the couple's suffering, nor a metaliterary statement on the impossibility of certain knowledge, and certainly not Nabokov tempting the reader into a *referential mania*. The first born son has leaped through a window, landed on his feet, run to a nearby gas station, negotiated a once-fearful gadget and telephoned his parents: *Mama, can I come home?*[30]

Unobserved, the Angel of Death passed over.

* * *

Appendix

Webster's New International Dictionary, Second Edition

cipher, n. ... fr. ar. *sifr*, empty, cipher, zero

1. *Math.* A character or symbols [written 0] denoting the absence of all magnitude or quantity however small; naught; zero. In the decimal notation ... it is used to fill out, and so to specify, the blank spaces, in the absence of any digits, which if present would occupy these places. Thus, in 5,070 the two ciphers signify that there are no units and no hundreds ...
   5. a] a method of secret writing that substitutes other letters or characters for the letters intended ... b] a substitution alphabet so used. c] a writing having the letters so substituted or transposed. Cf. CODE

fly, v. *Intransitive*
   1. a] To move in or pass through the air with wings, as a bird. b] To flee; as: [1] to run from danger; to take flight; to flee ... [2] To vanish; disappear; fade; as, a shadow *flies.*

knave, n.
   2. a tricky, deceitful fellow; an unscrupulous person; a rogue; a rascal ...
   3. a playing card marked with the figure of a servant or soldier, a jack.

sign, n.

I. A symbol
   1. A conventional symbol of emblem which represents an idea, as a word, letter, or mark; as the *sign* of the cross.
   4. a] A motion, an action, or a gesture by which a thought is expressed, or a command or a wish made known.
   6. In writing and print, an ideographic mark, figure, or picture ... conventionally used to represent a term or conception, usually technical. See *Arbitrary Signs and Symbols.*

II. Indication

8. Something serving to indicate the existence of a thing: a token; as, a *sign* of grace, wit, fear ...

9. A remarkable event, considered by the ancients as indicating the will of some deity; a prodigy; an omen ... a miracle; a wonder.

10. Presage; portent; omen; as, a *sign* of rain, of death, of victory.

III. Technical senses

14. *Math.* A character indicating the relation of quantities. or an operation performed on them; as the signs + [plus] ... etc. ... See *Arbitrary Signs*, in Appendix.

15. *Med.* An objective evidence of disease; that is, one appreciable by some one other than the patient ...

symbol, n.

2. That which stands for or suggests something else by reason of relationship, association, convention, or accidental but not intentional resemblance; esp., a visible sign of something invisible, as an idea, a quality or totality ...

3. In writing or printing, an arbitrary or conventional sign ... used instead of a word or words ... See *Arbitrary Signs and Symbols*, in the Appendix ...

The patterns of doom
Brian Quinn

Vladimir Nabokov is by far better known for his novels; however, he also deserves great stature for his 58 short stories that he wrote in both Russian and English. "Signs and Symbols" is one of his most remarkable and impressive works written in English. It is outwardly similar to many of his previous American short stories since it deals with many of the sad and difficult aspects of émigré life in America after World War II. It also mirrors many of the themes described by Isaac Bashevis Singer, who wrote similar stories at about the same time. Johnson perceptively notes:

> Dealing with the poorer and more desperate side of émigré life in America, it strikes an amazingly similar note to that sounded by Singer in his own stories dealing with the same topics—though of course the two writers also have in common their émigré status, their bilingualism, and the fact that they were both from eastern Europe.[1]

"Signs and Symbols" has many of the themes that Nabokov is famous for in both his other stories and novels, such as madness, narcissism, the cruelty of fate, the plight of poor émigrés, the exploitation of patterns and symbols to signify hidden meanings, and, finally, the theme of parents' love for their children and their dread of losing them. In fact, possibly the most poignant and dramatic moments of "Signs and Symbols" is indeed best observed in the tender and moving glimpses of love that are demonstrated by the elderly couple for their only son.

Theme of madness

One of the central themes of "Signs and Symbols" is the theme of madness, as demonstrated by the son's present disease. Nabokov is well known for his deep interest in various forms of madness; he often used madness in such novels as *Despair*, *Pale Fire*, and *Lolita*, often with grotesque and comic effect. In this story, the son's particular type of madness ("referential mania") has been invented by the author himself to achieve the desired effect in his story. Nabokov first came upon the idea for this type of madness in 1943 while writing his biography *Nikolai Gogol*, in which he stated:

> I shall have occasion to speak in quite a different book of a lunatic who constantly felt that all the parts of a landscape and movements of inanimate objects were a complex code of allusion to his own being, so that the whole universe seemed to be conversing about him by means of signs.[2]

The disease suffered by the boy is some type of complex schizophrenia which the author uses as one of the pillars of his story, but no medical explanations are given.

Interestingly, even though the symptoms and characteristics of the disease are carefully described by the author, the reader is given no descriptions of its possible cause. Therefore, the author leaves it up to the reader to discern what it might be. As a result, the overwhelmingly probable cause of this disease is the family's nomadic existence in which they have lost their country, language, friends, relatives, possessions, and status. One can easily assume that whatever eccentricities the boy may have had became sorely exacerbated upon his arrival to the USA. Thereafter, the stress of learning a new language and culture, while also watching his parents' continual suffering, may have very well led him to escape into some kind of personal fantasy world which, after a while, he was no longer able to control.

In fact, the reason for the boy's recent suicide attempts is apparently an effort to finally control his fantasy by permanently escaping from it. According to the text, the recent suicide attempt is not the first, but appears to be one of many such incidents. Nabokov shows the boy's intelligence while also indicating the severity of his mental state. The disease seems to have originated from the need to escape the grim reality of the world that he saw and perceived around himself. The author shows the circumstances under which the precocious boy grew up and from which he eventually decided to escape. In some ways, it might appear that due to the widespread murder, torture, and loss of human dignity that took place in the 1930s and 1940s in Europe, it may well have been quite natural

for some people to drift into insanity to escape the "insane" reality
of the world around them. The contrast of the fussy old Aunt Rosa
with the insane son seems to be intentional on the author's part.
The lives of both characters are somehow intertwined, with the old
woman endlessly worrying about the monsters and the horrors of
the real world and the boy worrying about those of his imaginary
world.

Johnson also supports this connection between the boy's
madness and the terrible tragedies suffered by his family over the
past 40 years: "There is a sense in which this is the second subject
in the story, running parallel with the first, which is the harshness
of the couple's life as émigrés."[3]

The title of the story, "Signs and Symbols," indicates a series of
patterns in the boy's life and in his disease as described by some
famous German doctor. Parker suggests that the disease of "referential mania" might also be some type of literary sickness that
readers can suffer from if they get too involved in a text and begin
to over focus on it at the expense of the real world around them:

> The young man suffers from "referential mania," a mental
> disorder in which the patient imagines that everything happening
> around him is a veiled reference to his personality and existence.
> The detailed description of the malady employs the words
> "signs," "alphabet," "patterns," "messages," "cipher," "theme,"
> "observers." It is the language not only of medical diagnosis but
> also of literature and literary criticism. The inference which can
> be drawn is that "referential mania" can also be an affliction
> of readers who get caught up in an over-reading of a literary
> text. "Signs and Symbols" not only suggests the possibility, but
> exemplifies, through a perfect merging of form and content, just
> how that might come about.[4]

As suggested by Parker, the signs and symbols of this story point
to tragedy in the past, present, and future for the protagonists.
In addition, the reader should be careful not to delve too deeply
into the morass of symbols of this story, since it may be a more
straightforward tale than the kind one usually encounters in
Nabokov's work.

The madness that is ever present in this story thus exists on
several levels, first of all on the level of the insane boy, next on

the level of insanity that modern history has continually dealt to certain countries and peoples in the 20th century, and finally on the level of the reader, who may have to occasionally enter into the realm of the insane mind to relate to those who have already escaped from the normal world.

Field suggests that the insanity experienced by the boy in this story is only another type of extreme narcissism, similar to that pervasive disease which afflicts many of Nabokov's main protagonists in both his novels and short stories:

> If one delves into the scientific literature on the subject, many of the outstanding features of Nabokov's writing are identified as characteristic of narcissism. B. Grunberger, for instance, one of the leading psychiatric theoreticians of narcissism, points out that the narcissist is constantly menaced by the world of things. That is only natural, since there is only one self and everything else is thing. This theme begins to play strongly in Nabokov's second novel, *King, Queen, Knave* (1926), and is more than a stylistic innovation that links him with the object-orientation French *nouveau roman* several decades later. For the narcissist, repetitions are absolutely necessary. They are a quest for the patterns of the past, and their very rhythm lulls disquiet. The narcissist may suffer referential madness, the theme of Nabokov's 1948 short story, "Signs and Symbols," in which everything in creation becomes a reference to oneself, which also explains *audition colorée* where language becomes privatized with unique colors in which letters and words are seen in the mind as they are said or read. Nabokov's mother experienced *audition colorée*, and she was also the extravagantly favored child in her own youth. It is less evident because the form and stylistic brilliance of his books vary so much from one another in comparison with most other writers, but Vladimir Nabokov really does have one tale to tell: the shadow that pursues or is being pursued by someone. That is the only story Narcissus knows.[5]

Therefore, according to Field, the boy in this story is just another in the line of extravagant heroes that make up Nabokov's oeuvre. For Field, the insanity described as "referential mania" in the story is just another version of narcissism. The presence of madness tends to be quite a usual occurrence in Nabokov's work.

Theme of tragic fate and impending doom

The reader is confronted with tragedy right in the first paragraph as Nabokov introduces the "problem" of the young man's "incurably deranged" mind (A9: 3). We understand the couple's tragic fate in the second paragraph, where we learn of their poverty and helpless financial and social condition. The sense of impending doom is hinted at in the third paragraph of the story: "That Friday everything went wrong" (A10: 22). The fourth paragraph ends with the couple observing a baby bird dying as they walk by: "A few feet away under a swaying and dripping tree, a tiny half-dead unfledged bird was helplessly twitching in a puddle" (A10: 40). The gloomy picture continues in the fifth paragraph as the sad wife notices a passenger on the bus crying in despair: "It gave her a kind of soft shock, a mixture of compassion and wonder, to notice that one of the passengers, a girl with dark hair and grubby red toenails, was weeping on the shoulder of an older woman" (A10: 48). Brian Boyd states:

> Detail after detail in the story seems impregnated with doom: That Friday everything went wrong. The underground train lost its life current between two stations. It is raining hard. They cannot see their son ... When they reach home, the husband finds himself without his key. His new dentures are hopelessly uncomfortable. He has just got to bitter crab apple when the telephone rings for the fatal third time.[6]

These unfortunate parents have led a life of continual tragedy and despair. Nabokov himself lost his family fortune when escaping from Russia in 1918 with his family, and later his father in Berlin. Thereafter, he lived in virtual poverty until he arrived in the USA in 1940. Many of his friends were like the elderly couple described in this story. It is not surprising, therefore, that "Signs and Symbols" impresses with its realistic air and compact style and, at times, appears to almost be journalistic in its mastery. Boyd declares that the story "works brilliantly as poignant realism, but what makes [it] such a masterpiece is the Nabokovian twist that turns the real world inside out and into an irresolvable enigma."[7]

Doom and gloom pervade this story. The ultimate tragedy, of course, occurs in the last scene when the phone mysteriously rings for the third time in the middle of the night. Logic says that it cannot be the same person who dialed the wrong number twice. The reader is left with almost no other conclusion than that the insane asylum is calling to inform the couple that their son has finally succeeded in committing suicide. Johnson notes:

> We are given no further information, but it is impossible to escape the implication that the call is from the hospital with news of another and this time successful suicide attempt. For if it were another wrong number there would be no relation at all between these calls and the remainder of the story. It is not possible to "prove" that this is the case, but it is quite obvious that Nabokov is inviting the reader to supply the missing explanation. Thus, the old man and his wife do have a further blow waiting for them, and the second link between the two subjects is made—in the reader's mind.[8]

The arbitrariness of tragic fate remains unabated and unstoppable in the modern world. We are left with both the feeling of frustration and sadness at the world's never-ending cycle of pain. However, Nabokov has shown us a glimpse of strength, love, and devotion as portrayed in two remarkable parents. Their love makes even this final tragedy seem not insurmountable.

Ways of knowing in "Signs and Symbols"

Terry J. Martin

Interpreters of Nabokov's "Signs and Symbols" disagree about the meaning of the story's enigmatic ending.[1] Is the third telephone call a portent of the boy's suicide, or simply another wrong number? More important, is it the key to determinate knowledge of some sort, like the ending of a detective story, which teleologically highlights some disguised pattern throughout? Or is it instead the apt figure of what is indeterminate and unknowable, like a promised message which never comes? By concluding on a note of such apparent uncertainty, Nabokov leaves the reader wondering not only what actually occurs, but also by what basis such knowledge can be ascertained. In other words, the story engenders an epistemological conflict in the reader, who must if possible determine on the basis of available evidence what the significance of the ending is. In this essay I will argue that this conflict is informed, even structured, by the two terms that form the title of the story, and that the story is centrally concerned with the problematic nature of our ways of knowing.

Most critics gloss the two terms "signs" and "symbols" as equivalent, but, as John Lane was the first to indicate, there is a commonly observed distinction between them.[2] According to the *Dictionary of Philosophy*:

> The meaning of "symbol" is often limited to a conventional sign: something constructed by society or by individuals and given a more or less standard meaning that members of that society agree upon or share. This restricted sense of "symbol" is contrasted with a natural sign, [which is defined as follows:] implied in saying that X is a natural sign of Y is their factual (causal) association together in a number of instances which allows one to anticipate or predict, or infer, that Y will be followed by X ... The relationship is not one which has been created by human convention.

The difference might be restated thus: a sign is an objective and natural indication of things, as smoke betokens a fire, whereas a symbol is a subjective and, to a certain extent, arbitrary representation of them, as the history of the swastika—which has meant everything from good luck to the greatest of moral atrocities—shows. Moreover, the sign evinces something about the nature of the world around us, while the symbol might be said rather to reveal more about the nature of the human mind or community and about its capacity for evaluating human experience.

The terms "sign" and "symbol" have an immediate bearing on the story, for they serve to frame its central interpretive problem. That problem, stated briefly, is whether (or to what extent) events in the story are governed by an objective and logical coherence, or whether they are merely a product of a given character's, if not of the reader's, mind. Indeed, as Lane indicates, "In ... 'Signs and Symbols,' causal ambiguity is the physical world's most salient feature" (A114). In effect, Nabokov introduces, *vis-à-vis* the title, two opposed and incommensurable ways of interpreting and forces us to choose between them. Nowhere is this more evident than in the case of the final telephone call, which may be seen at one extreme as a sign of the boy's death, and at the other extreme as a symbol of the absurd and meaningless (for not only are the first two calls wrong numbers, but the mother's explanation of why they occur also has nihilistic undertones in its reference to zero).[3] Moreover, in light of the way in which narrative endings teleologically determine the meaning of beginnings and middles, the two terms thus effectively structure the range of possible interpretations for the entire story as well. Indeed, it will be seen that no event in the story can be understood apart from the urgent question of its status as a sign (an objective and natural indication of things) or as a symbol (a subjective and arbitrary representation of them).

Of course, some readers are tempted to take the entire story as a kind of literary joke, a parody of the overworked conventions of the genre. In such a view, the significance of the distinction I am tracing here is, I suppose, minuscule, for Nabokov will simply be seen as poking fun at the very project of interpretation itself. There is much to be said in support of this view. For instance, as a number of critics have noted, the boy in his referential mania resembles no one so much as the reader, who by convention necessarily regards all things in the story as potential clues having some latent relevance to the solution to be adduced. Indeed, according to James Guetti, this way of reading is precisely what the conventions of detective fiction have helped to bring about. Moreover, like the boy, the reader may be said to encounter only himself in the text: thus, "Everything is a cipher and of everything he is the theme" (A11: 72). Finally, there are, of course, other works of Nabokov's, such as *Pale Fire*, which consistently mock both the methodology and pretentiousness of academic philology.

Nevertheless, "Signs and Symbols" contains a dark side which is not comic, and which cannot be subsumed by parody. For instance, the story alludes historically to some of the 20th century's worst crimes—crimes which Nabokov's own family was forced to flee from, including the violence of the Russian Revolution and the Holocaust. In addition, the picture that frightens the son, which contains "an old cart wheel hanging from the branch of a leafless tree" (A12: 124), may also be a reference to a notorious 16th-century persecution of Protestants, in which Philip II of Spain had victims tied to cart wheels and rolled over cliffs or burned.[4] Moreover, the tone of the story, which largely mirrors the mother's point of view, is bleak and pessimistic, and the story is full of images of mortality and suffering, including the boy's attempts at suicide, the dying bird, and the husband's swollen veins and brown-spotted skin. In short, if the story has parodic elements, it nevertheless contains material which goes beyond mere parodic play to suggest both an earnest examination of the inadequacy of our way of knowing and a grim portrait of human misery in a cruel and indifferent universe. Indeed, Nabokov "viewed ['Signs and Symbols'] as a very serious work" and was so angered by the fact that it had been "treated as an overwritten parody" by the editorial staff of *The New Yorker* that his friend and supporter Edmund Wilson "expressed surprise that he had not challenged someone to a duel."[5] The depth of Nabokov's response suggests that we not lightly dismiss the entire tale as a kind of elaborate joke.

The historical allusions to the Russian Revolution and to the Holocaust also underscore the need for the proper interpretation of signs. Whatever else the story may suggest about the potential insanity of the interpretive enterprise, it reminds us that there is objective evil that people must protect themselves against,[6] and it is of course necessary to recognize a threat in order to take action against it. In light of the fate of Aunt Rosa, we may presume that

the elderly Russian couple owes its very survival to the fact that
they correctly read the signs of their danger and emigrated. Indeed,
Nabokov's own family followed a similar trek, escaping first from
the Bolsheviks and later from the Nazis. Also, it is hardly a coincidence that the most equivocal sign in the story, the enigmatic third
telephone call, also bears a certain resemblance to the manner in
which the death of Nabokov's own father was reported. According
to Nabokov:

> On the night of March 28, 1922, around ten o'clock, in the
> living room where as usual my mother was reclining on the
> red plush corner couch, I happened to be reading to her Blok's
> verse on Italy—had just got to the end of the little poem about
> Florence, which Blok compares to the delicate, smoky bloom of
> an iris, and she was saying over her knitting, "Yes, yes, Florence
> does look like a *dimniy iris*, how true! I remember—" when the
> telephone rang.[7]

Thus, one's very life might be said to be at stake in distinguishing
between signs and symbols, or between what are real objective
threats and what are merely subjective constructions.

The story equally underscores the importance of distinguishing
signs from symbols by explicitly introducing the notion of responsibility. Just before the end of the story, the father realizes (too late?)
that he and his wife will have been responsible if their son succeeds
in committing suicide. Indeed, the tale abounds with the flagrant
signs of their neglect: they have placed him in an institution which
is so "understaffed" and in which "things g[e]t mislaid or mixed up
so easily" (A10: 34) that they are loath to leave their gift there; the
parents do not care for one of the nurses, who quite insensitively
("brightly") breaks the news about the boy's recent attempt on his
life; and, most telling of all, the boy has a history of similar attempts
while at the institution. Clearly, the boy is not receiving adequate
care, and the fact that the father does not have to explain to his
wife in what way both of them will be responsible suggests that she
is aware of it too, almost as if the two of them had been denying
to themselves all along the true significance of what they had been
witnessing. Indeed, the couple has, at least in regard to their son,
a history of willfully misreading signs, for they chose to ignore the
nature of the son's illness altogether, "stubbornly" misrepresenting

it to themselves as "the eccentricities of a prodigiously gifted child" until it was no longer possible to do so and "those little phobias of his ... hardened as it were into a dense tangle of logically inter-acting illusions, making him totally inaccessible to normal minds" (A12: 130). The father's admission of responsibility implies that the interpretation of signs is governed by a moral imperative and that as interpreters we are all thus morally accountable. In other words, we need to interpret correctly not only because it may be necessary to save our skins, but also because it is an aspect of our ethical obligation to others.

"Signs and Symbols" engenders a kind of interpretive paradox, however, for if it calls attention in a variety of ways to the need to interpret, it nevertheless simultaneously challenges our ability to do so. The story is a self-conscious and brilliantly constructed trap for interpreters, much like the chess problems that Nabokov loved to create. The analogy is apt, for Nabokov himself notes the affinity between composing chess problems and composing fictions:

> It should be understood that competition in chess problems is not really between White and Black but between the composer and the hypothetical solver (just as in a first-rate work of fiction the real clash is not between the characters but between the author and the world), so that a great part of a problem's value is due to the number of "tries"—delusive opening moves, false scents, specious lines of play, astutely and lovingly prepared to lead the would-be solver astray.[8]

"Signs and Symbols" especially resembles a chess problem in its final gambit—or is it rather a poisoned pawn?—which the reader is at liberty to accept or to refuse (i.e. to read the third phone call as a sign of the boy's death or not). Accordingly, different lines of play result from that decision. However, Nabokov has rigged it so the reader will find elements in the story that undermine the very epistemological assumptions upon which either interpretation rests. In effect, the story reveals flaws in our usual ways of understanding, which make any interpretation of the story at best tenuous and equivocal. It enacts this epistemological crisis in a number of ways, all of which call into question the implied contrast in the title.

One of the principal means that the story employs to challenge our confidence in the infallibility of the sign is by thematizing the role of chance. By revealing the first two telephone calls to be wrong numbers—and thus essentially meaningless accidents—the story invites us to consider the possibility that the third telephone call may also be the result of chance. It may, after all, be the same girl, who still has not gotten the number right, or it may be someone else who has made a similar mistake. It may, likewise, be a prank caller, or even an unexpected call from the Prince himself. In other words, nothing in the story guarantees that events are always the result of a conscious design, or even that they can, for that matter, be traced to an intelligible cause. Indeed, numerous other events in the story which present themselves to the reader as potentially significant may similarly be the meaningless products of chance. What, for instance, signifies the pattern of constant inter-ruption in the couple's efforts to visit their son, including the power failure in the subway, the delay of the bus, the hard rain which falls on their way to the asylum, the appearance of the disliked nurse who sends them away, and, finally, the forgotten key which makes the old man wait on the landing for his wife to let him in—a pattern which in some ways appears to echo that of the interrupted happiness of their entire existence? It is a revelation of the sinister character of the universe, a sign of some inscrutable cosmic malice which perversely governs human destiny, or is it only a random coincidence, entirely without purpose or significance? In this story, at least, there is no guarantee that any rational order underlies events.

Nabokov similarly questions the infallibility of signs by focusing on the manner in which perception is distorted by subjectivity. An event may, after all, have no significance beyond that with which our fears and desires invest it. Nowhere is this seen more clearly than in the case of the boy, whose extreme paranoia converts the entire world into a series of signs that endlessly and hieroglyphi-cally signify his own self; as the narrator observes, "Everything is a cipher and of everything he is the theme" (A11: 72). We may assume, of course, that the pathetic fallacy holds true in this case and that the boy is not warranted in regarding natural objects as objective indexes of his own nature; that is, clouds presumably do not "transmit to one another, by means of slow signs, incredibly detailed information regarding him" (A11: 67).

What the boy perceives are more properly deemed "symbols," which he has mistaken for signs. After all, clouds are not indicative of human nature in any directly causal way, but they can be representative of it. Nevertheless, the boy's tendency to discover a secret symbolic significance in everything no doubt serves as an apt warning to literary critics themselves, who at times seem equally prone to converting literary texts into symbols indiscriminately and without warrant. In fact, elsewhere Nabokov explicitly warns against this practice:

> My advice to a budding literary critic would be as follows. Learn to distinguish banality. Remember that mediocrity thrives on "ideas." Beware of the modish message. Ask yourself if the symbol you have detected is not your own footprint.
>
> Ignore allegories. By all means place the "how" above the "what" but do not let it be confused with the "so what." Rely on the sudden erection of your small dorsal hairs. Do not drag in Freud at this point. All the rest depends on personal talent.
>
> The symbolism racket in schools attracts computerized minds but destroys plain intelligence as well as poetical sense. It bleaches the soul. It numbs all capacity to enjoy the fun and enchantment of art.[9]

Moreover, it is hard not to suspect a further jibe at critics in the boy's arrogant blindness, who "excludes real people from the conspiracy—because he considers himself so much more intelligent than other men" (A11: 64). Thus, Nabokov suggests that solipsistic interpretation, in which the world (or the text) is reduced to some preconceived index of the self, is not only an exercise in futility but is itself a kind of madness.

Of course, the boy is something of a caricature in whom readers and/or critics never completely recognize themselves to begin with, and the extremity of his paranoia makes it easy to dissociate ourselves from him. However, the question of paranoia, and thus of subjective distortion in general, is not so simply put aside. It is especially exemplified by a brief description of Aunt Rosa, which might indeed serve as an analogue for the difficulty of interpreting the entire story. In this passage Nabokov subtly derides what can only be regarded as Aunt Rosa's paranoiac fixation on unfortunate events: "Aunt Rosa [was] a fussy, angular, wild-eyed old lady, who had lived in a tremulous world of bad news, bankruptcies, train accidents, cancerous growths ..." (A12: 115). The reader is clearly meant to see Aunt Rosa's concern with misfortune as excessive, and the description highlights this impression by emphasizing her eccentricity ("fussy") and lack of emotional and psychological stability ("wild-eyed"). The narrator even hints at the possibility of insanity, since Aunt Rosa is laconically said to inhabit "*a* tremulous world" (emphasis mine) as opposed to "*the* tremulous world" or "*our* tremulous world"), thus making it by implication a solipsistic and deluded world of her own making. This is an excellent example of what Wayne Booth has termed "stable irony," for we are invited to join the author in perceiving the foolishness and inadequacy of Aunt Rosa's way of understanding from the author's superior point of view (or "platform"), which we come to share with him. Who, after all, would prefer to remain below in Aunt Rosa's paranoiac world with her? However, Nabokov does not allow us the security of our shared platform for long, for if Aunt Rosa seems unwarrantably paranoid, the world that she inhabits turns out nevertheless to exceed her most nightmarish fears of it: Aunt Rosa's worries come to an end when "the Germans put her to death, together with all the people she had worried about" (A12: 117). The reader is thus forcefully left with the question of whether or not "paranoia" may not simply be a misconceived term for one who has better gleaned the nature of reality from the many immanent signs both of human evil and of cosmic indifference around her.

Moreover, it is surely no mere coincidence that the description of Aunt Rosa follows immediately after a description of the burgeoning paranoia of the boy at age four, who is "moodily, shyly, with puckered forehead, looking away from an eager squirrel as he would from any other stranger" (A12: 113). The juxtaposition of the boy's attitude with Aunt Rosa's nightmarish demise suggests that such acute distrust on the part of the boy is at least not as clearly groundless or insane as it might seem at first glance. The question of paranoia is even more difficult to determine in the case of the mother, whose point of view we share throughout most of the story, and who is indeed the most sympathetic character in the story, perhaps because she herself proves to be the most sympathetic to the suffering of others. Not only is she sensitive to the moods of her husband and compassionate toward the girl who is weeping on the subway, but she also identifies deeply with all victims, as in the following passage:

She thought ... of the incalculable amount of tenderness contained
in the world; of the fate of this tenderness, which is either
crushed or wasted or transformed into madness: of neglected
children humming to themselves in unswept corners; of beautiful
weeds that cannot hide from the farmer and helplessly have to
watch the shadow of his simian stoop leave mangled flowers in
its wake, as the monstrous darkness approaches. (A13: 135)

Because she articulates what amounts to the moral center of the
story, we cannot lightly dismiss her point of view.[10] But what, then,
are we to make of her quasi-paranoiac delusions? How are we to
understand references to "the endless waves of pain that for some
reason or other she and her husband had to endure," or to "the
invisible giants hurting her boy in some unimaginable fashion"
(A13: 137)? Is she simply projecting her fears on to the world in
paranoiac fashion, or is she instead somehow more highly attuned
to the way things really are? That is, is her image of the farmer
cutting the weeds simply a subjective representation of life—i.e. an
unconsciously poetic symbol forged out of her own paranoia—or is
it actually an objective indication—a sign—of a cruel and uncaring
universe? In some fundamental way, to know whether the third
telephone call is an announcement of the boy's death is simply to
know what kind of universe we are in. One thing we can say for
the mother is that she at least does not cosmeticize the world in the
manner of Mrs Sol, whose "face was all pink and mauve with paint
and whose hat was a cluster of brookside flowers" (A9: 16), or like
the nurse, who speaks "brightly" of the boy's latest suicide attempt.
These are clearly liars, whereas the mother displays a greater
willingness to face the truth, suggested by the way she presents
"a naked white countenance to the fault-finding light of spring
days" (A9: 17). Indeed, Hagopian concurs with both the boy's
and the mother's point of view, arguing that it is not "necessarily
paranoid to conclude that nature and the universe are enemies of
man" and "to want to 'tear a hole in [the] world and escape'."[11]
One cannot resist pointing out that Hagopian simultaneously
betrays a certain paranoid tendency himself when he claims, "The
post-modernists must not be allowed to kidnap Nabokov."[12] In any
event, we can no longer reject paranoia as a clearly demarcatable
form of madness that leads one to mistake signs for what are
actually symbols; rather, we must admit that we may be equally

mistaken in mistaking for symbols what are actually signs. That is, we can neither be certain that events in the story are not the result of objective causes, nor, conversely, that they are not simply a subjective delusion.

Finally, the very nature of the story itself challenges our ability to distinguish between signs and symbols. For if signs are natural and objective indications of things, their very appearance in—that is to say, their translation into—an essentially representational form such as fiction makes their status problematic. There is, after all, nothing that prevents the creator of the fictional world from suspending the normal physical laws under which we operate and thereby undermining the empirical authority by which signs derive their significance, as Nabokov claims that fiction may do with, for instance, the truths of mathematics:

> In this divinely absurd world of the mind, mathematical symbols do not thrive ... Two and two no longer make four, because it is no longer necessary for them to make four. If they had done so in the artificial logical world which we have left, it had been merely a matter of habit: two and two used to make four in the same way as guests invited to dinner expect to make an even number. But I invite my numbers to a giddy picnic and then nobody minds whether two and two make five or five minus some quaint fraction.[13]

Thus, in fiction, smoke may not betoken fire at all, and whether it does or not will depend simply on the rhetorical use to which it is put. In genres in which mimetic fidelity to empirical reality is pronounced, such as the realistic novel, signs will continue to operate as they do in our practical everyday life, and readers can continue to make inferences from them accordingly. There are, however, genres, such as allegory, in which mimetic realism is eschewed—indeed, simply cannot be tolerated[14]—and in which the appearance of smoke may have nothing to do with fire but may flow instead from the mouth of some abstract essence called Deceit, to suggest just one possibility. What this implies is that there can be no such thing as a natural sign in fiction, for its significance is already irreducibly a matter of artistry and of convention. As Nabokov himself puts it, "Raisins of fact in the cake of fiction are many stages removed from the initial grape."[15] Consequently, there is, at least according to our criteria of definition, no way to distinguish the sign from the symbol in fiction.

The cumulative effect of these techniques is to present what amounts to an intolerable interpretive dilemma to the reader. On the one hand, the story requires the reader actively to interpret by virtue of its open-endedness as well as by its thematic concern with the need for responsible interpretation. On the other hand, it portrays a world in which it is practically impossible to ascertain the precise nature of certain events so as to know what to make of them.

The interpreter's situation does not, however, seem to me to be hopeless. Indeed, the story reveals something about how *not* to interpret as well. In this regard I see the mother and the boy as representative of the two epistemological errors which Nabokov depicted in "The Art of Literature and Commonsense." The first error is what Nabokov disparagingly called "commonsense," a condition which is governed by, among other things, a myopic belief in "those farcical and fraudulent characters called Facts,"[16] and which sees no cause for optimism in the face of the harsh realities of 20th-century life. Another way of describing this might be the reduction of knowledge to the everyday logic of signs without the redeeming value of a kind of poetic insight. For instance, the mother lives passively in a world of nightmarish facts and lacks the ability to transcend them. Her life is dictated by "the loss of one joy after another, not even joys in her case—mere possibilities of improvement" (A13: 134). She is a victim of the "commonsense" view of life which measures human happiness in terms of external signs. She has lost faith in the goodness of life, because, despite her sensitivity, she has not discovered the value of poetic thought, which Nabokov describes thus:

Th[e] capacity to wonder at trifles—no matter the imminent peril—these asides of the spirit, these footnotes in the volume of life are the highest forms of consciousness, and it is in this childishly speculative state of mind so different from commonsense and its logic, that we know the world to be good.[17]

Where the mother sees only the bleak certainty of loss, Nabokov affirms his own unshakable optimism in the primacy and persistence of the life of the imagination, even in the worst imaginable circumstances. He writes,

Within the emphatically and unshakably illogical world which I am advertising as a home for the spirit, war gods are unreal not because they are conveniently remote from the reality of a reading lamp and the solidity of a fountain pen, but because I cannot imagine (and that is saying a good deal) such circumstances as might impinge upon the lovely and lovable world which quietly persists, whereas I can very well imagine that my fellow dreamers, thousands of whom roam the earth, keep to these same irrational and divine standards during the darkest and most dazzling hours of physical danger, pain, dust, dearth.[18]

For the reader who shares the mother's outlook, the logic of the final telephone call is doubtless the death of the son, for such a world is entirely unsupportive of the imagination. Such a world view conflicts, however, with "the irrational belief in the goodness of man," which is, in Nabokov's view, "a solid and iridescent truth."[19]

The second epistemological error is an equally disastrous tilt in the opposite direction, which is that of the unrestrained and indiscriminate play of imagination. The boy has supplanted normal causal reasoning with fantastic links between events and himself, and he is no longer able to distinguish his own solipsistic fancies from objective reality, having unknowingly turned the entire world into a symbol of the self. Nabokov is careful to distinguish between such a fruitless, misguided, and uncontrolled use of imagination, and the purposeful control of artistic creation:

Commonsense will ... remark that a further intensification of such fancies may lead to stark madness. But this is only true when the morbid exaggeration of such fancies is not linked up with a creative artist's cool and deliberate work. A madman is reluctant to look at himself in a mirror because the face he sees is not his own: his personality is beheaded; that of the artist is increased.[20]

Within the logic of the boy's way of interpreting, the final telephone call will mean simply whatever the reader (obsessively) takes it to mean. Thus, the narrative seems to leave us poised between two worlds—or, shall we say, between two world views, two ways of interpreting—which are equally sterile and nightmarish: the perversely fanciful, disconnected, solipsistic one of the boy and the bleak, unrelenting, deterministic one of the mother.

If those two ways of knowing stand in dialectical opposition to each other, there is a third way of knowing which in a manner synthesizes and transcends the other two: it is that of the artist. Indeed, it is Nabokov's view alone which, while not denying what is harsh and poignant in the lives of this poor immigrant family, nevertheless goes on to affirm the importance of the imagination and of serious artistic play. For what else does the final telephone call serve to inspire if not "this capacity to wonder at trifles— no matter the imminent peril—these asides of the spirit, these footnotes in the volume of life [which] are the highest forms of consciousness"?[21]

A funny thing about "Signs and Symbols"

John B. Lane

If Vladimir Nabokov ever entertained the notion that simple cause and effect provide an adequate explanation for the world in which human beings find themselves, he kept his moment of doubt to himself. All of his major fiction displays some kind of causal ambiguity, and in his short story "Signs and Symbols" causal ambiguity is the physical world's most salient feature.

The natural world in Nabokov's story is filled with signs and symbols which both reflect the characters' lives and foretell coming events. The old woman, who is the narrational focus of the story, is an astute observer, but she gives no conscious credence to the non-rational portents in the story. Her son's perception of them, on the other hand, is sufficiently acute to make the world's malevolence intolerable for him. When the old couple walks by "a tiny halfdead unfledged bird … helplessly twitching in a puddle" that is "under a swaying and dripping tree" (A10: 41), the incident is echoed in the description of the young man's illness, in which, the reader is told, "his inmost thoughts are discussed at nightfall, in manual alphabet, by darkly gesticulating trees" (A11: 70).

By means of such linkages of the world which the old couple inhabits with the world which the young man finds intolerable, Nabokov makes it clear both that it is a threatening world which the characters inhabit, and that the world's portentous nature is not just a product of the young man's deranged mind.

These different perceptions of the physical world and the device of the final phone call are significant elements in the story, but Nabokov is seldom if ever content with limiting his fiction to the milieu of his characters, and his tales invariably become a kind of literary chess problem (although an exception might be allowed for those in which a chess problem becomes a story). In writing on the composition of chess problems, Nabokov points out that "it should be understood that the competition in chess problems is not really between White and Black, but between the composer and the hypothetical solver (just as in a first rate work of fiction the real clash is not between the characters, but between the author and the world)."[1] In "Signs and Symbols" the struggle between the author and the world is very much in evidence, but Nabokov takes the struggle a step further and forces the reader from his or her comfortable position as spectator, drawing him or her into the conflict.

A striking feature of most Nabokovian texts is authorial foregrounding, but in "Signs and Symbols" it is, while still present, uncharacteristically ambiguous and restrained. This restraint clearly helps the genre gimmick of the final phone call to function effectively, but more importantly, it provides a strong incentive for a crucial rereading, with its concomitant involvement of the reader in the story's more profound problems. Without this restraint the story might be too easily read as diverging from the trick-ending genre of popular magazine fiction only by the tinge of parody supplied by Nabokov's distinctive strain of narrative intrusion. Instead, the shifting, ambiguous, and finally mysterious character of the story's narrator points the way toward a fuller understanding of the story by leading the reader to search both for a clear picture of the author/narrator and for reassurance that his initial interpretation of the final phone call is justified. The authorial foregrounding is effected by two different means. The first and most noticeable is the overt manipulation of the language of the story, and the second is the presence of allusions to both personal biographical details and to literary subtexts. In "Signs and Symbols" there are none of the startling narrative intrusions which occur in some of Nabokov's writing, and the diction is less playful than is often the case, but nonetheless, the reader's attention is still drawn to an author lurking within the story.

In the foregrounding, based on language manipulation, the narrator's changes in diction and syntax are closely linked with the story's overall structure. The story consists of three short, numbered sections. The first two sections are structurally very similar. They show a progressive development of literary style from a slow and highly objective beginning to a dramatic and subjective climax. The last section is uniform in style and deviates from literary transparency in only two minor ways.[2]

While both the first two sections begin in a highly objective tone, they are nonetheless distinctly different. In the opening of the first section, the word choice and grammatical structures are designed to remind the reader of the slightly awkward speech patterns which immigrants (like the old couple) often display. The opening of the second paragraph is a particularly good example:

> At the time of his birth they had been married already for a long time; a score of years had elapsed, and now they were quite old. Her drab grey hair was done anyhow. She wore cheap black dresses. (A9: 11)

The word order of "been married already for a long time" and the non-standard, literary use of "anyhow" are both calculated to link the narrator with the old couple. In the course of the first section the language gradually becomes subjective and highly lyrical. The diction, syntax, and imagery all differ dramatically from those which occur in the opening. The language ceases to be that of an elderly émigré couple and shows conscious "literary" artistry. The reader might be carried along by this gradual change and not notice the narrational change consciously, were it not for devices introduced to assure that the authorial presence is noted. The first such device is the extravagance of metaphor which creeps into a passage that begins as Doctor Herman Brink's strictly scientific description of the symptoms of referential mania. The second—an even more consciously literary device—is the triple use of alliterative word pairs which appears in the last third of the concluding paragraph of the first section:

> He must be always on his guard and devote every *minute and module* of life to the decoding of the undulation of things. The very air he exhales is indexed and filed away. If only the interest he provokes were limited to his immediate surroundings—but alas it is not! With distance the torrents of wild scandal increase in *volume and volubility.*
>
> The silhouettes of his blood corpuscles, magnified a million times, flit over vast plains; and still farther, great mountains of unbearable solidity and height sum up in terms of *granite and groaning* firs the ultimate truth of his being. ([A11: 78]; emphases mine)

The lyricism of the close of the first section is emphasized by the abrupt return to a calm objective tone in the opening paragraph of the second section:

When they emerged from the thunder and foul air of the subway, the last dregs of the day were mixed with the street lights. She wanted to buy some fish for supper, so she handed him the basket of jelly jars, telling him to go home. He walked up to the third landing and then remembered he had given her his keys earlier in the day. (A11: 87)

While the tone of this paragraph has much in common with that of the beginning of the story, it is different in that the émigré speech patterns are not in evidence, and the narrator is of the standard, invisible, and omniscient variety. However, once again, the prose gradually changes, and the second section ends in a climax which is even more lyrical and syntactically complex than the close of the first section. Even without obtrusive devices like the alliterative word pairs of the first climax, the final sentence of section two makes it apparent that there is an author behind the chameleonic narrator:

She thought of the endless waves of pain that for some reason or other she and her husband had to endure; of the invisible giants hurting her boy in some unimaginable fashion; of the incalculable amount of tenderness contained in the world; of the fate of this tenderness, which is either crushed or wasted, or transformed into madness; of neglected children humming to themselves in unswept corners; of beautiful weeds that cannot hide from the farmer and helplessly have to watch the shadow of his simian stoop leave mangled flowers in its wake, as the monstrous darkness approaches. (A13: 137)

There is no such development in the third section. The narrator remains virtually invisible; there is no change in tone, syntax, or diction. But there is no need for a change. The reader reads the "signs" given by the first two sections and anticipates a third climax without the necessity of a change in style to help him along. The tension created by the interplay between the steady tone and the reader's expectation serves to heighten the impact of the final phone call.

Although the tone is consistent throughout the third section, it contains several indications that a climax is coming. Two such indications occur in the final sentence. The first is the "yellow, green, red" succession of jelly colors, which suggest the caution, go, and stop colors of a traffic light. However, the sequence of lights is different from that which occurs in traffic lights, and the change reflects the story's dramatic sequence: the series of portents and the unhappy recounting of the family's history (yellow) is broken only by the old man's brief moment of enthusiasm (green), which precedes the final call (red). The second indication in the final sentence has been described by William Carroll as "the sequence of 'eloquent labels' from apricot to quince ... broken by the flat, cramped sound of 'crab apple,' fruit which is tart or sour" while the others are sweet.[3]

Other portents of the climax to come in the third section are the two allusions to mortality which occur there. The first comes in the opening of the section when the old woman hears her husband moan just before he staggers into the room—a description which would be more suitable for a heart attack than insomnia.

This impression is supported by his statement: "I can't sleep because I am dying" (A13: 151). The second occurs when the first phone call comes at "an unusual hour for their telephone to ring" (A14: 172). After explaining to the caller that she has a wrong number, the old woman's "hand went to her old tired heart" (A14: 179). These events serve as portents because they fit into a pattern of threes and twos anticipating a three, which recurs throughout the story. Many of these are obvious and some have already been specifically referred to, such as the three sections of the story, the three phone calls, the three uses of alliterative pairs of words, the three jelly colors, and the two suicide attempts, but they extend to much more subtle references. One such is the mention of three names in the story—Sol, Soloveichik, and Solov—which share elements of a root that is the Russian word for nightingale, and thus are linked to the "half-dead unfledged bird."[4] Another (and, like the allusion to a heart attack, it also occurs in the third section) is founded on the repetition of words by the old man. After he announces that he cannot sleep because he is dying, he says, "No doctors, no doctors ... To the devil with doctors! We must get him out of there quick. Otherwise we'll be responsible. Responsible!" (A13: 154). Aside from reinforcing the pattern of ominous threes and twos, this passage also lends credence to William Carroll's suggestion that the reader is him or herself at least partly "responsible" for killing the deranged young man by supplying meaning to the third ring.[5]

While the foregrounding through literary and personal references is, like the language-based foregrounding, not as prominent
as in some of Nabokov's other writing, it is still definitely
present. The cryptic line in the description of "referential mania"
("Everything is a cipher and of everything he is the theme") has
considerable relevance to the story, though it is far from clear in
which sense it is to be taken: Is it a code system? The key to such
a code? A message in code? Or a reference to the number 0 in the
second phone call? Nonetheless, it must have some foundation in
the delight Nabokov took as a child in his monomaniacal uncle,
about whom he wrote "Uncle Ruka ... prided himself on being
an expert in decoding ciphered messages ... we subjected him to a
test one day, and in a twinkle [he] turned the sequence '5.1324.11
13.169.13.55.13 24.11' into the opening words of a famous
monologue in Shakespeare."[6]

Another glimpse of the author is given in the ironic treatment of
the psychiatrist "Herman Brink," who writes an "elaborate paper
in a scientific monthly" on the nature of the young man's illness, a
problem which the old couple had puzzled out "long before." The
disdain the narrator displays toward Herman Brink is perfectly in
tune with Nabokov's many disparaging comments about Freudian
psychology. His comment in *Speak, Memory* is typical in tone:

> Let me say at once that I reject completely the vulgar, shabby
> fundamentally medieval world of Freud, with its crankish quest
> for sexual symbols (something like searching for Baconian
> acrostics in Shakespeare's works) and its bitter embryos spying
> from their natural nooks upon the love life of their parents.[7]

The most concrete biographical detail comes in the climax of the
story when the telephone rings for the third time, presumably
signaling the young man's successful suicide. The concluding few
lines bear more than a passing resemblance to Nabokov's account
of his own father's death:

> On the night of March 28, 1922 around ten o'clock, in the
> living room where as usual my mother was reclining on the
> red-plush corner couch, I happened to be reading to her Blok's
> verse on Italy—had just got to the end of the little poem about
> Florence which Blok compares to the delicate, smoky bloom of

an iris, and she was saying over her knitting, "Yes, yes. Florence does look like a *dimniy* iris, how true! I remember—" when the telephone rang.[8]

This telephone ringing ends the paragraph, and Nabokov gives no other description of the family's learning of his father's untimely death (he was killed while preventing the assassination of another speaker at a public meeting). The description provides a perfect reflection of the concluding paragraph of "Signs and Symbols" (the memoirs were written several years after the story), which is illuminating in that they both create ambiguities which are resolved only after some thought and rereading. In the memoirs, the specificity of the date and time seems incongruous when first read, falling as it does in a setting of apparently mundane reminiscence, but when the significance of the phone call dawns (somewhere in the following paragraph), the date and time suddenly make perfect sense. The same pattern occurs in the short story, but its resolution is considerably more difficult.

It seems clear in the story that there can be no happy resolution to the young man's difficulty. Paramount among the many indica-tions is the methodical description of the course of his disease: "as a baby he looked more surprised than most" ([A12: 109], indicating to the reader that he was abnormal from birth). An indication of the boy's early perception that the natural world is not benevolent is found in the comment "Four years old, in a park: moodily, shyly, with a puckered forehead, looking away from an eager squirrel as he would from any other stranger" (A12: 113). The information that at "age six ... he drew wonderful birds with human hands and feet, and suffered from insomnia like a grown up man" (A12: 118) suggests problems to come both through the physical symptom and through allusion to the "tiny half-dead unfledged bird." By age ten he is in a "special school" and causing his parents "shame, pity" and "humiliating difficulties." Finally, there

came a time in his life, coinciding with a long convalescence after pneumonia when those little phobias of his which his parents had stubbornly regarded as the eccentricities of a prodigiously gifted child hardened into a dense tangle of logically interacting illusions, making him totally inaccessible to normal minds.[9]

That the young man's fate does not hold any pleasant surprises also seems to be indicated by several references to his parents, such as the comment about his mother that "this, and much more, she accepted—for after all, living did mean accepting the loss of one joy after another, not even joys in her case-mere possibilities of improvement" (A13: 135), or the pathetic description of his father's patently unworkable plan for bringing the boy home to their two room apartment: "I have it all figured out. We will give him the bedroom. Each of us will spend part of the night near him and the other part on this couch. By turns. We will have the doctor see him at least twice a week" (A13: 166). In fact, the entire story is an agglomeration of signs and symbols pointing to the conclusion that there is no happy ending awaiting the characters. The indications seem to be unrelievedly bad, from the "cheap black dresses" of the first page to the succession of jellies which precedes the terminal phone call.

In addition to the several faint and one relatively strong autobiographical reference, there are also several faint allusions to Nabokov's own fiction, and two strong references to external subtexts, including one to a classic of Russian literature. When the narrator mentions "the ugly, vicious backward children, he was with in that special school," the description could apply just as well to the school for abnormal children where Adam Krug's son is killed in *Bend Sinister* and mention of the young man's "cousin, now a famous chess player" brings to mind Luzhin in *The Defense*. Aside from these allusions to his own literature, Nabokov includes an extensive reference to Puskin's short story "The Queen of Spades." It occurs in the third section in a short paragraph concerning the old woman:

> Bending with difficulty, she retrieved some playing cards and a photograph or two that had slipped from the couch to the floor: Knave of hearts, nine of spades, ace of spades, Elsa and her bestial beau. (A13: 163)

The pervasive use of the number three in "Signs and Symbols" and the succession of three cards ending in an ace suggest the analogous pattern in Puskin's story. Elsa and her bestial beau suggest Lizaveta and her suitor Hermann, and it is noteworthy that

Nabokov also gives the name Herman to the psychiatrist in "Signs and Symbols."[10] The "bestial beau" Hermann in Puskin's story becomes obsessed with the three cards which seal his fate, and the description of his thoughts is a perfect example of "referential mania":

> Two fixed ideas can no more exist in one mind than, in the physical sense, two bodies can occupy one and the same place. "Three, seven, ace" soon eclipsed from Hermann's mind the form of the dead old lady. "Three, seven, ace" never left his thoughts, were constantly on his lips. At the sight of a young girl, he would say: "How shapely she is! Just like the three of hearts." When asked the time, he would reply: "About seven," Every pot-bellied man he saw reminded him of an ace. "Three, seven, ace," assuming all possible shapes, persecuted him in his sleep: the three bloomed before him in the shape of some luxuriant flower, the seven took on the appearance of a Gothic gateway, the ace—of an enormous spider. To the exclusion of all others, one thought alone occupied his mind—making use of the secret which had cost him so much.[11]

The overwhelming impression of the signs and symbols in Nabokov's story is that the young man will die. There are, however, some less noticeable indications of the contrary, and the apparent time and date anomaly which Nabokov sets up and then resolves in his recounting of his father's death has an interesting parallel in this short story. In the course of the litany of minor disasters which befall the old couple while they are trying to deliver their gift, we are told that "that Friday everything went wrong." A technically literal interpretation would seem to indicate that the final phone call must also fall into the category of "everything." However, the third section of the story opens: "It was past midnight ..." and thus the phone call actually comes on Saturday morning.

A close reading of the story reveals a plethora of symbolic premonitions, but a dearth of hard facts. Only the matter of time comes as a straightforward statement from the omniscient narrator, and it only indicates that the call cannot be interpreted *with certainty* as coming from the hospital, although this is the conclusion which the structure of the story seems to dictate. The two previous wrong numbers heighten our interest in the final call, but actually serve to make its interpretation less sure; without them, we could justify no other explanation for the call.

The ambiguity of the final phone call forces the reader—after an initial leap to a conclusion which is too obvious to be satisfying—to go back and examine the story for signs and symbols which will make everything clear. The subsequent discovery that there is virtually no additional information in the story leads to a state of mind which the reader will sooner or later recognize as bearing an uncanny resemblance to the young man's "referential mania," a condition in which the sufferer imagines that

> everything happening around him is a veiled reference to his personality and existence. He excludes real people from the conspiracy—because he considers himself to be so much more intelligent than other men. Phenomenal nature shadows him wherever he goes. Clouds in the staring sky transmit to one another, by means of slow signs, incredibly detailed information regarding him. His inmost thoughts are discussed at nightfall, in manual alphabet, by darkly gesticulating trees. Pebbles or stains or sun flecks form patterns representing in some awful way messages which he must intercept. Everything is a cipher and of everything he is the theme. (A11: 63)

Nabokov was very distrustful of what he referred to as the "symbolism racket" of standard literary criticism. No doubt his attitude can be attributed at least partly to protectiveness toward his own creations; however, his remarks in an interview with Alfred Appel, Jr. seem to have particular relevance to "Signs and Symbols":

> My advice to the budding literary critic would be as follows ... Remember that mediocrity thrives on "ideas." Beware the modish message. Ask yourself if the symbol you have detected is not your own footprint. Ignore allegories. By all means, place the "how" above the "what" but do not let it be confused with the "so what." Rely on the sudden erection of your dorsal hairs. Do not drag in Freud at this point.[12]

There are footprints aplenty in "Signs and Symbols." Nevertheless, it eventually emerges that the story operates on three distinct levels: 1) the human story which the narrator describes, 2) a standard philosophical "second level" in which man's relation to the physical world is examined, and 3) a thoroughly Nabokovian object lesson for the *literati*.

The human story in "Signs and Symbols" is a simple, deft recounting of a day in the difficult life of an old émigré couple. With a few carefully detailed observations, Nabokov evokes a marital relationship in which the angularities of petty strife have long since been worn smooth. The old woman accepts her own suffering as being in the natural order of things, and she is solicitous of her husband, who cannot reconcile himself to the pain which their son's situation gives him. The old man's carefully structured plan reassures him, and formulating it allows him to relax, despite its obvious impracticality. The story is a beautifully drawn representation of that common condition among older couples, wherein the husband's assertiveness and orientation toward mechanical manipulation of the physical world has become a meaningless vestige of his productive years, while the wife's forbearance and compassion remain as the real foundation for their lives.

The story can also be read on a second level, which consists of a shift from the particulars of the characters' lives to the universal that is evidenced in them. This theme in "Signs and Symbols" mines an apparently inexhaustible mother lode: the relationship between a fixed, discrete, and causally determined physical world, and the mental construct of that world which is man's only means of perceiving it. The objective, scientific view is represented by Herman Brink's "elaborate scientific paper" and is given short shrift. His view that the young man's distrust of the physical is mere paranoia is refuted both by the objective milieu of the young man's world and by his links to the unfledged bird, an unambiguous symbol of the casual cruelty of a non-teleological, mechanically unfolding world which is, if not antagonistic, at least totally indifferent to suffering. Nabokov expressed his personal reaction to this world in an interview given late in his life: "nature expects a full grown man to accept the two black voids fore and aft, as stolidly as he accepts the extraordinary visions in between ... I feel the urge to take my rebellion outside and picket nature."[13]

"Extraordinary visions" are prominent in "Signs and Symbols," and the characters' responses to them vary considerably. Nabokov's years as a research entomologist probably left him more familiar than most writers with the world view that Herman Brink represents, but it can hardly be said to describe his own view of the natural world, which he presents in comments like: "I discovered in nature the nonutilitarian delights that I sought in art: Both were a form of magic, both were a game of intricate enchantment and deception."[14] Both this comment and his unhappiness with the "voids fore and aft" seem to place him much less in sympathy with Herman Brink than with the young man who wants "to tear a hole in the world and escape." Though the natural world in "Signs and Symbols" is full of "enchantment and deception," there is very little of "delight," and the humor which is so characteristic of Nabokov's other writing is not readily apparent. The world in this short story is grim and full of ominous portents. The old woman's awareness of them is indicated both by the fright she displays at the first phone call and by descriptions which show her powers of observation, such as "he kept clearing his throat in a special resonant way he had when he was upset" (A10: 38), and "During the long ride to the subway station, she and her husband did not exchange a word ... every time she glanced at his old hands (swollen veins, brown-spotted skin), clasped and twitching upon the handle of his umbrella, she felt the mounting pressure of tears" (A10: 43). They are not spared the cruelty of the world surrounding them, and the only balance to it is the familial love which they have, part of the "incalculable amount of tenderness in the world" which is fated to be "crushed, or wasted, or transformed into madness." Both as an entertaining narrative and as a fresh look at a standard literary/philosophical problem, the story is both readable and interesting, but it achieves its full stature through those elements which are directed specifically to the *literati*. Once the reader realizes that deciphering the signs and symbols is not going to yield the story's full meaning, and that he or she, as reader, is suffering from "referential mania," the story's meta-literary function begins to appear. Just as the old couple takes the young man "a dainty and innocent trifle" (the basket of jellies) which is calculated not to "frighten" or "offend," Nabokov presents a collection of discrete and multicolored literary devices for the reader's delectation.

There is a broad array of literary devices in the story, which tend to fall into discrete portions of the text. The openings and closings of the first two sections (quoted and described above) are good examples, each being a small sample of a distinct type of prose, but there are many others. In fact, the reader conducting such a survey soon feels like the protagonist in Nabokov's story "A Visit to the Museum," wandering from exhibit to evermore improbable exhibit, lost in an exposition hall of prose techniques.

Apart from the plentiful and readily apparent signs and symbols which contribute to "a dense tangle of logically interacting illusions" whose overall effect is to induce "referential mania," the story contains many other interacting references. These sometimes act as shaping devices, appearing at the beginning and end of paragraphs; in the opening of the story, for example, a phrase from the first sentence of the paragraph "for the fourth time in as many years," with its implied numerical repetition (reinforced by the homonym), is echoed by a phrase in the last sentence: "ten different fruit jellies in ten little jars." The jelly jars themselves also serve to help tie the whole story together by appearing at the beginning of the first two sections and at the end of the third.

Pairs of linked references occur throughout the story. One such pair, for example, links father to son through similar parenthetical insertions. A description of the son—"(his poor face blotched with acne, ill-shaven, sullen and confused)" (A10: 30)—is paralleled by that of the father—"his old hands (swollen veins, brown-spotted skin)" (A10: 45). The first of a pair of catoptric images alludes to the reflective properties of "glass surfaces and still pools" in such a way as to make them seem like symptoms of madness. The second is a grotesque image of the old man at the mirror where, "straining the corners of his mouth apart by means of his thumbs, with a horrible masklike grimace, he removed his new hopelessly uncomfortable dental plate and severed the long tusks of saliva connecting him to it" (A12: 97). In contrast to the first image, this one is readily acceptable as an objective description of reality despite the man/walrus metamorphosis which it describes.[15] The man/walrus combination is in turn one of a pair of man/animal combinations in the story, the other being the bird/man combination found in the young man's drawings (quoted above).

The photograph which introduces the "Queen of Spades" allusion also occurs twice in the story. Earlier, "from a fold in the album, a German maid they had had in Leipzig and her fat-faced fiancé fell out" (A12: 110). Despite the fact that the two descriptions are of the same photograph, and both have alliterative descriptions of the fiancé/beau, the reactions they evoke are very different: the first produces mild distaste, and the second loathing and apprehension. Such devices as these, and many others like them, are the structural units of the story, but alone they are only a collection of techniques. It is on the metaliterary level that they are given the coherence which makes them work as a literary unit.

Signs and symbols are the very stuff of language, both spoken and written, and they are so varied and complex a pair of ideas as to require 58 separate entries in *The Oxford English Dictionary*.[16] No comprehensive definition will be attempted here, but a consideration of some of the underlying notions is useful in attempting to understand Nabokov's short story. The two concepts are closely related, but their essential difference is that signs tend to be *indications* of other things and act as messages, while symbols are *representations* of other things. The two functions are rarely clearly separated, and one of the central problems which the story poses for the reader is founded on the tension which occurs between the two functions when the usage is ambiguous. The "tiny half-dead unfledged bird ... helplessly twitching in a puddle" is an image which is almost invariably alluded to in discussions of the story, but how is one to interpret it? As a representation, and therefore a symbol of the young man, as a symbol of the cruel indifference of nature, or as a portent of the young man's fate: a *sign* of things to come? When the old woman explains to the caller that she is confusing the letter O and the number zero—two very similar signs—is it a portent of the fatal call (third time's the charm), or is it a symbolic representation of the reader's difficulty in working out an interpretation of the story?

While such questions may have no definitive answer, they are central to the meaning of this story. All signs and symbols (and for that matter all perceptions) can be located somewhere between the two polarities which are referred to in such dichotomies as science/art, thinking/feeling, and rationality/intuition.

When the reader tries to interpret one of the images in Nabokov's story (or any sign or symbol), he or she quickly discovers that it is not obviously one or the other, but seems to be a muddy mixture of the two, with which he or she feels more or less comfortable. The initial inclination may be to attribute this difficulty to intentional perversity, and this would probably be at least partly correct, but there is also a serious point being made about the nature of signs, symbols, and human perception: a point which concerns the paradox inherent in both language and knowledge. The more scientific, exact, and concrete a sign or symbol, the less meaning it can contain, and therefore with perfect exactness comes perfect meaninglessness. The corollary is also true. The more meaning something carries, the less exact it must become, hence a thing which encompasses all meaning is also perfectly inexact. It is this epistemological fact which can make discussion about the arts so frustratingly inexact, and it is the state of affairs to which Nabokov alludes through the timing of the final phone call ("that Friday everything went wrong ... it was past midnight"): a precise description pertaining to an important event, but one which carries no relevant meaning. Nabokov causes the reader to compare this kind of information with such symbolic paradigms as the passage which speaks "of beautiful weeds that cannot hide from the farmer and helplessly have to watch the shadow of his simian stoop leave mangled flowers in its wake, as the monstrous darkness approaches" (A13: 142), which has broad implications and clear relevance to the story, and yet can never be reduced to a precise meaning.

The intricately interconnected and diverse signs, symbols, devices, and references in Nabokov's story may well induce "referential mania" in the meticulous reader, but they are not just a diabolically contrived labyrinth, but rather a carefully elaborated statement about the nature of perception and interpretation: a statement which encompasses both literature and epistemology.

The story is an effective trifle in a hackneyed genre, which simultaneously parodies that same genre, a philosophical trifle (in its evocation of the rational man/non-teleological nature conflict), and it is a leghold trap for heavy-footed symbolic racketeers. But it is ultimately founded on a thoughtful development of some of the basic concepts which underlie fiction and all language. While it abounds in those distinctively Nabokovian traits which result in amused delight or blind rage, according to individual temperament, it is at least as profound as it is playful.

The playfulness in the story is of an unusual flavor for Vladimir Nabokov, because it seems to smack more of grim cruelty than of the self-deprecating humor which one usually associates with his writing. Both this problem of the missing humor and the more overt problem of the meaning of the final phone call may well have no final solution, but there are two references which I believe shed some light on them. First are the biblical allusions in the names of Isaac and Rebecca, and the pseudonym for Isaac's brother: "the Prince." Two fainter biblical allusions occur in the following line: "that Friday everything went wrong. The underground train lost its current between two stations" (A10: 22). The stations of the cross are traditionally performed on Good Friday, the day on which Christ was crucified, and Rebecca's husband Isaac, son of Abraham and Sarah, was spared at the last moment when God—who had demanded that Abraham sacrifice his son as a demonstration of faith—struck the dagger from his hand.

The son spared at the last moment certainly seems to have a potential parallel in "Signs and Symbols" and it brings back to mind the allusion to "The Queen of Spades." The third card does not turn out to be the expected ace, and the description of Hermann's shock in Pushkin's story may well provide both the answer to the twin problems and the clearest glimpse of author and reader which "Signs and Symbols" contains:

> Hermann started: indeed, instead of an ace, before him lay the queen of spades. He could not believe his eyes, could not understand how he could have slipped up.
>
> At that moment it seemed to him that the queen of spades winked at him and smiled. He was struck by an unusual likeness ...[17]

Names
Yuri Leving

The defiant Nabokov expressively chooses to display the gaps both in the plot and the structure of his short story. As if this is not enough, he also leaves all its three main characters virtually unidentified. The readers of "Signs and Symbols" will never learn the names of either the parents or of their deranged son. There are, nonetheless, quite a few other names, which, for their part, build up an interactive system of "signs" and "symbols." Most of these names leave a trail of indirect allusions to either literary sources or biblical narratives, and can be viewed as functioning in a subtle unison. Below is an attempt to cover the fundamentals associated with the names mentioned in the text.

Brink, Herman

The earliest readers of Nabokov's story already seemed concerned with this name. The editor of *The New Yorker* wrote to him:

> One thing we need to know is whether Herman Brink is *a real name or not* and whether "referential mania" is a real disease or one you invented. If the name is that of a real doctor we might have to change it or reword to show he was not in charge of this boy's case. If the term 'referential mania' is invented, that presents more of a problem. (Katharine White to Nabokov on July 3, 1947; emphasis added; see A: 47)

Nabokov explained three days later: "The doctor is purely fictional. Should you discover that one of that name exists—which would be an odd coincidence—I would not object to a re-christening" (July 6, 1947).

The protagonist of Alexander Pushkin's "The Queen of Spades" (1833), who is also named Herman(n), goes mad after he becomes obsessed with the three cards which he hopes will win him a fortune. In three consecutive games Hermann tries to prove his theory but fails at the last attempt. The description of his mental process is akin to the symptoms of "referential mania" described by Nabokov.

Nikolai Gogol's short story "Diary of a Madman" (1835), notable for its curious numerological patterns and confusing dates, demonstrates the gradual mental deterioration of its own narrator. The madman is put into an asylum and the story ends with the high-pitched note of universal pity addressed to the narrator's mother: "Mother, save your son!" Nabokov used these final words as an epigraph to his own study on Gogol, written in 1944, just four years before the appearance of "Signs and Symbols." This plea resounds within the unrealized message sent by Nabokov's poor boy to his own parents. In the opening of the same book devoted to Gogol, Nabokov makes no effort to conceal his disdain for medical science, especially that branch dealing with the mental state of patients:

> The couple of diabolically energetic physicians who insisted on treating [Gogol] as if he were an average Bedlamite, much to the alarm of their more intelligent but less active colleagues, intended to break the back of their patient's insanity before attempting to patch up whatever bodily health he still had left ... Second rate German and French general practitioners still dominated the scene ...
>
> With as fine a misjudgement of symptoms, as clear anticipation of the methods of Charcot, Dr Auvers (or Hovert) had his patient plunged into a warm bath where his head was soused with cold water after which he was put to bed with half-a-dozen plump leeches affixed to his nose.[1]

Finally, Herman's last name, Brink, suggests the extreme radicalism of the doctor's ideas, bringing forth such connotations as the "edge," "border," or "verge."

Charlie

Charlie is a diminutive of *Charles*: masc. proper name, via the French *Charles*, from the Old High German *Karl*, lit. "man, husband." In Teutonic, "Charles" means "free man." The popularity of the name in continental Europe was due to the fame of Charles the

Great (742–814), commonly known as Charlemagne, a king of the Franks who came to rule over most of Europe. The name was subsequently borne by several Holy Roman Emperors, as well as kings of France, Spain, Portugal, Sweden, and Hungary. The name did not become common in Britain until the 17th century with the Stuart king Charles I, who was beheaded in 1649. Thanks to another "Charles," novelist Charles Dickens (1812–70), the phrase "King Charles' head" (featured in *David Copperfield*) became an allusion referring to some sort of obsession, particularly one that continually intrudes in matters where it is of no relevance. The midnight caller in "Signs and Symbols" uses name Charlie, while in Nabokov's *Pale Fire* the insane commentator's name is Dr Charles Kinbote, i.e. Charles II, last King of Zembla.

Elsa

Fem. proper name derives, via Greek *Eleisabet*, from German diminutive of *Elisabet* (Elizabeth), and has its origins in the Bible. This was the name of the wife of Aaron, *Elisheva*, denoting "God is an oath." In Hebrew, Eli means "my God"; sheva can stand for either "oath" or "sustenance."

Isaac

This is the name of another biblical patriarch, via Greek *Isaak*, from Hebrew *Yitzhaq* (lit. "he will laugh"). It is difficult to assert whether there is any link between Isaac and the ghostly appearance of Rebecca ("Whom did that woman resemble?") in the text, but there is a certain religious subtext that possibly connects them both (see the next entry).

Rebecca Borisovna

Rebecca (in English sometimes spelled as Rebekah) is the wife of Isaac, son of Abraham (Genesis 22.23). She was the sister of

Laban and daughter of Bethuel, the son of Nahor and brother of Abraham. The name originates from Hebrew: *rivkah*, which literally means "connection" (from Semitic root r-b-q: "to tie, join" or "to secure"). In the Torah she gives birth to Jacob and Esau. Rebecca and Isaac are one of the three couples buried in the Cave of the Patriarchs, the other two being Abraham and Sarah, and Jacob and Leah.

Rebecca Borisovna's patronymic is obviously a Russified variant of her father's Jewish name, *Barukh* (meaning "blessing"). However, being a fusion of two distinctly Jewish and Russian names (Rebecca + Boris), it might also suggest the assimilative nature of the generation she belongs to, along with the old couple—the protagonists of the short story.

Rosa, Aunt

Etymologically, the name Rosa is derived from Latin and comes from the field of botany (*rosa* = "rose"), where it is a taxonomic genus in the family *Rosaceae*—the roses. As a female given name it is featured in William Shakespeare's *As You Like It*, written in 1599; Celia says: "and when I break that oath, let me turn monster. Therefore, my sweet Rose, my dear Rose, be merry" (Act I, Scene II; *cf.* with *Elisheva* as an oath). Rose became a popular girl's name among English speakers in the 19th century (along with a number of flower names that came into use for girls, such as Daisy and Lily), but Nabokov's Rosa, pronounced ROH-zah, may rather reflect the Slavic or Yiddish influence. In the mystical garden of our protagonist's phobias, the rose seems to reverberate with the "idyllic landscape" and "beautiful weeds." Lolita will be later placed in a rosarium of her own—in the class list, Dolores Haze is surrounded by Mary Rose and Rosaline.

Sol, Mrs, see *Soloveichik*

Solov, Dr, see *Soloveichik*

Soloveichik

The name recurs three times in the short story, twice in truncated, Americanized, versions: *Solov* and *Sol* (Mrs Sol, the next door neighbor; Dr Solov, the family's doctor; and Soloveichik, whom the daughter of Rebecca Borisovna married in Minsk). Soloveichik crowns the pattern; it derives from the Russian *solovei*, meaning "nightingale." As a common Jewish last name it may lead to numerous traps. Here are just a few "mnemonic knots" to consider:

1) A certain Soloveichik was among Nabokov's real classmates. Sergei Soloveichik was born in 1896, and we know with certainty that he studied at the Tenishev school at least until 1914 (Nabokov started on 7 January, 1910). Sergei's father, Solomon Mikhailovich Soloveichik, was a *doctor* (Doctor Solov?), and his mother, Vera L'vovna, is recorded as a "free artist" (from the personal file at the Tenishev school archive, St. Petersburg).

2) Dr Mark Soloveichik was a member of Russian Zionist Organization along with Israel Rozov, the father of another Nabokov classmate and his best friend at Tenishev, Samuil Rozov.[2]

3) Yet another well-known personality in Russian émigré circles, S. M. Soloveichik, was a secretary of the Berlin-based newspaper *Days* [*Dni*]. This publication, edited by Alexander Kerensky, was ideologically close to *The Rudder* [*Rul'*], the newspaper associated with V. D. Nabokov. S. M. Soloveichik later moved to America, where he became a professor at the university in Kansas City and continued writing for the New York newspaper *New Russian Word* [*Novoe russkoe slovo*].

4) Rabbi Joseph B. Soloveichik (1903–93) is the one who probably embodies Nabokov's network of references most perfectly. Soloveichik was one of the 20th century's most preeminent and influential Jewish scholars. Born in Belarus into a family renowned for its Talmudic prowess, he graduated from the University of Berlin with a doctorate in philosophy in the early 1930s. Afterwards Soloveichik accepted the position of Chief Rabbi of Boston—the same city where Nabokov's "Signs and Symbols" was written. Soloveichik wrote numerous highly influential essays and Torah discourses. His essay "American Jewish Experience" describes the kind of choices the elderly parents of "Signs and Symbols" dealt with: the great traumatic experience of the European Holocaust and its impact on American Jews.[3]

5) Finally, we must not exclude the philosopher and poet Vladimir Solovyov (1853–1900). The founder of the Russian Symbolist movement (adding further poetic flavor to the title of Nabokov's story), he became famous for his metaphysical poetry. One of his texts, "Memory" (1892), contains a curious call: "Onward, Memory!" ("*Dalee, pamiat'*!"), as well as the following lines in tune with the Nabokovian Muse: "Life is a game of shadows," and "My dear friend, don't you see, / All that is visible / Is just a reflection, mere shadows / Of something that no eye can catch?" (*cf.*: "Clouds in the starring sky transmit to one another, by means of slow signs …").

Alexander Dolinin points out that the triad of names is charged with numerous possibilities for multilingual word-play:

> In Russian the initial *solovei* (nightingale), losing a syllable, turns into *solov* (a form of the adjective *solovyi*—dull, dazed, limp; *cf.* also the verb *osolovet'*—to become dazed) and then into *sol'* (salt). The paronomasia on *solovei* / *osolovet'* was used by Marina Tsvetaeva in her poem "A i prostor u nas tatarskim strelam" (1922): "Ne kurskim solov'em osolovelym."[4] The word *solov* is a palindrome of *volos* (hair; *cf.* a line in Khlebnikov's palindromic verse "Koni, topot, inok": "Solov zov, voz volos")[5] as well as an anagram of *slovo* (word). In Nabokov's drafts of the second volume of *The Gift*, Fyodor puns upon *slovo* / *solovyi*, exclaiming: "O russkoe slovo, solovoe slovo …" ("O the Russian word, the dull word …"). In English *solov* can be read as *so love* while *sol* suggests solitude (from Latin *solus* as in the title of Nabokov's story "Solus Rex"), the sun (and gold as used in alchemy) and, palindromically, a loss.[6]

Considering the multiplicity of implied meanings listed above, Dolinin believes that the triad allows two contradictory interpretations: on the one hand, it parallels the boy's pitiful devolution from the "bird phase" to the dazed state of insanity and the ultimate loneliness of death, but, on the other, heralds a metamorphosis through Logos and Love to the sun/gold of spiritual rebirth.[7]

PART THREE
Muscles of the Story

Objects

Five known jars
Carol M. Dole

When the phone rings the third time, who is calling? Most discussions of Vladimir Nabokov's "Signs and Symbols," whether in literary journals or freshman English classes, center around this question. One line of criticism, best represented by John Hagopian,[1] has been to take up the invitation of the title to puzzle out the significance of the phone call by examining the extraordinary number of images imbedded in the story, most obviously the many references to death: the ace of spades, the "tiny half-dead unfledged bird," (A10: 41) the train that "lost its life current between two stations" (A10: 22). Another line, established by William Carroll in the first full-length essay on the story,[2] has been to take that procedure one step further and conclude that the identity of the caller is irrelevant; Nabokov's insistence that we rely on our knowledge of literary conventions to solve the puzzle is also the insistence that we recognize the fictionality of the story, and that we recognize our reading strategy as very much like the son's "referential mania," a disease in which "the patient imagines that everything happening around him is a veiled reference to his personality and existence" and so must put all his energy into "decoding" the messages of the phenomenal world (A11: 62).

Regardless of critical position, then, readers seem to have found that they cannot analyze the story without taking careful account of its numerous "signs and symbols." A good deal has been written on these symbols, and one commentator, Larry Andrews, has analyzed their interplay in exhaustive detail. Yet no one has fully accounted for the most insistent apparent symbol in the story, the "ten different fruit jellies in ten little jars" that the elderly couple purchases as a birthday present for their institutionalized son (A9: 9).[3] As Andrews has noted, the conspicuous placement of the jelly jars in the story—in the first paragraph, at the beginning of section two, and in the last three sentences of the final section—argues for their symbolic significance. Yet the reader finds it as difficult to arrive at the meaning of the jelly jars as the characters find it to get the jelly jars to their intended destination (not only are the parents unable to deliver the gift to their son, but the father also finds himself locked out of their apartment when he tries to return with the jellies). The "luminous" little jars seem unreadable rather than illuminating. Might Nabokov, then, have been hinting at their very *lack* of meaningfulness when he introduced the basket of jellies as an "innocent trifle" (A9: 9), something that even the referential maniac son wouldn't construe as a threatening cipher? Might he be taunting us for hunting symbols in a way that is suspiciously like the maniac son's?

As soon as we start calling the jellies an innocent symbol, though, we face another problem. The jelly jars may not stand for something else in the way symbols conventionally do, but to cite them as proof that objects are no more than they appear is, after all, to accept them as signs, not mere objects. Indeed, in labeling them "innocent" Nabokov uses the jelly jars as a signpost pointing to his theme: our impulse to restructure a random world into a meaningful pattern, an impulse most evident in our response to fictional worlds. His other clues to this theme—the description of referential mania (the extreme extension of such an impulse), the story's title, the mysterious final telephone call that insists we put our pattern-finding skills into practice—seem to me sufficient argument that the story is about creating and interpreting as well as about a crazed boy and his pitiable parents. But, for the unconvinced, Nabokov has hidden in the final lines of the story still another clue to his theme; a clue available only to the reader painstaking (and manic?) enough to decipher his more extravagant riddles.

Nabokov alerts us to this clue by hinting that we should do as the father does and look again at that recalcitrant symbol, the jellies: "he put on his spectacles and re-examined with pleasure the luminous yellow, green, red little jars" (A14: 197). Having dropped this hint, Nabokov immediately concludes the story with a focus on the jellies so conspicuous that we can hardly resist puzzling over it:

> "His clumsy moist lips spelled out their eloquent labels: apricot, grape, beech plum, quince. He had got to crab apple, when the telephone rang again" (A14: 198).

Puzzle long enough, and at last the jelly jars yield a final clue to what Nabokov is up to. We must join the father in spelling. Nabokov, whose fondness for puns and puzzles is well known, has concealed an anagram in the list of "eloquent labels." The last letters of the four jellies in the list (apricot, grape, beech plum, quince) form the word *theme*.

Are the jellies, then, somehow the theme? Once again, they are a signpost, directing us to the part of the story in which the theme is most evident: the paragraph describing referential mania. It is there, at the very center of the paragraph, that the word *theme* makes its single appearance in the story. And it is there that the activities of reader, writer, and referential maniac reveal their affinities. And so the jellies, unlike the many symbols in the story that seem to point to a meaning within its fictional world, point outside it, to the realm of fiction making and fiction breaking.

Five missing jars

Gennady Barabtarlo

It is worthy of note that "Signs and Symbols" (May 1948) is the only English short story Nabokov wrote in regular third person—in a quiet, compassionate, but firm voice originating outside the story. None of his short stories has commanded nearly as much attention of some of the most astute Nabokov students as this one.[1] Nabokov's biographer considers it "one of the greatest short stories ever written ... a triumph of economy and force, minute realism and shimmering mystery."[2] Economy indeed: in the course of 118 uncharacteristically short sentences that make up the story, Nabokov carefully avoids naming any one of the 3 principal characters—a difficult feat that he had already attempted in the vaster space of "The Enchanter."

Moreover, the main personage never appears on stage. He is the only son of two elderly Russian émigrés, a young man of twenty, who for the last four years has been kept in a mental asylum. His peculiar insanity, called *mania referentia*, consists in relating outside objects and phenomena to his person in a menacing way, as if he were a focal point of continuous and hostile ecological scrutiny and machinations. He had attempted, not for the first time, to take his life on the eve of his parents' visit on his birthday, so that they were not allowed to see him and had to take back with them the present they had brought—ten little jars of assorted fruit jellies. Around midnight that very Friday, after they have decided to bring their son home next day, a sudden telephone ring, then another, imps their old hearts with fright. In each case, the caller misdialed, it appears. They sit down to their late tea, and as the father is reading the jelly labels, the phone rings for the third time, and the curtain-fall-hushed audience lingers: Has the young man finally torn "a hole in his world and escape[d]"? Or perhaps, as one acute interpreter has recently suggested, the reader is invited to imagine "a moment of panic prolonged to infinity, with the telephone still ringing and the mother's hand still stretching towards the receiver"?[3] Several others have cleverly argued that Nabokov mesmerizes the reader into seeing the disaster beyond the story's boundary by infecting him or her with exactly the sort of referential mania that clouds the young man's mind, so that the sharper and more attentive the reader the surer he or she is enmeshed. For all its magnetic ingenuity, this line of argument discounts the importance of evidence pointing to the tragic end, which comes about through a chain of secret signals and not by force of a crafty syllogism. The title once again carries a double load, meaning as a set phrase a chart of referential codes appended to an atlas. Not only does Nabokov shirr the length of the story with a series of omens, but he also tells the reader that the signs are all mapped and coordinated. Some of them are trivial (it's a Friday; the subway train suddenly loses its "life current"), or obvious (an attempt at suicide on a birthday; the father's twitching hand resembling the half-dead, twitching bird fallen out of a nest and seen a moment earlier); others are vague (the "kind shock" at the sight of a girl weeping on the bus) and tenuous (the letter O that Charlie's girlfriend erroneously dials for the zero: incidentally, this o—zero, the ovoid emblem of a void, appears later in *Lolita* and *Pale Fire*,[4] but together they all unite to confer a designative value on themselves. One signpost tends to be underestimated, although its value increases greatly for the fact that it is the very first *and* the very last item in the series of the story's internal references: if nothing else, Nabokov's propensity for rounded structures alone should warrant our redoubled attention to the set of jelly jars. But it is not simply a frame. When the woman hands her husband the basket with the jellies but not the keys to their flat, thus making him wait on the stair-landing for her return, the incident seems to be more than yet another mishap of that sad Friday: it assumes in retrospect a queer symbolism, as though that undelivered gift *were*, in another dimension, a key to the invisible over-plot. In the last sentence the old man is halfway through the labels on the jars when the final call comes, and the reader should not fail to realize that the jellies are arranged in the order of increasing astringency, from pungent–sweet to tartish to tart. The five flavors somehow answer the five photographs of her son that the woman examined an hour earlier; and those pictures recorded the five stages of the incremental occlusion of his mind (baby, then aged four, six, eight, and ten). The gift had been selected as a "dainty and innocent trifle," one that would not frighten the young man by an evil reference, as any "man-made object" inevitably would. Instead, the old couple decides not to leave it in the sanitarium and brings home the basket of jars that perhaps is charged with ominous reference to other signs and ultimately to the tragic outcome their concordance predicts.

Nor is the double entendre of the title an "innocent trifle," nor even the curious string of uniradical names of otherwise unrelated marginal characters, the Soloveichiks—Dr Solov—Mrs Sol, that may imply that the pre-charted coincidences are not "man-made." Or does it imply more? For instance, that the doctor and the neighboring lady are of Russian extraction and may even be related to the Soloveichiks (their names being typical New World dockings of long Slavic names, this one meaning "little nightingale") whom the old lady recalls in a spasm of compassion, in the depth of her own grief? Whether leading to a secret passage or a cul-de-sac, these signals can hardly be taken for a word game or a reference-hunt game, in a story welling with pain, love, and gentle sympathy, a story bemoaning the waste of "the incalculable amount of tenderness contained in the world." Nabokov later would single out "Signs and Symbols" as an example of a story with a second plane "woven into, or placed behind, the superficial semitransparent one."[5] The "superficial" story paints an unforgettable picture of piercing sadness. Here is how the invisible *main* story envelops the obvious:

> From within the parents' world, their son's death seems simply more jagged glass on the pile of miseries that makes up their life. But from outside their vantage point, we can see that *if* the boy has died, then the story bears the mark of a tender concern that shapes every minute detail of a world that from within seems unrelieved, meaningless tragedy. The final blow of death, in one light so gratuitous, in another seems the very proof of the painstaking design behind every moment of their lives.[6]

One can see here a scantling of the concentric pattern that all of Nabokov's English novels would reproduce to a much larger scale.

The last jar

Joanna Trzeciak

Although "Signs and Symbols" has been scrutinized for every possible bearer of symbolic significance, there is one about which little has been said: the ten-jar sampler of fruit jellies that opens and closes the story. Although it is one of the story's most important symbols, it escapes close scrutiny unless attended to from the standpoint of the story's silences. The parents, while trying to navigate their way through their son's interpretive mania, settle on this apparently innocuous gift, yet a closer look reveals symbolic echoes. At the end of the story, the father begins to mouth the names on the labels of the ten fruit jars, stopping, when the phone rings, with crab apple. Brian Boyd has ascertained that Nabokov was partial to the Gerber's brand of fruit jellies. My research has shown that unlike apricot, grape, beech plum and quince, crab apple was not one of Gerber's assorted fruit jellies. If one removes crab apple, the names of the jellies in the story—apricot, grape, beech plum, quince—form an anagram. That is, by taking the final letter in each name and reconfiguring the letters, one can create the word "theme."[1]

It has escaped comment that the Linnean polynomial for the crab apple is *Malus pumilla paradisiaca* and that the common Russian name is *raiskoe iabloko* (lit., paradise apple). This apparently innocuous gift echoes the story of Adam and Eve. Within this symbolic paradigm, mouthing the names on the jars seems to be a gesture toward reenacting the first act of naming, while the fruit jars bear a distant, vague resemblance to the forbidden fruit, a symbol of the origin of human suffering.

Trees and birds

Larry R. Andrews

The jellies are part of an intricate system of images and symbols which add a second dimension to Nabokov's title. On one level, the signs and symbols of the title are those mysterious sources of apparent meaning that afflict the son in his referential mania. On another level, they are the literary signs and symbols which the reader or critic must interpret in order to find meaning in the story. One cluster of such signs—in both senses—is the tree images. Trees are among the elements of "phenomenal nature" which supposedly conspire against the son in his delusions: "His inmost thoughts are discussed at nightfall, in manual alphabet, by darkly gesticulating trees" (A11: 69). "Groaning firs" on mountainsides also participate. The jellies are an indirect extension of this tree imagery—they come from fruit trees—and can be seen as insidiously infiltrating the relatively treeless city and sterile sanitarium walls in the hands of the well-meaning parents. The names of the jellies are singled out for special emphasis at the end, as the old man's "clumsy moist lips spelled out their eloquent labels: apricot, grape, beech plum, quince." The stress on "eloquent" and the focus on the words themselves recall the "manual alphabet" of the trees. The father's act of pronouncing the words may in fact signal the son's death. Certainly the emphasis on external forces as bearers of secret coded messages puts us on the alert as to Nabokov's own tricks of language and imagery in the story.

The imagery of sinister trees is echoed elsewhere in the story. Immediately after leaving the sanitarium, the parents encounter a "swaying and dripping tree" with "a tiny half-dead unfledged bird" under it (the bird image will also soon prove momentous). The "swaying" motion here recalls the "manual alphabet" of the "gesticulating trees" mentioned above, as well as the general description of the hostile forces as an "undulation of things." An unpleasant tree also figures prominently in the exposition of the son's increasingly phobic childhood. At the age of eight, he was "afraid of a certain picture in a book which merely showed an idyllic landscape with rocks on a hillside and an old cart wheel hanging from the branch of a leafless tree" (A12: 123). Since leaflessness suggests lifelessness, this tree is perhaps intended to foreshadow the son's death, The tree images may even be reflected in the metaphor of "a dense tangle of logically inter-acting illusions" (jungle?) and in the references to the "swollen veins" in the old man's hands and the prominent vein on his head (leaf venation? roots?). Several other key objects in the story with sinister overtones are also products ("man-made objects") of trees—the Russian newspaper, the playing cards, the album and photographs, the wallpaper, the picture book, the cart wheel, and even the labels on the jelly jars (not to mention the paper on which the story itself is printed). Finally, the only animal life mentioned in the story occurs in passages on the son's mania, and consists, with perhaps the exception of the bees suggested in "hives of evil," of species that inhabit trees: the squirrel in the park which the four-year-old boy was "looking away from" in the photograph; the primate in the metaphor of the scything farmer's brutal "simian stoop"; and, most importantly, the numerous references to birds.

While the tree images tend to be negatively colored and to function as hostile forces, the bird images that pervade the story are ambivalent and may suggest either freedom or entrapment. A bird image with the former connotation appears in the description of one of the son's recent suicide attempts. Nabokov tantalizingly refuses to elaborate on this attempt, saying only that it was a "masterpiece of inventiveness" and that an "envious" inmate interpreted it as an attempt to fly. That it was indeed an attempt to fly—to escape from persecution by emulating a bird's freedom—is suggested by the later reference to the son's drawings of "wonderful birds with human hands and feet" (A12: 119). This image, combined with the "envious" inmate's interpretation of the suicide attempt, hints that the son's final, successful suicide, if it occurred, also took the form of some ingenious emulation of flight. (The father's concern to keep knives locked up after their son returns to them shows the parents' misunderstanding of him.)

A conspicuously negative bird image, suggesting death and entrapment, occurs in close conjunction with the sanitarium. After failing to see their distraught son, the old couple encounter the "tiny half-dead unfledged bird ... helplessly twitching in a puddle" cited earlier. Clearly this bird is a symbol of the son himself, who has never properly grown up and who is at the mercy of the sinister forces represented by the "swaying and dripping tree" overhead and the inescapable puddle. It also refers to the recent suicide attempt and foreshadows the possibility of successful suicide at the end. The son does not have wings and cannot escape, yet he perhaps tries to fly out a window at the sanitarium and is destroyed in the attempt.

Still more bird references infiltrate the story in clever disguises. On the bus from the sanitarium the boy's mother notices "a girl with dark hair and grubby red toenails ... weeping on the shoulder of an older woman. Whom did that woman resemble? She resembled Rebecca Borisovna, whose daughter had married one of the Soloveichiks—in Minsk, years ago" (A10: 49). The name "Soloveichik" is a diminutive of the Russian word for nightingale, *solovey*, subject of many popular songs, poems, and legends, in which it connotes persecution and sorrow. This nightingale reference is echoed in the names of the doctor ("Solov," a truncated form of the same word) and next-door neighbor (Mrs "Sol," a still further shortened form of the word, which may refer simultaneously to "sun," as we shall see).

In addition to the tree and bird images, there is a host of other "signs and symbols" seemingly at work in the story. The suggestion that the son in the sanitarium is like a caged bird is related to a whole series of claustral images, which in turn reinforce the idea of a sinister conspiracy directed against and enclosing the son. The sanitarium, the parents' flat, and the building that contains the flat are oppressive enclosures. The son has tried to flee the institution.

The flat is small and will seem even smaller if the son moves in, and it has a "narrow yard." The power failure in the subway causes temporary enclosure and entrapment and is the first example following the foreboding statement "That Friday everything went wrong" (A10: 22). The crowded bus, the hard rain, the umbrella, the bus-stop shelter, the puddle with the struggling bird, the landing on which the old man waits ten minutes, and the "unswept corners" of neglected children also serve to circumscribe and hem in. Even the jellies are imprisoned in jars, which in turn are enclosed in a basket. All of these images, besides commenting on the stifling and dehumanizing atmosphere of the city, reflect the son's mania: to him the whole world is an enclosure he wants to "tear a hole in ... and escape." Death images form another branch of the conspiracy and also serve as foreshadowing devices in the plot. The mother wears "black dresses" (A9: 13); the stalled subway is described as having "lost its life current"; the bird in the puddle is "half-dead" (A10: 41); the anonymous neighbor seen through the window is a "black-trousered man" (A12: 106) lying, in a deathlike posture, "supine on an untidy bed" (A12: 108); Aunt Rosa was obsessed with death and catastrophe and was herself put to death; and the old father comes out of the bedroom saying "I can't sleep because I am dying" (A13: 151). The midnight hour and the crucial zero of the telephone number also intimate death. And in general, the imminence of death and decay pervades the old people's lives, from her heavy "trudging" up the stairs to his swollen head vein and the "horrible masklike grimace" in the mirror when he removes his dentures.

Photographs
Maria-Ruxanda Bontila

Nabokov's story can function as an epitome of the writer's "ethics of aesthetics," that is, an example of Nabokovian poetics both of reading and of writing. My argument is meant to explain how the writer is building, in this particular story, the "ethics of discomfort" as a condition of being in the world, of finding oneself one piece of the "pile of debris" that Walter Benjamin called history. This is magnificently achieved in the story by means of fictional photography, as when the distressed mother chooses to spend her time with her "old albums" ("she remained in the living-room with her pack of soiled cards and her old albums" [A12: 103]). What follows is a loop in time on an itinerary established by a photographic album. My contention is that, at the semantic level, photograph reading, i.e. the fictional photograph, succeeds where text cannot; it offers the "unsymbolizable," where the threshold to the "real" of the past can be crossed.[1] The photograph, through its appeal to "the absolute particular,"[2] can communicate what language fails to, and in doing so, it assumes the superior function of bridging both souls and minds, but it may also provide "counter-narratives" as long as there is potential for alternative readings and ways to construe identity.[3] In this particular case, fictional photo-graph is charged with the status of tragedy by the way constitutive thought is retrieved in its search for an ordering pattern.

The Romantic consciousness on the watch in this very passage ("When he had gone to bed, she remained in the living-room with her pack of soiled cards and her old albums ... This, and much more, she accepted—for after all living did mean accepting the loss of one joy after another, not even joys in her case-mere possibilities of improvement" [A12: 103]), voices despondency by admitting to loss at both the empirical level (contingency), and the universal level (history). Photographs *and* album, within the aforementioned fragment, are, simultaneously, celebrations of the uniqueness of every moment of being, every configuration of shadow *and* an elegy upon them ("As a baby he looked more surprised than most babies" [A12: 109]; "From a fold in the album, a German maid they had in Leipzig and her fat-faced fiancé fell out" [A12: 110]). Photographs, in this text, are as heavily mediated as paintings are, depending on light, camera angle, the grain of paper, the mood of the artist, but mostly, the mood of the viewer ("a slanting house front badly out of focus" [A12: 112]; "Four years old, in a park: moodily, shyly, with puckered forehead, looking away from an eager squirrel as he would from any stranger" [A12: 113]).

Nabokov will make us see that photographs of the same person taken by different/same people, at different moments, become different utterances not only about the play of light and mood, but also as epiphanies of transience. The present revaluation of "Aunt Rosa" ("a fussy, angular, wild-eyed old lady, who had lived in a tremulous world of bad news, bankruptcies, train accidents, cancerous growths-until the Germans put her to death, together with all the people she had worried about" [A12: 115]) is the empirical turned typical, life turned history.

The photograph showing the son "[a]ged six—that was when he drew wonderful birds with human hands and feet, and suffered from insomnia like a grown-up man" (A12: 118) creates what Walter Benjamin calls "dialectics at a standstill."[4] The mother's first thought bespeaks her quest for the essence of the beloved son, her second thought spells out repressed worry; the juxtaposition re-signifies the mother–son relationship, in offering some not-yet-uttered truth.

As in a film, photographs precipitate the "never again" of the fleeting moments into a dialectical movement fraught with contradictions: the pageantry of "not even joys in her case—mere possibilities of improvement" and "endless waves of pain," pain let loose in images and words. The mother's search for the essence of her son intensifies in a space of "monstrous darkness" in which time stops and thought moves: "This and much more, she accepted …" The "ethics of discomfort" as key to this fragment returns us to the photograph as repository of the "unspeakable," "unrepresentable," "inexplicable" of "past" and "present."

Before proceeding to "examine" the photographs at the beginning of the fragment, the woman pulled the blind to protect herself from the image of "a black-trousered man," "lying supine on an untidy bed," whom she could see framed in a "window … blandly alight" (A12: 107). I read this image or live photograph as both "sign" and "symbol." The former in light of "the monstrous darkness" accumulating within the story, the latter in light of a by far more disturbing thought that the photograph shapes into being: to what extent the story of my life is my own creation or a mere intertext compiled by all the members of the community I am a part of. The photograph allows this thought into being (Barbara Harrison's "counter-narrative"), a thought that finds philosophical backing in MacIntyre's narrative theory of identity and virtue philosophy.[5] Whatever plausibility this theory of concurrent narratives as identity might have, it certainly does not free us from worries since, both in real life and fiction, we can hardly choose the stories to figure in. Thus, the "second (main story)," as Nabokov would say, is this, our being framed to become our own theory as well as the idea that the very best aim of art is incarnation concretized within our own experience through the act of narration. This definitely replicates Nabokov's warning: "In order to enjoy life, we should not enjoy it too much."[6]

Cards

Pekka Tammi

In an interesting essay on "Signs and Symbols," Larry R. Andrews has sought to establish the literary subtexts for the passage where the old woman picks up from the floor the following three cards: knave of hearts, nine of spades, ace of spades (A13: 165). The playing cards belong to a larger network of "symbols" in the story, designed to anticipate the fate of the deranged protagonist (his suicide). According to Professor Andrews, this symbolism derives from three literary sources: Carroll's *Alice's Adventures in Wonderland* (likewise referring to a "knave of hearts"); Baudelaire's "Spleen" (*"Le beau valet de coeur et la dame de pique"*); and Nabokov's own *King, Queen, Knave,* where the three court cards are given a somewhat similarly emblematic function.

He may be right, but I would still suggest another source, perhaps better suited to the Russian émigré background of the story. The motif of "three cards" figures also in Pushkin's "Pikovaia dama" ("The Queen of Spades"). Here it is Hermann, the protagonist of the story, who is supposed to make three draws in a game of bank (faro)—if his third card is an ace of spades, he will gain a considerable fortune. Instead, he draws a queen, which causes him to lose his mind, and the rest of his days are spent in a mental institution.

The parallel with the insane hero of "Signs and Symbols" is an obvious one. It becomes still more enhanced when we remember that in Tchaikovsky' opera (1890), based on the story, Hermann actually commits suicide after his third draw.[1]

Consequently, the card motifs in Nabokov's story are seen to enter its narrative system also via a Pushkinian linkage.[2]

Telephone
Andrés Romero Jódar

> The telephone destabilizes the identity of the self and other, subject and thing, it abolishes the originariness of site; it undermines the authority of the Book and constantly menaces the existence of literature.
>
> Avital Ronell, *The Telephone Book*, p. 9

The telephone is without doubt one of the most important "artifacts" invented in the last century that has blurred boundaries, especially those imposed by distance. The ringing machine has become a mythical bridge between people and nations, disturbing the time/space duality that relativized the *Weltanschauungen* of the older conceptions of the world. The appearance of the telephone has given voice to the cravings of urban citizens who now have a soothing solution to their loneliness. The telephone has become more than a simple object for chatting: its creation responds to the human quest for an eternal line of communication and information. An age of tele-existence (from Greek *tele-*, meaning "distant," especially "transmission over a distance") has plunged the individual into a web of cybernetic space where information is shared through communicative devices. As pointed out by Joseph Tabbi, "human beings become unique precisely because they inhabit and therefore can connect different kinds of space."[1]

On the other hand, the telephone may become the instrument of the Other. The notion of uncertainty marks the very lifting of the receiver; answering the call makes it an acceptance of the Other's reality entering one's life. In Vladimir Nabokov's fiction, the telephone often functions as a metaphorical device exposing this duplicity when it comes to the realities of the receiver of the call. Nabokov's telephone becomes a symbol that carries different but interconnected meanings over which one prevails: the impossibility of communication.

Nabokov creates a complex "mirror" world which strikes the reader with similarities to both the real world and to Nabokov's own life. As Beverly L. Clark affirms, "the mirror reflects the world, but not mimetically. Instead, the mirror distorts the merely tangible to increase its historical resonance. The mirror multiplies images, madly doubling, tripling, fracturing the realistic surface."[2] In Nabokov's writings there are many resonances of the "real" world, but it is the multiplication of images that fractures the "realistic surface" of the new existence, exposing the artificiality of the text. Among the images that are continually doubled and repeated, the telephone occupies an outstanding position. In "Signs and Symbols" it acquires a depth of meaning which goes over and beyond the written frame of the story.

The external reality in "Signs and Symbols" is responsible for the boy's mental illness. But aren't we—as readers—plunging the "referential maniac" into suicide by picking up the telephone and interpreting the third call as the notification of the son's suicide? According to Patricia Waugh, the telephone is a "frame-break" which, "while appearing to bridge the gap between fiction and reality, in fact lays it bare."[3] Thus, the telephone not only seems to implicate the reader in the fictional world, but it also elucidates the fact that all the interpretations given to the text are part of ontology outside the borders of fiction. The reader enters into the world of fiction, shattering the boundaries which differentiate the real from the mirror creation. The telephone bridges reality and fiction, although there is no one on the other end of the line to "answer" the reader.

The literary representation of a telephonic communication is its symbolic paradigm: "Technically speaking, the narrator's art of integrating telephone conversations still lags far behind that of rendering dialogues conducted from room to room, or from window to window across some narrow blue alley in an ancient town."[4] The idea of introducing other media inside a text is what Joseph Tabbi calls "mediality": "Mediality refers to the ways in which a literary text inscribes in its own language the effects produced by other media."[5] The telephone in many of Nabokov's narratives becomes the element of mediality that introduces the new space created by the telephone inside the text. But what is important for our analysis is the meaning this artifact acquires: the telephone becomes a recurrent element reaching the level of a symbolic figure—just like the puddle in *Bend Sinister* or the squirrel in *Pnin*.

As a symbol, the telephone serves to contribute to the reader's understanding of the difficulties of communication between characters. It also brings to the fore the unexpected nature of the events to come and the characters' indeterminate future. This, in turn, creates for the reader the image of the author as a God-like figure.

The difficulty of communication inside the mirror world is highlighted in Pnin's first phone call to the Clements' house:

> When Joan, in her brisk long-limbed way, got to the compelling instrument before it gave up, and said hullo [...], a hollow quiet greeted her; all she could hear was the informal sound of a steady breathing; presently the breather's voice said, with a cozy foreign accent: "One moment, excuse me"—this was quite casual, and he continued to breathe and perhaps hem and hum or even sigh a little to the accompaniment of a crepitation that evoked the turning over of small pages.
>
> 'Hullo!' she repeated.
>
> 'You are,' suggested the voice warily, 'Mrs Fire?'
>
> 'No,' said Joan, and hung up.[6]

The recurrence of mistaken phone calls haunts the characters of Nabokov's stories. Here, Pnin is unable to achieve communication with Mrs Clements. Pnin, like many other Nabokov's characters, craves to be understood. Such characters suffer from anxiety to express themselves inside the mirror world of letters. This is a kind of existentialist *Angst* which goads them to keep on moving, in this case, to keep on making calls. They have to phone themselves into existence.

This alien, uncontrollable world of the telephonic space is often the source of anxiety for Nabokov's characters. In *Laughter in the Dark* (1937), it causes distress to Albinus, who is waiting for the never-coming call from his young lover, Margot.[7] The telephone numbers in late Sebastian's old notebook are supposed to provide the symbolic keys to the doors of the outer world in *The Real Life of Sebastian Knight* (1941);[8] they are characterized as "dead telephone numbers" (*cf*.: "telephone numbers proved delusions.")[9] The telephonic space is the dead simulacrum of a delusion, a fantastic world that does not solve any of the individual's sufferings.

A hindrance frequently prevents Nabokov's characters from

establishing a telephonic link to the source of knowledge; for example, in *The Real Life of Sebastian Knight*:

> I went to the telephone instead. I thumbed the soft greasy book. [...] Starov ... ah, there it was: Jasmin 61–93. I performed some dreadful manipulations and forgot the number in the middle, and struggled again with the book, and redialled, and listened for a while to an ominous buzzing. I sat for a minute quite still. [...] Again the dial turned and clicked back, five, six, seven times, and again there was that nasal drone: donne, donne, donne ... Why was I so unlucky?[10]

In *Pnin*, the telephone projects foreign realities outside the focalized world (what are "foreign realities"?):

> He said he was sure foxy old Pnin had not really left yesterday, but was lying low. So why not telephone and find out? He made the call, and although there was no answer to the series of compelling notes which simulate the far sound of actual ringing in an imaginary hallway, it stood to reason that this perfectly healthy telephone would have been probably disconnected, had Pnin really vacated the house.[11]

The characters in Nabokov's novels are not only subject to a search for the outer reality, but they are also the victims of the uncontrollable world percolating through the fissures of fiction. The telephone, as a medium between the mirror world and the foreign realities, creates a schism in the mirror world and becomes the source of the unexpected and the unpredictable. As Ronell affirms, the call is "something which we ourselves have neither planned nor prepared for nor voluntarily performed, nor have we ever done so. [...] 'It' calls, against our expectations and even against our will."[12] It cannot be known when the outer reality is going to perturb the characters. Thus, in many cases the telephone becomes the symbol of the premonition of a future fiendish omen, as in *Bend Sinister*: "Adam Krug too, he too, he too, unclipped his rusty wobbly fountain pen. The telephone rang in the adjacent study [...] [His fingers] trembled more than usually because it was after midnight and he was unspeakably tired."[13] *Cf.* in "Signs and Symbols":

The telephone rang.
It was an unusual hour for their telephone to ring. [...] Having more English than he did, it was she who attended to calls. [...]
    "It frightened me," she said. (A14: 172)

In both examples the telephone becomes a disturbing presence because of the late hour of the calls. After midnight, a phone call can be expected to bring bad news, especially if one awaits it. However, while in "Signs and Symbols" the reader is offered some information in the first two calls, in the passage from *Bend Sinister* quoted above, neither the reader nor Adam is informed of the subject of the telephone conversation. The author is the only one who seems to control the message:

The telephone emitted a discreet tinkle. Paduk attended to it. His cheek twitched as he listened. Then he handled the receiver to Krug who comfortably clasped it and said "Yes."
    "Professor," said the telephone, "this is merely a suggestion. The chief of the State is not generally addressed as '*dragotzennyi*'."
[...]
    The telephone rang again. Paduk listened.
    "You are not supposed to touch knives here," he said to Krug as, with a sigh, he replaced the receiver.[14]

Paduk's agents search for Adam Krug's lost son and Kol, an official, asserts: "There are four hundred telephones in this building. Your little lost child will be found at once."[15] The world of Paduk and Krug is controlled by an external agent, unknown to the characters and to the reader; this agent manifests itself in the literary world by means of the telephone. The artifact, thus, becomes the link between different levels of knowledge. While the author remains outside the novel (although Nabokov occasionally places himself within the novels), the mythical bridge between reality and fiction is established through the telephone.
    Most of Nabokov's characters are deceived by the telephone. In *Laughter in the Dark*, *Bend Sinister*, and *Pnin* the ringing artifact turns out to be a source of mystery, anxiety, and perturbation. In "Signs and Symbols," it acquires a symbolic status as both a metafictional and a metaphysical device.
    "Donne, donne, donne ..."[16]

PART FOUR
Nervous System

The importance of reader response
Paul J. Rosenzweig

Unlike such dazzling baroque constructions as *Ada* or *Pale Fire*, which threaten to inundate the reader in their rich texture of detail, intricate cross references, and recondite literary games, "Signs and Symbols" may prove initially puzzling largely because it does not seem to work in a Nabokovian way at all. However, once the richness of its simplicity is appreciated, the story demonstrates how quietly and economically Nabokov works. The danger of his more elaborate artifices is that their surfaces dazzle and involve the reader, blinding him to the more subtle shimmering resonances that underlie the glitter and are essential to Nabokov's purpose. For instance, in *Pale Fire* the reader may be so caught up in trying to pin down the various mergings and primacy of identities—whether the King of Zembla, Kinbote, Shade, or Botkin subsumes one or all of the other identities in the novel—he may fail to realize that in his failure to resolve these puzzles he has not failed at all. His failure comes only when, instead of relating his own experience as reader of the novel to the themes and characters, he insists on forcing one solution—one identity, one interpretation—upon the work. In much of his fiction, Nabokov undercuts the traditional distances among the realities of author, reader, and text by forcing the reader to become both a character in and author of the text. His themes are thus often principally illustrated through the subtle interplay between the reader and the text, and the reader has entered another dimension in reading Nabokov when he begins to take note of his own reactions to the text.

This step is essential to a proper reading of "Signs and Symbols." While the ending by itself, with its as yet-unanswered third call, may seem to fall flat, prove puzzling, or seem trite, it is the probable reader reaction to this last call rather than the call itself that provides Significance, which echoes throughout the story, changing both its structure and meaning.

Therefore, it is necessary first to examine the reader's initial response to the last call—a response which, as I shall show, will probably be more standard than might at first seem likely. The response should prove threefold. The call should seem to be 1) a call from the mental institution bringing the tragic news of the successful suicide attempt of the couple's son; 2) merely a third wrong number by the same inept young caller; 3) ultimately ambiguous. It is likely, too, that the reader's response will occur in the above order, even if her responses occur almost simultaneously.

The first response is the most conventional, the most deeply ingrained and therefore the most natural, even if Nabokov were not manipulating the reader to insure this response. The reader automatically and unconsciously adopts the convention of entering the world of the fiction and treating it as reality. Paradoxically, she assumes from the outset that this fictional reality has a pattern and meaning to it which the plot, structure, and language are all promoting, even though in the real world, she may never consciously operate on this assumption.

Nabokov exploits these tendencies for all they are worth. The entire story is imbued with the symbolism of impotence and doom, so that as we read we anticipate the son's suicide as an appropriate part of the pattern of the story, even though in more logical retrospect we should see there is no reason to assume this fatality since the symbolism, of course, has no necessary relation to the son's fate, whatever that might ultimately prove to be. The old parents have been trapped on the underground train that "lost its life current" (A10: 22). As they leave the hospital, they find "a tiny half-dead unfledged bird … helplessly twitching in a puddle" (A10: 41). This helplessness and mortality is subtly shifted to the couple themselves. The wife notices her husband's "old hands (swollen veins, brown-spotted skin), clasped and twitching … She felt the mounting pressure of tears" (A10: 45). Later, while her husband sleeps, she thinks of

> the endless waves of pain that for some reason or other she and her husband had to endure … of beautiful weeds that cannot hide from the farmer and helplessly have to watch the shadow of his simian stoop leave mangled flowers in its wake, as the monstrous darkness approaches. (A13: 136)

In the third section, the melodrama heightens as Nabokov takes us through a series of stock situations from which he can assume a universal stock response: mounting fear and pity ("I can't sleep because I am dying," the old man moans [A13: 151]); the complete realization of peril ("We must get him out of there quick. Otherwise we'll be responsible. Responsible!" [A13: 155]); and the hope of safely resolving the perilous situation, which, however, is just beyond one's grasp ("'All right,' she said quietly, 'we shall bring him home tomorrow morning'"; "He returned in high spirits ... "I have it all figured out. We will give him the bedroom. Each of us will spend part of the night near him ...'" [A13: 166]). Interwoven with these dramatics are more subtle incidental details that are no less manipulative in their intent. "Bending with difficulty," Nabokov writes, "she retrieved some playing cards and a photograph or two that had slipped from the couch to the floor: knave of hearts, nine of spades, ace of spades, Elsa and her bestial beau" (A13: 163). The ominous quality of these elements is so subtle—the bestiality echoing the "simian stoop," the choice of the ace of spades and the use of the word "knave" —that we probably won't consciously notice their symbolic effect.

But Nabokov has set us up for the telephone's three calls, at each of which our hearts will jump a bit, and he is in no hurry to resolve our anxiety: "The telephone rang. It was an unusual hour for their telephone to ring. His left slipper had come off and he groped for it with his heel and toe as he ... childishly, toothlessly gaped at his wife ... The receiver was gently cradled. Her hand went to her old tired heart" (A14: 172). In short, each piece of apparently objective description becomes fraught with ominous portent. As we read the last long and detailed paragraph, we are poised waiting for the axe to fall. Of course, it never does; that is Nabokov's game, but we have been thoroughly conditioned to impose on that third call a tragic meaning.

However, at the same time that Nabokov is employing many of the stock conventions of a sentimental melodrama, he is under-cutting them, although this second, contrary line probably will not—and ideally, should not—become evident until after we have finished the story. The two previous calls, which might at first seem to be merely another tool to heighten the suspense, have another purpose as well—to make probable the mistaken nature of the third unidentified call. The caller's identity as a child, and the nature of her dialing mistake, the substitution of the letter "O" for a zero, lend concrete detail to this contrary line. In fact, all rational analysis points to the probability that the call is yet a third mistaken call by the girl. Yet even such detailed analysis is not likely to end the reader's sense that the last call is ominous. Much of our intuitive insistence that the last line implies tragedy is our sense about the traditional shape of a story—the fact that the last sentence of a story be given greater import than it would otherwise command by its content alone.

In short, after his immediate reactions, the reader will find himself pulled in two contrary directions. He may well search for clues to support one interpretation or another and it is at this point that he will find himself in a similar position to the reader of *Pale Fire*, who, lost in its more intricate maze, searches for clues to determine who indeed wrote the novel he holds. Like him, our reader will be able to find signs and symbols to support either interpretation and, similarly, he should resist the temptation to force a resolution to this ambiguity. The meaningless calls (be they two or three) occurring at what promised to be the moment of truth, seem to mock both the old couple and us.

At some time during the reader's floundering attempt to find meaning, he may notice when rereading the description of the son's condition that he is reading a description of his very own state. (We cannot notice this analogy on a first reading because it does not yet exist, and for this reason Nabokov came to address his audience in his last novels as "rereaders.") The story, "a man-made object," has seemed to the reader a "hive of evil, vibrant with a malignant activity" (A9: 4). Both the story and the reader's deciphering of it have proven "masterpieces of inventiveness," and "everything happening around him" (all the events and words in the story) suddenly seem "a veiled reference to his personality and existence." As the reader begins to see, "of everything he is the theme" (A11: 72). Not pebbles or stains or sun flecks, but phone calls, and the weather, and the number and suit of particular cards all seem to "form patterns representing in some awful way messages which he must intercept" (A11: 71). Even the little jelly jars and the order in which the old man spells out their labels seem to have some hidden meaning, for they are the son's gift, and his spelling them out is the last activity he engages in before the last phone call. Like all good critical readers, he has found himself "always on his guard," devoting "every minute and module of life to the decoding of the undulation of things" (A11: 78). In themselves, these parallels may seem only a cute coincidence which relies solely on the reader's own ingenious, aberrant reading, but this feeling will only make the parallel more exact. Like the son, the reader "excludes real people" (other readers and people outside the world of the story which he has entered) "from the conspiracy—because he considers himself to be so much more intelligent than other men" (A11: 65) and the reader's interpretation, therefore, "totally inaccessible to normal minds" (A12: 132). She may even feel when rereading the sentence describing the son's desire "to tear a hole in his world and escape" (A11: 58) that that character has succeeded, extinguishing himself in the story in order to step out of the paper world of the story (like his Nabokovian predecessor, Cincinnatus, in *Invitation to a Beheading*) and become the reader. Only when she realizes that, quite to the contrary, this correspondence between character and reader is the very key to the meaning of the story and an effect purposely induced by Nabokov will the story will begin to acquire an appropriate, though untraditional, meaning.

In fact, this correspondence between the son's illness and the reader's own state of mind is induced three times over, and on each level the effect induced is an initial desire for an insistence on pattern and meaning followed by the frustration of that desire. First, we are led to assume the old couple's point of view and their own referential mania that is mocked by the meaningless calls; as naive readers, we initially supply stock, sentimental responses to what we automatically and unconsciously assume to be the predictable patterns and expectations of traditional fiction-responses we find inappropriate when the ambiguity of the final call frustrates a melodramatic ending; as critics, we search the story—this time consciously—attempting to impose a meaning that the story does not yield.

By springing upon us the covert analogy between our experiences as readers or creators of art and a state of mental illness, the story forces upon us the relativity of apparent absolutes, the provisional nature of all labels, categories, and conventions. We are made aware of how unconsciously and automatically we change frames of reference, accepting each frame as absolute rather than relative. By coining the neutral term, "referential mania," to describe the son's paranoia, a term Nabokov avoids, the author encourages us to inspect that state of mind anew; the neutrality of the term also allows us to apply it outside of its original context of mental illness. The analogy applies as well to our normal empathetic responses in everyday situations; this very characteristic that we label abnormal in the son and that distances us from him, when possessed by the old couple in their stressful situation, seems normal, indeed, a sign of their humanity, and a factor in our identification with them.

The story first leads us toward a heightened concern for symbolism and meaning and then frustrates it in order to show us our own pervasive tendency to illogically search for meaning where rational thought alone suggests none. Such meaning may, of course, exist. The symbolism in the story does in the end prove meaningful, even if not in the way we initially expected, and the paranoia we may feel at some point that the story has us as its center is merited. But the patterns and meaning in Nabokov's fiction and the world he depicts are never those of our stock realities. For Nabokov, the reality we ultimately live in and the only one we can surely know is that of the mind; and its richest function, the imagination, is the essential ingredient of humankind's humanity. The person of imagination, the artist, will not be content in accepting the stock version of any reality, for conventional realities are too simply patterned either to convince or entertain. In Nabokov's fiction one is often reminded of Shakespeare's comparison of "the lunatic, the lover, and the poet ... of imagination all compact,"[1] for Nabokov typically employs the union of these three roles to exemplify his themes of the perception or creation of multiple realities by the imagination.

Since art by means of the imagination creates its own reality, the function of art can never be and should not try to be mimetic. The surface realism that this story seems to create is subtly parodied and the correlation between life and art is undercut. The title reflects this concern for correspondences between these two realms, for the signs that the son sees as portents of his fate, that we all to some degree tend to see in our daily lives, are analogous to the symbols of the artist and critic; yet our responses to them prove different. The son is not the only one to see correspondences. His mother sees in a fellow passenger in the subway a likeness to an old acquaintance: "Whom did that woman resemble? She resembled Rebecca Borisovna" (A10: 52). And while the son's early preoccupation with bird-like men or men-like birds—"wonderful birds with human hands and feet" (A12: 119) —should seem strange to us as it does to his doctors, it is exactly this correspondence that we ourselves have created when, a few pages earlier, we see in the half-dead helpless bird a likeness to first the son and then his father. We accept without a blink Nabokov's creation of a tusked boar-like man ("He removed his new hopelessly uncomfortable dental plate and severed the long tusks of saliva connecting him to it" [A12: 98]) and a woman with a sun as a face ("Mrs Sol ... whose face was all pink and mauve with paint and whose hat was a cluster of brookside flowers" [A9: 14]). By naming them metaphors, we assure ourselves of their normality. Indeed, it takes two prior calls to create an ambiguity about the final call, whereas in life the one call alone would suffice. The conventions of fiction would immediately impose upon that solitary ring a quite definite, unambiguous, and tragic meaning, and, so, within the story it takes two additional rings to counter in part our conventional assumption.

By being a parody of a traditional story with its stock characters, sentimental emotions, and tired ending, "Signs and Symbols" also suggests the inadequacy of hackneyed art to inform us about an external reality. Most traditional forms, from which we may unimaginatively derive our version of reality, are really only shadows of shadows. The story demonstrates how the very conventions of the fictional world impose a distorting order on our perceptions that is so insidious we normally fail to notice its subverting influence. Insanity of one sort or another is inescapable; yet we are truly insane—in a negative sense—only when we lack the imagination to step outside ourselves and our conventions to see, self-consciously, our own insanities.

The Jewish quest

Yuri Leving

Martin Amis has stated recently that in Nabokov's fiction, to his knowledge, the writer touched upon the Holocaust at paragraph length only once,

> in the incomparable *Pnin* (1957). Other references, as in *Lolita*, are glancing. Take, for example, this one-sentence demonstration of genius from the insanely inspired six-page short story 'Signs and Symbols' (it is a description of a Jewish matriarch) ...[1]

Among literary scholars, Leona Toker was first to identify the potency of the Jewish theme in Nabokov's "Signs and Symbols." While admitting that the name of the old man's younger brother, Isaac (alias "the Prince"), may or may not have biblical connotations, she posited as a much more decisive factor the fact that the characters are Jews.[2] Despite the fact that the emigration from Europe to America on the eve of World War II was a multinational phenomenon, it is particularly relevant that the old couple was Jewish, which is

> significant for placing the plight of their son in a historical context. The specific mental malady of this young man is a morbidly condensed expression of the Jewish experience in Europe at the time of the Holocaust.[3]

Toker calls attention to the story's composition date—1948—and its opening ("For the fourth time in as many years"), which means that the onset of the young man's irreversible madness overlapped with the time of the Holocaust in Europe. The boy's madness developed from his earlier phobias:

> [I]t is as if some time before the Holocaust he could already sense what was brewing on the inner agenda of the times. And his horror is not mitigated by the security of the geographical remove: "with distance the torrents of wild scandal increase in volume and

volubility" [A11: 82]. The alliterating "volume and volubility" invoke the image of the radio, another man-made object, a hive of evil, "vibrant with a malignant activity which he alone [can] perceive" [A9: 4]. Reports that he cannot understand refer, like everything else, to himself: as if what is known as the Final Solution were summed up in terms of "granite and groaning firs" as the "ultimate truth of his being" [A11: 85].

Joanna Trzeciak advances a reading that foregrounds the story's "silences."[4] Once she turns to deciphering the silences, three focal points emerge from the narrative details, in order of increasing scope: parental love and the fear of loss; the tragedies of the Holocaust; and the fragility and finitude of life. Trzeciak brings another, earlier, Nabokov story into the balance: "Breaking the News" (1935). Both stories present the drama of Russian Jews in exile, depicted as a snapshot of their everyday drab émigré existence. Trzeciak suggests that "Signs and Symbols" can actually be "viewed as a post-Holocaust reprise of 'Breaking the News,' with the shift in backdrop effecting a change in the character of the silences in the two stories."[5]

Anthony Stadlen has continued this line of thought on Nabokov and Jewish issues, offering an innovative interpretative angle.[6] This proved especially useful in addressing the mystery of the short story's finale. "For those who would like the young man not to have killed himself and would prefer the third telephone call still to be from the sign-instead-of-symbol-dialling girl, because the only alternative they can envisage is an official call announcing his suicide," Stadlen writes, "please note that this would entail, as Alexander Dolinin indicates but, oddly, does not mention, the girl's dialling three uncalled-for sixes—the ominous mark of the Beast."[7] In other words, Stadlen argues that (as a result of the presumed error, whether made by one or two people, three times in succession) the sixes could be understood either "Christianly" as 666 (i.e. the number of the Beast, the Antichrist, death, etc.) or "Jewishly" (by Gematria) as $6+6+6 = 18 = Chaim$ ("*Life*" in Hebrew).[8] Citing the difficulty of drawing specific conclusions from this ("The sixes are completely ambiguous. One can deduce precisely nothing from them"), Stadlen speculates:

Surely both these symbolisms are beside the point, except the point that they and the other beside-the-point signs and symbols are, ultimately at least, beside the point.

My own point was simply that, while of course we don't know who was "really" making the third call, there is, corresponding to the boy's presumed "referential mania" of attributing human agency to non-human events and referring them to himself, a kind of reciprocal "NON-referential mania" into which we readers can be seduced by the story, whereby we overlook even the possibility that a post-midnight telephone call to his parents might originate from the boy himself as human agent. I wondered if this might have been one of Nabokov's points, too.[9]

Alexander Dolinin responded to Stadlen's remarks:

When I discuss "Signs and Symbols" with my American students, they often raise similar questions about Shabbat and Saturday as the "sixth day" of the week. It seems to me that the details noticed by Dr Stadlen (the woman buys and cooks fish when it is already dark, whereas a traditional Jewish woman would have prepared the Sabbath meal long before dusk, etc.) show that the couple are non-practicing Jews who had actually lost their religion. It is a phenomenon typical for educated Russian Jews of their generation. My grandfather, who was born in 1880 in a shtetl, left his Jewish community beyond the pale when he was about 20 years old, studied abroad and in St. Petersburg, got his University degree and eventually became a free-thinker with very strong connections to Russian culture and customs. He never rejected (or tried to hide) his Jewish ethnic origins and because of that was a target of numerous anti-Semitic attacks in the USSR but the Jewish religion didn't mean anything for him: he would never celebrate Shabbat and his calendar was Christian and/or secular. Most of the Jews Nabokov knew in the emigration, I think, belonged to the same type and, portraying the Jewish couple in "Signs and Symbols," he was true to reality.[10]

In addition to his "Death/Life" theory based on sixes, Anthony Stadlen raises the question of whether Nabokov intended for his readers to be aware that the mother was buying fish, and later making tea (and perhaps cooking the fish) after dark, when it was already the Jewish Sabbath, when observant Jews would do none of these things. Stadlen's and Dolinin's assumptions about the old Jewish couple's detachment from their traditional roots are probably accurate; however, stating that the wife "wanted to buy some fish for supper," Nabokov does not necessarily imply that she would start cooking it. Considering the husband's "hopelessly uncomfortable dental plate" (A12: 98), it is likely that the product meant here is a "gefilte fish" (from Yiddish: "stuffed fish"). A poached fish mince stuffed into the fish skin, this has been a dish common in the Ashkenazi Jewish community since the World War II. Gefilte fish is typically eaten on Shabbat, the seventh day of the week, because the numerical equivalent of the word "fish" in Hebrew ("*dag*") is seven. Curiously, the *Shulkhan Aruch*, compiled in the 16th century and to this day the most authoritative legal code of Judaism, draws a parallel between fish and judgment: "Just as fish are caught in a net, we are caught in the net of death and judgment. The realization of this concept should make us thinking of repenting" (*Kitzur Shulkhan Aruch* 123. 27).

Alexander Drescher detects an interesting coincidence, namely that Good Friday and Erev Pesach (the first Seder evening of Passover) coincided in 1947. For his part, Stadlen has counted the number of paragraphs in the three parts of story (7, 4, 19), and suggested that this could be taken to indicate the year of the text's composition. The opening ("For the fourth time in as many years"), therefore, points to the date 4/4 (4 April or April 4) of Good Friday/Passover 1947. In the article reproduced in this collection, Drescher offers further evidence to support this hypothesis, and even reveals that Nabokov's short story appeared in *The New Yorker* on the same day that Israel officially became an independent state, May 15, 1948.

A quarter of a century earlier, the author's father, Vladimir Dmitrievich Nabokov, would prophetically warn against the dangers of the mass persecution of the Jewish population in Europe. In this article, triggered by the pogroms in Ukraine, he wrote not long before his own tragic death: "How scary, inhuman, and intolerable for normal human nature are these manifestations of brutality, and so infinitely pitiful are their miserable and innocent victims."[11]

Symbols

Signs of reference, symbols of design
Geoffrey Green

In the years immediately before the World War II, as Nabokov began to experiment with other languages, he also began to modify his notions of the relation between the form of a work of art and its stylistic assertion. Previously, the works had offered—through style, authorial manipulations, characters, plot devices—the primacy of the subjective, creative, affirmative authorial imagination over all destructive opponents (including banal history, mundane chronological time, sexual dullards—all forces that worked against living as a process of creating); but now, in his experimentation, Nabokov considered the idea of allowing the entire novel to serve as the embodiment (not merely the vehicle for expression) of his affirmative assertions about the power of the imagination. The novel would not only be about artistic creation in relation to the structures of the world, it would itself be an example, a demonstration, of imaginative reordering that yet exists as a structure of the world.

Despite being extremely insecure about his use of the language in his first English novel, *The Real Life of Sebastian Knight* (1941), Nabokov eventually overcame this uncertainty to the extent that he was able subsequently to write and publish many English-language novels. But still, as late as 1967, when asked whether he had any "conspicuous or secret flaw as a writer," he answered:

> The absence of a natural vocabulary. An odd thing to confess, but true. Of the two instruments in my possession, one—my

native tongue—I can no longer use, and this is not only because I lack a Russian audience, but also because the excitement of verbal adventure in the Russian medium has faded away gradually after I turned to English in 1940. My English, this second instrument I have always had, is however a stiffish, artificial thing, which may be all right for describing a sunset or an insect, but which cannot conceal poverty of syntax and paucity of domestic diction when I need the shortest road between warehouse and shop.[1]

Nabokov was shrewd enough to realize that when ideas and images are presented as part of a network of intermingled levels and shades of meaning, their intrinsic naked state becomes elusive, more difficult to isolate and refine. Fortunately, his artistic conceptions of memory, creation, and imagination were evolving in a similar direction, emphasizing the complex relativity, the persistently increasing ambiguity of the differentiation between imaginative creation and realistic experience. Thus, partly because of artistic inclination, and partly to obfuscate what he believed was a fragility and vulnerability of language, Nabokov in his English works continually exploited the method of veiling his fictions and ideas in multiple layers of elusive, ironic gauze.

Accordingly, it can be seen that Nabokov's repeated assertions after 1940 that his work was devoid of meaning, idea, or application other than its own aesthetic appearance (which completely enticed a generation of literary critics) accomplished, for him, two desired ends: 1) his fictional creations had to be understood exclusively in relation to Nabokov, on his own terms; 2) the degree of ambiguity and intricate entanglement in his work was greatly intensified, thus minimizing the likelihood that one of his ideas or phrases might be found to be inelegant or crudely expressed. Still, he was never completely satisfied with these devices and conceits and late in his life, he was eager to adjust the prevalent mode of appreciating his work. When asked what "literary sins" could he someday be accountable for, he replied: "Of having spared in my books too many political fools and intellectual frauds among my acquaintances. Of having been too fastidious in choosing my targets."[2] And he suggested that in the future his work would be regarded in a considerably different manner, one closer to his own authorial intent:

In fact, I believe that one day a reappraiser will come and declare that, far from having been a frivolous firebird, I was a rigid moralist kicking sin, cuffing stupidity, ridiculing the vulgar and cruel—and assigning sovereign power to tenderness, talent, and pride.[3]

In 1948, Nabokov published one of his first English language short stories, "Signs and Symbols," in *The New Yorker* (later collected in *Nabokov's Dozen*); at first that magazine was reluctant to publish the story, believing it to be an overwritten parody of a psychiatric study.[4] An examination of the story provides apt illustration of the meticulous care and the extraordinarily elaborate construction which typify Nabokov's English language works. In the briefest space (fewer than 3,000 words), the complexity of texture and the intensity of effect are remarkable. The story is constructed around the idea of symbolic designations referring back to, but always approximating in representation, an original concept; also significant is the maxim that one occurrence is chance, two occurrences are coincidence, but three signify design.

An investigation of such a perspicacious work—produced early in Nabokov's transition to his primary identity as an English language author—provides a unique vantage point, a special detached perspective, with which to evaluate what would become his abiding structural mechanism. Further, its value as an exemplary indication of his authorial path is supported by his confidence about the work compared to his relative insecurity about the language of such earlier works as "Cloud, Castle, Lake," "Spring in Fialta," "That in Aleppo Once ..." and *The Real Life of Sebastian Knight.*[5]

An elderly and poor Russian émigré couple now living in Boston, after years of residence in Europe, are going to pay a birthday visit to their son, institutionalized because he is "incurably deranged in his mind." A birth day is the anniversary of the actual day of one's birth; the present they choose, a basket of assorted fruit jellies, is a "trifle" which will be completely meaningless to the boy, but will be symbolic of his parents' love for him. Although the father had once been financially prosperous, he is now wholly dependent upon the support of his brother, who is nicknamed "the Prince." Their son suffers from "referential mania." Along the way to visit their son, the couple's progress is halted by various malfunctioning machines: they are forced to be passively subjected to the whim of these devices, much as they are "subjects," in a sense, of the Prince. Upon their arrival, they are informed that their son has again attempted suicide. Their presence might further upset him.

It is raining as they make their way home. While they are waiting for the bus, "a few feet away, under a swaying and dripping tree, a tiny half-dead unfledged bird was helplessly twitching in a puddle" (A10: 40). The baby bird, of course, will die through no fault of its own, but as a result of the whim of nature: it was not yet able to fly, so the rain which fell on the tree, which dripped it onto the sidewalk forming a puddle, became for the bird a death trap. Riding to the subway station, the narrator observes the husband's umbrella (which shields him from the rain), and his hands, which "twitch" like the dying baby bird. The "swaying and dripping tree" under which the bird is suffering is repeated in the description of the boy's mania: "darkly gesticulating trees." So, too, in that passage, are there references to the rain which kills the bird ("clouds in the staring sky," "running water, storms") as well as the puddle he suffers in ("still pools"). The wife notices, in "wonder," that another passenger is crying: the wonder of seeing another cry establishes the realization that everything in the world does not refer back to oneself.

The previous suicide attempt of the boy had been "a masterpiece of inventiveness": like Cincinnatus C. in *Invitation to a Beheading* and Luzhin in *The Defense*, the boy wanted to "tear a hole in his world and escape" (A11: 58). In the second of the story's three parts, the couple "emerge from the thunder and foul air of the subway" (A11: 87); the "thunder" again associates with the rain motif, and the "foul air" echoes the boy's exhaled air, which he indexes in the description of his mania. At home, the husband prepares for sleep, but before retiring, he first removes his false teeth and tears the "long tusks of saliva" (A12: 99) which trail from them: this animal-centered task establishes another link (after the umbrella) with the bird; earlier, we had been told to notice his "brown-spotted hands" (A10: 45), which, like the bird's inability to fly, were marks of birth. And when the boy had tried to tear open his world, he was saved by a jealous patient who thought he "was learning to fly" (A11: 57). Looking out at the rain, the woman pulls down the blind in an effort to lock out the external world, hints of which we encountered in the bus: the woman next to the girl who was crying reminded her of another person she had known long ago in Minsk. She sits down and examines the family album:

As a baby he looked more surprised than most babies. From a fold in the album, a German maid they had had in Leipzig and her fat-faced fiancé fell out. Minsk, the Revolution, Leipzig, Berlin, Leipzig … Four years old, in a park: moodily, shyly, with puckered forehead, looking away from an eager squirrel as he would from any other stranger. Aunt Rosa, a fussy, angular, wild-eyed old lady, who had lived in a tremulous world of bad news, bankruptcies, train accidents, cancerous growths—until the Germans put her to death, together with all the people she had worried about. Age six—that was when he drew wonderful birds with human hands and feet, and suffered from insomnia like a grown-up man. (A12: 109)

We notice the small details in this passage begin to trigger massive associations within the story: the "fussy, angular, wild-eyed" description of the aunt can also apply to the squirrel; the husband had been financially comfortable, but was now "bankrupt"; the "bad news" of the day was the boy's suicide attempt; the day's "train accident" was that "the underground train lost its life current between two stations" (A10: 22); the spots on the man's hands might well be "cancerous growths." Most importantly, there is the fine padding of referential details which partially hides the powerful, but subtly understated, point of the passage: "until the Germans put her to death, together with all the people she had worried about." Aunt Rosa's world had been fatally destroyed, not for any reason which concerned her, or which she had worried about, but destroyed, rather, as the baby bird's existence had been: brutally, absolutely, for no cause or reason, almost whimsically. And the boy's drawing of birds with human hands and feet reminds us of the husband's hands, which twitch, as did the dying bird. Slowly, detail upon detail, the trappings of a life accumulate, and then are annihilated. The effect of this horror is similar to the description of the time in the boy's life when "those little phobias of his which his parents had stubbornly regarded as the eccentricities of a prodigiously gifted child hardened as it were into a dense tangle of logically interacting illusions, making him totally inaccessible to normal minds" (A12: 129).

In the third section, the husband complains of insomnia (as did his son at age six); he claims he can't sleep because he is "dying" (A13: 151), dying of life, as do all animate beings, for reasons that "are totally inaccessible to normal minds," but like the rain, are dictated from above. Bravely, the husband decides that they will reverse the order of things: they will make a brazen attempt to seize control by removing the boy from the hospital and caring for him at home. They would simply watch him at all times, and keep the knives locked up: "even at his worst he presented no danger to other people" (A14: 184) —but neither did the bird or Aunt Rosa.

In the midst of these deliberations, the telephone rings: a girl asks for Charlie; the woman informs her that she has dialed incorrectly. The call frightens them because it is late at night, after midnight. Then the phone rings again: it is the same voice, requesting Charlie. This time, however, the woman provides the caller with the precise information which explains her error in dialing—there is no reason, now, for her to make the mistake again. They sit, sipping tea, at the table, and the narrator calls attention to "a large birthmark" (A14: 194) on the man's head; that mark, like the bird's in ability to fly at the moment of the shower, is a random designation of birth, made by God. While he drinks, the man examines the designation on the labels of the jars (of "preserves") they had bought for their son. During his observations, the phone rings again, for the third time.

The third call—presumably no accident—provides the order by which all the minute, precise details of the story can be coherently viewed. And we recall the meditation of the woman earlier:

> This, and much more, she accepted—for after all living did mean accepting the loss of one joy after another, not even joys in her case—mere possibilities of improvement. She thought of the endless waves of pain that for some reason or other she and her husband had to endure; of the invisible giants hurting her boy in some unimaginable fashion; of the incalculable amount of tenderness, which is either crushed, or wasted, or transformed into madness; of neglected children humming to themselves in unswept corners; of beautiful weeds that cannot hide from the farmer and helplessly have to watch the shadow of his simian stoop leave mangled flowers in its wake, as the monstrous darkness approaches. (A13: 133)

Like Enricht, the mad landlord in *King, Queen, Knave*, the boy with referential mania is only partially correct: he is mistaken in his belief that the elaborate network of references signifies only him, and in his exclusion of "real people" from his conspiracy.

By the end of the story it is evident that all living things—humans, birds, "beautiful weeds," flowers—are ineluctably linked to each other by the very fact of their being alive. The patterned flow of their lives is "a dense tangle of logically interacting illusions," but the ultimate key, the explanation that would demystify the tangle of references, is "totally inaccessible to normal minds"; instead, it is controlled by forces we cannot know or understand: inexorable, implacable powers who reveal ominous signs and symbols but no original referent; who inflict "endless waves of pain" upon all forms of life "for some reason or other"; who act out of a funereal whimsy, "crushing" and "wasting" the tenderness of life and "transforming it into madness," "mangling flowers," drowning tiny birds; who initiate wars, force people to leave their homes and homelands; who execute people in malevolent concentration and work camps; who crush lives as if they were "weeds that cannot hide from the farmer" —in short, they are the malevolent energies of "monstrous darkness" who work to snuff out the light of life, imagination, and all creative impulses.

The beauty and the power of "Signs and Symbols" —which Nabokov claimed was one of his favorite works[6] —is conveyed through the scrupulously refined and repetitive images, details, and motifs which are intricately designed and fashioned so that the experience of reading the story is simultaneously an experience of an interlocking network of signs and symbols. The story, then, becomes the primary example of what it is about; it not only describes and refers to imaginative structures, but demonstrates them, proves their validity, by being itself a structure of the highest imaginative artistry. And it is this eloquent and influential function of language which characterizes Vladimir Nabokov's works of fiction in American prose. Certain examples indicate how this is so.

Bend Sinister (1947), like "Signs and Symbols," constructs an elaborate referential system in order to pit the realms of imaginative creation against the threat implicit in realistic experience. The novel contains, in Nabokov's words, "certain reflections in the glass" of "the idiotic and despicable regimes that we all know and that have brushed against me in the course of my life: worlds of tyranny and torture, of Fascists and Bolshevists ..."[7] The fictional text is "interlaced ... with bits of Lenin's speeches, and a chunk of the Soviet constitution, and gobs of Nazist pseudo-efficiency."[8] To read the novel, then, is to sort through the actual trappings of recent European history in order to experience a book about an imaginary European country under totalitarian siege.

Recalling the mechanism of "tear[ing] a hole in the world," the plot describes a spiral from the childhood relationship of Paduk (the mad dictator) and Krug (the mourning widower) to the ominous political manifestations of their prior friendship to the all-encompassing authorial whimsy of Nabokov as he composes the novel we are reading in his Cambridge, Massachusetts, apartment in 1946. The text contains numerous references to a rain puddle, meant to signify "a rent in [Krug's] world leading to another world of tenderness, brightness and beauty"[9] —the world of art and converted memory. The puddle, first seen from a hospital window, reappears as an ink blot, an ink stain, spilled milk, "the infusoria-like image of ciliated thought," a footprint, and "the imprint of a soul."[10] There are allusions to Shakespeare, Melville, Werfel, Sholokhov, Mallarme. Thus, these "rents" in the historical reality of the fictional text refer to the primacy of the enduring world of literary art by physically incorporating actual examples of literary art into the pages of the novel. By establishing correlations between the references of the text and the events of his recalled life, the reader imaginatively recreates his own recent history and culture along with the author—which is, of course, the point of the book.

The recognition of these principles of design in Nabokov's subsequent work serves to emphasize the associative continuities. That the true ending of *Pnin* (1957) is not to be found in the fleeting disconsolation that characterizes the book's closing pages, but in the midst of *Pale Fire* (1962: there, Timofey Pnin's quiet, enduring dignity achieves ultimate vindication in his appointment as Head of Wordsmith College's "bloated" Russian Department) further emphasizes the fact that we are meant to regard Nabokov's American *oeuvre* as a fictional network of "logically interacting illusions," conceived by an author who believes that his characters are as entirely dependent upon his artistic determinations as are all mortals dependent upon the ultimate contingencies of Fate or the creative energies of their Deity.

Similarly, *Lolita* (1955) evokes an interrelated reticulation: Lolita is Humbert Humbert's creative conceptual vision of the actual Dolores Haze; Dolores is a reflection of a girl earlier in time who was Humbert's childhood playmate; Humbert is in prison for murdering his double, Clare Quilty. Humbert's jail confession is interpreted by psychologist John Ray, and his introduction and Humbert's manuscript are enclosed by Nabokov's comment, "On a Book Entitled *Lolita*." The intricate involution of characters formulates a progression from innocent past experience (Humbert's original playmate) to coincidental replication (Dolores) to deliberate recreation (Dolores as Lolita, Humbert's playmate) to spurious repetition (Quilty's Dolores) to explication (Ray's rendition of Lolita) to art (Nabokov's Lolita, and ours). The particular incidental details "harden"—like the reader's perceptions in "Signs and Symbols"—into an active synergy of designation which is the novel.

The boy's referential mania is expanded to epic proportions in *Pale Fire*, a novel which itself refers back to its two antecedent fragments, "Solus Rex" and "Ultima Thule."[11] Here we are presented with a series of characters, each of whom believes that "everything is a cipher and of everything he is the theme." *Pale Fire* describes the magnificent tapestry of Zembla, a hypothetical land envisioned by the poet John Shade, "a poet who deliberately peels off a drab and unhappy past and replaces it with a brilliant invention."[12] The novel is perhaps Nabokov's most lucid embodiment of the notion that the structure of a work of art reflects and contains its subject: "our poet suggests here that human life is but a series of footnotes to a vast unfinished masterpiece."[13] So writes the editor, Charles Kinbote, commenting on Shade's poem; but in that maze of commentary, Kinbote becomes Charles the Beloved, deposed King of Zembla, who in turn becomes V. Botkin, crazed professor at Wordsmith University, all of whom are the shadowy creations of John Shade: and it is Shade's mock-assassination, during a lecture, which refers back to the actual murder of Nabokov's father in Berlin, 1922. Indeed, the very structure of *Pale Fire*—a novel disguised as a poem with a foreword and commentary—is, in actuality, a series of self-reflexive references and designations.

The publication of the colossal and labyrinthine *Ada* (1969) marked Nabokov's most exhaustive and definitive proclamation of the intricate and symbiotic mirror-image relationship between the physical, tangible world, and the conceptual, shadowy, invented world.

Thus we see that from a language system of referential design, in "Signs and Symbols," it is but a brief and exultant interval to the buoyant and incandescent imaginative constructions of *Bend Sinister*, and from there to the serpentine form and circuitous structural patterns of Vladimir Nabokov's finest novels: *Pnin*, *Lolita*, *Pale Fire*, *Ada*. In the process of imagining his novelistic landscape, he attained an awareness of the myriad potentialities of art as simultaneous shape and shadow, that fervent propensity to exploit the relative degrees of self-reflexive complexity, that jubilant tonality which best suited his creative vision.

Sacred dangers: Nabokov's distorted reflection

David Field

Vladimir Nabokov began his lectures on literature by claiming that "the real writer, the fellow who sends planets spinning and models a man asleep and eagerly tampers with the sleeper's rib, that kind of author has no given values at his disposal: he must create them himself."[1] Like the God of creation, the artist faces an amorphous world and must impose form on it:

> The material of this world may be real enough (as far as reality goes) but does not exist at all as an accepted entirety: it is chaos, and to this chaos the author says 'go!' allowing the world to flicker and to fuse. It is now recombined in its very atoms, not merely in its visible and superficial parts.[2]

Nabokov thus seems to acknowledge that artists are supreme egotists who vie with Jehovah's power to create a world.

But that god-like creative act involves a tremendous risk because the artist may merely possess the insane notion that he or she is God. Such delusions of grandeur lead to a false sense of creation, for insane artists lack the power to recombine the world "in its very atoms" and must settle instead for an order that distorts reality, an order that they discern in the "visible and superficial parts" of the world. And that false order inevitably replicates the insane artists' imaginations because the chaos merely reflects elements of their own minds.

There is, nevertheless, a point of tangency between the hubris of the artist and the delusions of the insane, and Nabokov repeatedly acknowledged his sympathy for highly personalized and eccentric imaginations.[3] In a lecture he gave his classes at Cornell, for example, Nabokov lashed out at "commonsense" (one word) and praised those who break from shared reality:

> It is instructive to think that there is not a single person in this room, or for that matter in any room in the world, who, at some

nicely chosen point in historical space-time would not be put
to death there and then, here and now, by a commonsensical
majority in righteous rage. The color of one's creed, neckties,
eyes, thoughts, manners, speech, is sure to meet somewhere
in time or space with a fatal objection from a mob that hates
that particular tone. And the more brilliant, the more unusual
the man, the nearer he is to the stake. *Stranger* always rhymes
with *danger*. The meek prophet, the enchanter in his cave, the
indignant artist, the nonconforming little schoolboy, all share
in the same sacred danger. And this being so, let us bless them,
let us bless the freak; for in the natural evolution of things, the
ape would perhaps never have become man had not a freak
appeared in the family.[4]

Because such freakish, insane-appearing minds may reach more
sacred insight than those who accept society's shared reality, the
only "real" worlds are highly personal imaginative creations:
"What I feel to be the real modern world is the world the artist
creates, his own mirage, which becomes a new *mir* ('world' in
Russian) by the very act of his shedding, as it were, the age he lives
in."[5]

Nabokov's short story "Signs and Symbols" illustrates this
complex relationship between imagination and insanity. Criticism
has focused on the way that the reader's attempt to decipher the
story's own signs and symbols—especially the reader's quest to
determine whether or not the third phone call reports the boy's
suicide—duplicates the very nature of the boy's insanity. William
Carroll says that in the story "a Nabokovian character's self-
consciousness resembles, though in a distorted manner, our own
self-consciousness as readers."[6] He claims that "referential mania,"
the disease from which the insane boy suffers, "'is a critical disease
all readers of fiction suffer from" (A245). Like Carroll, David
H. Richter finds that "Signs and Symbols" engages the sensitive
reader in a plight similar to that of the main character: "through
Nabokov's device of narrative entrapment, we become collaborators not only in crime but in creation."[7]

Larry R. Andrews carries such reasoning further and, after
arguing for a reading in which he deciphers the story's ending to
show how signs point to the boy's suicide, he unravels his own and
all other interpretations to reduce the story to "a configuration

of black marks on the page," an abstract aesthetic pattern, "the higher sphere of the artist's fictive world (in which we are characters too)."[8] And Paul J. Rosenzweig insists that "Nabokov undercuts the traditional distances among the realities of author, reader, and text by forcing the reader to become both a character in and author of the text."[9]

Standing in stark contrast to such reader-response critics is John V. Hagopian, who argues that "no legitimate artist produces randomness."[10] For Hagopian, the signs and symbols in the story all point to the boy's suicide; the story cannot metamorphose with each reader's interpretation, and a careful and scrupulous reading can yield its meaning. An example of the signs that alert us to the impending tragedy occurs in the story when the couple comes home: "The underground train lost its life current between two stations" (A10: 22), and then, when they've left the subway to walk the rest of the way home, they see "a tiny half-dead unfledged bird" which is "helplessly twitching in a puddle" (A10: 41). Their plan to bring the boy home puts him, in a sense, "between two stations." His childhood drawing of "wonderful birds with human hands and feet" (A12: 119) and his effort to fly when attempting suicide both associate him with the helpless bird. Hagopian uses such evidence to infer that the boy does, in fact, commit suicide and that the third phone call conveys the bad news from the hospital.

But even Hagopian must grapple with the issue of meaning that inheres in details, and he must express faith in the order of the world of art. The other critics, in fact, acknowledge the evidence that Hagopian presents but refuse to believe in his conclusions. Nevertheless, all the interpretations move from the question of whether or not the boy commits suicide to a consideration of the very foundation of knowledge: can anyone know anything definitely? Are there any principles for determining reality? Are we not in fact all insane as we try to make order of the world? Or, as Nabokov's former student Thomas Pynchon puts it, "life's single lesson" may be that "there is more accident to it than a man can ever admit to in a lifetime and stay sane."[11]

Is the boy in "Signs and Symbols" merely a misunderstood artist, a combination of all the freaks a commonsensical mob might put to death—prophet, enchanter, schoolboy, artist? His first attempt at suicide is "a masterpiece of inventiveness" and his desire to fly into a transcendent world through somehow connecting himself to nature links him with Romantic poets. His active imagination, like all creative fancy, colors what he sees and performs a major transformation when it observes nature. According to Dr Brink's diagnosis, in "referential mania":

> the patient imagines that everything happening around him is a veiled reference to his personality and existence ... Phenomenal nature shadows him wherever he goes. Clouds in the staring sky transmit to one another, by means of slow signs, incredibly detailed information regarding him ... Everything is a cipher and of everything he is the theme. Some of the spies are detached observers, such as glass surfaces and still pools; others, such as coats in store windows, are prejudiced witnesses, lynchers at heart ... He must be always on his guard and devote every minute and module of life to the decoding of the undulation of things. (A11: 62)

As the reader-response critics have pointed out, the boy's quest resembles critical and poetic inquiry as well as insanity. Carol T. Williams extends the argument and calls Nabokov's technique "self-directed irony" because he is "a writer devoted to the 'decoding of the undulation of things.'"[12] Even Nabokov speaks explicitly about the importance of imaginatively connecting himself to "phenomenal nature." In *Speak, Memory*, after recounting the origin of his first poem, he relates that writing the poem was "a phenomenon of orientation" and explains that all poetry involves the attempt "to express one's position in regard to the universe embraced by consciousness." He goes on to say that "[t]he arms of consciousness reach out and grope, and the longer they are the better. Tentacles, not wings, are Apollo's natural members."[13] Like the boy, Nabokov sends out his imaginative tentacles to the universe, enveloping "reality" with his own consciousness.

This similarity with the boy in "Signs and Symbols" goes even further, for Nabokov, too, saw messages to himself in the clouds. In Chapter Ten of *Speak, Memory*, he recalls a "particular sunset" and describes it as a "prodigious ovation in terms of color and form": "There it lay in wait, a family of serene clouds in miniature, an accumulation of brilliant convolutions, anachronistic in their creaminess and extremely remote; remote but perfect in every detail; fantastically reduced but faultlessly shaped; my marvelous tomorrow ready to be delivered to me" (213). This, then, is almost an exact analogue to "referential mania," in which "clouds in the staring sky transmit to one another, by means of slow signs, incredibly detailed information" regarding the boy.

But, as Nabokov's John Shade acknowledges in *Pale Fire*, "resemblances are the shadows of differences,"[14] and, despite the similarities, there are several key differences between Nabokov and the boy in "Signs and Symbols." First, Nabokov repeatedly calls for the importance of scrupulously exact observation of nature. He is scathing toward those who do not recognize the differences between butterflies, trees, birds, and other creatures in nature. In *Speak, Memory* he lambastes his governess for not recognizing the difference between the butterflies which she accidentally destroyed by sitting on them and the completely different ones with which she tried to replace the rare originals (128).

Nabokov's character Fyodor in *The Gift* goes even further in praising scrupulous observation. He condemns the Russian materialist Chernyshevski, whose simple-minded materialism becomes the brunt of Fyodor's sharpest criticism: according to Chernyshevski, "We see a tree; another man looks at the same object. We see by the reflection in his eyes that his image of the tree looks exactly the same as our tree. Thus we all see objects as they really exist." Fyodor's summary of Chernyshevski's false materialism stands as Nabokov's own analysis of the defects of abstract thought: "All this wild rubbish has its own private hilarious twist: the "materialists'", constant appeal to trees is especially amusing because they are all so badly acquainted with nature, particularly with trees."[15] Fyodor goes on to point out the ways that "materialism" leads to abstraction:

Look what a terrible abstraction resulted, in the final analysis, from "materialism"! Chernyshevski did not know the difference between a plow and the wooden *soha*; he confused beer with Madeira; he was unable to name a single wild flower except the wild rose; and it is characteristic that this deficiency of botanical knowledge was immediately made up by a "generalization" when he maintained with the conviction of an ignoramus that "they [the flowers of the Siberian taiga] are all just the same as those which bloom all over Russia!" (255–6)

Chernyshevski becomes especially relevant for "Signs and Symbols" because his son suffered from an intense form of this inability to deal with the material world and contracted a mental illness requiring that he enter a nursing home. The son "was afraid of space, or more exactly, he was afraid of slipping into a different dimension" (309), a fear realized by the boy in "Signs and Symbols," who wants to tear a hole in his world and escape.

Nabokov stands in stark contrast to his governess and Chernyshevski because, when he infers messages from nature, he precisely describes what he sees and refuses to reduce nature to a beautiful garden or a transcendental message board. He claims that he permanently damaged his eyesight by spending long hours examining butterflies' organs under the microscope at Harvard's Museum of Comparative Zoology. Even when he does detect messages in nature, he alludes to the importance of scrupulous observation. He describes one cloud-filled sunset in which he "could pick out brightly stained structural details of celestial organisms, or glowing slits in dark banks, or flat, ethereal beaches that looked like mirages of desert islands."[16] This description at once contains his future as a lepidopterist and implies the importance of meticulous observation of nature, for he describes the cloud as if it were a microscope slide with carefully stained and prepared butterfly organs on it. Even "the mirages of desert islands," his created artistic worlds, contain a paean to a reality principle, referring, as we have seen, to the Russian word for "world."

In analyzing paintings of insects, moreover, Nabokov criticizes artists who do not carefully scrutinize the world they paint:

> One simple conclusion I have come to is that no matter how precise an Old Master's brush can be it cannot vie in artistic magic with some of the colored plates drawn by the illustrators of certain scientific works in the nineteenth century. An Old Master did not know that in different species the venation is different and never bothered to examine its structure. It is like painting a hand without knowing anything about its bones or indeed without suspecting it has any. Certain impressionists cannot afford to wear glasses. Only myopia condones the blurry generalizations of ignorance. In high art and pure science detail is everything.[17]

He insists that "the artist should *know* the given world" (his emphasis) and claims that "[i]magination without knowledge leads no farther than the back yard. of primitive art, the child's scrawl on the fence, and the crank's message in the market place."[18] Criticizing John James Audubon's portraits of butterflies, he asks, "Can anyone draw something he knows nothing about? Does there not exist a high ridge where the mountajl1side of 'scientific' knowledge joins the opposite slope of 'artistic' imagination?"[19] Mountains convey a different message to the boy in "Signs and Symbols" because he sees his own form in them: "great mountains of unbearable solidity and height sum up in terms of granite and groaning firs the ultimate truth of his being" (A11: 84). To Nabokov, on the contrary, mountains are a perilous challenge, for he must balance along their narrow ridges.

A second factor differentiating him from the boy in "Signs and Symbols" is Nabokov's self-awareness of the role of imagination. The fact that he could write a story like "Signs and Symbols" reveals his keen recognition of the perversions to which intellect is subject. He claims that "being aware of being aware of being" separates humans from animals.[20] This self-consciousness also applies to the imaginative perception of all reality: as long as he is aware of being aware, as long as he knows that his imagination is at work, Nabokov protects himself from taking the messages in the clouds too literally. In the lecture on commonsense, Nabokov says, "A madman is reluctant to look at himself in a mirror because the face he sees is not his own: his personality is beheaded; that of the artist is increased."[21] A sane artist may risk insanity, but he can put the world back together in an ordered fashion:

> Lunatics are lunatics just because they have thoroughly and recklessly dismembered a familiar world but have not the power—or have lost the power—to create a new one as harmonious as the old. The artist on the other hand disconnects what he chooses and while doing so he is aware that something in him is aware of the final result.[22]

The very act of undercutting "reality" and making his art self-conscious about its technique qualifies Nabokov's deciphering of the world's signs and symbols. According to all our information—however tentative that information may be—the boy sees literal

messages to himself in nature. And we don't need to depend on the
shadowy Herman Brink, because the parents have figured out the
boy's problems for themselves.[23]

Finally, Nabokov differs radically from the boy because his own
quest for an imaginative order originates in his love for his family.
The very imaginative act which connects him to the universe also
connects him to others in a deep and significant way. He makes
explicit the fact that his desire for order and meaning in a world
beyond this one comes from love, from a desire to believe in a
world where seemingly immortal feelings can endure. Nabokov
once claimed that the vividness of his memories "is all a matter
of love: the more you love a memory, the stronger and stranger it
is."[24] He says that his autobiography originated with his love for
his wife, his parents, and his son. This love created his desire to
explore the universe with his poetic tentacles:

> Whenever I start thinking of my love for a person, I am in
> the habit of immediately drawing radii from my love—from
> my heart, from the tender nucleus of a personal matter—to
> monstrously remote points of the universe. Something impels me
> to measure the consciousness of my love against such unimagi-
> nable and incalculable things as the behaviour of nebulae
> (whose very remoteness seems a form of insanity), the dreadful
> pitfalls of eternity, the unknowledgeable beyond the unknown,
> the helplessness, the cold, the sickening involutions and inter-
> penetrations of space and time.[25]

In other words, Nabokov's love connects him to his family and
others, just as surely as the boy's self-absorption in "Signs and
Symbols" isolates him from his parents: the boy's "dense tangle
of logically interacting illusions" makes him "totally inaccessible
to normal minds" (A12: 131). Nabokov recognizes the danger
inherent in his own connection—the "very remoteness" of those
distant regions "seems a form of insanity," and there is something
dreadful about this quest, which forces him to face pitfalls and a
sickening unknown.

The threat of illness—and of insanity—lies close to the heart of his
endeavor. The boy in "Signs and Symbols" falls prey to this threat,
cuts himself off from his family, and becomes almost entirely solipsistic; Nabokov uses his aesthetic to achieve communication—not

just with an abstract and anonymous audience but with those he loves most. In short, "Signs and Symbols" shows how artistic imagination can become distorted and turn to insanity, preventing any communication. It shows the necessity for the artistic imagination to include an attention to natural reality, a scrupulous concern for detail. It also shows the importance for an artist of a keen awareness of his or her own limitations. Nabokov recognizes that his own imagination could become distorted or ill; that insanity lurks just beneath the surface of his artistic achievement.

Focusing on the boy's possible suicide is a false trail that has misled critics—we cannot know whether he commits suicide or not, but we *can* know that he is insane. As Carol T. Williams has recognized, the identity of the final caller "is irrelevant, for alive or dead, the young man cannot live in this world" (A344). The boy may resemble Nabokov, but he also differs from him in deep and significant ways. Finally, just as Nabokov is not the boy in "Signs and Symbols," so we readers need not be that boy. We need not suffer from "referential mania" so long as we remain meticulous in our attention to detail, so long as we recognize the imaginative nature of the inferences we draw, so long as we respect the quirkiness and individuality of artists and their art.

Numbers

The mysticism of circle

Mary Tookey

Although the title of Vladimir Nabokov's "Signs and Symbols" has invited readers and critics to seek and interpret symbolism, one meaning involving the cipher has been overlooked. The geometrical figure representing a cipher, which either is a circle or closely resembles one, is symbolically ambiguous, thus presenting the reader with a paradox in the incident involving the wrong numbers at the climax of the story. This paradox becomes a key to an ironic theme.

Critics William Carroll, John Hagopian, and Carol Williams have mentioned the cipher as well as other symbols including the ace of spades, a traditional omen of death; the "tiny, half-dead unfledged bird ... helplessly twitching in a puddle"; (A10: 41) and the "mangled flowers" of "beautiful weeds" (A13: 143). The bird and flowers represent the unfortunate deranged young man and others like him. Carroll notes Nabokov's words, "Everything is a cipher" (A11: 72), and comments on a double meaning of the term:

> The primary meaning of "cipher" here is "secret writing based on a system ..." But "cipher" also means, of course, "the mathematical symbol (0) denoting absence of quantity," or zero. This is the more frightening possibility; it suggests that everything is a zero, meaningless, without substance.[1]

Carroll believes that the wrong phone numbers indicate Nabokov's desire to leave the reader puzzling as to whether the cipher is a clue to hidden meaning or signifies no meaning. "Does it matter?" Carroll asks.[2] The cipher does not matter greatly in his interpretation of this work since Carroll's thesis is that Nabokov engenders in the reader the same mental disorder that afflicts the son—referential mania, in which "the patient imagines that everything happening around him is a veiled reference to his personality and existence" (A11: 62).

Hagopian disagrees, saying, "Indeed, the central thematic question of the story is: Is it necessarily paranoid to feel that nature and the universe are enemies of man?"[3] He also differs from Carroll's view that the wrong number is plausible because there is no hieroglyphic difference between the letter and numeral. Hagopian says that the letter O "is a perfect circle, whereas the number zero is a vertical oval."[4] These comments are used to support his view that the third call is surely not a wrong number. Neither Hagopian nor Carroll has noted the traditional symbolism of the circle.

The hieroglyph at the climax of "Signs and Symbols" has just the sort of multiple meaning that has seemed to delight Nabokov. The geometrical figure cannot be the cipher in the sense of something with hidden meanings but can be the zero—nothing— or the circle—everything, or perfection. Through many centuries in both East and West, the circle has been an important religious symbol.

In Taoism, the separate elements of yin and yang exist within a circle representing primordial unified being. In Hinduism and Buddhism, the circle stands for the absolute, the primal couple before the division that created the universe. H. M. Raphaelian not only comments on the circle as symbolizing "the absolute, the perfect and unknowable" but adds that it is sometimes a symbol of the sun.[5] George Ferguson says that in the Judeo-Christian tradition:

> The circle, or ring, has been universally accepted as the symbol of eternity and never-ending existence. As the monogram of God, it represents not only the perfection of God but the everlasting God ...[6]

With this symbolism of the circle in mind as well as the meanings of the cipher, how should a reader interpret the wrong numbers?

The child is an anonymous young person. She could be any young person. She asks for Charlie, a name meaning a man of the common people. She too is probably a common person. She telephones, dialing the circle. Is Nabokov suggesting that she wants everything—perfection, God, a transcendent being? The older woman, the deranged boy's mother—a displaced person, as was Nabokov himself, impoverished in both her family life and her economic situation—gently tries to straighten out the confusion. The girl has been dialing the circle and should have been dialing the zero, the symbol of nothing.

Is Nabokov trying to make a statement about the disillusionment confronting humanity, especially youth who attempt to hold a religious or mystical world view? Certain names in the story support that possibility. The father's brother is named Isaac and referred to as "the Prince." Both appellations suggest the Judeo-Christian tradition. There is a Mrs Sol, noted as having brookside flowers, and a Dr Solov (love of the sun?), who might represent the sun or nature and early traditions of nature worship. At a point of suspense in the climax, the crab apple jelly is mentioned, reminding the reader of the Garden of Eden and humanity's unfulfilled hopes first of enjoying the Garden and then of becoming like gods.

Thus, Nabokov appears to use the ambiguous O—which as a cipher may represent either hidden meanings or nothing and as a circle may represent everything, the absolute, God—to suggest a nihilistic theme. One may compare Nabokov's thinking to that of Nietzsche, who, according to Martin Heidegger, defines European nihilism as the historical process whereby the dominance of the transcendent ("God" standing for "transcendent" in general and in its various meanings) "becomes null and void, so that it loses its worth and meanings."[7] Nabokov expresses not philosophically but symbolically the similarity, even identity, of the everything and the nothing.

The semiotics of zero

Meghan Vicks

"Signs and Symbols," despite its short length (it amounts to a modest six pages in my edition), contains a close examination of a patterning (and therefore, meaning-making) mechanism, analogues of which are found in many of Nabokov's works. This mechanism, known as "referential mania," has a zero—a signifier of nothing—at its very core. A careful reading of this short story reveals how the patterning produced by referential mania constructs both meaning and madness. The following discussion will demonstrate how nothing itself functions and appears in "Signs and Symbols," as well as how it makes possible the creative moment. I will then turn to a close analysis of referential mania, which operates by means of zero. Throughout this analysis, I will look at the various versions of referential mania that are found in Nabokov's other works, and that together figure as a dominant aesthetic motif in his literary corpus.

When we strip away the language, imagery, and symbolism of "Signs and Symbols," and analyze only the skeletal plot structure, what we find is a series of canceled happenings, thwarted wills, and *almost* incidents that *always* end at nothing—an example of a naught-ward narrative. Most basically, the short story covers one day in which a number of nullified events occur: an émigré couple want to bring a birthday present to their mentally deranged son, *but* are turned away because the boy attempted to commit suicide earlier that day, and their presence may further trouble him; later that night, the husband makes plans to take his son out of the mental institution, *but* is interrupted by three telephone calls; the first two telephone calls are wrong numbers, and the phone rings a third time just as the narrative closes, thereby "signing" the ending with a call that is never picked up, or a textual and symbolic abyss. Even minor events in the story are marked by nullification: for instance, the train loses its "life current" as the couple are on their way to the sanitarium (A10: 23); the husband wants to unlock his door, *but* realizes that his wife has taken the key with her; he wants to sleep, *but* cannot. What we have here is a plot that follows an equation that may be best described as _will to do "x"_ + _but "y"_ = _0(x)_; or, in other words, it is the zero and zeroing in the most literal sense that move the story along. The zeroed event nonetheless pushes the story forward, which indicates that while "will to do x" was reduced to zero, the story has still moved to a new position not despite, but because of this deletion. It turns out that these canceled aspirations and incidents do not merely create, but their tracings also form a line that draws attention to the value and power of the zero in the text.

Furthermore, nothingness and negation distinguish the characterization of the central characters: a triad of husband, wife, and son, none of whom are named. Their anonymity is heightened by the fact that other, minor characters _are_ given names; for instance, Mrs Sol, the next-door neighbor who is only mentioned in a parenthetical aside, the psychiatrist, Herman Brink, who writes of their son's disease in a scientific journal, a stranger on the bus who resembles an old friend Rebecca Borisovna, or even Charlie, the person that the mistaken caller repeatedly asks for, as well as many others (Aunt Rosa, Dr Solov, Elsa). Those who do have names cannot really be called characters, as they are all only fleetingly mentioned, never make actual appearances in the narrative, and have no real bearing on the story other than to highlight the nameless-ness and vacuity of the central figures. Nabokov therefore peppers this story with a number of unseen characters who nevertheless do have names in order to construct a sharp dichotomy against the central characters who remain anonymous. Moreover, it is these named absences (Mrs Sol and company) that define through contrast the unnamed and ghostly presences (husband, wife, son). Here, for example, is how the story introduces husband and wife:

> Her drab gray hair was done anyhow. She wore cheap black dresses. Unlike other women of her age (such as Mrs Sol, their next-door neighbor, whose face was all pink and mauve with paint and whose hat was a cluster of brookside flowers), she presented a naked white countenance to the fault-finding light of spring days. Her husband, who in the old country had been a fairly successful businessman, was now wholly dependent on his brother Isaac, a real American of almost forty years standing. They seldom saw him and had nicknamed him "the Prince" (A9: 13).

In the above passage, Nabokov describes both husband and wife in terms that tell us more about who they are not, than about who they are. The wife is *unlike* women of her age, is *anything but* Mrs Sol, who is characterized with an overabundance of bright colors and clustered flowers that resonates in her name, and whose excess is even more firmly established by the run-on sentence in which she is animated; in short, the wife *is not*. Likewise, the husband is characterized by what he used to be, but no longer is (a sort of characterization by erasure), and also by his dependence upon his brother who is significantly doubly named (Isaac and "the Prince"), and mostly absent. Second, those attributes that are given to the wife—"drab gray hair," "cheap black dresses," "naked white countenance"—together imply a being that is ghostly, insipid, and deathlike, which further imbues the wife with a sense of nothingness. In regards to the husband's appearance, other passages underscore his toothless mouth, his "horrible masklike grimace" as if he lacks a human face (A12: 98), the silence that seems to accompany him wherever he goes, and his preference for "the old overcoat with the astrakhan collar" (A13: 147), which subtly associates him with one of the most famous nonentities of Russian literature, Akaky Akakievich of Nikolai Gogol's "The Overcoat." In sum, husband and wife appear in "Signs and Symbols" as nothings that have taken center-stage; it is nullification that characterizes both husband and wife, and that saturates the contours of their (non)beings.

Their son—the figure that is the narrative's central catalyst—is even more of a nonentity than his parents. He never makes an appearance; in his stead stands a discussion of his illness. Defined as "referential mania," his disease is distinguished by a perception of patterns and phenomena that are (seemingly) not there, but highly conspired and meaningful:

In these very rare cases the patient imagines that everything happening around him is a veiled reference to his personality and existence. He excludes real people from the conspiracy—because he considers himself to be so much more intelligent than other men. Phenomenal nature shadows him wherever he goes. Clouds in the staring sky transmit to one another, by means of slow signs, incredibly detailed information regarding him. His inmost thoughts are discussed at nightfall, in manual alphabet, by darkly gesticulating trees. Pebbles or stains or sun flecks form patterns representing in some awful way messages which he must interpret. *Everything is a cipher and of everything he is the theme* (A14: 170; italics mine).

We should pause here to recollect the multi-faceted meanings of the term "cipher," which variously signifies a code or secret message, and zero. These meanings are simultaneously relevant here. Regarding the former, the boy's mania is marked by these ciphers as cryptograms, and by the notion that he must uncover the secret of their message. With this definition, the sentence translates to read, "Everything is a cryptogram, and of everything he is the theme of the cryptogram's message." Regarding the latter, the answer to the code is repeatedly revealed to be a zero, which enables and personifies not only the boy's mania, but also the various contours of the story (character development and plotline), as demonstrated above. With this second definition, the sentence translates to "Everything is zero and of everything he is the theme (which is also zero)." The cipher is both the secret message and the zero—or meaning and meaninglessness. In "Signs and Symbols," the son himself represents the gap at the center of the story that catalyzes not only the text (the story is, after all, about him), but also the world around him (the world of the story very much reflects the vision of his mania, as will be discussed below). He is the zero that produces both word and world.

"Signs and Symbols," then, is a story of the world produced by the son's referential mania: hence the "zeroing" of the plot, and the zeroed-nature of the central characters, both of which are symptoms of a world that has zero as its theme and creative force. These ideas help us to understand the mechanics of the boy's referential mania, and also provide an explanation for the paranoia and fear that plague the boy as a result of this dementia. We cannot overlook the fact that the boy is suicidal (he is a nonbeing who desires to not be), that he wants nothing more than to "tear a hole in his world and escape" (A11: 58), and exploring the zero's role in his referential mania helps explain his torment. It is not just that he sees conspiracies or that he is besieged by paranoia, but that he is trapped at the mid-zone between being and nonbeing. This is dangerous because it unravels the seams of his world, disallows him any solid ground to stand on. If he does crack the code, he paradoxically winds up at zero: meaning has been reduced to zero, or zero enables meaning; everything is about him, but everything is zero. He has no way of positioning himself or securing his own meaningful boundaries, as either way, he is caught in this liminal tension between the tick and tock of nothing and everything. It makes sense, then, that he longs "to tear a hole in his world and escape": the only way to "escape" is not to escape at all, but rather to embrace the paradox and give himself over to the contradictory void—the hole—that is everything.

And what is a liminal realm, if not the space of zero? In his groundbreaking study, "Betwixt and Between: The Liminal Period in *Rites de Passage*," Victor Turner designates the liminal state as a structural—if not physical—invisibility or nonexistence, which is responsible for the liminal's twofold character. The liminal is "at once no longer classified and not yet classified,"[1] and is therefore, on the one hand, symbolized by death, corpses, decomposition, menstruation—that which has a negative tinge. But it is also, on the other hand, symbolized by gestation and parturition, "likened to or treated as embryos, newborn infants, or sucklings."[2] The symbolic renderings of the liminal contain within them both the positive and negative aspects of existence due to the fact that the liminal position is structurally not there—it is a nothingness in the system. Thus, nothingness and nonbeing are the common denominators of all liminal realms; zero is one of their ambiguous symbolic renderings.

"Signs and Symbols" also harbors a human theme that is purposely hidden in the text—or signified through its quiet invisibility—due to the nature of the theme itself: that trauma, especially the trauma of the innocent, cannot be iterated. Trauma is something that often eludes straightforward articulation in art and literature, and Nabokov's works, including "Signs and Symbols," are no exception. Here, we find that trauma cannot be transcribed in a definitive manner within the text; rather, it is paradoxically represented in the text's silences and voids, those moments of zero. "Signs and Symbols," Nabokov said, is a story with both an inside and an outside, in which "a second (main) story is woven into or placed behind, the superficial semitransparent one" (*Selected Letters* 117). The second hidden story is only pieced together with seemingly non-sequitur details, which add up to indicate a Holocaust background to the main events in the story.

For instance, in "Decoding Nabokov's 'Signs and Symbols,'" John Hagopian argues that the malignant forces that plague the boy are not just his horrifying and insane imaginings, but are very much a real part of his world: "The family's history [aunts exterminated in concentration camps, suicidal cousins, bullies at school], fully justifies the feeling that they live in a malevolent universe" (A302). Likewise, Leona Toker, in "'Signs and Symbols' In and Out of Contexts," says, "The specific mental malady of this young man is a morbidly condensed expression of the Jewish experience in Europe at the time of the Holocaust" (A165). "Signs and Symbols," then, contains a hidden background of trauma that is too unspeakable to be represented in language, or too "barbaric" to be captured in poetry. And so, instead of the trauma, the ciphers are found in its place. When the narrative ends in the middle of the third phone call, silence takes the place of language, thereby indicating we have once again entered the realm of trauma—the boy has achieved his goal of disappearing into a hole. But the silence and abyss that punctuate the story's ending are the only creative way to articulate that trauma; it cannot be circumscribed by language, for that would imply it could be contained or appeased, and perhaps is not so very traumatic.

All of these ideas come to a brilliant point in the final scene of the story, when the phone rings for a second time. The wife tells the young voice on the other end of the line, "'You have the incorrect number. I will tell you what you are doing: you are turning the letter O instead of the zero'" (A14: 198). It is through the wife's kind advice that Nabokov directs his own "callers"—his readers—to turn to the zero. This is a directive that has been ignored, undervalued, and disputed by many critics of "Signs and Symbols."[3] The common interpretive strategy has been to decode a set and finite meaning in the narrative, the result of which finds the son dead at the story's conclusion.[4] Critics have searched for secret messages in the patterns of numbers and images permeating the narrative,[5] have hypothesized a hidden significance behind the labels of the jelly jars,[6] and have checked the first letter of every word or line to see what meaningful words they may form.[7] (And who, as William Carroll first asked, has "referential mania"?[8] I will revisit this question.) The critical literature has repeatedly denied the wife's directive to turn to zero; whereas the caller has been misdialing, we have been misreading if we have not turned to zero for answers.

"Signs and Symbols" demonstrates how zero is that which allows the patterning of referential mania to take place. It is the *gap* in the system, and the *lack* of an absolute significance, that causes the proliferation of patterns that make meaning. This is an idea that touches a deep chord in metaphysics: the zero between positive and negative numbers (modern mathematics), the *clinamen* in the laminar flow of atoms (atomic physics), the play in the system (Derridian deconstruction)—these gaps are all needed for creation and structures (be they mathematics, the physical world, or language) to exist at all. While it is not within the scope of this essay to fully summarize and unpack the theories listed above, some brief remarks on these ideas will demonstrate their kinship to referential mania and zero. Modern day mathematics grants zero a special and paradoxical status as both a number, and the marker of a number's absence; mathematically, zero functions to generate the full plane of numbers, and as a number itself. Because of this, mathematicians have been forced to ask, "Is [zero] to be the mark of the empty, or the empty mark? The first keeps it estranged from the numbers, merely part of the landscape through which they move; the second puts it on par with them."[9] It seems that zero carries with it the moment of exception; it produces the plane of numbers, but also stands outside of that plane.[10] This is quite similar to the structure's de-centered center that Jacques Derrida discusses in his famous piece, "Structure, Sign, and Play in the Discourses of the Human Sciences." Here, Derrida puts forward the notion of a deferring center that gives form to discursive structures. Like the zero in mathematics, the unstructured center controls the meaning-making of its system, while remaining exempt from its own laws and functioning; this center is at once intrinsic and external to the system. Finally, twentieth-century developments in atomic physics demonstrate that atoms themselves are not the building blocks of the universe, but rather it is the gaps and irregular spaces, which randomly occur in the laminar flow of atoms, that create worlds. In *The Birth of Physics*, Michel Serres dubs these gaps and wavers in the laminar flow of atoms *clinamen*. Defined by Serres, the *clinamen* "is the minimum angle of formation of a vortex, appearing by chance in a laminar flow."[11] And it is through such indiscernible deviancies from the laminar flow that that the world emerges. Serres writes, "This idea goes to the heart of philosophy, that is, metaphysics. If we had only the principle of identity, we would be mute, motionless, passive, and the world would have no existence: nothing new under the sun of sameness."[12] The failure of perfect order—a failure that is caused by the gap in the laminar flow of atoms—creates the meaningful world. In each of these theories, a form of zero is needed for the existence of the system or the world. Referential mania is another version of this idea, that words and worlds are produced by virtue of a patterning that is born from something that is not there—a zero that is the element of freedom and chaos present in the system.[13]

Variations of referential mania abound throughout Nabokov's work, and their main attributes are usually the same: patterning that produces meaning or madness, and that is catalyzed by nothing. An early rendition of it is found in *The Defense*, wherein the protagonist Luzhin, as many critics have noted, has a mania similar to the boy's in "Signs and Symbols." Luzhin perceives signs and symbols in the world around him that indicate he is ensnared in a life-sized chess game, which consumes him entirely: "The only thing that really interested him was the complex, cunning game in which he somehow had become enmeshed. Helplessly and sullenly he sought for signs of the chess repetition, still wondering toward what it was tending."[14] It is tending toward nothing, of course, because there is no chess game behind the patterning. Luzhin's perception of patterns is at once his gift and his madness. On the one hand, it allows him to expertly control the chessboard and ingeniously solve the puzzles of chess, thereby creating a beautiful and ordered realm that contrasts his spontaneous and chaotic existence. On the other hand, his perception controls him, renders him a slave, and reduces all to the imagined movements and fantastical intrigues that happen along sixty-four nonexistent squares. Like the boy in "Signs and Symbols," Luzhin's mania is both meaning-making and meaning-annihilating, and is derived from something that is not there.

In *Pale Fire*, referential mania takes the form of the ingenious madness of Charles Kinbote. When Kinbote acquires John Shade's final work, he expects that it will depict his imagined life as King of Zembla. Shade's poem, however, says nothing of Kinbote or of Zembla; it is instead an autobiographical meditation on life and, in particular, on the "abyss" of death. Nevertheless, Kinbote creates a long and detailed analysis of Shade's work in which he demonstrates, by means of loose word patterns and tenuous textual evidence, that the poem is indeed about Zembla, and about his own exile from that land. In Shade's poem, Kinbote discovers patterns that give shape to a world that is not actually existent in lines of Shade's work; in other words, Kinbote's mania reads patterns in nothing, and creates a world out of what doesn't exist.

In *Ada*, referential mania appears in the madness of Aqua and other Terra-believers, who are "afloat in infinite non-thingness"[15]—these characters feel as though Anti-Terra is unreal, a realm of nothing, and they therefore envision a truer, Terra realm. Their madness gives shape to Terra, and is described as a patterning mania in which "Man-made objects [lose] their significance or [grow] monstrous connotations."[16] As in referential mania, meaning is reduced to naught, and meaning burgeons to infinity. Everything is both meaningless and meaningful at the same time. Moreover, these believers in a terrestrial otherworld—which is likely *our* own world, the world of Nabokov's readers—are attuned to the extra-textual realm, as if they occupy a literal space between fiction and reality, between word and world. In *Ada*, then, Nabokov renders our own reality the ravings of the insane; "reality" is once again in quotation marks, the product of the imaginary impulse. There is still another way in which referential mania appears in *Ada*: in Ada's own metaphysical system of towers and bridges, which functions by perception of patterns and coincidences in one's life, patterns which create meaning and "supreme rapture,"[17] but are otherwise not there. Like the Terra-believers, Ada produces meaning through patterning of phenomena that do not exist outside the realm of her perception and imagination. Her towers are creations of her imagi-nation, just as Terra is the collective dream of madmen. Both Ada's towers and Terra provide a meaning and an ethos that are sorely lacking in Anti-Terra existence; they provide something "real" to make up for Anti-Terra's reality that is "non-thingness."

Referential mania later becomes "Transparent Things" in the novel of the same name. Hugh Person, another Nabokovian protagonist who is "harrowed by coincident symbols,"[18] can perceive the histories and stories of objects around him, these "transparent things, through which the past shines."[19] By the end of the novel, Person's capacity to see the past—to view those trans-parent things—has reached its full potential: the past comes to life in the form of his deceased wife's footsteps, and Person dies in a fiery blaze having resurrected the past in which his wife lives, and thereby erasing a present in which he strangled his wife in her sleep. Person's perception of the past through transparent things becomes synonymous with a resurrection of the past; his vision that peers through transparent things to find "coincident symbols" recreates a world that takes the place of his current existence.

In Nabokov's last novel *Look at the Harlequins!*, referential mania becomes the play of "looking at harlequins":

> "What harlequins? Where?"
> "Oh everywhere. All around you. Trees are harlequins, words are harlequins. So are situations and sums. Put two things together—jokes, images—and you get a triple harlequin. Come on! Play! Invent the world! Invent reality!"[20]

There is also a darker version of referential mania in this novel: Vadim's chronic illness, dubbed the "numerical nimbus syndrome" (Vadim himself asserts "that 'nimbus' means nothing"[21]), causes him to read a dreadful meaning into the most minutia of things— dots in the light, heartbeats, blinking eyelashes. As his first wife deduces, his madness is brought about by a "good clean zero,"[22] and she forbids him from engaging in exercises that exhibit the relativity of existence, that demonstrate how nothing actually means anything at all in the absence of human consciousness. Thus, in his last novel, Nabokov has split up referential mania into its positive and negative poles: "Looking at harlequins," the patterning of which generates meaning and reality; and "numerical nimbus," which incites an erasure of signification and a paralysis of being.

Finally, there is also a metafictional aspect of referential mania that is not only at play in "Signs and Symbols," but also throughout Nabokov's literary corpus: the reader of the text participates in his own kind of referential mania. "Signs and Symbols" provides an excellent illustration of this. Because the end of "Signs and Symbols" is stamped with a yawning hole (the telephone continues to ring as the narrative closes, thereby leaving the reader with no clear indication who is calling), and moreover because it is patterned with multiple numbers, signs, and symbols that bait the eager reader's deciphering, the careful readers of this story fool themselves into becoming "referential maniacs." What's more, if we interpret all of the codes to indicate something about the boy, then we legitimate his dementia. He is indeed trapped in a world in which "everything is a cipher and of everything he is the theme," and his belief of this could be regarded as an awareness of Nabokov's pen, and of the various readers and critics who pore over his story and continually reinterpret it. His referential mania, then, is otherwise understood as his tuning into the scratchings of Nabokov's thick pencil along the page (scratchings that literally shape his existence), and his reception of the wavelengths of the readers' thoughts (thoughts that give his life meaning). A wormhole is thus opened up between reader and text: our reading of "Signs and Symbols" does indeed exacerbate the boy's attunement to the conspiracy that is constantly hounding him, thereby insinuating a symbiotic relationship between reader and character. If our reading of "Signs and Symbols" is provoking the boy's referential mania, and if the text is likewise turning us into referential maniacs, always through the double-edged cipher, then who can say what is fiction and what is reality?

We have arrived at Nabokov's "reality" in quotation marks.[23] Referential mania, in all its various forms found throughout Nabokov's narratives, is the moment in which nothingness becomes a creative force, and the sign of the creative mind—be it the mind of a genius, or the mind of a madman. It is our ability to create patterns out of nothing that is our greatest gift, for this patterning is the source of all—both the word and the world. As Nabokov tells us in *Speak, Memory*:

> There is also keen pleasure (and, after all, what else should the pursuit of science produce?) in meeting the riddle of the initial blossoming of man's mind by postulating a *voluptuous pause* in the growth of the rest of nature, a lolling and loafing which allowed first of all the formation of *Homo poeticus*—without which *sapiens* could not have been evolved.[24]

This voluptuous pause—this zero in time and space—enables the formation of the poet, who in turn enables the creation of the world. We *are*, because we are referential manics.

PART FIVE
Dissection

Web of contexts

"Signs and Symbols" in and out of contexts
Leona Toker

"Signs and Symbols" has been frequently discussed in critical literature and widely admired by the general reader. The critical articles usually deal with the subtle metafictional inquiry indirectly conducted in the text, perhaps because the moving "human interest" of "Signs and Symbols" is self-evident and does not demand comment. What still does demand comment, however, is the relationship between the two major layers of significance. I shall attempt to show that this relationship is both functional and thematic.

I

The self-reflexive layer of the story's meaning consists in its probing of interpretive conventions. Whereas "Recruiting," "Torpid Smoke," and "The Leonardo" are devoted to different aspects of literary creation, "Signs and Symbols" examines the other side of the process, viz. the problem of careful reading.

This problem is riveted on the story's patterns of recurrence and its open ending. In the last sentence, the telephone rings for the third time in the apartment of an elderly immigrant couple, late at night. Two calls had come from a girl who had dialed the wrong number.

During the second call the wife had patiently explained to the girl that she had dialed the letter O instead of the zero; hence it is unlikely that the girl should make the same mistake again. And yet it is not impossible: the girl is confused; her voice is described as "dull" (A14: 177), "toneless," and "anxious" (A14: 186). Is the third call another mistake or is it coming from the psychiatric sanitarium in which the couple's son is confined? The young man has already made two suicide attempts: is the third midnight call a sign that he has made a success of the third one? This question is left open in the text; its answer largely depends on the interpretive procedures the individual reader chooses to apply to the patterns of recurrence that run through the story.

A recurrence is an equivalent of "redundancy" which, as information theory tells us, can ensure a successful communication of meaning. In a short and condensed work like "Signs and Symbols" repetition or recurrence is a particularly powerful attention pointer. There are three kinds of recurrence in the story: the numerical pattern, the pattern of irony, and the pattern of recurrent imagery. All suggest that the last telephone call is a death message, but the evidence that they supply is inconclusive.

The numerical pattern consists in sequences of three homogeneous items. The story is divided into three sections: America is the elderly couple's third abode; their apartment is on the third landing; three cards fall out of the old lady's pack. The pattern is fatidic: as David H. Richter has observed, in folklore "two false starts [are] followed by an effective third try. And so we expect that two wrong numbers will be followed by a genuine call, that the boy's two failed suicide attempts would next time be successful."[1] Yet the third call may be viewed in terms of a different interpretive convention: as Paul Rosenzweig notes, "it takes two prior calls to create an ambiguity about the final call, whereas in life the one call alone would suffice. The conventions of fiction would immediately impose upon that solitary ring a quite definite, unambiguous, and tragic meaning, and, so, within the story it takes two additional rings to counter in part our conventional assumptions."[2] In other words, the third call may be regarded as ambiguous precisely because it is not the only one.

The pattern of irony consists in the so-called irony of fate. In section 1, after having painstakingly picked out an inoffensive birthday present (a basket of ten fruit jellies) for their son, the parents never get to deliver it because the hospital staff does not allow them to see him: he has to be kept quiet because that morning he tried to take his life for the second time, as the nurse explains "brightly" (A10: 32). In section 2 the old lady looks at the photograph of Aunt Rosa "who had lived in a tremulous world of bad news, bankruptcies, train accidents, cancerous growths until the Germans" cavalierly liberated her from her anxieties by putting her to death, "together with all the people she had worried about" (A12: 118): an individual world with its cosmic tendernesses and tremulous cares for the loved ones is dwarfed by a genocidal wave. In section 3, the old couple decide to take their son out of the sanitarium; as they sit down together to their "unexpected festive midnight tea," we almost expect this moment of joy to be taken away from them by the death message. Yet whether or not the third call is a death message, the irony is still in force: the call would not fail to frighten them and disrupt their quiet celebration.

The most important and the most problematic of the three patterns is the sequence of recurrent images and motifs related to death: the underground train loses "its life current" (A10: 23), a "half-dead unfledged bird" is helplessly twitching in a puddle (A10: 41), the third of the cards on the floor is the ominous ace of spades, and just beneath it there is a picture of a young German couple, the maid Elsa and her "bestial beau" (A13: 165), whose career during World War II could be easily imagined. In the troubled imagination of the heroine, "beautiful weeds ... cannot hide from the farmer and helplessly have to watch the shadow of his simian stoop leave mangled flowers in its wake, as the monstrous darkness approaches" (A13: 142). Are we supposed to interpret all these plausible narrative details as "signs and symbols" of the young man's death at the end of the story? Not necessarily. As William Carroll was the first to suggest, if we do so, we may, in a manner of speaking, find ourselves trapped in the young man's own "referential mania" (A11: 61).[3]

"Referential mania," the story explains, is a patient's belief "that everything happening around him is a veiled reference to his personality and existence" (A11: 61). The idea of reference is widely known in literature, from a Puritan's search for signs of salvation to a Romantic poet's "egotistical sublime." This quasi-animistic vision becomes morbid if the reference is, in all earnestness, interpreted as hostile:

Everything is a cipher and of everything he is the theme. Some of the spies are detached observers, such are glass surfaces and still pools; others, such as coats in store windows, are prejudiced witnesses, lynchers at heart; others again (running water storms) are hysterical to the point of insanity, have a distorted opinion of him and grotesquely misinterpret his actions. (A11: 72)

There are no causal links between a power cut in the subway, a fledgling pushed out of his nest, and a potentially successful suicide attempt of the old couple's son. Yet events in a work of fiction do not always depend on causality.[4] Jorge Luis Borges claims that words and images have the power to attract, as if by sympathetic magic, words, and images like them.[5] As a result, though one usually expects the author to flesh out his or her story with images appropriate to a character's fate, this fate may be an outcome of the development of images ("I am a slave of images," thinks, in another connection, Adam Krug of *Bend Sinister*,[6] echoing Nabokov's famous remark that his characters are "galley slaves").[7] This effect is, Borges would suggest, akin to sympathetic magic, or rather to the atavistic beliefs in sympathetic magic that survive in the most civilized segments of the modern world: if one enacts an event, rehearses it, the image of the event may attract, through contact or imitation, the event itself. Thus, the death of a character, such as the insane young man in "Signs and Symbols," may be brought about not by a chain of causes and consequences in the plot but by a structural pattern, by the presence of a slot for the motif of death in a chain of homogeneous recurrences.

And yet even this technique loses its "magic" as soon as it turns into an interpretive convention. To balance it, one may recall, as does John Hagopian, that the focal consciousness of "Signs and Symbols" is that of the mother,[8] that the narrative details (though not the language) reflect the selectiveness of her attention on the day presented in the story. The news of the boy's suicide attempt naturally lowers the threshold of her consciousness to whatever is related to trouble, helplessness, and death. Significantly, the young girl who is crying on the shoulder of an elderly woman is only *one of* the passengers in the bus that the couple takes on their way home (A10: 49). And if the images of death reflect the workings of the heroine's consciousness, the expected final reference to death may be confined to her imagination and panic as she stretches her hand to the receiver.

The whole question of how the reader is expected to understand the ending of the story presupposes the existence of a "proper" or "implied" reading of the Nabokovian text. It posits a closure, while a closure is belied by the very openness of the ending. Nabokov usually forms and cancels his fictional worlds in such a way as to make them capable of a residual motion after the curtain falls; yet this motion is not endless. In our dynamic century "reality" has become a matter of multiple perspectives: few of us can still afford to believe that we hold the "ultimate truth" of culture or ideology. "Strong opinions" are a rare luxury; and most of the fortunate people who hold them are becoming aware that the assumptions on which these opinions are based are a matter not of knowledge but of feeling or choice of belief. A literary text is a part of this "reality." We may, if we wish, discontinue our imaginative construction of the story's world after conjuring up either 1) a mistaken call or 2) a death message, or we may 3) stop earlier, with the horror of the old couple, with the painful suspense that poisons their night. Any one of the choices largely depends on the interpretive strategies that we choose to apply.

II

My choice is in favor of the third option, viz. of imagining a moment of panic prolonged to infinity, with the telephone still ringing and the mother's hand still stretching towards the receiver. This choice is based on the following considerations.

The debate concerning the recurrent motifs of death in the story largely hinges on their contextualization: should they be read in the narrower context of the old lady's consciousness or in the broader context of the master discourse? Yet the story being so short (combining, as it were, economy of effort with emphasis on defamiliarization), its other recurrences must also be meaningful. Thus, when close to midnight the father, having decided to bring the boy home in the morning, says "We must get him out of there quick. Otherwise we'll be responsible. Responsible!" (A13: 56), the repetition not only expresses the old man's precariously controlled feelings, but also emphasizes the words "responsible" for the benefit of the reader.

The words pronounced by a fictional character may, in addition to a direct deictic significance (what the character means), have also an indirect paradigmatic significance as ingredients of the story's overall conglomeration of motifs. In its immediate context, the word "responsible" means "answerable as the primary cause, motive, or agent," guilty of not having done enough to prevent the son's suicide. In a broader context, the word may be read in the meaning of "trustworthy," "able to respond or answer for one's conduct and obligations." It also has the ethical meaning of "having a character of a free moral agent."[9] Indeed, the reader of "Signs and Symbols" is not coerced into any definite position. We remain free intellectual agents, so long as we are "responsible" for what we say about a work of art, so long as we avoid hastiness of thought. Or, on another plane, of action. The potentially lethal effect of irresponsible telephone calls in the middle of the night is well known to those who have received such calls at times of private anxieties. The telephone is a useful gadget, yet it can turn into one of the "hives of evil, vibrant with a malignant activity" (A9: 4) that the insane young man considers all human-made objects to be. The old lady's hand goes to her heart after the first call. "It frightened me," she says (A14: 181), and the "quick smile" (A14: 182) of her husband expresses his sympathy, relief, and his awareness of the cause of her fright.

Carroll suggests that if under the influence of the recurrent imagery of death (an "overdose of meaning") we, the readers, decide that the young man does commit suicide, then it is we who "kill" the boy,[10] or rather become "responsible" (in the sense of "answerable as the primary cause, motive, or agent") for this death. Though this striking statement can be accepted only "in a manner of speaking," its rejection of the need for the kind of finality often represented by a character's death is within the spirit of Nabokov's philosophy. In a seminal paper, "Nabokov's *Invitation:* Literature as Execution," Dale Peterson shows that the fate of the character may be a matter of "execution" in both the conflicting senses of this word: the killing and the artistic performance.

Nabokov does not belong to the realistic writers who reject happy endings on principle and "kill" their characters in order to impress the "full meaning" or "meaninglessness" (as the case might be) of their lives on the reader. It seems that he would rather side with Kierkegaard's belief that "to regard death as a conclusion is a deceitful evasion."[11] Indeed, Hemingway's repeated presentation of a character's death as the highest expression of his identity in *For Whom the Bell Tolls* may have been one of the reasons for Nabokov's dislike for this novel.[12]

The ambiguous ending of "Signs and Symbols" is similar to that of *Invitation to a Beheading* where Nabokov dismantles the fictional world a moment before the gory execution of the protagonist can take place. He rejects physical death, while he also rejects the possibility of a reconciliation, of a false promise of "improvement." He does not allow us to forget "that all that comes into being must be ready for a sorrowful end," yet his open ending effects a muted variation on what Nietzsche calls the "metaphysical comfort" of tragedy:[13] it reminds us that the individual identities of the characters are but illusory bearers of the experience that can also be our own. The illusion of their discrete identities is cancelled just before they can be exposed to the most crushing blow.

The cancellation of the dramatic illusion (through say, the ambiguity of the open ending) is a metafictional technique that has replaced the tragic and the melodramatic heightening in modern literature. It is not for the sake of an exercise in self-reflexivity that the narrative of "Signs and Symbols" inquires into our interpretive conventions: the metafictional layer of significance places at an anesthetic distance (and thus cushions, controls, and makes bearable) the "endless waves of pain" that engulf the old couple, as well as the thoughts of

> the incalculable amount of tenderness contained in the world; of the fate of this tenderness, which is either crushed, or wasted, or transformed into madness; of neglected children humming to themselves in unswept corners; of beautiful weeds that cannot hide from the farmer and helplessly have to watch the shadow of his simian stoop leave mangled flowers in its wake, as the monstrous darkness approaches. (A13, lines 138–44)

At the same time the metafictional game prolongs the span of our attention to the story, thus keeping the waves of emotion on the near side of the threshold of consciousness.

III

Yet the significance of the story's metafictional inquiry is not merely functional. The criticism to which this inquiry subjects the reader's potentially excessive preoccupation with symbolism is a counterpart of the criticism to which the "human-interest" plane of the story subjects a potentially excessive literalization.

The literal, "human-interest" plane of "Signs and Symbols" is the narrative of an immigrant family and, in particular, of the waves of emotion that rise and break in the experience of the mother. The details of this story, a matter of brilliant artistic "execution," have some symbolic reverberations yet should also be read as subtly appropriate to its subject and cultural–historical setting.

Indeed, the "third landing" (A11: 90) on which the old couple lives may be read as symbolic: America is their third abode after White Russia and Germany. Yet this detail can, and should, also be read as an appropriate touch: the old couple lives not on the convenient second landing nor yet on the fourth, where they would risk heart attacks every time they climbed the stairs on their way home. The "hopelessly uncomfortable dental plate" (A12: 99) which the husband removes as soon as he gets home is likewise a symptom rather than a symbol. An uncomfortable plate is better than none at all, even though it is used for going out into the street rather than for eating (the lady serves "pale victuals" that require no teeth [A12: 101]). Obviously, the brother Isaac, on whom the couple depends, has financed the dental plate as well as their other minimally decent comforts, yet they cannot claim money for improvement.

The material culture of the new world is still alien to the old couple: the husband prefers his old coat to his nice blue dressing gown and the wife ignores fashions and cosmetics. The name of the neighbor, Mrs Sol, is significant not only as a symbol of solitude or a reference to the sun but rather as a symptom of the immigrants' adaptation (at a price, perhaps) to the new country: names are truncated from "Soloveichik" through "Solov" to "Sol." The wife's black dresses may be read as mourning, yet women in straightened circumstances know the value and versatility of plain black. The husband's being locked out of the apartment while the wife is shopping for supper may be read as a symbol of an exile's condition (he is also kept away from his detached son and from

an estranged brother), yet it is more significant as a symptom of
his absent-mindedness—in their silent grief both the husband and
the wife forget that she has his keys. The brief episode, moreover,
conveys their tacit and forgiving mutual understanding. The name
of the younger brother, Isaac (alias "the Prince"), may or may not
have biblical connotations; yet it is much more important in its
suggestion that the characters are Jews.

In the century of the greatest migration of peoples the predic-
ament of the old couple is not uniquely Jewish, especially since
the move from Europe to America on the eve of World War II was
made by people of many nations. Their being Jews is, however,
significant for placing the plight of their son in a historical context.
The specific mental malady of this young man is a morbidly
condensed expression of the Jewish experience in Europe at the
time of the Holocaust.

A little more than 100 years before Nabokov wrote his major
works, Søren Kierkegaard wrote a book about a mad preacher
whom he regarded as "a transparent medium for seeing the
confusion of [his] age."[14] The 19th century had entered the era
of rapid transition that gained vertiginous momentum in our
times: its resulting loss of ideological confidence was, according
to Kierkegaard, reflected in Magister Adler's life and work. In a
sense Kierkegaard may have recognized his own "secret sharer" in
Adler, and, since Adler was mad, his case acquired a particularly
problematic poignancy.

Some of Nabokov's works contain characters who seem to
respond to the slow processes that take place on the "inner
agenda" of the culture while remaining indifferent to the "outer
agenda"[15] reflected in media brainstorms. One of these characters
is the mad chess player Luzhin in The Defense. He is alluded to in
"Signs and Symbols": the insane young man's cousin is "a famous
chess player". Thematically, indeed, Luzhin is a related case, a
"cousin" of the emigrant couple's unfortunate boy.

The Defense indirectly reflects the intellectual confusion into
which Europe, and, in particular, its Russian population, was cast
by World War I and the Revolution. Paradoxically, the protagonist
of the novel, the chess player Luzhin, is minimally affected by the
irreversible changes in his fatherland: had the revolution never
taken place he would, most probably, still spend the greater part
of his life shuttling between the chess cafes of Middle and Western

Europe. And yet Luzhin is the kind of person whose fate literalizes the fate of his generation.

Both Luzhin and the young hero of "Signs and Symbols" are presented as having been mysteriously gifted children (the parental bias of the couple in the story is supported by the hospital staff's testimony that the boy's first suicide attempt was "a masterpiece of inventiveness" [A10: 55]) whose "secret stir"[16] of talent verges on madness. In Nabokov's works madness is usually associated with prophetic insight. In his pampered pre-revolutionary pre-school days young Luzhin's fear of the "unknown and therefore hideous"[17] outside world is far more intense than that of a regular sensitive child. He seems to fear the incipient chaos long before the historical cataclysm breaks upon the consciousness of ordinary people. Feeling intensely that the chaos is associated with violence and pain, Luzhin seeks substitute harmonies to counteract the "burning mist"[18] which the outside world forces upon his senses. He finds them in the involute game of chess, a harmonious world nested within a disharmonious reality. Since the place which the chaotic perceptual and moral data occupy in his consciousness gradually dwindles, a nervous breakdown makes him reverse the nesting and turn perceptual data and personal relations into moves in a cosmic game of chess. Thus, in an attempt to evade pain, Luzhin, like so many of his contemporaries, imposes an abstract, artificial system of relationships upon the complex multiform flow of contiguities. Yet unlike most of the contemporary followers of doctrines, dogmas, and ideologies, he takes this tendency to its extreme: the system of his choice is more abstract and schematic than any ideology, and it is in the most literal sense, not by way of any generalizing hyperbole, that he imagines it taking over his world. In other words, Luzhin's case, like the case of the young man in "Signs and Symbols," is not an allegory on the experience of his fellow wanderers but a *literalization* of the metaphors through which one interprets this experience.

In "Signs and Symbols" the young man responds not so much to the chaos as to what he interprets as the hostility of the universe. The photograph of the old couple's former maid Elsa and her "bestial beau" suggests that this alien world had come very close to the boy in his early days. Like all children, he endows phenomenal nature with conscious life, yet unlike most children, he finds this life strange and threatening. At the age of eight he is afraid of the image of a cart wheel hanging from a branch of a leafless tree. Such fears, normal in younger children who cannot distinguish surrealistic pictures from representations of reality, signal his tendency to confuse perception with imagination. Under the influence of "the shame, the pity, the humiliating difficulties" that fall to the lot of immigrants, of the hostility of the "backward children" in a special school (A12: 127), and the delirium of pneumonia, the boy eventually places himself not in the world of fortuitous sensations but in "a dense tangle of logically interacting illusions" (A12: 131) in which he is constantly persecuted by monstrous transfigurations of the surrounding world.

The story bears the date of 1948, and its first words, "For the fourth time in as many years," show how long the boy has been in his present state. This means that the onset of his irreversible madness roughly coincided with the times of the Holocaust in Europe,[19] a period which Humbert Humbert likewise (symbolically) spent shuttling in and out of psychiatric sanatoria. The shape that the madness takes is not inappropriate to the period when simian prejudice, lynch, distorted opinions, and grotesque misinterpretations were the order of the day, when the "dark gesticulation" transmitted awful messages, when nations, armies, classes, and societies conspired against the Jewish population, predatory spies watched its moves, and organized insanity conducted its destruction with such a scientific thoroughness that the very air it breathed seemed to be "indexed and filed away" (A11: 80).

The boy's madness has developed from his earlier phobias: it is as if some time before the Holocaust he could already sense what was brewing on the inner agenda of the times. And his horror is not mitigated by the security of the geographical remove: "with distance the torrents of wild scandal increase in volume and volubility" (A11: 83). The alliterating "volume and volubility" invoke the image of the radio, another human-made object, a hive of evil, "vibrant with a malignant activity which he alone [can] perceive" (A11: 82). Reports that he cannot understand refer, like everything else, to himself: as if what is known as the Final Solution were summed up in terms of "granite and groaning firs" as the "ultimate truth of his being" (A11: 85).

Though this type of madness is a response to its times, it is, nevertheless, madness. Hitler, his henchmen, and their apprentices are not "the world"; and an earnest belief that "the world is hostile" is a literalization of a hyperbole. And if such a belief includes phenomenal nature, then by advancing it we fall into the trap of the young man's animism even as we evade the trap of "referential mania." Phenomenal nature is neither hostile, nor friendly, nor indifferent: human qualities cannot be ascribed to it otherwise than by way of cautious personification expressive of an individual mood or state of mind. A responsible use of language avoids undue literalization just as it avoids an obsessive quest for symbols.

Despite its semiotic title, however, the story is not solely concerned with the uses of language. The moral universe is not so "hostile" if it contains as much tenderness, sympathy, and mutual understanding as transpires through the actions and thoughts of the old couple. The young man's tragedy is that in his "sullen" and "confused" (A10: 30) detachment he makes himself inaccessible to his parents' love.

The mother's interpretation of the boy's suicide attempt is vaguely in tune with the cautious metaphysics that runs through the whole of Nabokov's fiction: the young man tries to "tear a hole in his world and escape" (A11: 58), as if his world were a canvas painted by a wicked demiurge, while beyond it there stretched, perhaps, the unsullied transcendent eternity. In the language of *The Gift*, our days here are "only pocket money ... and ... somewhere is stocked the real wealth, from which life should know how to get dividends in the shape of dreams, tears of happiness, distant mountains."[20] The "solidity and height" (A11: 85) of distant mountains is unbearable to the young man in "Signs and Symbols," yet Nabokov's healthier characters love them, as they would love all phenomenal nature, with its puddles, its fruit trees evoked by multicolored jellies, and its clusters of "beautiful weeds" (A13: 142) haunted by miraculous butterflies. For Nabokov, the fragment of the divine within every human being belongs not only to the transcendent dimension but also to this very real world of ours: the "inner" mystery of feeling, genuine love, tenderness, stoicism, considerateness, and mutual understanding bind the two worlds.[21] It is not for nothing that Nabokov paints the young man's father as a bald-headed irritable old gentleman with badly fitting false teeth, and with age spots on his hands. It is not for nothing that the mother's hair is done anyhow and that she presents her wrinkled face frankly to "the fault-finding light of spring days" (A9: 17).

Nabokov is a painter of reality that is "part jewel, part mud"[22] and the reader shares his responsibility not only for transforming the "mud" into an intricate texture of significances but also for recognizing the jewel. The "jewel," however, is another figure of speech, perhaps another necessary symbol for the ineffable "something" that presents Nabokov with his "inner problem" and that makes itself known not through a literal presence or unambiguous name but rather through symbols and signs.[23]

"Breaking the News" and "Signs and Symbols": silentology

Joanna Trzeciak

"Signs and Symbols," by far the most studied of Nabokov's short stories, has been analyzed for its symbolism, its metafictional aspect, and more rarely for the links between its metafictional and narrative levels. In its most basic outline, the story concerns an unnamed Russian Jewish émigré couple and their birthday visit to their mentally ill son.

The emphasis of most scholars on interpreting the story's symbols in light of its open ending has privileged the symbolic level and perhaps has under-emphasized its equally rich literal level. Many have focused on exploring either the hermeneutic or the metafictional implications of the story's ample symbolism in order to derive a meaning for its open ending.[1] Moreover, because of the seductive analogy between the son's referential mania[2] and the reader's quest for symbols, in most studies of this story—those of Leona Toker and John Hagopian being notable exceptions—the emphasis has been placed on the son rather than on his parents.[3] A possible explanation for why readings have tended to focus on the son is the inconspicuousness of the pervasive, mutually acknowledged silences the couple share throughout the story.

An interpretation that offers the promise of a shift in emphasis from the story's symbolism can be found in Michael Wood's *The Magicians Doubts:*

> What seems to me most striking about the story is its immense shadowy background of pain and frightening possibility; not its secret, but its silence. It is full of things not said, fuller than Nabokov's writing often seems; and it may help us to see what's not said elsewhere; to see that even such a talkative, explicit writer has his silences, that his silences may be larger, more eloquent, than we reckoned.[4]

Following up on Wood's insightful and suggestive remark in this chapter, I advance a reading that foregrounds the story's silences, favoring its literal level over its symbolism and metafictional possibilities, with a bias toward the parents and away from the son. I then undertake a reinterpretation of the story's symbolism from the point of view of the silences, attending primarily to the half-said and the unsaid. Such a reading elevates the surface-level narrative to something suggestive of a much larger picture of unspeakable suffering rather than a mere "human-interest story" that serves as a vehicle for Nabokov's metafictional game of narrative entrapment. Once we turn to deciphering the silences, three foci emerge from the narrative details. These are, in order of increasing scope: parental love and the fear of loss; the tragedies of the Holocaust; and the fragility and finitude of life.

To elucidate the themes of parental love, the unspeakability of loss, and the emotional content of silence in "Signs and Symbols," the story will be compared with its 1935 predecessor "Opoveshchenie" ("Breaking the News"), which initiates these themes. Nabokov himself set the stage for such a comparison in a bibliographical note to "Breaking the News" in his 1973 collection of translations, *Russian Beauty and Other Stories*, in which he explicitly pointed up the correspondence in theme and milieu between the two stories.[5] As in "Signs and Symbols," the theme of "Breaking the News" is parental love and the unspeakability of loss, and both stories are set on/ cold spring days in the life of Russian Jewish émigrés. In fact, "Signs and Symbols" can be viewed as a post-Holocaust reprise of "Breaking the News," with the shift in backdrop effecting a change in the character of the silences in the two stories.[6]

The pervasive silence of "Breaking the News" is an unknowing silence. The story's main character, Eugenia Isakovna Mints, is a widowed Russian Jew who has adapted well to life in pre-World War II Berlin. Proud of her coffee, duck-footed, opinionated, eccentric, and gregarious, she is a well-liked member of an extended network of elderly Jewish émigrés. Severely hard of hearing, an impairment she uses to her advantage, she is able to "silence" whomever she wishes with a simple flick of the switch on her hearing aid. Hers is a world steeped in silence, where sounds are not heard but, rather, misattributed to things (for example, she takes the bun of her blood to be the hum of the town), lending the story a surreal, carnival-like air.[7] While surprisingly unproblematic and routine for her, her deafness presents a grave problem for those close to her, who pace, "akh, and

218 ANATOMY OF A SHORT STORY

"tsk" their way through various tribulations as they grapple with how to break the tragedy of her son's death gently.

At the outset of the story, the reader is laconically informed that, unknown to the widow, her son has just died. This gives the reader a narrative advantage prerequisite for the dramatic irony at work throughout the story. At nearly every turn, the widow meets symbols foreboding death, signs to which she is not at all attuned. In a telling instance, she receives a postcard with a loving note from her overworked son that uncannily reflects the manner in which he has fallen to his death: "*[I]a po-prezhnemu po gorlo zaniat i po vecheram priamo valius' s nog.*" In the Nabokovs' 1973 English translation, the irony comes across more strongly: "I continue to be plunged up to the neck in work and when evening comes I literally fall off my feet."[8] Likewise, to the reader, the gesture of a loving mother checking on her son's broken watch, in for repairs, highlights her blissful ignorance of the harbingers of death that crop up in the course of the day's errands. As she attends to her activities, reveling in the low-level hum of a world to which she is quite well accommodated, the reader anticipates the moment in which not only the news but also the silence will be broken. The silence of her world, which is initially used to somewhat comic effect, comes to signify her tragic obliviousness and ultimately the tragic obliviousness of the Jews in Berlin of 1935.[9]

In "Signs and Symbols," which falls under the long shadow cast by the Holocaust, the situation is quite different. The reader is given no epistemic advantage over the characters. The couple learns—along with the reader—of their son's attempted suicide early in the story. The narrative point of view, most closely allied with that of the mother, picks out the details of their day foreboding death. The parents' love for their son and their grief at his attempted suicide inform the pervasive undercurrent of silences.

The silences in which the couple engages are rooted not in obliviousness but in a shared tacit acknowledgment of the depth of suffering their lives have seen and in all likelihood will continue to see. Descriptive details suggest that the transition to the New World has been marked by loss and discomfort—Ellis Island's elisions have clipped the storied rabbinical family name Soloviechik to Solov, and even to Sol.[10] Unlike the émigré widow of "Breaking the News," who is able to indulge in the joys of good food (wonderful bananas, fruit jellies, fresh pastry) in the company of her friends, the elderly Jewish couple of "Signs and Symbols" is reduced to mere subsistence in the New World. Financially dependent on a successful brother from whom they are estranged, the woman is relegated to wearing cheap black dresses and going without makeup, and the man must endure a poorly fitting dental plate.[11] Companions silently sharing soft, pale meals, they quietly struggle with private memories of the past. Some scholars have treated the Jewish couple as oblivious,[12] but such a reading can occur only if the undercurrent of non-verbal communication between the two is taken for obliviousness. While the silences convey mutual acknowledgment of shared pain, it is the narration that gives the reader intimations of what they are silent about.[13] The wife knows her husband's moods, but it is not until late in the story that she learns, along with the reader, that it is the thought of bringing their son home that he has been mulling over.

The reader gleans from the couple's silent activities the extent of their loving preoccupation with their son—the husband's throat clearings (which his wife silently and tacitly understands) and the couple's inability to sleep (the mother stays up sifting through old pictures and the father arises from an unsuccessful attempt at sleep). Contact with their son has been made difficult by his illness—he is at both a physical and a mental remove. Critics have justly treated the childhood onset of the son's referential mania as a mad response to the (instinctively sensed) signs of impending doom preceding the Holocaust.[14] Likewise, his ongoing conviction that he is the semiotic center of the universe is a perversion of all of nature's unidirectional reference to God found in Psalms (especially Psalm 19) and the El Adon prayer. But neither the messages encoded in nature nor the process of decoding are joyous, and the unrelenting need to intercept nature's encryptions becomes such a torturous task that suicide seems the only escape. With distance, the son's torrents of torture "increase in volume and volubility," hence the parents' desire to bring their son home, hoping that close proximity will ease his suffering. Yet the real tragedy is that the son is ultimately detached (as Leona Toker has pointed out) and thus unable to acknowledge his parents' love or recognize their suffering.[15] The parents' world is marked by prolonged silences. Not only is the son unable to inhabit this space of shared pain, but he is trapped in a solipsistic world without silence, surrounded by the ceaseless drone of malevolent buzzing.

What allow the couple's silences to work so powerfully are the glimpses Nabokov provides into what they are silent about. The reader is left to extrapolate from a half-told personal history to the full-blown tragedy of the Holocaust. As the woman flips through her photographs, we are offered, as a backdrop to an abbreviated history of the son's descent into mental illness, a few snapshots of the family's life in Europe. These photographs, if enlarged and brought into focus, could well be the Russian Jewish émigré world of "Breaking the News" (a German maid and her fat-faced fiancé; a slanting housefront; "an old, fussy, angular, and wild-eyed Aunt Rosa who had lived in a tremulous world of bad news, bankruptcies, train accidents, etc." [A12: 115]). Moving toward a more literal reading of this passage—one contrary to some commentators' interpretations—the photograph of Aunt Rosa is not merely one of the story's many omens of the son's successful suicide attempt. Rather, it is above all the last remnant of someone who succumbed, along with "all the people she worried about," to a fate that the old couple escaped.[16]

The narration of "Signs and Symbols" moves between a point of view closely allied to that of the characters (principally the woman) and third-person omniscience. In the most lyrical passage in the story, the distance between the narrator's point of view and that of the woman is nearly obliterated. This exposes a train of thoughts and images in the woman's mind the likes of which presumably lurk behind her silences elsewhere in the story. Taken together, these thoughts belie what seems to be her worldview. Although much scholarship has focused on interpreting the rich imagery of this passage in light of the symbolism that appears in the rest of the story, I will examine it from the perspective of silence:

> This, and much more, she accepted—for after all living did mean accepting the loss of one joy after another, not even joys in her case—mere possibilities of improvement. She thought of the endless waves of pain that for some reason or other she and her husband had to endure; of the invisible giants hurting her boy in some unimaginable fashion; of the incalculable amount of tenderness contained in the world; of the fate of this tenderness, which is either crushed, or wasted, or transformed into madness; of neglected children humming to themselves in unswept corners; of beautiful weeds that cannot hide from the

farmer and helplessly have to watch the shadow of his simian stoop leave mangled flowers in its wake, as the monstrous darkness approaches. (A13: 133)

Multiple layers of silence suggest themselves in the language of this passage. First, these thoughts are unspoken—they lie behind the woman's silence and are given voice by the narrator. The train of thought here takes the form of silent protest, perhaps even silent resignation. Second, at least within the narrator's description, these words fall short of their target, an acknowledgment that pain lies somewhere off the coast of the signifiable, yet the words themselves are beautiful and moving in their incapacity.[17] A coherent, articulate discussion of pain would be too monstrous.[18] Finally, the linguistic markers—"this and much more," "endless waves of pain," and "incalculable amount of tenderness"—convey that the pain prompting these thoughts has an unfathomable, unquantifiable aspect.

Because many of the narrative details in "Signs and Symbols" seem to point to one another, much of the critical commentary on the story would have us believe that they constitute an interpretive key that leads to the solution of what appears to be the final riddle— the significance of the third telephone call. This is particularly true of the often and eloquently discussed numerical references.[19] Two assumptions have guided analysis of the symbolism in "Signs and Symbols." The first is that the third call is a puzzle that has an answer. The second is that the function of the symbols is to point the way to that answer. Both assumptions can be rejected. Although there is no denying that, in "Signs and Symbols," these symbols are richly woven into patterns of cross-referencing, it has often been tacitly advanced that the only mode of symbolism at work in the story is foreshadowing and that this Nabokovian technique of narrative entrapment might well lead down a blind alley. This is the so-called metafictional game. This engaging but ultimately fruitless search for an answer to the story's open ending (most critics agree that there is no one answer) suggests that the reader consider an approach other than the interpretive key framework.[20] The story's signs and symbols certainly play many roles, but they may be best understood as coordinates marking out the tragedy of people's lives, not as harbingers of impending doom referencing one specific event.

One is struck by the solitude and remoteness of the old couple's life in "Signs and Symbols." Their world is sparsely populated by other survivors whom they seem to know only barely. This can be gleaned indirectly from how few names are given: the estranged brother Isaac; a woman on the bus who—in characteristically Nabokovian fashion—bears a vague resemblance to Rebecca Borisovna, "whose daughter had married one of the Soloveichiks in Minsk" (A10: 52); the overly made-up fellow émigré Mrs Sol; and the family doctor, Dr Solov. The couple does not interact with any of these people in the course of the gray day presented in the story contrast this with the 1930s Berlin of "Breaking the News," in which a Gogolian cast of characters parades into the story one by one to inform and console the widow: the obese Chernobylski, who must throw his fat face back and out of the way as he fiercely bares his teeth to fasten his collar; Madame Shuf, "a vivacious lady with a somewhat exaggerated make up";[21] and Miss Osipov, "a tiny creature, almost a dwarf."[22]

When the unnamed couple in "Signs and Symbols" flees Europe for the New World, it is such people who remain and perish. Two emendations in the 1973 English translation of "Opoveshchenie" heighten its historical contrast to "Signs and Symbols." First, in the English translation, Nabokov explicitly sets "Breaking the News" in 1935, the year in which, not coincidentally, the Nuremberg statutes were put in place, severely limiting the freedom of the Jewish population in Germany.[23] Second, Nabokov chooses to render "*umer, umer, umer!*" (lit., "he's dead, he's dead, he's dead!") in the last sentence of "Opoveshchenie" as "dead, dead, dead!," broadening its scope. Through the grave irony of history, the phrase can be taken to apply to all of the Jewish characters in the story. In the world depicted in "Signs and Symbols," their absence is palpable.

Conclusion

The narrative and epistemic advantage enjoyed by the reader of "Breaking the News" is withheld from the reader of "Signs and Symbols." Rather than being made privy to the story's hermeneutic fulcrum early in "Signs and Symbols," the reader encounters it only at the end. Even there, it is not a crucial piece of knowledge but its suppression that drives reader response. Because of the open nature of the ending of ""Signs and Symbols," the prospect of the son's third suicide attempt echoes *backward* through the story. Of course, all of Nabokov's stories are written for rereaders and re-rereaders, but "Signs and Symbols" is a story that *provokes* rereading by virtue of its ending. The final act of silence, in denying the reader knowledge of what will happen next, is not trivial; nor is it an act of cruelty toward the reader. It is a way of letting the reader know that following the path of signs and symbols leads nowhere. And at the end of the story it is the parents who will "live on" to know the outcome of the third phone call, while the reader will not.

Pnin and "Signs and Symbols": narrative entrapment

David H. Richter

All of literature is potentially subversive in that its ironies lie in wait like traps to be sprung by the overly literal reader. Even the most attentive among us are likely to blunder into such traps more often than we know, since we only learn of our errors when we compare our responses with those of other readers.

But cleverness and agility are not sufficient to salvage our self-respect. As Umberto Eco, among others, has pointed out, a certain kind of text "lures its Model Reader into an excess of cooperation and then punishes him for having overdone it."[1] The author in effect makes the reader his ironic victim by seeming to license a response, then turning and attacking him for this presumptuous collusion. As readers, we repeat the mistake of Timofey Pnin, Nabokov's comic hero and "absent-minded professor"; we fall into the trap not because we are unobservant, but because we are "perhaps too wary, too persistently on the lookout for diabolical pitfalls, too painfully on the alert."[2]

In an article on irony in Laurence Sterne, I outlined three forms of narrative entrapment.[3] The simplest involves eliciting mistaken judgments or inferences—merely jumping to the wrong conclusions. Next in complexity comes the evocation of an inappropriate emotional response, like laughing at a dirty joke that turns out to be no joke at all. The most elaborate involves enticing the reader into a special mode of decoding the text, which the author then subverts.

Historically, these techniques began with Swift and Sterne in the 18th century, were largely neglected in the 19th, but have become major narrative devices in the 20th. Examples of narrative entrapment recur in elicited misjudgments in Albert Camus' *The Fall*, inappropriate programmed emotional responses in Nathanael West's *Miss Lonelyhearts*, and through a subverted reader involvement in Jerzy Kosinski's *The Painted Bird*. But if there is a 20th-century Laurence Sterne, a novelist whose impact depends primarily on ironic victimization and reader entrapment, it is surely Vladimir Nabokov. His use of these techniques may derive directly from Sterne, though perhaps a more likely line of influences would be through his compatriot, the ironist Nikolai Gogol.[4] The techniques explored here, in the novel *Pnin* and the short story "Signs and Symbols," are also apparent elsewhere in Nabokov's works.

Narrative entrapment is a form of moral corrective irony, and attributing to Nabokov such an intent goes strongly against the grain of critical fashion. His art has usually been treated as an abstract patterning of language, with minimal bearing on the sentient life that Nabokov, like all novelists, was immersed in. Nabokov has said, in his Afterword to *Lolita*, that he is "neither a reader nor a writer of didactic fiction," that for him "a work of fiction exists only insofar as it affords me what I shall bluntly call aesthetic bliss."[5] Moreover, it would be disingenuous of me to cite the "intentional fallacy" against Nabokov inasmuch as the following analysis of the ironic structures presumes that Nabokov had very definite intentions and knew quite well how to carry them out.

Nevertheless, we may want to inquire just what Nabokov means by the didacticism he despises and by its opposite quality of aesthetic bliss. Nabokov's notions of didacticism may be gathered from his essays on Maxim Gorki and on "Philistines and Philistinism" in *Lectures on Russian Literature*, supplemented by his views on the literary criticism that sees moral and social sermons everywhere—in the sheaf of "reviews" of Godunov-Cherdyntsev's biography of N. G. Chernyshevski, in The *Gift*.[6] While we must certainly heed Nabokov's plea not to read his narratives as social sermons, we need not turn him into a mere manufacturer of crossword puzzles and chess problems. In Nabokov's own analysis of the qualities that make up aesthetic bliss—"curiosity, tenderness, kindness, ecstasy"—three of the four have moral and emotional, and not merely intellectual significance. And thus it seems to me that, though Nabokov is not a moral writer in the obvious and brutal way that Dostoevski and Gorki were, he was as much a moralist as the writers he most admired: Pushkin, Gogol, and Chekhov. Chekhov's "The Lady with the Pet Dog" provides an example of the techniques and purposes of literary entrapment. In order to foster our involvement in the existential dilemma of Gurov's impossible love, Chekhov must first entrap us into misjudging Gurov as a shallow lecher. When the depth of his personality is ultimately revealed, as much to Gurov himself as to us, we become alienated from our false assumptions and from our former narrow perspective and the more engrossed in Chekhov's wider one. With Nabokov, as with Chekhov and Sterne, narrative entrapment entails the reader's mortifying self-exposure of intellectual and moral inadequacy, though it merely draws the reader further into the author's circle of greater generosity and broader understanding.

While some of Nabokov's harder-edged fictions may appeal to intellect more than the emotions, the qualities of aesthetic bliss seem especially appropriate to *Pnin*. But *Pnin*, like *Lolita*, is constructed around a single device of narrative entrapment—arousal and frustration—which is played out, like variations on a theme, again and again. This device in *Pnin* might be called the interrupted pratfall. Professor Timofey *Pnin* is placed in a situation which appears to be leading to some comical disaster, which the reader is forced to anticipate with *Schadenfreude*; at the last moment, however, the disaster is averted, or postponed, and we are made to feel not only a slight embarrassment but a conviction of the more complex patterns life weaves over the simpler codes of comic art. These ethical and intellectual issues, moreover, are finally related to an integral problem which the narrative presents: the truth of the story itself, which is told through a morally ambiguous dramatized narrator.

The interrupted pratfall is presented in its purest form in the opening chapter. There Pnin, dressed in clownish motley, is en route from Waindell College to the Women's Club at Cremona to deliver a lecture. He has been told which train to take, but in a misguidedly clever attempt to save half an hour, he has consulted an out-of-date timetable and chosen a train that no longer stops at his destination. Landing at a nearby town, he checks his bag and waits for the Cremona bus. When it arrives, Pnin finds that the station attendant has temporarily left his post, so that he must choose between his bus and his luggage. Pnin chooses the bus, but has not gone far before he discovers that he has taken with him a student's essay and left his prepared lecture in the valise. The professor gets off the bus quickly and emerges, sweating and terrified, in the public park of a strange town. Wrong train, wrong papers, lost luggage—where will this comedy of errors end? The reader, by this point, must be expecting something climactically ludicrous: that the lecture has been cancelled, or that Pnin has come on the wrong day. But in this he is anticipated:

> Some people—and I am one of them—hate happy ends. We feel cheated. Harm is the norm. Doom should not jam. The avalanche stopping in its tracks a few feet above the cowering village behaves not only unnaturally but unethically. Had I been reading about this mild old man, instead of writing about him, I would have preferred him to discover, upon his arrival in Cremona, that his lecture was not this Friday but the next. Actually, however, he not only arrived safely but was in time for dinner.[7]

And the reader who has without much difficulty anticipated disasters finds himself associated with the archly clever narrator, who finds anything short of Pnin's total mortification a breach of aesthetics on the part of the universe.[8]

One may find some variation on the interrupted pratfall in almost every chapter. In chapter 3, for example, the impending disaster involves Pnin's rented room in the home of Professor and Mrs Clements, which Pnin secured with much difficulty in the previous chapter. The setup involves Mrs Clements' visit to her married daughter, who is living in "a Western state"; soon after, a telegram summons Professor Clements to join them. By this point, any reasonably attentive reader has inferred a domestic tangle, an impending divorce, and the return of the daughter to Waindell, which will dislodge Pnin from his comfortable accommodations. Pnin has not only failed to pick up these signals himself, but he even disregards the warning given him by a friendly librarian ("I wonder if poor Isabel will really get divorced … I suppose we'll have to find you another room, if they bring her back with them").[9] Pnin is not deaf, but he fails to hear the warning because of his rage at the recall of a Slavic journal he needs, which—true to form—Pnin has by mistake recalled *from himself*. And one last turn of the screw, for the reader who has bothered to pay close attention to the narrator's clamorous hints, is that Pnin's eviction is scheduled for his birthday. Completely oblivious to all this, Pnin does research, attends the movies, retires for the night, and has "all but lapsed into velvety oblivion" when the invasion we have anticipated occurs. We hear the taxi arrive and leave, the key in the

lock, the voices of all three Clementses, but the narrator closes the
scene with a calculated anticlimax:

> ... a pair of young feet tripping up steps so familiar to them,
> and one could already make out the sound of eager breathing.
> In fact the automatic revival of happy homecoming from dismal
> summer camps would have actually had Isabel kick open—
> Pnin's—door, had not her mother's warning yelp stopped her
> in time.[10]

In this case, as we later find out, the disaster does actually occur;
Pnin, when we meet him next, is living in a different house. But not
only is Pnin spared the midnight eviction, we are kept away from
whatever scene may have occurred. Like the semi-pornographic
rhythms of Lolita that are turned, for the reader at least, into *coitus
interruptus*, in *Pnin* the reader is deprived of the expected scene.[11]

Later, in chapter 6, still another variation is played out, centering
on a beautiful flint glass punchbowl—an expensive antique—which
Pnin's stepson has given the eccentric professor. Pnin values the
bowl because Victor, the closest thing to a son he has, has given it
to him, but he assumes that the thing is of no intrinsic worth, that
it cost perhaps a dollar. When we learn, along with Pnin, that the
bowl must have cost hundreds, we begin to expect that the bowl,
by chapter's end, will be a mass of shards. By then, in fact, the rest
of Pnin's life is in splinters. At a party he gives to celebrate moving
into a new rented house he hopes ultimately to buy, Pnin is told
by his department head that he will be losing his job and will have
to leave the town—much less the house—to continue his exiled life
somewhere else. It is while washing the dishes from his party and
contemplating his fate, *sans* wife, *sans* son, *sans* house, *sans* job,
that a soap-slippery nutcracker drops through Pnin's fingers into
the sink, "where an excruciating crack of broken glass followed
upon the plunge."[12] But once more, the pratfall is interrupted just
where the reader expects it to be completed:

> He looked very old, with his toothless mouth half open and a
> film of tears dimming his blank unblinking eyes. Then, with a
> moan of anguished anticipation, he went back to the sink and,
> bracing himself, dipped his hand in the foam. A jagger of glass
> stung him. Gently he removed a broken goblet. The beautiful

bowl was intact. He took a fresh dish towel and went on with his household work.[13]

The chapters that do not have obvious variations of this pattern—like chapter 5, in which Pnin, taking a backroad "short cut" to a mountain retreat, unexpectedly manages to find his way back to civilization—have subsurface versions of it, disasters that are in fact triumphant escapes. Chapter 2, for instance, contains Pnin's long-anticipated reunion with his ex-wife Liza, whom he still loves. She turns out, in fact, to have come to Pnin for financial help for her son Victor; she is about to leave her second husband for a younger lover. Pnin wails after she is gone, and is sure she has no feeling for him. Yet both we and Pnin have seen "her cruely ... her vulgarity ... her impure, dry, sordid, infantile soul" and are glad that "there is something in ... life" that keeps them apart.[14] Pnin has gotten off cheap at the cost of a little heartbreak.

Again, in chapter 4, during Pnin's meeting with Victor, another disaster threatens. Pnin has bought for the 14-year-old boy a soccer ball and a Jack London novel, unaware that Victor is uninterested in games and is already reading Dostoevsky. He greets a little seven year old who gets off the bus instead of the gangling adolescent Victor, feeds the lad a meal he doesn't want, discusses obscure Russian etymologies with him, and concludes the evening by taking a genuine pratfall down a flight of stairs. And yet despite Pnin's oblivious eccentricities—or, rather, because of them—some real human link between them is forged. Victor, an insomniac at home and at school, falls asleep instantly his first night at Pnin's, and the flint glass punchbowl we see two chapters later is mute testimony to the love Victor feels for his fantasy-father.

Finally, in the last chapter, we see Pnin leaving Waindell a "superfluous man" (as the Russian tradition has it), detached from and rejected by his society. But the last predicate, "free at last," more nearly defines the mood of the last chapter. The narrator, Pnin's acquaintance and nemesis, whose meddling in Pnin's life has caused much of his misery,[15] and who has been hired to replace Pnin at Waindell, becomes trapped among the dim and incompetent colleagues who have made up the backdrop of the novel, trapped especially by his host and boss, who continually mimics Pnin's mangled English and his Slavic gesticulations. But while the narrator is stuck with his "British breakfast of depressing kidney and fish" accompanied by Jack Cockerell's parodies of Pnin, Pnin himself is off to some new place "where there was simply no saying what miracle might happen."[16] The pratfalls have always been interrupted; the Chaplinesque hero, despite his real sufferings, has landed on his feet. We are not surprised to hear once more of Pnin, in Nabokov's *Pale Fire*, as the head of the Russian department of another university.

If *Pnin*, structurally, is made up of this sequence of interrupted pratfalls, they are not phenomenologically equivalent as the reader experiences them. At the outset, we watch a clown's performances detachedly; the reader may be genuinely disappointed that Pnin's ultimate disaster is withheld. But as the innocent and suffering protagonist is further revealed, we are more likely to feel a keen pang of pity at his anticipated misfortunes, and to be relieved more than disappointed as the sequence continues. This progressive sympathy with Pnin is matched and balanced by a progressive alienation from the other figure who runs through the story: the narrator himself.[17]

One of the more peculiar features of the narrative in *Pnin* is that its seemingly omniscient mode is gradually revealed to be the product of a fully dramatized narrator who has played a part in the protagonist's life. As a result, the reader likely begins the novel taking the narrator's condescending comments about Pnin very much at face value. So few clues are initially given about the discrepancies between the author's values and those of the narrator that at least one critic has called the latter by the former's name.[18] Not until ten pages into the story is there a concrete indication that the narrator is actually a fictional character.[19] But the pretense of omniscience continues throughout the story: the narrator reports in vivid detail what Pnin does, says, thinks, remembers, and dreams about, without being, until the last chapter, physically present on the scene.

By the conventions of realism, the reader must posit the accuracy of the narrative. But as we respond to the hints that the narrator is a fictional character who has helped Pnin write a letter to the *Times* or vacationed at the same rural retreat, we sense the conflict between the intimacy of the narrator's vision and his absence from the private scenes he recounts.

In fact, there have been two major intersections between the narrator's life and Pnin's. The second, already mentioned, occurs when the narrator is hired to replace Pnin at Waindell: the narrator offers to allow Pnin to continue to serve under him. Pnin firmly and proudly refuses and his reasons have to do with their first connection. Around 1925, the narrator had been Liza's lover, and had subsequently rejected her. As a result Liza had attempted suicide and, after her recovery, married Pnin on the rebound. The narrator, then, has been indirectly responsible for some of the suffering Pnin has endured.

Aside from that, the narrator and Pnin have apparently been casual acquaintances and perhaps less than that. The narrator describes meeting Pnin around 1910 at the home of Pnin's ophthalmologist father and seeing him five years later on the estate of the narrator's aunt. These minor incidents are described in vivid detail. We are told, however, that when the narrator recounted them (around 1923) to show off "the unusual lucidity and strength of my memory," Pnin "denied everything," insisting that he and the narrator had in fact never met. Later on, Pnin warns a mutual acquaintance: "Now, don't believe a word he says, Georgiy Aramovich. He makes up everything. He once invented that we were schoolmates in Russia and cribbed at examinations. He is a dreadful inventor (*on uzhasniy vidumshchik*)."[20] While the final chapter accounts for some of the narrator's surface knowledge about Pnin's circumstances—the narrator has known Liza, her second husband Eric Wind, Pnin's émigré friends, and the Waindell people who have known Pnin—it fails utterly to account for the narrator's inside views into Pnin's private actions, memories, fantasies, and dreams. The only way we can rationalize the narrative is to presume that the narrator has, as Pnin himself says, made up everything; that Pnin is in part a fictional character created by Nabokov and in part a metafictional construct of the fictional narrator's.

But even more important than the philosophical paradoxes implicit in *Pnin's* dual authorship is the reader's entrapment by a narrative whose truth and moral authority are called in to question. On the one hand, the reader is alienated from the narrator who casually condescends to Pnin's harmless eccentricities. But on the other hand, to respond to Pnin independently of the narrator's comments about him is to grant Pnin a "real" existence which the narrative itself increasingly invalidates. While it becomes increasingly clear the Pnin's inward life must be (as we have seen) the narrator's invention, even the factual details the narrator recounts are accepted doubtfully.[21] The novel's ending, which released Pnin from that narrator's scrutiny and restores him to his freedom, at the same time releases the reader from the tightening grip of this narrational paradox. But the paradox itself is never resolved within the story, regardless of its interest in the context of contemporary metafictions in general and Nabokov's obsession with dualities and distorting mirrors in particular.

In *Pnin*, then, the more attentive the reader is, the more that narrative threatens to dissolve into a "dreadful invention" on the part of the dramatized narrator. The reader can escape, however, from the horns of Nabokov's dilemma. He can, like Page Stegner, ignore the complications of the narrative technique by positing that the narrator "is finally an unimportant figure in the novel."[22] Or he may, like Ambrose Gordon, Jr., dissolve the distinction between author and narrator, treating the work as a standard omniscient narrative with a chatty and self-conscious authorial presence reminiscent of Fielding and Thackeray.[23] While neither route is really acceptable, both at least free the reader from the paradox in which he would otherwise be trapped. To cut off both escape routes, one would need to omit the dramatized and self-conscious narrator; this would force the reader rather than the narrator to become the collaborator of the author. This is precisely what Nabokov has done in his 1948 short story "Signs and Symbols," where we are forced into decoding symbolic messages and are in consequence made highly uncomfortable about the meanings our own fabrications have helped to create.[24]

Our collaboration is further insured by the fact that any literal reading of "Signs and Symbols" is unsatisfactory. The story, as it would appear to a literal mind, concerns a day in the life of an émigré couple who try to pay a birthday visit to their son, who is an institutionalized paranoid schizophrenic. Upon their arrival at the hospital, they are told that the boy has attempted for the second time to take his life, and that a parental visit might prove too disturbing for him. The couple return home, prepare and eat dinner, and spend the evening reflecting, with the help of their mementoes, upon their own history and that of their son. Late at night, the father proposed bringing the boy home from the institution and watching over him in shifts. The mother agrees, and while they are discussing the arrangements, the telephone rings.

It is a wrong number. The same wrong number is dialed a few minutes later. As the telephone rings a third time, the story ends.

What is principally unsatisfying about this literal reading is the denouement. Had the story ended with the mother's agreement to bring her son home, we might have been willing to accept this as a plausible resolution of the instabilities of the plot, but the telephone calls disturb such a conclusion. The first two calls are wrong numbers, but what can the third be? It could be the same wrong number once more, despite the mother's elaborate explanation of the caller's mistake. Or it could be a different wrong number, or some friend calling with an urgent problem of his own. But given the brevity and economy of the story, the conclusion we are most likely to reach is that it is the hospital calling with news that the son has attempted suicide a third time—this time successfully.

Once we have jumped to this conclusion, a great many of the story's details, inert matter before, can be seen to foreshadow it. First, there is the pattern, almost universal in naïve narratives from folk tales to jokes, of two false starts followed by an effective third try. And so we expect that two wrong numbers will be followed by a genuine call, that the boy's two failed suicide attempts would next time be successful. Second, the mother is said to be wearing black, prefiguring her mourning. Third, the story takes place on Friday, the day of the crucifixion of Christ. Fourth, the subway train the parents take to the hospital "lost its life current between two stations" (A10: 23). Fifth, the mother sees, as she leaves the hospital, "a tiny half-dead unfledged bird helplessly twitching in a puddle," which may be seen as symbolic of her child. Her mementoes focus, sixth, upon an aunt put to death during World War II by the Germans, an aunt whose tremulous habits of worry about vague threats resemble the son's paranoia. Seventh, the playing cards dropped by the mother while picking up the mementoes include the emblem of death, the ace of spades. Finally, the boy's father is nearly desperate to remove his son from the hospital: "We must get him out quick. Otherwise we'll be responsible. Responsible!" (A13: 155). If we stop here, we are safe. But Nabokov has made it unlikely that we can stop hunting for symbols here. The story, short as it is, contains an immense mass of realistic detail which, once we have started, we continue to sift and examine for a significance that remains suggestive but elusive. What will we make of the parents' neighbor, Mrs Sol? Her name means

"sun" or "alone" —and what of that? What will we make of the
biblical name of the father's brother, Isaac? Is the father therefore
an Ishmael, an accursed exile? Can we understand anything from
the photograph, twice mentioned, of the parents' German maid
whom they employed in Leipzig? Or a fellow-passenger on a bus
with the mother, who resembles a woman she had known before
the Russian Revolution? If the ace of spades represents imminent
death, what is signified by the two other cards that the mother
drops at the same time: the knave of hearts and the nine of spades?
This way madness lies—and that is just the point, for this process
of symbol-hunting assimilates us readers to the schizophrenic son
himself, whose disease is described as "referential mania":[25]

> In these very rare cases, the patient imagines that everything
> happening around him is a veiled reference to his personality
> and existence ... Phenomenal nature shadows him wherever
> he goes. Clouds in the staring sky transmit to one another, by
> means of slow signs, incredibly detailed information regarding
> him ... Everything is a cipher and of everything he is the theme
> ... He must be always on his guard and devote every minute
> and module of life to the decoding of the undulations of things.
> (A11: 62)

Referential mania has become our disease as well, the story's
details a cipher whose meaning we decode and whose roots lie in
traditions exterior to the story itself.

But as we milk each detail of its meaning, our inevitable failure
to decode each physical fact and every gesture is bound to bring
us to self-conscious awareness of what we have been doing. And it
is then that we see that, if the boy's referential mania has ended in
his death, it is we who, in a sense, have killed him. In effect, rather
than allow Nabokov's story to end with a pointless phone call, we
have insisted for aesthetic reasons that still more suffering come to
the blameless and sympathetic parents who have already in their
lives suffered so much. In our symbol hunting, we have become
Nabokov's accomplices, trapped by the immortality of art.

Nabokov's use of narrative entrapment in "Signs and Symbols"
can be compared to the other cases of entrapment to which I
earlier alluded. With Camus, West, and Kosinski, this technique is
something more than a mere artistic device, ironic victimization;

there is a subversive political act, one which seeks to undermine our naïve confidence that we can remain guiltless in a fallen world, able to display clean hands and dissociate ourselves from the misery, crime and brutality our world produces.[26] There is some of this rage in Nabokov too. When we are entrapped into collaborating in the crimes of Hermann (of *Despair*) or Humbert (of *Lolita*), we are forced to acknowledge ourselves hypocrites lecteurs, likenesses and brothers. And when we participate in the pathetic destinies of Pnin and the émigré couple of "Signs and Symbols," this awareness of our own subterranean reserves of cruelty and indifference, brings us back into the fiction with renewed "tenderness" and "kindness"for those who, like ourselves, are Nabokov's chosen victims.

But for all this, there may yet be something more in Nabokov's use of narrative entrapment, something allied to the purely aesthetic "ecstasy" of which the author spoke in his Afterword to *Lolita*. William Carroll speaks of Nabokov's games with his reader as being like a chess problem in which

> the solver reenacts the creative process of the composer ... The solver must become ... the composer's double, his co-author, in effect. The relationship established between solver and composer, reader and author, is thus a bond of sharing, not an irreconcilable division. (A249)

The result, where the reader succeeds in rising to the occasion, is that "we share with Nabokov, for a moment, the incomparable eminence of the view from on high."[27] What this suggests is that through Nabokov's device of narrative entrapment, we become collaborators not only in crime but in creation.[28] As active participants and co-authors in making these jeweled fictions, we are privileged to see the narratives, not as simple imitations of life but as disciplined forms, shaped in aesthetic detachment out of the raw materials of painful desire and fallible memory.

Pnin and "Signs and Symbols": narrative strategies

William Carroll

My characters are galley slaves.[1]

The design of my novel is fixed in my imagination and every character follows the course I imagine for him. I am the perfect dictator in that private world insofar as I alone am responsible for its stability and truth.[2]

— *Vladimir Nabokov*

Being a character in one of Vladimir Nabokov's fictions is evidently not much fun. Arbitrarily created, the character leads a life inherently fragile; he is continually jostled, transported in space and time, forced into exile at the stroke of a pen, capriciously tortured, driven into madness at the last moment,[3] or abruptly "cancelled." As William H. Gass puts it, Nabokov's characters

> are his clowns. They blunder comically about. Clubbed by coincidence, they trip when most passionate. With rouge on their pates and wigs on their features, their fundaments honk and trousers tear. Brought eagerly, naively near, beauty in a boutonniere pees on their faces.[4]

As flies to wanton boys are we to our authors—they kill us for their plots. Or so it seems to a series of characters in Nabokov's novels and short stories, characters whose very position as characters-in-a-story seems to be one of the subjects of the stories in which they appear, and one of their own preoccupations there. Labyrinths, receding concentric circles, vertigo: Nabokov's fiction spawns special critical vocabularies and diseases in those who attempt to account for its persistently odd effect.

One way to a clearer perception of the aims of these fictions is to look closely at a few instances—especially at *Pnin* and the deranged boy in the story "Signs and Symbols"—in which a

Nabokovian character's self-consciousness resembles, though in a distorted manner, our own self-consciousness as readers. I am not invoking the term "identification": the laughter from Montreux would sweep it away anyhow. But these situations, these carefully arranged structures of self-consciousness, do seem, in curious ways, to be "archetypal" (another word Nabokov would never use). That is, our own sense of ourselves—lapsed believers in order unable to embrace disorder, dimly aware of coincidence and patterns in experience but trying to ignore their import—is often like these characters' self-awareness.

In *Pnin*, for example, Timofey Pnin tells Dr Hagen that "the history of man is the history of pain!"[5] The novel demonstrates the validity of that comment as it applies to Pnin himself beginning with Pnin's very name, in whose explosive pronunciation reverberates the word "pain."[6] His name also alludes to an 18th-century Russian poet whose most famous work was *The Wail of Innocence.*[7] The outer events of Pnin's life are painful enough: political exile, flight from two totalitarian states, the hopelessness of his marriage with Liza, above all the death of Mira Belochkin (and others) in the Nazi Holocaust.

> In order to exist rationally, Pnin had taught himself, during the last ten years, never to remember Mira Belochkin ... because, if one were quite sincere with oneself, no conscience, and hence no consciousness, could be expected to subsist in a world where such things as Mira's death were possible. One had to forget.[8]

And yet, of course, Pnin cannot forget. The world continually reminds him of all of this suffering, adding new refinements every day. At Waindell College, the suffering is more comic, but no less real to Pnin: loafish students, dull classes, obnoxious colleagues, confusion over American arcana such as railroad timetables. The worst of his colleagues at Waindell is Jack Cockerell, who cruelly parodies everything about Pnin that is different, from his clothes to his accent. In the process, Cockerell invents or reproduces legends and anecdotes about Pnin that never happened. The novel ends with one of Cockerell's errors—that Pnin brought the wrong lecture to the Cremona Women's Club—and it begins with a different version of the same story, in which Pnin was on the wrong train. But he did arrive and give his lecture.

The pain in Pnin's life originates outside of him. His inner world of linguistic research, mythography, and Russian history is secure, comfortable, friendly. But his pain results from an uninterrupted series of cruel intrusions from the various worlds in which must live. Perhaps the greatest intrusion, gradually revealed through the novel and most clearly seen in chapter 7, is made by the narrator.[9] Careful re-readers of the novel have seen that the narrator has turned up in Pnin's life suspiciously often: he helped Pnin write a letter to the *New York Times*;[10] he possesses one of Pnin's love letters to Liza[11] and his letter of proposal to her;[12] he too has previously been at the émigré retreat The Pines;[13] he has apparently had an affair with Liza before her marriage, who when dismissed by the narrator attempted suicide, then married Pnin;[14] and it is the narrator, as *he* tells us, "a prominent Anglo-Russian writer,"[15] "a really fascinating lecturer,"[16] who has come to take over Pnin's position at Waindell, a prospect which repels Pnin: "I will never work under him."[17]

Pnin's objections to the narrator appear to be twofold. In addition to the more obvious interferences mentioned above, Pnin distrusts the narrator's ability to tell the truth about him. The narrator's self-confidence—"Do I really remember his crew cut, his puffy pale face, his red ears? Yes, distinctly"[18] —is not shaken by Pnin's denials. When he tries to remind Pnin of former meetings between them and amuse him and others

> with the unusual lucidity and strength of my memory ... he [Pnin] denied everything. He said he vaguely recalled my grandaunt but had never met me. He said that his marks in algebra had always been poor ... he said that in *Zabava (Liebelei)* he had only acted the part of Christine's father. He repeated that we had never seen each other before ... noticing how reluctant he was to recognize his own past, I switched to another, less personal topic.[19]

The trouble is exactly that Pnin cannot recognize "his own past" in the distortions and fabrications of the narrator. At a dinner in Paris, while telling other anecdotes about him, the narrator is interrupted by an angry Pnin: "Now, don't believe a word he says ... He makes up everything. He once invented that we were schoolmates in Russia and cribbed at examinations. He is a dreadful inventor *(on uzhasniy vidumshchik)*."[20]

Pnin, in other words, finds himself the subject of still another cruel intrusion from the outside, another invasion of his privacy. He is the subject (as we eventually realize) of a kind of biography, a version of his life told by a faulty artist, a "dreadful inventor" who adds his own details, transforms others, and plays fast and loose with the truth. Which is exactly what Nabokov—and every other artist—does. It is the very definition of an "inventor," dreadful or not. It is this power of transformation which we praise and admire in our favorite inventors. Yet Nabokov has maneuvered us into the curious position of condemning the same power in the narrator (who is necessarily distinguished from Nabokov himself). We *do* believe, with Pnin, that the narrator is "dreadful." The suffering and pain in Pnin's life have been made so powerful, so convincing, so "real," that we resent the narrator's intrusion. Vertigo sets in again when we remind ourselves that the narrator is also a fiction, that Pnin is a fiction, and that our feelings against the narrator's inventions are in a way a condemnation of Nabokov's similar power of invention, the power which has convinced us of the "reality" of these figures in the first place. And on and on in circles.

At one point, rejecting the personal intrusions of psychoanalysis, Pnin makes another wail of innocence: "Why not leave their private sorrows to people? Is sorrow not, one asks, the only thing in the world people really possess?"[21] Yes, we say, our sympathy fully engaged. Yet Pnin's sorrow is not private; it is the substance of the novel. And it is the reader, as well as the narrator, who has violated Pnin's privacy. Those "private sorrows" are what have engaged us so deeply in Pnin's plight, and have engaged our anger against the narrator. Curiouser and curiouser. The act of reading the novel is thus itself an intrusion.

We are spared the worst violation of Pnin, mercifully. After the big party he gives in chapter 6, Pnin is told by Hagen that he will be replaced in his job by the narrator. When everyone leaves, Pnin washes the dishes, which include an aquamarine glass bowl, a gift to Pnin from Victor Wind, Liza's child by her second marriage. When Liza was pregnant with Victor, Pnin "was not only ready to adopt the child when it came but was passionately eager to do so,"[22] and a father–son bond has grown between them. The bowl is an emblem of that bond. While washing the dishes, a distraught Pnin drops a slippery nutcracker: "He almost caught it—his fingertips actually came into contact with it in midair, but this only helped to propel it into the treasure-concealing foam of the sink, where an excruciating crack of broken glass followed the plunge."[23] The pain of this moment, this apparent cruelty, is unbearable:

> Pnin hurled the towel into a corner and, turning away, stood for a moment staring at the blackness beyond the threshold of the open back door. A quiet, lacy-winged little green insect circled in the glare of a strong naked lamp above Pnin's glossy bald head. He looked very old with toothless mouth half open and a film of tears dimming his blank, unblinking eyes. (*Pnin* 129)

Nabokov, lurking as close to the surface as that suspicious green moth, pulls back from this worst of cruelties, though one which seems inevitable to the reader. "Then, with a moan of anguished anticipation, he went back to the sink and, bracing himself, dipped his hand deep into the foam. A jagger of glass stung him. Gently he removed a broken goblet. The beautiful bowl was intact. He took a fresh dish towel and went on with his household work."[24] The bond between Pnin and Victor, like the bowl, will remain intact throughout the novel; but this is virtually the only outside link Pnin can endure, and it is fitful and fragile at best.

As he has done in the past, Pnin makes an attempt to flee this inventor and his other intruders at Waindell. In the final scene, after a cruel anonymous phone call from Cockerell and the narrator during the night, Pnin drives out of town early (to avoid meeting the narrator). Walking in the town, the narrator sees his subject leaving. He emits "a roar of greeting," but Pnin doesn't hear him:

> I hurried past the rear truck, and had another glimpse of my old friend, in tense profile, wearing a cap with ear flaps and a storm coat; but next moment the light turned green, the little white dog leaning out yapped at Sobakevich, and everything surged forward—truck one, Pnin, truck two. From where I stood I watched them recede in the frame of the roadway, between the Moorish house and the Lombardy poplar. Then the little sedan boldly swung past the front truck and, free at last, spurted up the shining road, which one could make out narrowing to a thread of gold in the soft mist where hill after hill made beauty of distance, and where there was simply no saying what miracle might happen.[25]

A character in "flight ... from his author,"[26] Pnin breaks away, "free at last." The actual scene is a fitting emblem for Pnin's life, sandwiched in between two versions of the story about the lecture: "truck one, Pnin, truck two." It also suggests his larger imprisonment in the novel, between Nabokov and the narrator.[27] He is seen in a "frame" which both emphasizes and limits his situation; a "frame" which is an artifact. But Pnin "boldly" move out of the sequence, the rigorous pattern, and as he disappears into the mist, where distance has been made "beauty," we feel at least one miracle has already happened. On the last page of the story of his life, on his birthday no less (February 15), he leaves us— Nabokov, narrator, reader—and recedes into a spatial, temporal, and esthetic "distance." At the novel's end, he escapes the narrator to enter the world as a living, breathing fiction.[28]

The narrator, though, leaves us with only the parody of Pnin: Jack Cockerell telling an inaccurate anecdote. When we begin to examine the narrator's stories, compare the different descriptions of the same scenes and people, and realize his interference in Pnin's life, then we must begin to wonder whether Pnin hasn't escaped us too, whether the version of Pnin we have come to believe in, through the narrator, is any more authentic than Jack Cockerell's imitation. We can take refuge in the reply that Nabokov, after all, has created all of this, that he is the master inventor. But we have been led, in the process of reading this invention, into the bizarre position of questioning the right of one "inventor" to create stories. We sense there is a moral difference between the narrator and Nabokov; and there is. But there is no esthetic difference. It is godlike to create; it is unbearably human, and inferior, to be the subject of someone else's creation. The web of human inter-relationships insures that each human being will inevitably interact with others, will be, by turns, both creator and creature, master and servant. Nabokov's characters are "galley slaves" in that they know themselves subject to inhuman and autocratic powers; and we (and a few of them) know that the "galley" is both humankind's physical situation and the printer's proof taken from composed type. One's labor in life is analogous to labor in printed type.

Pnin's plight is sad enough, but that of the unnamed boy in the story "Signs and Symbols" is far more serious. A victim of incurable derangement apparently from birth ("As a baby he looked more surprised than most babies" [A12: 109]), with "no desires," the boy perceives in the world about him nothing but "malignant activity that he alone could perceive" (A9: 4). His parents are dull, sad people who are merely oblivious where he is paranoid. The boy lives in a closed system of signs, all of which point, malevolently, toward him. He suffers from "referential mania," as "Herman Brink" calls it. His situation thus resembles that of a character in an incredibly complex fiction, in which every single word, every image, every nuance, is carefully related to that character's life; existing only inside the system, the character cannot know what the signs are pointing to, can only dimly guess at the outside referents. Thus, in Nabokov's story, what the boy "really wanted to do was to tear a hole in his world and escape" (A11: 57). Death is apparently the only way open to him; his parents, trying to visit him, learn instead of his latest suicide attempt, "a masterpiece of inventiveness." An envious fellow patient seeing (apparently) the boy's desperate clawing motion, "thought he was learning to fly—and stopped him" (A10: 56). It is inevitable that the boy's cousin is "a famous chess player," a participant in another closed system of signs. The chessmaster Luzhin, in *The Defense*, like the boy here, attempts to escape his world through suicide, but fails: an eternity of dark and pale squares, another chessboard, "obligingly and inexorably spread out before him."[29] As a child, we are told, Luzhin, working through classic chess games, "gradually ceased to reconstruct actually on the board and contented himself with perceiving their melody mentally through the sequence of symbols and signs."[30] Nabokov clearly links the two cases together.

Referential mania is the ultimate, insane extension of the act of personification. Lunatics and poets are, as they say, of imagination all compact. The boy believes that

> Phenomenal nature shadows him wherever he goes. Clouds in the staring sky transmit to one another, by means of slow signs, incredibly detailed information regarding him. His inmost thoughts are discussed at nightfall, in manual alphabet, by darkly gesticulating trees. Pebbles or stains or sun flecks form patterns representing in some awful way messages which he must intercept. Everything is a cipher and of everything he is the theme. (A11: 66)

Signs, patterns, messages, cipher, theme: these are terms of literary analysis. The boy is the "theme" of all reality and of the story. The primary meaning of "cipher" here is "secret writing based on a system"; the system, the master writer, remains unknown. Bad literary criticism is a hunt for "keys" in this sense, making of literature something arcane and elite. But "cipher" also means, of course, "the mathematical symbol (0) denoting absence of quantity," or zero. This is the more frightening possibility; it suggests that everything is a zero, meaningless, without substance. The boy does attribute meaning, and it is this need to make such an attribution, a need we all feel, which, taken to an extreme, results in insanity. The intercepted messages may be in a code that reveals nothing.

After the cipher–theme comment, the unknown narrator of the story tells us of the "spies" who are "staring" and "gesticulating" at the boy:

> Some of the spies are detached observers, such as glass surfaces and still pools; others, such as coats in store windows, are prejudiced witnesses, lynchers at heart; others again (running water, storms) are hysterical to the point of insanity, have a distorted opinion of him and grotesquely misinterpret his actions. He must be always on his guard and devote every minute and module of life to the decoding of the undulation of things. The very air he exhales is indexed and filed away. (A11: 73)

The boy conceives of three different kinds of "spies"[31] or "inventors," then, those who have created and who monitor the closed system in which he suffers. And these three correspond to the kinds of rhetorical narrators used most commonly in modern fiction since James; the boy's personifications are the personae Nabokov himself uses throughout his fiction. The "detached observers" do not intrude into their stories in obvious ways; they simply hold the mirror up to nature, as the formula has it, and their emblems here are "glass surfaces and still pools," calm, neutral reflectors of the world around them. Nabokov's earliest novels and stories, like *The Defense*, are written from this point of view. The second kind of "spies" are those "prejudiced witnesses," seen *through* the glass now, not content with passive reflection, taking some active part in the ordering of things. One thinks here of the narrators of *The Real Life of Sebastian Knight* (an ultimately beneficent "prejudice") and *Pnin* (a malevolent one). The third type of narrator is "hysterical to the point of insanity," completely unreliable, one who "grotesquely" misinterprets the subject's actions. Their emblem is not the calm reflective mirror of the "still pools" but the turbulence of "running water, storms"—a version of the pathetic fallacy. The insane narrator is Nabokov's own special province: Smurov of *The Eye*, Hermann of *Despair*, Humbert Humbert of *Lolita*, Kinbote (for the sake of argument)[32] of *Pale Fire*. Mad artists, deflected or warped imaginations, offer oblique but spectacular perspectives on the nature of art, on the idea of transformation and distortion of "reality,"[33] and Nabokov uses them with increasing frequency in his work. As avatars of the imagination, these figures are our only means of seeing the world about them. Few other narrators in modern fiction are so astonishingly, so interestingly, unreliable.

The narrator–spies represent sheer terror for the boy, however; he is another character attempting to escape from his authors. But there is no escape:

> If only the interest he provokes were limited to his immediate surroundings—but alas it is not! With distance the torrents of wild scandal increase in volume and volubility. The silhouettes of his blood corpuscles, magnified a million times, flit over vast plains; and still farther, great mountains of unbearable solidity and height sum up in terms of granite and groaning firs the ultimate truth of his being. (A11: 80)

The "still pools," already given way to "running water, storms," are now "torrents of wild scandal." It is the extension, the completeness, of the system which is so terrifying: "a dense tangle of logically interacting illusions, making him totally inaccessible to normal minds" (A12: 131). The boy is the ultimate solipsist, dying from an overdose of meaning. The existence of one object which did not seem to point to him would represent the necessary "hole in his world," through which he might now and then seek relief. But there is none.

The boy thus lives continually in a world which seems governed by an all-powerful deity disturbingly like Descartes' famous "evil genius":

I shall then suppose, not that God who is supremely good and
the fountain of truth, but some evil genius not less powerful
than deceitful, has employed his whole energies in deceiving
me: I shall consider that the heavens, the earth, colors, figures,
sound, and all other external things are nought but illusions and
dreams of which this genius has availed himself in order to lay
traps for my credulity.[34]

The casualness of the "availed," the ubiquity of the "traps,"
increase the horror. Pnin has known this kind of a world, too, not
only because of the narrator's actions, but as a result of childhood
illnesses as well. The wallpaper in his room possessed patterns of
oak leaves and purple flowers which tormented young Timofey:
"he could not find what system of inclusion and circumscription
governed the horizontal recurrence of the pattern."[35] This childhood
fascination with pattern led Luzhin to the glories and terrors of
chess, but for Pnin it leads only to terror:

> It stood to reason that if the evil designer—the destroyer of
> minds, the friend of fever—had concealed the key of the pattern
> with such monstrous care, that key must be as precious as life
> itself and, when found, would regain for Timofey Pnin his
> everyday health, his everyday world; and this lucid-alas, too
> lucid-thought forced him to persevere in the struggle.[36]

"Evil genius," "dreadful inventor," designer," "friend of fever":
this is the artist seen from within his artifact, from within a world
in which paranoia is normality and the *deus absconditus* is a vain
dream. Descartes imagined such a world but turned away from it;
Nabokov imagined it and found a way for us to experience it with
him.
     "Referential mania" is a critical disease all readers of suffer
from. Our duty as critics is to explicate and analyze signs which
point to a single meaning outside the work itself, as in allegory,
or to another word inside the work, and the symbols which point
to various meanings simultaneously, both inside and outside the
work. Over-reading is another, milder form of referential mania,
and Nabokov has insured, through his rhetorical strategy, that the
reader will succumb to the same mania that afflicts the boy. The
story is studded with apparent signs and symbols that the gullible

reader—that is, any reader—will attempt to link together in a "meaningful" pattern. Most of these signs point to the probably successful suicide of the boy. On the way to the hospital, for example, the parents take the underground train; but it "lost its life current between two stations, and for a quarter of an hour one could hear nothing but the dutiful beating of one's heart and the rustling of newspapers" (A10: 22). Other things lose their "life current" and fall into darkness that day. The parents go to a bus stop, after learning of their son's latest suicide attempt: "A few feet away, under a swaying and dripping tree, a tiny half-dead unfledged bird was helplessly twitching in a puddle" (A10: 40). This seems inevitably to be a "foreshadowing" of the son's death, the sort of symbolist anticipatory detail found in traditional fiction. Confronted with a similar vision in *Ada*, though, Van Veen has a more skeptical attitude, one which we might well emulate: "A dead and dry hummingbird moth lay on the window ledge of the lavatory. Thank goodness, symbols did not exist either in dreams or in the life in between."[37]

The rest of the parents' day is filled with similar omens. A picture of Aunt Rosa reminds the mother that "the Germans put her to death." She dimly senses a larger power behind such events; but her vagueness is the opposite of her son's hyper-sensitivity. She has no idea of any source: "she thought of the endless waves of pain that for some reason or other she and her husband had to endure; of the invisible giants hurting her boy in some unimaginable fashion; of the incalculable amount of tenderness contained in the world; of the fate of this tenderness ... of neglected children ... of beautiful weeds" (A13: 137). The existence of cruelty and death are indeed without apparent "reason," they are "unimaginable." Yet they are here, in an imagined fiction, as in the world. Nabokov gives us all sorts of signs that death is near, and we learn next how it is the fate of the "beautiful weeds" that they helplessly have "to watch the shadow of [the farmer's] simian stoop leave mangled flowers in its wake, as the monstrous darkness approaches" (A13: 143).

That "darkness" seems imminent in the third and final part of the story; it is "past midnight" when the parents resolve to bring the boy home from the mental hospital, to care for him themselves. Another symbol of death appears when the mother picks up from the floor some playing cards and photographs: "knave of hearts, nine of spades, ace of spades, Elsa and her bestial beau" (A13:

165). The mother is oblivious to the ace of spades, a familiar harbinger of death, but she is startled then by the telephone, ringing at "an unusual hour." It is a wrong number. "It frightened me," the mother says. The telephone rings again, again a wrong number, asking for Charlie. The mother replies: "You have the incorrect number. I will tell you what you are doing: you are turning the letter O instead of the zero" (A14: 188). Absorbing the implications of *this* idea will take a moment. While it is a plausible explanation of the wrong number, the fact remains that there is no hieroglyphic difference between the letter and the number. We may recall an earlier line in the story: "Everything is a cipher and of everything he is the theme." Nabokov has placed us in the position of the boy here—is the O a letter or a number? Does it matter? Is this confusion a cipher—a clue to a hidden meaning? Or is it just null, a zero, without substance? It could be either.

The moment for our decision arrives quickly. After the second call, the father looks over the gift for his son: the ten little jars, each containing a different fruit jelly. He "re-examined with pleasure the luminous yellow, green, red little jars. His clumsy moist lips spelled out their eloquent labels: apricot, grape, beech plum, quince. He had got to crab apple, when the telephone rang again" (A14: 197). And so the story ends. What has happened? Who is calling? Surely most readers of the story will feel that the hospital is calling to tell them of their son's suicide, an event the mother anticipated at the first call. This is the *third* call, a most prophetic and ominous number. The sequence of "eloquent labels," from apricot to quince, has been broken by the flat, cramped sound of "crab apple," fruit which is tart or sour while the others are luscious and ripe; it is an easy step to conclude that the sequence of wrong numbers has also been broken by the "right" number, bringing bad news. And surely short stories aren't supposed to end with something as inconclusive as a wrong number? It seems that Nabokov has engendered in the reader (who eagerly assists him) a serious case of referential mania. A "cipher" can be a nullity just as easily as it can be a key, but most readers will see it as a key; we will conclude that the third call is from the hospital. In so doing, we will have assigned a meaning to the signs based on something outside the closed system; we will have, in effect, participated with Nabokov in killing the boy. The overdose of meaning is our own; we can't accept a third random phone number, but must see the "death-pattern" completed, because that is the way our minds work. Nabokov made use of the same fact when he seemingly broke Pnin's punch bowl; but the pattern there, as here, was completed only in the reader's mind, not in the work itself. Enough for Nabokov to have suggested the possibility. This strikes to the very nature of a created, fictional world, and the kind of relationship a reader has to it. We have felt pity for the boy, sympathized with the parents, but probably separated ourselves from the boy's mania. It is our very participation in that mania, however, the need to see a completed pattern, that has "killed" the boy. It is just as plausible to argue, though, that the signs and symbols of death have no logically inherent and inescapable conclusion; that they point to nothing finally, and are as "meaning"-less as a sequence of random numbers. It is this ambiguity which makes the story so profoundly eerie. The "cipher" is constructed so that we have to supply a key, constitutionally unable to admit the possibility that there is none. As in *Pnin*, we find ourselves, as fully engaged readers, seemingly exemplifying what we would prefer to reject, and vice versa. Both fictions encourage a denial of the power that informs them. Where is the essential paradox to be located, then—in the reader or in the author?

Both. (The coward's answer.) There obviously *are* patterns in Nabokov's fictions.[38] In *Speak, Memory*, Nabokov himself, moreover, after relating a coincidence involving a Russian general and a match, says that "the following of such thematic designs through one's life should be, I think, the true purpose of autobiography."[39] We perceive similar themes in every novel, every story. As Joan Clements, speaking of an unknown author, pants in *Pnin*: "But don't you think—haw—that what he is trying to do—haw—practically in all his novels—haw—is—haw—to express the fantastic recurrence of certain situations?"[40] Undoubtedly, we answer, for we have seen them. The rhetorical strategy of "Signs and Symbols" and, less clearly, of *Pnin* is first to offer "meaning" and "theme," to give us signs and the "fantastic recurrence of certain situations" and then deny or limit the pattern to refuse to complete it and ask, with the innocence of a child what pattern? It is yours, not mine. So we not only are *not* put off by coincidence and fantastic recurrence, by a pattern of signs; we are instead implicated in the pattern more deeply than we ever thought possible.

The author's self-consciousness in these cases does *not* distance us, as critics tell us it usually does; rather, it draws us into the web of esthetic responsibility, and our anger at the cruel fates which torment Pnin and the boy deflects from the author and redounds on ourselves, his co-authors. The most remarkable thing about the whole process is that, somehow, we participate in both worlds, in that of the character and the author, creature and creator.

Nabokov tells us in *Speak, Memory* that

> competition in chess problems is not really between White and Black but between the composer and the hypothetical solver (just as in a first-rate work of fiction the real clash is not between the characters but between the author and the world), so that a great part of a problem's value is due to the number of "tries"—delusive opening moves, false scents, specious lines of play, astutely and lovingly prepared to lead the would-be solver astray.[41]

The metaphors Nabokov employs here—"competition," "clash" —are, for once, misleading, for they suggest an absolute barrier between author and reader, an off-putting haughtiness. Thus Gass misconstrues the distinction between game and problem: "it's ourselves the moves are made against: we are the other player. Most of Nabokov's novels ... are attacks upon their readers."[42] This is too crude, I think. In a game, the competition is everything; in a problem, the solver reenacts the creative process of the composer, preferably in the same sequence of moves. The solver must become, as far as is possible, the composer's double, his or her co-author, in effect. The relationship established between solver and composer, reader and author, is thus a bond of sharing, not an irreconcilable division. The greater authority is still on the author's side, admittedly, in *Pnin* and "Signs and Symbols": at least, we share with Nabokov, for a moment, the incomparable eminence of the view from on high. It is a complex, and breathtaking, accomplishment. The nature of the trick is, I think, impossible to achieve in more traditional forms of fiction.

Through this labyrinthine process, finally, Nabokov has shown is what it is like to live in his world, and simultaneously reminded us of our position in our own. *Ada* tells Van of a similar feeling:

In "real" life we are creatures of chance in an absolute void—unless we be artists ourselves, naturally; but in a good play I feel authored, I feel passed by the board of censors, I feel secure, with only a breathing blackness before me (instead of our Fourth-Wall Time), I feel cuddled in the embrace of puzzled Will (he thought I was you) or in that of the much more normal Anton Pavlovich, who was always passionately fond of long dark hair.[43]

In "Signs and Symbols" or *Pnin*—in virtually all of Nabokov's fiction—we are required to become "artists ourselves," to assign and to be assigned meaning, with the result that the "monstrous darkness" the mother in "Signs and Symbols" fears is mitigated, at least, into a "breathing blackness," one which is not merely a "void," but a blackness which may also be a cipher that is a sign, a letter (and hence a meaning) instead of a zero. All of us, everything, is "authored" in one sense or another. It is the special achievement of Nabokov's fiction that it induces a confirmation of this in us, that it represents a confirmation in itself. Better to be a "galley slave," laboring in service of the printed word, than not to feel "authored" at all. It is a very small affirmation, to be sure, but we are grateful for all such things these days.

Pale Fire and "Signs and Symbols"

Vladimir Mylnikov

Nabokov's short story "Signs and Symbols" can be read as a paradigm of the writer's poetics. Extremely laconic, the piece is marked by an incredible depth of meanings, as well as a striking delicacy regarding human feelings and emotions. These two aspects marvelously complement one another. The story is extraordinarily lyrical, tender, and poetic—characteristics all the more impressive given the relative absence of rich metaphors and verbal interplay. The story's voice is appropriately calm, meditative, and in a somewhat minor key in accord with its subject matter and theme. But having read (or, better, reread) it, one senses that death does not exist in terms of objective reality: "Death is but a matter of style," the style in which destiny lays out human lives.

The major theme of the story is man's fate and the modalities of its realization. The theme is developed at different levels; biographical, subtextual, textual, and semantic. The levels interweave to achieve perfect balance and harmony. The biographical level is based upon a tragic event, the death of Nabokov's father on March 28, 1922. The level of literary allusion is connected with Pushkin's tale, "The Queen of Spades." The story's characters and plot constitute the textual level, while the semantic level is the summation of all these levels.

The key is the story's title, "Signs and Symbols." The ontological status of the "signs," as well as the "symbols," depends entirely upon our own perspective. Any event can be viewed as either a *symbol* or a *sign*, but the difference between the two is important. If the symbol, as a phenomenon, is connected to a person's perception, then the sign deals mostly with the message that destiny is sending us. Destiny speaks to us in the language of signs, but we often understand the messages by "translating" them into the language of symbols. But this does not mean that we cannot "read" them correctly. Generally, a single fact can be read as a sign or a symbol because its reality is encoded into signals which can represent the sign or, vice versa, the symbol. It is the directional vector (to or from the viewer) that creates these phenomena. The problem with human perception is that we often mix or substitute signs for symbols and vice versa. Real understanding of phenomenological reality, or even a step toward it, can be achieved only when we try to perceive the meaning of the sign without restricting ourselves to the superficial significance of the symbol. It does not, of course, mean that genuine comprehension of the sign automatically entails the correct solution. The sign is only an instrument, a tool, that helps us to decipher the message and to perceive its meaning through an interpretation. In its turn, the interpretation depends upon our aim and intentions.

The telephone is one of the most important thematic focal points in "Signs and Symbols." Its function and roles highlight the story's central theme—Destiny. It integrates all of the tale's levels. The phone can be read as a metaphor that combines two realities—Space and Time. It is the instrument of their connection. The phone, as a personage in the narrative, delivers a message that, in a sense, determines the story's textual meaning. It creates the atmosphere of mystery and suspense. It is not out of place, I think, to point out that the telephone has an analogous functional and ontological status in *Pale Fire* where its role is still broader, including such themes as television and electricity, which are also connected with the theme of destiny and death.

The third and last phone call is indeed ominous since the developing pattern bodes ill for the old couple: their unsuccessful visit to the hospital, the old man's negligence over his keys, his insomnia and foreboding of death, as well as still other small intimations. Brian Boyd's question, "Is it the sanitarium this time, calling to say their son has succeeded in killing himself," is reasonable, if perhaps rhetorical. We can, I think, provide an answer, but only if we will rely on semantic rather than textual reality: in other words, *we must read the phone call as a sign and not as a symbol.* On the textual level there is no answer, but on the level of the sign, there is. It is not the hospital calling.

Telephone calls and telephones in general hold, as we know, great significance for Nabokov. First, because of the grim news that he and his mother received on March 28, 1922. (This is perhaps why Nabokov disliked phone calls in general.) That day was, according to Nabokov himself, the most tragic in his life. Another parallel between biography and story is that the events take place in spring time. The young man in "Signs and Symbols" is, like

Nabokov at the time of his father's death, 22 (I disagree with Boyd, who thinks he is a year younger). These parallels are, of course, conventionalities and do not imply exact verbal or even textual compliance. In other words, it is incorrect to read signs as symbols by equating them. It is wrong first of all because it equates the present and the past and, in the case at hand, incorrectly substitutes present for past.

Pale Fire provides a similar thematic and compositional theme: the "death" of John Shades' 22-year-old daughter, Hazel; the spring setting (March); and, finally, a telephone call. These all correspond to the facts of "Signs and Symbols." Thus, from a biographical point of view, it is tempting to assume that the final telephone call *was* from the sanitarium. But first, a question: How did Nabokov respond to his father's death? Did he actually believe he was dead? No. His father's death does not exist in his poetical reality and probably not in his mental life. Perhaps the best answer is in Nabokov's poem "Easter," which was dedicated to his father's death. Just after the event Nabokov wrote: "But if all the brooks sing anew of miracle ... then you are in that song, you are in that gleam, you are alive." This view is found throughout Nabokov's life and works. It is even proleptic: Véra Nabokov was to die at Easter tide. Nabokov's genius transformed the fatal event into a different reality. On that fatal day, Destiny sent Vladimir and his mother a message, but Nabokov recreated the symbol as a sign.

"Signs and Symbols" is a story, a text, and the decipherment of the final phone call should not be carried out as it was on the biographical level. It is wrong to read past as present because we need not observe the established ordering of real or textual realities. This is why I would argue that the phone call does not come from the hospital.

The card theme provides another clue that Nabokov drew the story's events from those of March 28. Nabokov's diary records that on that evening he was reading a small volume of Blok's poetry while his mother was laying out a game of patience. "Signs and Symbols" also has its card scene. Just before the first phone call, the young man's mother picks up three cards that have fallen from the sofa to the floor. They are the knave of hearts, the nine of spades and ace of spades. The literary illusion is unmistakable. The three cards and their sequence is identical with those given to Pushkin's Chekalinsky by the old Countess, the "Queen of

Spades." Chekalinsky wins, but Hermann who has forced the secret from the Countess and caused her death, loses when the spade ace on which he has staked all of his winnings is replaced by the fateful queen of spades. Herman goes mad.[1]

Nabokov's "Signs and Symbols" shares the three themes of Pushkin's "Queen of Spades": cards, madness, and destiny. The same elements occur in Nabokov's story, but the role of cause and effect is quite different. The problem is to read the elements correctly, to avoid confusing sign with symbols. In Nabokov's view, it is clear that Herman went mad because he took a sign as a symbol. He wanted to "unlock" the real world with the wrong key. He simplified reality by reducing it to a secret code. In Nabokov's story the boy's madness, called "referential mania" by psychiatrist Herman(!) Brink, offers the reverse point of view. The young man, or more accurately, his mind, is in the external world and he wants only to flee from it. Suicide is his way out. We can assume he is finally successful, but, again, there is no textual proof. The story's semantic level tends to point to a different conclusion.

Death for Nabokov was a mask over reality, a false sign. The human mind cannot fully decipher this code without creating new terms for realities. There is presumably only one power that can do so—Destiny. But Destiny sends us only signs which we tend to convert (and often mis-convert) into symbols. Herman's madness is caused by his need to get in touch with the otherworld and he ultimately finds atonement. His obsession causes the death of the Countess and this is yet another cause of his madness. The textual terms in "Signs and Symbols" apply to the other interpretation of his madness. His "referential mania" may be understood as a form of genius, reading reality as signs without confusing them with symbols. But Nabokov's character lacks creativity and even, to some extent, personality. He lives in a totally different reality. Hence:

> Clouds in the staring sky transmit to one another, by means of slow *signs* [emphasis added], incredibly detailed information regarding him. His inmost thoughts are discussed at nightfall, in manual alphabet, by darkly gesticulating trees. Pebbles or stains or sun flecks form patterns representing in some awful way messages, which he must intercept. Everything is a cipher and of everything he is the theme.

John Shade creates a similar poetic expression of existence in his poem "Pale Fire." Canto Two opens:

> There was a time in my demented youth
> When somehow I suspected that the truth
> About survival after death was known to every human being:
> I alone Knew nothing, and a great conspiracy
> Of books and people hid the truth from me.
> There was the day when I began to doubt
> Man's sanity: How could he live without
> Knowing for sure what dawn, what death, what doom
> Awaited consciousness beyond the tomb?

Finally, I would like to point out that here again we find three thematically connected themes—death, doom, and consciousness. They are framed by the sign that is the symbol in question.

PART SIX
DNA Testing

Cracking the code

The signs and symbols in Nabokov's "Signs and Symbols"
Alexander Dolinin

In his famous letter to Katharine A. White, the chief editor of *The New Yorker*, while explaining the intricate riddle-like structure of "The Vane Sisters," which had been rejected by the magazine, Nabokov mentioned that some of his stories written in the past had been composed according to the same system "wherein a second (main) story is woven into, or placed behind, the superficial semitransparent one."[1] As an example, he named another story with such an "inside"—"Signs and Symbols," which had been published in *The New Yorker*.

Thanks to Nabokov's explanations, the "inner scheme" of "The Vane Sisters" has become a common property. It is a story of the intervention by gentle spirits (or ghosts) into the reality of the narrator, "a callous observer of the superficial planes of life," crowned by the secret message in the finale that can be decoded by the rules of acrostic reading. To quote the letter to Katharine A. White again, "everything in the tale leads to one recurring end, or rather forms a delicate circle, a system of mute responses, not realized by the Frenchman but directed by some unknown spirit at readers."[2] Yet numerous critics of "Signs and Symbols" so far have failed to discover a similar "inside" in the story, which, as everybody believes, should hinge upon a mystery of the third, unanswered telephone call at the very end and its interpretation. While one line of criticism has been to focus on the obvious patterning of images and incidents in the narration and to read them as ominous "signs and symbols" indicating that the third call is a death notice from the sanatorium,[3] the majority—from William Carroll's pioneering article of 1974[4] up to Irving Malin's recent coquettish blabber[5] — has chosen the reader-response approach. Most of the critics have embraced William Carroll's provocative idea that those readers who interpret numerous "signs and symbols" in the story as clues allowing one to solve the puzzle are guilty of "referential mania" and therefore bear an "esthetic responsibility" for the boy's death. In spite of Nabokov's attesting to the presence of a "second (main) story" behind "the superficial semitransparent one" in "Signs and Symbols," they either deny its existence or question its relevance. Thus, in his book *The Magician's Doubts*, Michael Wood writes that Nabokov's comment makes "the work sound more like a riddle than it probably is" and reads it as a vague metaphor. In his view, a second story in "Signs and Symbols" concerns not the characters—"the old Jewish couple and their sick boy"—but us, the readers, and our response to the mystery of the third telephone call: "In the second story, the young man's world invades ours; his clouds and trees become our telephone, and a new pain, the pain of a new uncertainty, is visited upon the innocent and the guilty alike."[6]

Contrary to the prevailing line of criticism, I take Nabokov at his word and argue in this article that "Signs and Symbols," like "The Vane Sisters," is constructed according to a specific "system" of concealment and does contain a neat soluble riddle whose function is similar to the acrostic puzzle in the later story.

To understand what Nabokov means by his "system" of two superimposed stories, it can be helpful to recall a classical dichotomy of *siuzhet* (the plot) and *fabula* (the story) introduced by the Russian formalists. In their parlance, *fabula* is the sum total of interconnected textual events (or motifs) in chronological and causal order, in contrast to *siuzhet*, which consists of the same events as they are actually presented in the narrative. As Boris Tomashevsky wrote,

> the place in the work in which the reader learns of an event, whether the information is given by the author, or by a character, or by a series of indirect hints—all this is irrelevant to the story.

But the aesthetic function of the plot is precisely this bringing of an arrangement of motifs to the attention of the reader.[7]

Nabokov's peculiar strategy that he used sparingly but persistently throughout his mature work is to create a discrepancy or a tension between *siuzhet* and *fabula* of a text through enigmatizing certain important elements of the latter. He constructs the narrative in such a way that it does not contain any direct or even indirect reference to an important, usually pivotal event (or a number of events) of the fibula and disguises this ellipsis. For example, instead of presenting such climatic events as death of the protagonist in "Lik," a betrayal and murder out of jealousy in "That in Aleppo Once ..." or supernatural intervention in "The Vane Sisters," the plots of these short stories deliberately conceal them, superseding the textual "reality" with false or incomplete accounts of it. However, narration of this kind not only hides or masks the important event, but also provides the reader with adequate means to deduce it and thereby construe the *fabula* in its entirety. Relevant information related to the omitted event (or events) is encrypted in the *siuzhet* as a kind of intratextual riddle (often supported by intertextual references), and specifically marked clues to the pertinent code are implanted into the text.

That is exactly what Nabokov had in mind when he wrote to Katharine White that the reader of "The Vane Sisters" "almost automatically slips into" the discovery of an encrypted message from the other world if he pays attention to "various allusions to trick-reading" in the story.[8] Actually, the narrator of "The Vane Sisters" refers to the forming of words from the initials of words three times. First, he mentions the acrostic puzzle in connection with the death of Cynthia's friend, an eccentric librarian called Porlock who had been engaged in examining old books for miraculous misprints such as the substitution of "l" for the second "h" in the word "hither." When Cynthia, "on the third day after his death," read a quotation from Coleridge's "Kubla Khan," "it dawned upon her that 'Alph' is a prophetic sequence of 'the **initial letters** of Anna Livia Plurabelle' ... while the additional 'h' modestly stood, as a private signpost, for the word that so hypnotized Mr Porlock."[9] After that, the narrator talks about a "novel or short story (by some contemporary writer, I believe) in which, unknown to the author, the **first letters of the words** in its **last paragraph** formed, as **deciphered** by Cynthia, a message from his dead mother."[10] When a friend informs the narrator of Cynthia's death, he finds himself plunging into Shakespeare's sonnets and "idiotically checking **the first letters** of the lines to see what sacramental words they might form."[11] These allusions to procedures of deciphering and acrostical reading conjoint with the theme of death serve as invitations to decoding: they are supposed to alert the reader to the acrostical code used for encrypting the relevant information and make him apply it to the stylistically marked passage at the very end of the story. Likewise, numerous allusions to anagrams in *Bend Sinister* signalize the presence of a hidden anagrammatic message in the novel that can be found and deciphered by the reader.[12] Of course, omitted or veiled events and codes used for solving an intratextual riddle would be different in each text, but "the system" of encrypting always remains the same: the text itself incorporates a set of clues that indicate which code is needed to decipher encrypted information and to fill a gap in the *fabula*.

Let us see how this system works in "Signs and Symbols," a story that in comparison to "The Vane Sisters" presents a much more difficult case, because it alludes, both directly and obliquely, to several interpretative codes, and our primary task is to select the one that can be applied to a riddle hidden in the text. Critical attention so far has been focused, of course, on the "referential mania" of the insane protagonist, who believes that "everything happening around him is a veiled reference to his personality and existence":

> Phenomenal nature shadows him wherever he goes. Clouds in the staring sky transmit to one another, by means of slow signs, incredibly detailed information regarding him. His inmost thoughts are discussed at nightfall, in manual alphabet, by darkly gesticulating trees. Pebbles or stains or sun flecks form patterns representing in some awful way messages which he must intercept. Everything is a cipher and of everything he is the theme ... He must be always on his guard and devote every minute and module of life to the decoding of the undulation of things.[13]

Some critics argue that Nabokov, planting patterned, symbolically charged details, deliberately entraps the reader of "Signs and Symbols" into a sort of over-interpretation similar to the "referential mania" of the insane character, making us read the story as if everything in it were a cipher. Yet the idea of seeing a model for the reader's response in the boy's pan-semiotic approach to reality, however tempting, should be rejected from the very start for several simple reasons. First, "referential mania" is limited to natural phenomena (clouds, trees, sun flecks, pools, air, mountains) and random artifacts (glass surfaces, coats in store windows), but "excludes real people from the conspiracy," while the story deals with human beings in the urban setting and focuses upon cultural systems of communication and transportation: the underground train, the bus, the Russian-language newspaper, the photographs, the cards, the telephone, the labels on the jelly jars. The only exception is the image of "a tiny half-dead unfledged bird" helplessly twitching in a puddle "under a swaying and dripping tree" —a symbolic parallel to the sick boy's situation and his parents' perception of him.

Second, the boy's reading of the world is auto-referential and egocentric (every alleged signifier refers only to the boy himself), while the story concerns three major characters and a dozen minor ones, whether named or unnamed.

Last but not least, "referential mania," unlike the "allusions to trick-reading" in "The Vane Sisters," does not point at any applicable code, as the boy himself is unable to decipher secret messages: he surmises only their "theme" (himself), their intent (evil, malicious, threatening), and their validity (they misinterpret and distort), but not their actual content. So the description of "referential mania" cannot serve as a "prompt" suggesting some way of identifying and solving a textual riddle; instead of providing a specific clue, it sets metafictional guidelines, introducing a group of semiotic motifs that refer to the structure of the text itself. If cleared of their psychiatric smokescreen, the key words in the passage form a kind of instruction for the reader to "puzzle out" an inherent "system" of the story, to look for a "veiled reference" to the boy's fate—its central "theme," to "intercept" and "decode" some "transmitted" message containing "information regarding him," to crack a "cipher" encrypted "in manual alphabet." The boy's paranoia (and, by implication, a fallacy of symbolic reading) lies not in the processes of his thought, but in their misapplication: to comprehend any sign one must first ascertain the signifying system in which it functions.

The metafictional commentary is complemented by Nabokov's stock auto-allusions. It has been noted that the boy's cousin, a "famous chess player,"[14] "is perhaps a projection of Luzhin in Nabokov's *Defense*, who is also a victim of referential mania."[15] A metaphorical description of the boy's failed suicide as an attempt "to tear a **hole** in his world and escape" (A11: 58) parallels the final episode of *The Defense* in which Luzhin makes a "black, star-shaped **hole**" in the frosted window glass and "drops out of the game."[16] In addition, the image of "wonderful birds with human hands and feet" that the boy drew at the age of six (A12: 119) can be interpreted as a "veiled reference" to Nabokov's Russian penname, Sirin, derived from the name of a fairytale bird with a human head and breast.[17] This implies a connection between the character and the author of the story, but, again, does not allow us to deduce a hidden event.

There is also a strong hint at a divinational code, as the three cards that slip from the couch to the floor are conspicuously named (knave of hearts, nine of spades, ace of spades) and form a standard fortune-telling packet or triad. If interpreted according to a traditional Russian system, they seem to foretell some tragic loss (ace of spades), grief and tears (nine of spades) with respect to a single young man (knave of hearts).[18] At first glance, the triad refers to the boy and therefore predicts his imminent death, to be announced by the third telephone call. Yet in cardomancy, to quote the *Encyclopaedia Britannica*, "the same 'lie' of the cards may be diversely interpreted to meet different cases," and much depends on the position of a card representing the object of fortune telling. It is significant that Nabokov's divinational "packet" of three cards is "laid" side by side with photographs of the couple's German maid Elsa and her "bestial beau," who in the context of the story personify forces of evil responsible for the suffering of the innocent, for the death of Aunt Rosa and "all the people she had worried about," and for the Holocaust. Their representations then should be regarded as an integral part of the whole "lie"—as quasi-cards standing for the "inquirers" of fortune telling. It is to the dismal fate of blondes Besties at the end of World War II that the ominous combination of spades refers: the cards foretell the "monstrous darkness" of disaster and death not to the boy and his parents but to their torturers and butchers, while the fate of the innocent remains untold.

The sequence of three cards and two photographs, however, brings us to the last potential code suggested by the text—to numerical cryptography and numerology. From the very start the narration in "Signs and Symbols" registers and emphasizes numbers (cf.: "For the **fourth** time in **as many** years," "a basket with **ten** different fruit jellies in **ten** little jars," "a **score** of years," "of **forty** years standing"); all the major incidents, images and motives in the text are arranged into well ordered patterns or series. There are allusions to and short sequences of three based on the universal paradigm of birth/life/death and corresponding to the three sections of the story. The couple lives on the third floor; they go through three misfortunes on their way to the hospital (underground, bus, rain), and encounter three bad omens on their way back (a bird, a crying girl, and misplaced keys); the name of Soloveichik (from the Russian for nightingale), the old woman's friend, is echoed twice in the truncated, Americanized versions Solov and Sol; as we have seen, three cards fall to the floor and, of course, there are three telephone calls in the finale.

Even more prominent are sequences of five, some of which result from addition (three cards + two photos; three "nightingale names" + two images of birds). The story begins on Friday, the fifth day of the week; the life of the couple has passed through five locations (Minsk, Leipzig, Berlin, Leipzig, New York); the woman looks at five photographs of her son that represent five stages of his descent into madness—from a sweet baby to a sour, insane boy of ten, "inaccessible to normal minds"; in the end the father reads five "eloquent labels" on the fruit jelly jars—apricot, grape, beech plum, quince, and crab apple, a series that mimics the deterioration of the boy from the sweetest to the sourest (A12: 132).

At last, there is the longest and singular sequence of "**ten** different fruit jellies in **ten** little jars" (A9: 9), which is connected to a theme of birth (after all, it is the birthday present) and is mentioned five times in the text.[19] Critics have noted that the recurrence of the motif and its conspicuous placement at the most marked points of the text—in the first paragraph, in the beginning of section two, and in the finale—suggest some symbolic significance, but so far

have offered mostly vague and sometimes preposterous interpretations.[20] Only Gennady Barabtarlo, who was the first to notice that
the five named flavors of the jellies "are arranged in the order of
rising astringency and somehow answer the five photographs of
her son that the woman examined an hour earlier," has ingeniously
suggested that the set of ten jellies serves as "the key to an invisible
over-plot" of the story, though he stopped short of using the master
key to unlock a hidden *fabula*.[21]

Discussing the enigma of the little jars, it is necessary to keep
in mind that the sequence of labels is "spelled out"[22] only to the
middle point, and we do not know what fruit comes after crab
apple. In numerical terms, it means that ten is presented here as
the double of five, which implies the duality of being, its split into
the known/unknown halves. The only thing we can more or less
safely bet on is that the jellies in the jars from number six on won't
be bitterer than crab apple in the fifth one. If projected upon the
life-stories of the insane boy and his parents, this duality infers
a jarring question: is there anything for them beyond the misery of
their present situation but "the monstrous darkness of death"? As
in the case of the ten jars, we know the meaning of the five stages
in their lives but do not seem to have any clue to their future.

However, I believe that there is such a clue in the story and that
it is succinctly "spelled out" by the old woman when she answers
two after-midnight telephone calls from a nameless girl:

> "Can I speak to Charlie," said a girl's dull little voice.
> "What number you want? No. That is not the right number." [...]
> The telephone rang for a second time. The same toneless anxious
> young voice asked for Charlie.
> "You have the incorrect number. I will tell you what you are doing;
> you are turning the letter O instead of the zero." (A14: 177)

The very word "number" repeated three times by the old woman
indicates that the reader should give more consideration to her
seemingly casual remarks than it has been done in previous
criticism. What is most amazing about the old woman's response
is that she confronts the nuisance as a kind of a numerical riddle.
The woman actually subjects Charlie's number misdialed by the
girl to scrutiny and notices that it differs from their own only by
the presence of zero in it (the Arabic *sifr*, from where we get cipher,

means zero). So she comes to the conclusion that the cause of the mistake is the replacement of the needed numeral by the letter O— or, in other words, a substitution of a sign for a symbol as, according to dictionary definitions, letters or alphabetical characters are **signs** while figures and numerals (ciphers) are **symbols**.

Looking for a plausible explanation of the wrong number, the old woman, in fact, draws attention to the properties of a standard American telephone dial as a crude coding system that consists of 10(!) symbols (digits from 0 to 9) and 24 or 26 signs (the English alphabet, sometimes without Q and Z). Since every numeral on the dial from 2 to 9 is equivalent to three or four letters, it can be used for converting letters into digits and vice versa—that is, for enciphering and deciphering. While the woman converts a digit into the letter O, the reader can (and must) go backwards and find out what "cipher" the girl "is turning." With the help of a telephone, this riddle is easily solved: **instead of the "empty" zero, the girl dials six**, which on the telephone dial corresponds to three letters—M, N, and O.

I don't think that the shadow of OMEN in this combination is just a coincidence, because if we look at the numerical value of letter O as a cipher, the girl's mistake becomes literally ominous (in the meaning of "having the significance of an omen"). She knows the correct number for Charlie,[23] she is anxious to talk to him, she calls after midnight—which implies the matter is urgent—yet she dials a six instead of a zero not once but twice, which is hardly plausible. It seems that she is acting like a medium (hence her **toneless** voice), transmitting a secret message in code, the cipher 6, addressed directly to the old woman and her husband. The very fact that the misdialed digit is not named in the text but must be deduced by a simple decoding procedure turns her mistake (like most mistakes in Nabokov's fiction) into the most important clue leading us to the hidden central event of the story, to its "inner scheme."

In the context of "Signs and Symbols," with its emphasis on numerical sequences and patterning, the transmitted six acquires several meaningful connections and implications. It should be noted at once that the ciphered message comes after midnight, when Saturday, the sixth day of the week, has already begun. The Holocaust background of the story suggests an association with the Star of David, a six-pointed symbol that signifies a union of humankind with a divine principle. The cipher obviously alludes to the photo of the boy "aged **six** [...] when he drew wonderful birds with human hands and feet and suffered from insomnia like a grown-up man," which not only evokes his dream of a flight and a bird-headed Sirin, but also echoes the old man's insomnia during the immediate present of the narration. What is even more significant, though, is the relation of the sixth slot on the **ten-digit** telephone dial to the set of **ten** jars and, by implication, to the future of the boy and his parents. It parallels the sixth, unread "eloquent label" of the series that comes after "crab apple" and presumably promises a sweeter continuation[24] —the next stage of metamorphosis that will follow the misery of madness, persecution, old age, and despair. The cipher seems to tell the old woman (and the reader) that her fears (and ours) for "the fate of tenderness" and love in the world are premature, and that her thinking of death as "monstrous darkness" is short-sighted. In other words, it informs her (and the reader) of the central event of the *fabula*—the eventual death of the boy, though not as annihilation, the meaningless and empty zero, but as transformation, the mystery of rebirth (hence the motive of birthday and the "conspicuous" birthmark in the final paragraph), the meaningful, albeit unnamed "sixth step" in the open, incomplete, unfolding sequence.

The last question to be answered is who is sending the secret message from the other world. The text itself offers the reader only two options. We can choose either the boy or Aunt Rosa—an old lady who "had lived in a tremulous world of bad news, bankruptcies, train accidents, cancerous growths—until the Germans put her to death, together with all the people she had worried about" (A12: 116). The characterization of Aunt Rosa gives some ground for supposing that she is trying to intervene from the beyond and to warn her relatives about a death in the family, all the more so that a parallel to Aunt Maud's sending encoded messages in *Pale Fire* is self-evident. Yet the connection between the telephone code and the birthday present points to the boy, whose mind is felt in the cunning use of the available signs and symbols. His obsession with codes, alphabets, veiled references, and secret messages makes him capable of inventing an ingenious and simple method to transmit the news of his rebirth, using the available means of communication and the set of ten jars chosen for him as a token of love and care—the last symbolic bond uniting him and his parents. If the boy has escaped, flown away from the prison of his madness and reached a mysterious beyond, in Nabokov's world this would imply that he has regained and expanded his consciousness, and with it, his ability to love, to feel compassion. He sends the message to his parents at a moment when they are planning a reunion with him, and the cipher six reciprocates their selfless sacrifice, indicating that the reunion will soon happen—only not in this life.

This reading of the story is strongly supported by its poetical subtext, alluded to at the end of the second part when the old woman is thinking of

> the incalculable amount of tenderness contained in the world; of the fate of this tenderness, which is either crushed, or wasted, or transformed into madness; of neglected children humming to themselves in unswept corners; of beautiful weeds that cannot hide from the farmer and helplessly have to watch the shadow of his simian stoop leave mangled flowers in its wake, as the monstrous darkness approaches. (A13: 138)

The image of helpless, innocent children as beautiful but useless flowers mowed or reaped by the simian farmer echoes Henry Wadsworth Longfellow's poem "The Reaper and the Flowers," which Nabokov must have read in his childhood (a volume of Longfellow's complete poetical works is listed in the catalogue of V. D. Nabokov's St. Petersburg library):

> There is a Reaper whose name is Death,
> And, with his sickle keen,
> He reaps the bearded grain at a breath,
> And the flowers that grow between.
> [...]

> "My Lord has need of these flowers gay,"
> The Reaper said, and smiled;
> "Dear tokens of the earth are they,
> Where He was once a child."
> "They shall all bloom in the fields of light,
> Transplanted by my care,
> And saints, upon their garments white,
> These sacred blossoms wear."
> And the mother gave, in tears and pain,

The flowers she most did love;
She knew she should find them all again
In the fields of light above.
    Oh, not in cruelty, not in wrath,
The Reaper came that day;
'Twas an angel visited the green earth,
And took the flowers away.[25]

Nabokov's imagery reworks, refreshes and to a certain extent subverts Longfellow's sentimental and trite rhetoric, but the concealed "inside" of the story retains and even strengthens the theodicy of the poem. Like the Reaper whose name is death, Nabokov takes the sick boy away not in cruelty, not in wrath, but in hope for his meeting his loving parents in "the fields of light." This is what the protagonists, unaware, celebrate by their "unexpected festive midnight tea," enjoying "the **luminous** yellow, green, red little jars." As is often the case with Nabokov's narratives, "Signs and Symbols" plays a cunning trick upon the reader, making him or her mad at some unnamed malign force of cruel chance, "friend of giants and farmers" that "is using the mistaken girl" to torture the poor helpless old people. The culprit is, of course, the omnipotent author who inflicts pain upon the innocent and lets them (and us) remain forever suspended in anxiety and fear when the ominous telephone rings for the third time. Is it that stupid girl again? Is it the hospital with news of death?[26] Breaking out of this trap and finding the hidden "inside" encrypted in the plot reverses our perception of the story and reveals Nabokov's design. The very wrongness of the telephone number that seemed so cruel becomes benevolent if we discover the secret encoded promise—the ultimate sign and symbol of the text; and the uncertainty about the third call becomes irrelevant, because whoever dials the number this time, the message we have already received and deciphered will never change.[27] If it is the girl, it means that the cipher 6 is being sent again; if it is the hospital—well, we have already heard the news from the dead man's mouth, which makes it not so bad, after all. As for the old man and the woman who, in contrast to the reader, are unable to decipher the message, their tears and pain for the son "they most did love" will be real, but their sorrow won't last long. Having broken the code, we can be certain that in the fictional universe where Nabokov is God, they too will be allowed to pass through and meet the sender of the secret message.

In the final analysis, the inner scheme of "Signs and Symbols" is, *mutatis mutandis*, similar to that of "The Vane Sisters," though the earlier text is much more dramatic and artistically complex. While "The Vane Sisters" seems to have been composed for the sake of an elegant puzzle, the elegant riddle in "Signs and Symbols" was composed for the sake of the narrative. Discovering and solving it does not undermine existing ethical, historicist, and psychological interpretations, but challenges stale clichés of reader-response criticism. Those who refuse to look for a hidden closure beneath the deceptive openness of "Signs and Symbols" are more guilty of a "referential mania" than their opponents because they, like the insane boy, believe that everything in the world created by Nabokov refers to them and they are free to project their own doubts, uncertainties, and fears upon it. As "clouds in the staring sky" do not "transmit to one another" any information regarding the deranged boy, so Nabokov's texts with an "inside" do not refer to the smug, theory-clad critic—but only to themselves and their creator, though they do allow a "peep unto glory" for the reader who is ready to accept and obey the rules of their game.

The castling problem in "Signs and Symbols"

Yuri Leving

Chess as the story's matrix

In one of his earlier stories, "Christmas" (1924), about a father grieving the death of his son, Nabokov employed a particular chess problem as a structural matrix. He described it as a *sui-mate* (self-mate).[1] As far as I know, no one has yet tried to consider applying the chess key as a potential solution to the mystery of his later short story, "Signs and Symbols." This move seems especially apt because of a clue that Nabokov tacks amidst the dense description of the young man's developing phobias: his cousin is "now a famous chess player" (A12: 120). Addressing the "double solutions" involved in resolving the sui-mate problems, the authors of a beautifully written book on chess (published not long before Nabokov's birth) have observed that the sui-mates'

> difficulty is of a different order altogether to that presented by a direct mate problem, especially when the sui-mate is effected in several moves, because at the beginning we must see the end, the beginning and end, as it were, meeting as in a bracelet. There is a kind of topsy-turvydom in the whole process which is something like looking through a telescope the wrong way.[2]

Although the "bracelet" paradigm neatly describes the pattern of many of Nabokov's works, from *The Gift* to *Pale Fire*, the question remains whether its ends are destined to meet also in this short story. I would like to suggest that Nabokov's "Signs and Symbols" is also built around a specific chess problem with a "double move," albeit a different one this time.

Who, when, why?

Terry J. Martin in "Ways of Knowing in 'Signs and Symbols'" came the closest to breaking the story's secret code, but stopped short of asserting the final solution that the story arises out of a specific series of chess moves that fascinated the author.[3]

So far the debate over Nabokov's short story has focused on various possibilities for the denouement, sprouting from its missing solution: who is calling and what is the message? In a somewhat paradoxical reading of "Signs and Symbols" I would like, first, to recalibrate its central thematic concern: I believe that this is a story not so much about the death or survival of the old couple's son, but mainly about the suffering of his father (hereafter referred to as Husband) and the existential choice that he makes. The Mother is a more passive agent in the story and she seems to misread the signals sent to her, but I will address this issue later.

My reading is based on a combination of two patterns that have been lately used to approach Nabokov's riddles in *Pale Fire* and *Lolita* respectively. For *Pale Fire*, supernatural forces have been drawn into the game[4] —something justified by Nabokov himself, who prompted us to read the last paragraph of "The Vane Sisters" as something akin to a telekinesis session. In the case of *Lolita*, it has been proposed that Lolita's death takes place not beyond the timeframe of the narrative but, in fact, right inside of it, during her stay at the Elphinstone hospital, while the rest of the story— including Humbert's searches for her and Quilty's murder—is the product of the unreliable narrator's creative imagination.[5]

In the same vein, I will argue that the Husband eventually dies in the story's timeframe and his death coincides with its textual end ("I am dying," he warns earlier in the evening [A13: 151]), right before the third call is answered. The Husband's decision is an ethical one: he withdraws himself from this world, freeing their tiny two-room apartment for the son to return and thereby also relieving his brother, "the Prince," from any additional financial burden. What is more, the Husband withdraws from the scene in a conscious attempt to strike a winning combination in life's conundrum: if his son has survived, then the Husband has created the conditions for his successful return; if the son has committed suicide, then this is the Husband's escape into a safe place where he can reunite with the deceased. In other words, one hero moves aside in order to save another. A similar scheme is known in the game of chess as *castling*.[6] It is also called "the King's move" and it not only ensures the King's safety but also brings another piece, the Rook, into active play. The name of the move itself is poetic and metaphoric at the same time: castling "provides the King with an escape into his castle."[7]

Many have observed the significance of the Husband's brother, Isaac's, nickname—the "Prince." This might be a clue to the Husband's role as a "King" in the castling problem superimposed over the story's design. Castling is a special move involving the king and either of the original rooks of the same color and it is the only move in chess in which a player moves two pieces at the same time. But what is especially curious here is the way the actual moves are recorded: the notation for castling, in both the descriptive and the algebraic systems, is O–O with the kingside rook and O–O–O with the queenside rook.[8]

This was a common practice during Nabokov's lifetime as well: not long before he had composed "Signs and Symbols," Jos Raul Capablanca (1888–1942), noted for his technical mastery, published a popular manual of chess. In this book, *A Primer of Chess* (first brought out in 1935 by Harcourt, Inc.), Capablanca explains the fundamentals and provides diagrams; of castling he says:

> When castling one must specify which side, and write thus: castles King's side or castles Queen's side, according to the side of the board on which castling takes place. This is also written sometimes as follows: O – O for castling on the King's side and O – O – O for castling on the Queen's side.[9]

Nabokov followed Capablanca's career (at the age of 28 he wrote a review of Znosko-Borovsky's *Capablanca and Alekhine* and the poem "The Chess Knight" about a chess master who goes mad and is hospitalized in a psychiatric clinic),[10] but castling could also be an appealing device in and of itself: in Russian it is called *rokirovka*, with a clear homophonic root *rok*, meaning "fate."[11]

This metaphysical dimension is in line with Alexander Dolinin's breakthrough discovery of the word "Omen" in the dialed number

6 (the six on the telephone dial corresponds to three letters—M, N, and O). In his analysis, Dolinin suggests that the properties of a standard American telephone dial can be seen "as a crude coding system that consists of 10(!) symbols (digits from zero to nine) and 24 or 26 signs."[12] The caller, therefore, according to Dolinin, is

> acting like a medium (hence her "toneless" voice), transmitting a secret message in code, the cipher 6, addressed directly to the old woman and her husband. The very fact that the misdialed digit is not named in the text but must be deduced by a simple decoding procedure turns her mistake (like most mistakes in Nabokov's fiction) into the most important clue leading us to the hidden central event of the story, to its "inner scheme."

All three calls constitute a deliberate message to the parents, but it is the Husband who interprets (or instinctively guesses) the meaning. As readers, we do not hear the full contents of the conversation, but we can approach all three calls as a set of signals, not unlike Morse code, which transmits textual information as a series of on-off tones, lights, or clicks, where each character (letter or numeral) is represented by a unique sequence of dots and dashes.[13] The difference between the set of two blank calls (be it all zeroes or letters "O") and the set of three blank calls is a variation between two and three 0/Os in a row. Graphically, this can be rendered exactly as a chess notation used for castling:

(a) O–O
(b) O–O–O

Metaphysical key

Now let me get back to the initial role of the Husband in this riddle. From his standpoint it does not matter what the third call is about, because castling presumes the double move either as the kingside (O–O) or the queenside (O–O–O) rook.

Death in Nabokov's universe is often a kind of salvation (as in *Invitation to a Beheading* or *Bend Sinister*). If the Husband escapes into death (like Luzhin in *The Defense*), this means that dying is his safe place. The son might be already there in tranquility, where no one can reach him, along with Aunt Rosa, Rebecca Borisovna, and the Soloveichiks.

The girl's voice acts like a medium, but, contrary to Dolinin's conclusion, I do not see the call to Charlie as a mistake. Charlie *does not* exist because he is beside the point here and, in fact, there is no real girl either—only *a girlish voice of the son's ghost.* The girl's repeated attempts to connect with a certain "Charlie" forms a clue to yet another letter, disguised like the 6 behind the zero. Indeed, when transmitting and receiving voice messages by radio or telephone, code words and names are acrophonically assigned to letters in the English alphabet (Alfa for A, Bravo for B, etc.). Common among *all* of the existing systems[14] at the time of Nabokov's writing of his short story was that "Charlie" designated the letter C.

Developing Dolinin's ingenious explanation,[15] one should realize that the letter C on a telephone dial is assigned to the digit 2, which expands the already known formula by one crucial element in consecutively "misplaced" calls.[16] Hence, the *known* digits that emerge in the phone conversation are 6, 0, and 2. Adding 6 + 0 + 2 results in 8. The *sign* eight is a *symbol* of eternity (∞).

The call frightens the Wife, but not the Husband ("'It frightened me,' she said. He smiled a quick smile and immediately resumed his excited monologue" [A14: 181]). Possibly, this is because earthly intrusion is not a part of his reality as he has already made his choice. Some scholars, most notably John Hagopian, have previously noted that all we know about the boy's peculiar sickness in the story is mostly delivered through his mother's sole agency.[17] The Wife filters the narrative of the child's obsession through her own suppressed fears (scientists studying genetic factors in mental diseases claim that some schizophrenia is inherited[18]). Even more so, the Wife not only fails to understand the "dull voice's" message, but arrogantly tries to correct the caller. In fact, it is she who, instead of prompting her interlocutor to dial 0 instead of 6, had to "convert" the name *Charlie* into 2. Had she done this, she could have been spared from the problem of the third call as she would have probably realized—as her husband has—that even if something terrible had happened, there was nothing to fear anymore.

We cannot understand and explain the process of dying, neither is it possible to clarify the nature of life after death. But if there is something we cannot understand directly, using an analogy can help. Rabbi Yitzchak Vorst uses the example of television, which Nabokov also did in *Pale Fire*:

> A person sits and watches a program on a television screen. The set has received the program, and it appears clearly on the screen. However, even before it reached the screen, for an instant, the program already existed in the form of waves, sent through the air by a transmitting station.
>
> The operation of television can thus be divided into three parts: (1) the transmitting station; (2) the waves; and (3) the receiver.
>
> Suppose that suddenly, for sonic reasons, the person doesn't see the picture anymore. Something went wrong, and the set no longer shows the program on the screen. That part of the television system has ceased to exist. Yet the other two parts of the system continue to exist. The station continues to transmit and the program is still present in the form of waves. But the man before the set cannot see them. As far as he is concerned the program is gone ...[19]

Analogously, Rabbi Yitzchak Vorst states that the totality of a person consists of a body *and* a soul *and* the "region" between the two. A material event like a car accident cannot terminate the total existence of a person. The physical bond between two persons can be broken by a bullet, but not their spiritual relationship. Judaism recognizes the concept of reincarnation. Hence, there should be no contradiction in that even if it is the son who is calling, physically he might already be dead, because his soul can establish contact with the parents through a phone call. Nineteenth-century materialism, according to Vorst, tried to explain all experiences of the soul as phenomena of the brain, as physical functions, just like breathing and digestion, but failed to explain the phenomenon of "man" in a fully satisfactory manner. (Diminutive "Charlie" in this context could mean and mock only Darwin.) Moreover, such phenomena as telepathy, telekinesis, and bilocation, which have been empirically proven to exist, remain strong evidence for the existence of both body and soul.[20]

Solution

So what does the Husband's death, if we assume that it takes place in the finale of the story, add to our understanding of "Signs and Symbols"? What Nabokov seems to suggest in his moral tale is that, while the Hereafter is important, even more important is the Before-hereafter—one's decisions here and now, in this world. The father assumes personal responsibility ("We must get him out of there quick. Otherwise we'll be responsible. Responsible!" [A13: 155]) and is instantly rewarded (let's say the omnipotent author grants him something like a heart attack): in the very last sentence of the story he "had got to crab apple ..."—but who promised that the knowledge would be sweet?

Was his choice correct? From the ethical point of view, this question is also irrelevant because it comes as a result of his personal choice. What about the Wife? Attempts to contact her have been made also: the Queen was invited to the otherworld but refused to absorb the message.

The graphical representation of eternity (figure 8 on its side) is a combination of two zeroes or "O"s.[21] Likewise, two "O"s are encoded into Nabokov's last name, which, in Russian, means "on the side"—pretty much like the King's move when castling.

Reading madly
Irving Malin

I want to read "Signs and Symbols" in a detailed way, but I am not sure about "close reading." At what point does "close reading" become obsessive, mad, "deranged" (to use a word found in the first paragraph of this story [A9: 3])? You can already observe that my questions about reading imply the question (or the answer?) mentioned in the story. I am, if you will, trying to interpret the words used by Nabokov, to study his "signs and symbols."

But "Signs and Symbols" is an ambiguous title. Are all words "signs"? What is the difference between a "sign" and a "symbol"? Since I assume that Nabokov has deliberately chosen his words, I believe they are "clues" to his fictional world. I am a bit uneasy about the two "s" words because they may contain hidden meaning, meaning that is clear only after I have studied the text. Bear with me!

The first sentence of the story is wonderfully strange. "For" is the first word; it implies a "connection" between itself and the "fourth" time. What should I make of the repetition of four (as "for"), a repetition that is, at one and the same time, double. "For" and "four" —odd, isn't it? And the phrase in "as many years" doesn't really clarify things. Notice there is emphasis on time: it is always (?) present in a Nabokov story. I'll assume this "birthday present" is a sign of respect, love, duty? But I am troubled by the possible play with "present." Is "present" duplicitous? Is it ""connected" with time?

These questions are a "problem," to use another Nabokov word. Thus the story begins with a kind of mirror effect; its "birth" is, perhaps, related to the "birthday" gift. The sentence is "arranged" to stress the "deranged" mind of a "young man." Who is the "young" man? How "young" is he? And who are "they"? What is their *connection*? The first sentence is a "confrontation" for me as it is for "they" (them)? I keep staring at the words "confrontation" and "problem"; they seem to take control of the sentence. And in this sentence about time "confrontation" sneaks in the notion of "front" —space. But "front" is a temporal word as well. No? I have written at least several hundred words, seeing things—shall I call them signs? —that may not even be present. My mind may be—what? "Incurably deranged"? Or subtly arranged?

The second sentence offers some relief (some "cure")? It consists of just four words: "He had no desires." But four words uncannily refers back to "four" in the first sentence—the sentence *before*. Who cannot have any desires? Not having any desire may be *desirable?* I don't know.

The third sentence is full of ambiguous referents, signs. "Man-made" objects were "hives of evil." "Hives" brings into play "bee." But "bee" also brings into play "be." Notice that "hive" is a container of sorts—like the mind (A9: 3). I am informed that "he" perceives life and death in the activity—"vibrant" with a "malignant activity." I am told that "he alone" could perceive the activity. Who is telling us this? Is it Nabokov? Yes. He "alone" knows that "he" [the "young man"] "alone" knows. Of course, authority rests in the storyteller.

But don't I stand above him? Don't I "alone" give meanings to his words? But I must move on to the rest of the sentence. The "young man" may find "gross comforts," but the "gross comforts" are not useful in his "abstract world." What is an "abstract world"? Isn't every world non-abstract? Is the young man "incurably" ill because he "lives" in an abstract world? Then I (and you?) am "deranged," seeing meaning in words not usually read this closely.

Nabokov's story—his present—is beginning to unnerve me because I am not sure of the "limits" of his narrative world (a tautology?). I'll continue, searching for enlightenment. The next sentence is the last one in the paragraph. It is the longest one so far. It is full of problems. A number of "articles" and pronouns bring me back to numerology ("four"). And I wonder about the word "article" (Pun?).

And the pronouns! "Him" is repeated twice in quick succession—the word almost makes "him" an "it." What in heaven's name is a "gadget line"? And does "for instance" deliberately take me back to the "for"—the first word of the story? And is "stance" to be read as a shadowy position? "They" are now seen as "his parents"—notice how Nabokov has waited to clarify the relationship, the *connection* of "he" and "they." Unlike their son, they can choose things—even an "innocent trifle." They choose a "basket"—not, I hope, to be taken as a "hive." The basket has "ten little jars" with ten different jellies. "Ten" is repeated—the word need not have been repeated. Is there any connection of "jellies" to "honey" produced by bees? Probably I am seeing more than Nabokov wants me to. I have a *strong desire* to perceive the world he has created. But I am "alone."

I realize that I am reading madly; I identify in part with "him" but at the same time, I recognize that his parents read—interpret—his need for a "gift." And Nabokov is also writing "madly"; he is employing every word he can to create symbols. Therefore, there are at least four interpreters, readers, perceivers: "him," "they," I, Nabokov.

I look now at the second paragraph to clarify "things." But I'm uneasy because of my desire or compulsion. The first sentence repeats the "birthday"—origins, "Eden." And the *time* references take on added meaning. (Time is additional?) What is a long time? What is "quite old"? "Score" of years? Score as number—"score" related to "scare"? Some "word golf" ("gulf")? The second sentence is short in contrast to the first. "Gray" troubles me by its lack of clarity. (And I think of "gray" in *Pale Fire*.) "Anyhow" *seems* to be easy, a throw-away word—I distrust it. I'll have to come back to it. "Black" seems to be the only interesting word in the next sentence. Gray, black—indeterminate, gloomy colors. The next sentence mentions "Mrs Sol," a neighbor. I was right. What kind of name is "Sol"? Does it signify sun (son?), sole, soul? And her colors are "pink" and "mauve"—very bright, but they are "painted." Is she *hiding* her "real" colors? That hat—it is described as a "cluster of brookside flowers." Cluster—back to "hive," *containers?* Mrs Sol "presented a naked white countenance to the fault-finding light of spring days." Is white naked? Isn't it all colors? That damn *Moby-Dick!* "Presented" underscores present (another pun—two in one underlies a pun ... hmm!). "Fault-finding." Isn't Nabokov offering "fault" so far? Who is at fault? Let's *find* out. The young man is "at fault" for disturbing his parents by his madness. Mrs Sol is "at fault" for being so "cheery" in this dark story. But in the light of things aren't we all at fault finding fault with so many "people"?

That husband! He had once been "fairly successful in the old country." But he doesn't *fare* well now. The old country! Time again! And the husband is dependent on his brother Isaac. In this faulty world it's hard to find freedom, independence. Why not create *your Own World*? That task is desirable, perhaps necessary. "Isaac." But the Bible makes him a sacrificial son. Did Nabokov know Hebrew? "Isaac" means "he will laugh." How ironic! In this story there's not much fun. Isaac is a "real American." America is the new (knew?) country. But is it really new? "Isaac" is said to be in a "real America" for almost forty years. *Forty!* Four, before, for—I'd better stop this kind of linkage; I'm finding meaning in every word. Surely Nabokov couldn't have meant these bonds. And he surely couldn't have me see in the next sentence a possible pun in "the Prince"! Nickname! "Nick"—is this connected to fault, scar the devil? That's "crazy." I'll pretend I don't really believe my interpretations, but I'll leave them "standing," to use a word from the previous sentence. Do you understand? I'm just presenting you gifts. And you—I know you! —are finding fault with my "enlightened" meanings. What a world!

In the next paragraph "everything went wrong." "Everything"? I'm not surprised by the imperfect world. "Friday"? Why Friday instead of Monday, or better yet, *Sunday?* I don't know.

I am making much of "underground" things, like the train that "lost its life current between two stations." Current—another pun? Can a train have a "life current"? It's *not human.* And, of course, it seems to be there a *"quarter* of an hour"—four! And there are two noises: the "dutiful beating of one's heart" and "the rustling of newspaper." The heart beats *dutifully*—it's just like the duty they are performing by visiting their son. They should be in the newspapers. What good parents!

And the bus in the next sentence "kept them waiting for ages." "Ages." "Ages." Time is a *weight!* I can't keep interpreting every word. Is this criticism? Or is it madness? What's your "strong opinion"? "Continue" it to yourself—what do you know? You'll probably expect me to relate "crammed" to "confine," to "contain."

I'm not *that* crazy. I'll show you. *I won't even analyze the next sentence!* After the missing sentence I can't *resist* assigning meaning to the repeated "waiting" or the "instead" nurse—the nurse who enters instead of their "boy." Their "botched" boy—where is he? Here they come all the way and they get a nurse they "did not care for." She "appeared at last" (lost?). She "brightly explained he had again attempted to take his life." "Brightly"? Consider the kind of world this is. A "boy" tries to kill himself *again*; and he is the subject of a bright explanation. What kind of explanation did you expect? I've already explained to you—at length!—that the world is painted (like Mrs Sol's face) with every kind of false interpretation. And nobody sees this. I do! I'm not "disturbed"—a word I "visit" in the next sentence—by the lack of truth the "mix-up," the "miserable" lies people use. And I assume that the parents understand this. I'd better stop. I'm beginning to think of them as people, not as "nicks" on a page. "Next time" I'll restrain my feelings; *instead* I'll be a better commentator by looking at "*words*," not at "*people*." But I must write that it's so easy to start identifying with words, signs, giving them *life*! After all Nabokov is giving me a *present* of fiction.

But it's so easy to *care* for these words. The poor parents! Look at the next paragraph. She waits in the rain for her husband to open the umbrella. And he keeps clearing his throat "in a special resonant way he had when he was upset." (And that's a sign, isn't it?) Certainly there's a "special resonance" for her interpretation—and for mine. She reads him well. She knows him well.

When in the last sentence—oh, I've missed one; should I revisit it? I see the "half-dead bird," twitching in the "puddle," and I'm almost tempted to cry. Nabokov is *swaying* me. (He's a tyrant, a real rex.) I'd better continue my emotions. I've never read any other story in this emotional way. I don't know why I'm acting this way. Maybe it has "special resonance" for me.

Onward! I'm not revealing myself to strangers. I'll close just like the umbrella. In the next paragraph they don't "exchange a word"—they don't have to speak; they know each other so well. But she notices his aged hands, which are described as "twitching" upon the handle of the umbrella, and she feels the "mounting pressure" of tears. Have you noticed all the present participles, all the activity these verbal forms suggest?

The next sentence reinforces my "referential mania." I see a rhyme of "look," "shock." I place "something" in relation to "everything" and "anything"—words used previously. And I notice the word "mind." It assumes significance in every Nabokov work because he is "obsessed" with "consciousness," perception, epistemology. I like the odd joining of "soft shock," the manner of quick "closure," in the "ock." Am I over-reading the second because I associate it (un)consciously with *clock*? "Mixture"—the word has already been used. I notice the "girl with dark hair" and "grubby red toenails." "Grubby" is "gross"—*it faults* the hair and the nail. What's her problem? Why is she weeping? The fact that she is with "an older woman"—her mother—is a kind of *reflection* of the son (who is too crazy to weep) and his parents. She is disturbed when she looks at the girl and mother. She sees a resemblance. And Nabokov uses a question mark! That woman "resembled Rebecca Borisnova," who lived in "Minsk years ago." Rebecca? Is the biblical reference here? Is Rebecca related to "Rachel"? Does she suggest the caring woman? And does "Rachel" relate to a Hebrew word meaning pity?

I'm pleased that the next paragraph is short. (Is there something going on with the length of contrasting paragraphs?) I read that "the last time" he tried to kill himself he used a method that was "a masterpiece of inventiveness." (This story is "a masterpiece of inventiveness"; I'm mad enough to think that my essay is one.) He tried to "fly" according to an "envious fellow patient"; the patient stopped him. I admire the last sentence: "What he really wanted to do was to tear a hole in his world and escape." Does the patient know this? Does the doctor know this? Does the young man? Let's move slowly. (I'm joking.) "Tear"—is it related to weeping to tears? "Hole"—the story is, as I have implied, full of mysterious hints, holes, gaps of interpretation.

It is "wholly" "holy" (the biblical references, the parable-like effects). So then we have a story of hole and/or wholes. It's little wonder that the young man wants to escape the word and world! Don't you? Then why are you reading my mad criticism? Stop before you suffer from "referential mania," "special resonance."

And now I turn to the last and longest paragraph in section one, the birth of the story. We learn that the young man had been the subject of an "elaborate" scientific article. He was a "text," a text in a text. And, of cause, he is in this text (my essay) of a text by Nabokov.

What a "puzzle"! But the parents had "long before" figured his condition. Now what *exactly* is this condition? Is it "referential mania," the term used by Herman Brink, the author of the text. "Herman"? I should go back and check the hero's name in *Despair*. I'll merely read "Herman" in this text. Herr and man—both are the same if we accept the German. But if I read "Herman" as "her man," then I can say that "her man" refers to the wife's subject, her husband. She's been doing a lot of reading! And "brink"?

Obviously, I can't resist seeing "brink" as "edge." But I want to notice more meaning—"blink" and "blank." I love world gulf—I mean "word golf."

I'm slipping: punning is *dangerous*. We are told that the sufferer of "referential mania" is so narcissistic that everything that happens is a "veiled reference" to him. I think that I've caught his illness! Or given mine to him or to Nabokov's world?

The next sentence really alarms me. I distrust "real people" reality itself. In fact, I distrust real words. My consciousness is over-determined. Or under-determined? I've been putting so many question marks into this essay because I'm not sure of *anything*. But this statement is one of certainty. What a maze! What a Haze! My—I mean *Nabokov's*—next sentence is wonderful: "*Phenomenal nature shadows him wherever he goes.*" "Phenomenal" is the "name" included in the word. It is—dare I say it?—a "shadow."

I must think ("brink"). "Shadow" implies two things a person and a twisted or distorted reflection. Does one need sunlight to have strong shadows? Is sunlight forcing me to go back to "Sol"? Is it forcing me to go back to son? Is it—the previous reference—shadowing my consciousness? Or am I creating shadows? Make what you will of my mania, my "misreading." I know that you are analyzing my analysis.

You are a shadow critic!

The next sentence humanizes "clouds." It is ironic to join "clouds" and "staring"; they are, in effect, contradictory words. The two objects—"sky and clouds"—"transmit" detailed information regarding him. I assume that "transmit" carries a hint of "transit," but I'm probably incorrect. Perhaps I should ask the trees that communicate in "manual alphabet" his "inmost thoughts." But I don't know what a "manual alphabet" means. The trees are *assigning* meaning by gestures. There is a linkage (link-age?) of "alphabet" and "gesture" and "manual." Is Nabokov suggesting the progression of madness or of language from glyphs to alphabet?

In the next sentence "stains" appear. I think of "the world's slow stain" in Shelley. Surely we decay slowly, not even recognizing our progression towards death, the *final strain*. "Fleck" and "form" alliterate. Do you see a shadow of "flock" (rhyming with shock) in fleck? Am I *intercepting* invisible messages? Am I forming patterns? Or are the patterns forming (deforming, performing, reforming?) me?

I guess that the answers depend on free will and/or fate. The next sentence is oddly structured. Subject and object are conjoined; "everything" is repeated. All the world represents him as "theme." But is "he" the central "theme" or character in the narrative? Or is he merely the object of interpretation?

There are "spies" everywhere. (Think of *Pale Fire*.) Some are "detached"—from *what*? Others—"coats in windows"—are not so detached; they are indeed "prejudiced witnesses." Do you see the mention of "glass" and "window"? Do you think, as I do, of the first line of Shade's poem? The spies increase; the sentence seems out of control. It is as "hysterical" as his interpretation (and mine). Does "insanity" have a "point"? What is the point? What is the *boundary* between sanity and insanity? Can we reasonably chart the *lines*? Or are we "always" incorrect? ("Always"— always) I need help; I "alone" am interpreting the signs. Probably I am "grotesquely" distorting Nabokov's words. Help me! Reader, respond!

I, like the young man, "must be always on guard"; I must *decode* everything, including the wavering, "undulating" syllables. In the next sentence Nabokov uses the word "air." It has been mentioned previously—in a shadowy manner—in sky, in the movement of bees. Is "air" a slant pun on "heir"? Probably not. Is there a connection between "holes" and "files" because of the "I" in the middle? Is there some play with "files" and "heir"? Probably not.

The next sentence informs me—and you? —that he *provokes* the interest, that he *creates* it. Consider the choices. Would you rather live in a world you create or one created for you? Which world would be more interesting, less dangerous? I'm begging the question because there is no objective world; it is created by personal perceptions. "With distance" in the next sentence reintroduces the notion of connection. They go from their apartment (pun?) to the asylum. They cross distances. But, in order to understand him, they must enter his world. And they can't. Consciousness and distance are bound together; we want to bring the world closer. "Torrents" takes us back to "undulation," to water as clement. Notice the alliteration of "vol" in "volume" and "volubility," the possible pun in "volume."

Now we reach the last line in the first section. The line requires close reading. How bizarre is the notion of "silhouettes of his blood corpuscles." "Silhouettes" are "shadows"; they off "rhyme" with flit." Note the alliteration of "magnified" and "million." "Referential mania" always magnifies things seeing "worlds in a grain of sand." But so does close reading. "Solidity" and "granite" are "terms" that suggest *weight*. They oppose airy objects. It is fitting that the very last words in the sentence are the "ultimate truth of his being." Don't we all want to know the ultimate truth? But is there one? And how can we be sure that it exists? The sentence sums up the various strategies in the texts; it is a kind of "summa."

Now that I have read the first section, I have to make a choice. Should I move forward to find out the ultimate meaning? But if I do progress I will probably prolong my agony, my mania. I am placed in the young man's position. I want to tear a hole in the narrative or in interpretation (which is, in its own way, my narrative).

I am at a crossroad. If I continue, I suggest that I will drive you into more "madness" (or boredom?). Thus I choose to *resign*. I stop while I'm relatively "sane." Call me "coward." Call me "hero."

If you risk reading the remainder of the narrative—a mere two pages—perhaps you find "closure." But I rest my case as I *fly* from the complete (?) text.

Deciphering "Signs and Symbols"

Larry R. Andrews

In his little story about a family of émigré Russian Jews called "Signs and Symbols," Vladimir Nabokov suggests that the son is destroyed by the very forces he fears in his "referential mania." At least he tantalizes us with this possibility, yet all the while he is chuckling at us, and particularly if we are symbol-hunting critics, for momentarily believing in it. It is the intention of this study to demonstrate how Nabokov foreshadows by hidden clues an ending he does not reveal explicitly—the mad son's suicide, perhaps by defenestration.

It will conclude by exposing the irony that makes these clues ultimately false.[1] On a first reading we may find the story superficial, with its shameless exploitation of suspense and clichéd, indeterminate ending.

Can the author be *serious?* Yet the tone is quiet and unsensational. The characters' situation is compelling. Something leaves us vaguely uneasy. Upon further examination we perceive the narrator's wayward, Gogolesque eye for seemingly trivial and insignificant details. We notice the odd focus at both the opening and close of the story on the parents' birthday present of jellies for their insane son.

In the first paragraph of the story, Nabokov emphasizes the difficulty of finding the son a "safe" birthday present in view of his "referential mania":

> For the fourth time in as many years they were confronted with the problem of what birthday present to bring a young man who was incurably deranged in his mind. He had no desires. Man-made objects were to him either hives of evil, vibrant with a malignant activity that he alone could perceive, or gross comforts for which no use could be found in his abstract world. (A9: 1)

The parents, however, are confident that they have found a proper gift:

> After eliminating a number of articles that might offend him
> or frighten him (anything in the gadget line for instance was
> taboo), his parents chose a dainty and innocent trifle: a basket
> with ten different fruit jellies in ten little jars. (A9: 6)

The jellies will come to seem anything but innocent, as we shall
see, and Nabokov's emphasis on them here (end of sentence, end of
paragraph, repetition of number) helps to establish their important
role in the story.

Nabokov slyly reminds us of the jellies twice again in the
middle of the story. When the parents are turned away from the
sanitarium after learning of their son's latest suicide attempt, they
bring the present back with them to save for the next visit, because
"the place was so miserably understaffed, and things got mislaid
or mixed up so easily" (A10: 34). And later, on the way home, the
mother gives the father the basket of jellies to take home, while she
stops to buy fish.

Then in the last paragraph the jellies loom large again. At the
couple's "festive midnight tea" celebrating their decision to take
their son out of the institution and care for him at home, "the
birthday present stood on the table." The father is in the act of
fondling the jars and spelling out the names of the jellies when
the telephone rings for the third time. With the third ring of the
telephone the story breaks off, raising the possibility—but leaving
it only a possibility—that the call is from the sanitarium and brings
the news that the son has finally succeeded in killing himself. At
the same time that Nabokov seems to be treating the jellies as
"innocent," he has carefully linked them in the structure of the
story to the son's fears, to his unsuccessful suicide attempt, and to
the possibility of a final, successful suicide.

We do not know whether the late phone call at the end will be a
wrong number again, a death notice from the sanitarium, or some
other call. It could be either trivial or ominous. Yet the parents
are frightened by the first call: "it was an unusual hour for their
telephone to ring," the husband gapes in suspense at his wife, and
the wife clutches "her old tired heart" and says, "It frightened me."
Clearly, they fear that their son has succeeded in killing himself.
When the second call comes, the wife is much more matter-of-fact
about it. By the third call they are completely relaxed over the
pleasure of the tea and the "luminous" little jars. Their confidence

makes them ripe for disaster. Nabokov has emphasized this confidence in the opening and closing paragraphs in order to make the
reader suspect dramatic irony and conclude that the final call will
report the son's death. The proof is that in both scenes he links
the *jellies* to the parents' feelings of self-assurance. He thus leads
us to suspect that the jellies are not "innocent" but are in some
mysterious way a *cause* of the supposed death. An overwhelming
irony becomes apparent in what appeared to be a rather plotless
and inconsequential story: the parents, who have tried to please
their son with a birthday gift, and who have decided to bring him
back home to *save* him from suicide, may in fact have helped to
cause his death. They may have been used unwittingly as part of
the conspiracy of mysterious forces which the son has long learned
and attempted to escape by suicide. But suicide in this context
would, of course, be a self-defeating gesture, less a liberation than
an ultimate entrapment signaling the triumph of the hostile forces.

The parent–child relationship is a persistent pattern in the
complex conspiracy of the story, stressing an element of parental
responsibility for the offspring's unhappiness or death. Was it right
to place the son in the caged institution that "was so miserably
understaffed," where "things got mislaid or mixed up so easily"?
This innocent language refers to the jellies but obliquely suggests
that the son himself has become a "thing" that the parents have
"mislaid" and is now even more "mixed up" than before. The
father suddenly decides to bring the son home, because he feels
guilty over the latter's suicide attempts:

> "We must get him out of there quick. Otherwise we'll be respon-
> sible. Responsible!" he repeated and hurled himself into a sitting
> position, both feet on the floor, thumping his forehead with his
> clenched fist. (A13: 155)

The parents *are* indirectly responsible for the son's condition, not
just because they have put him in an asylum or have been unable
to understand him, but because the jellies and every other object
they come into contact with seem to use them to persecute him.
This responsibility is implicit in the distance between parents and
son. They were unusually old when he was born, and now 20 years
later they are aged. They are also physically separated from the
son. No direct communication between them and their son occurs

in the story or even in the snippets of exposition from the past (photographs mingled with reminiscence).

The budding child prodigy had become not only "difficult to understand" at eight but "totally inaccessible to normal minds" in his teens. The sanitarium nurse turns the parents away for fear that their "visit might disturb him." Even their various migrations through Europe and America in flight from revolution, world war, and pogrom must have had a disturbing effect on the child. Again there are concealed clues to reinforce the monstrous suspicion that the story's end portends a suicide for which the parents are responsible. The story is filled with images of parental distance and neglect. The "unfledged bird" that symbolizes the son has been neglected by its parents—neither guarded closely nor trained for survival in the world on its own. The raven-haired girl on the bus is weeping on an older woman's shoulder and reminds the mother of another mother and daughter from the past. The girl here is unhappy and unkempt, with "grubby red toenails" (A10: 150). Earlier the "garrulous high-school children" (A10: 27) on the bus exist in isolation from parents and are annoying to the old couple. Later the mother muses on the "neglected children" of the world with impotent sorrow (A13: 141). The reference to the father's prosperous brother Isaac recalls the similar prosperity of the biblical Isaac and underscores two other parallels with that story:

1) the extreme age of Abraham and Sarah when Isaac was born is a parallel to the age of the father and mother in the story;

2) the divine test in which Abraham nearly slew his son as a sacrifice is a parallel to the parents' implicit responsibility for their son's condition and his attempted suicides.

The son's tragic wish to fly also reminds us of the Icarus myth, in which the father, Daedalus, is responsible for *his* son's death, while the latter survives.

Other, less conspicuous symbolic patterns arise through the use of doubling.[2] We have seen that the black-trousered man is the son's double, because he *is* used to foreshadow the son's death. The son's cousin also serves as a double. *This* cousin is a "famous chess player" and *is* perhaps a projection of Luzhin in Nabokov's *The Defense*, who is also a victim of referential mania and who commits suicide by defenestration. There are other doubles for the parents and son in addition to the parallel sets of parents and children mentioned in the preceding paragraph. The insensitive nurse at the sanitarium is yet another reflection of the "irresponsible" mother. And two pairs of details link the son with the father: 1) at age six the son is described as having "insomnia like a grown-up man," and in the last scene we see that the father is unable to sleep for anxiety over his son; 2) the son *is* referred to as "ill-shaven," and one of the last details in the story shows that "although (the father) had shaved that morning, a silvery bristle showed on his chin." Furthermore, both the father and the son are imprisoned and dying. These details suggest that the son's condition is partly due to his similarity to his father, thus again implying the father's responsibility for the son's possible death.

Doubling is not only applied to character: there is also a doubling of images, such as those of trees and birds discussed earlier. In fact, almost every hostile image in the long paragraph describing the son's referential mania is doubled elsewhere in the story. Below is a list of such images:

Description of mania	*References elsewhere*
"clouds in the staring sky"	the cloudy; rainy day; "rain tinkled **in the dark**," "**monstrous** darkness"
"pebbles," "granite," "mountains,"	"rocks on a hillside"
"stains"	"blotched with acne," "brown spotted skin," "soiled cards," "large birthmark"
"sun flecks"	"Mrs Sol," "fault-finding light of spring days"
"glass surfaces"	the mirror the father uses, "his raised glass," "his spectacles in the jelly jars"
"still pools"	the puddle, the tea
"coats"	"*old* overcoat"

Description of mania	References elsewhere
"store *windowsill*" lynches at heart	"windows were blandly alight and in one of them a black-**trousered man could be seen**," allusion to window in description of son's suicide attempt "cart wheel hanging from the **branch of a leafless tree**," "**one** could hear nothing but the dutiful **beating of one's heart**," "her hand went to her old tired **heart**," "**knave of hearts**"
"running water", "torrents"	"raining hard," "dripping," "circular motion" of the tea
"storms"	"raining hard," "thunder"
"Undulations of things"	"swaying," "waves of pain"
"air he exhales is indexed and filed away"	"foul air of the subway", "pneumonia"
"groaning"	"moan"

Other pairs of images include the newspapers rustling on the subway echoed in the father's Russian newspaper at home and the "twitching" of the bird echoed in the "twitching" of the father's old hands. The sinister implications here are again monstrous. The real world of the parents and even the language of the story seem to be infiltrated by the hostile elements of the son's mania. Furthermore, the extraordinary emphasis on images of language codes ("veiled reference," "transmit," "alphabet," "messages," "cipher," "decoding") invites us to consider the story itself as a code with a sinister meaning.

Another pattern emerges from the numerological symbolism of the story, which brings us to the deck of cards and the telephone number. The numbers that dominate the story tend to be even:

2—"two-room flat," "twice a week"
4—"fourth time in as many years," "quarter of an hour," "four years old"
6—"age six," father reading sixth label when phone rings at end
8—"aged about eight"
10—"ten different fruit jellies in ten little jars," "ten minutes later," "aged ten"
12—"scientific monthly," "midnight"
20—"a score of years," age of son
40—"American of almost forty years standing"

Yet a few odd numbers infiltrate with particular suspiciousness. The mystic number three shows in the three sections of the story, three landings on the stairs, three cards on the floor, three telephone calls at the end, and three suicide attempts specifically mentioned or suggested. The knave of hearts and the nine and ace of spades, the cards that accidentally fall to the floor with the picture of Elsa and her beau, are also suspicious, since Nabokov's careful eye selects them for naming. The nine is yet another mystic number, the square of the mystic number three, which occurs regularly in the story. The ace of spades is a traditional omen of death. The knave of hearts contains at least three allusions, all of them relevant to the concerns of the story: 1) an allusion to guilt, since the knave of hearts is the stealer of tarts in Lewis Carroll's *Alice's Adventures in Wonderland*, which Nabokov translated into Russian and published in Germany in 1923; 2) an allusion to conspiracy and death, since in Nabokov's early novel *King, Queen, Knave* the "knave" conspires to murder his lover's husband; 3) an allusion to the rainy, claustrophobic setting of Baudelaire's first "Spleen" poem and to its description of an old deck of cards with dirty odors:

Heritage fatal d'une vieille hydropique,
Le beau valet de coeur et la dame de pique
Causent sinistrement de leurs amours defunts.
Fatal inheritance from a dropsical crone,
The handsome knave of hearts and the queen of spades
Chat sinisterly of their dead loves.

These lines echo the story's pervasive imagery of death and decay and also the son's fantasy that things are communicating with each other in sinister ways about him.

When we hear of the "wrong number" on the first two phone calls, we are suddenly convinced that the texture of numbers in the story is part of the conspiracy against the son. All we know about the wrong number is that the girl is "turning the letter O instead of the zero." On the third try, presumably the girl dials the correct number, the zero. If so, the third ring is not hers and is perhaps the sanitarium's. Zero is a death omen as well as a "veiled reference" to the "cipher" of the referential mania: "cipher" can mean "zero" as well as "code" and "symbolic image." The zero is thus a part of the son's mania, and all the numbers seem to be a part of the code used by the hostile forces. The telephone itself becomes a sinister threat because of the numbers on its dial, because of the prominence of zero among those numbers in the story's final episode, and also because it is the most obvious example in the story of the sort of man-made "gadget" mentioned in the first paragraph as "malignant" and hence "taboo" as a birthday gift.

Another important detail in the phone call is the mention of the name "Charlie." It seems strange that Nabokov refuses to name the three leading characters in the story but gladly offers up the names of minor characters who do not even appear (Mrs Sol, Herman Brink) and finally names a seemingly irrelevant "Charlie," who is asked for by someone dialing a wrong number! The namelessness of the main characters has, however, at least two purposes: it suggests their lack of clear identity, especially in the case of the son; and it also suggests, when set in the context of the extensive naming of others, that the world outside is strong and threatening and that names are a part of its sinister code. As in the case of the numbers, however, the hostile Significance of the names is not always clear.

By now we have surely come to see the story as a gothic tale. The images that have symbolic overtones in the story sometimes occur with similar overtones in Nabokov's other work: Humbert fears the conspiracies of poplar trees and lovebirds in a cage; and Pnin is paranoiac about his oak-leaved wallpaper. The conspiracy finally extends beyond the world of this particular story to include characters in earlier novels (such as Luzhin) and also, proleptically, characters in the later novels as well. We are implicitly invited to read those novels in terms of this story and this story in terms of those novels, so that Nabokov's entire career gradually takes on the appearance of an elaborate code with an intricate symbolic meaning.

As we perceive the intricate system of hidden clues in the story, apparently planted by Nabokov to convince us that the son's paranoia is justified and the conspiracy real, we momentarily suspend our disbelief and see the world through the son's eyes, the sane and insane visions now reversed. The dull, gray world of the parents now seems impossible, unreal, insane, and tainted by mortality, while the son's imaginary world is intensely alive.[3] The fictive world viewed by the son has taken over the "real" world of the parents in our eyes and in the fabric of the story. Everything in the story seems to corroborate the son's feeling of total vulnerability. The world has become a projection of his self turned inside out ("The silhouettes of his blood corpuscles, magnified a million times, flit over vast plains'"). It is astonishing how Nabokov has involved us in this vision in so short a space. Yet, in retrospect, such a paranoiac view of the world seems preposterous, no matter how plausibly the fiction justifies it. The suggestion that occult influences have affected even the linguistic texture of the story seems, in retrospect, particularly absurd. The idea is slightly more credible in "The Vane Sisters" and "Scenes from the Life of a Double Monster," because of their first-person point of view. But here, after being momentarily mesmerized by Nabokov's skillful imagery, we emerge from the trance realizing that the sly author has played a joke on us again. Not only do we realize that the son is, after all, mad and the "conspiracy" his delusion, but we also realize that the question of which world (the son's or the parents') is real has become irrelevant, since both are equally unreal fictions of the author.

The artificiality of the ending, with its suggestive withholding of the story's climax, reminds us of the artificiality of the whole. Furthermore, there are many crucial elements of the plot that are either denied us by the artifice of the story or filtered through secondary, unreliable sources, thus calling further attention to the story's receding levels of artifice. The narrator seems objective, yet he withholds a great deal of straightforward information we are sure he possesses. Exactly what was the "masterpiece of inventiveness" of the son's recent suicide attempt? We are told only that "an envious fellow patient thought he was learning to fly-and stopped him." The son himself never appears in person. We go to visit him with the parents but are turned away. His childhood is glimpsed only in impressionistic fragments through the medium of photographs.

Most of the details of the story are seen through the eyes of the parents: the jellies, sanitarium, rain, bird, people on the bus, neighbors, cards, photographs, and telephone (e.g., "she glanced at his old hands"; "she ... examined the photographs"; "he put on his spectacles and re-examined ... the ... little jars" [A10: 44]). The description of the son's mania, which is central to the image patterns, is itself of doubtful "reality."His symptoms and the term "referential mania" are not related directly by the narrator but through the medium of "an elaborate paper in a scientific monthly." Undercutting the seriousness with which we may take the article is the light mockery of its author as a comic stereotype of a German psychiatrist in the adjective "elaborate" and in the name Herman Brink, with its reminder of the thin borderline between sanity and madness, reasonable and arbitrary interpretations, fiction and "reality." Further undercutting the authority of the report is the fact that the parents had "puzzled it out for themselves" long before (but this puzzling out produces, of course, still another subjective view). Finally, much of the mania is described in imagery of art, making us aware of the artifice of the scientific paper and of the story itself ("reference," "alphabet," "patterns," "*messages*," "theme," "misinterpret," "indexed and filed," "silhouettes," "sum up ... the ultimate truth of his being" in addition to the similar terms cited earlier). Brink's scholarly article can be seen as a fiction about the son, just as Nabokov's story is a fiction about Brink and the son, and just as this essay is a fiction about Nabokov's story. Where lies "reality"?

In his essay on the story, William Carroll argues that

a "cipher" can be a nullity just as easily as it can be a key, but most readers will see it as a key; we will conclude that the third call is from the hospital. In so doing, we will have assigned a meaning to the signs based on something outside the closed system; we will have, in effect, participated with Nabokov in killing the boy.[4]

Carroll also points out that it is "just as plausible to argue ... that the signs and symbols of death have no logically inherent and inescapable conclusion." He nonetheless insists that "most readers" (and this presumably includes Carroll himself) automatically complete the pattern of symbols, assume that the third call is from the sanitarium, and therefore "kill" the boy by mentally writing their own ending to the story. Such a view does not take full account of the story's aesthetic implications. As soon as we appreciate that the story is a fiction and that all its clues are therefore false, the "reality" of the boy and his mania is shattered, and it is no longer possible to speak of our participation in his "world." There is no ambiguity left at the end about the significance or meaninglessness of the symbols in the story, and speculation about the boy's possible suicide is irrelevant, since the world of the story has ceased to exist with the story's final punctuation mark. It has been translated, so to speak, from our perspective to the higher sphere of the artist's fictive world (in which we are characters too) and ultimately to a configuration of black marks on the page. The reliability of *all* the information about the boy is questionable. Carroll's argument to the contrary notwithstanding, we *are* ultimately distanced from the story and hence even from what Carroll calls an "esthetic responsibility" for the boy's death.[5] This is the final stage of deciphering "Signs and Symbols," the stage that goes one step beyond Carroll's otherwise convincing interpretation.

This stage reminds us of the "Hegelian syllogism of humor" practiced by Axel Rex in *Laughter in the Dark*:

> Uncle alone in the house with the children said he'd dress up to amuse them. After a long wait, as he did not appear, they went down and saw a masked man putting the table silver into a bag. "Oh, Uncle," they cried in delight. "Yes, isn't my makeup good?" said Uncle, taking his mask off. Thus goes the Hegelian syllogism of humor. Thesis: Uncle made himself up as a burglar la laugh for the children); antithesis: it *was* a burglar laugh for the reader); synthesis: it still was Uncle (fooling the reader).[6]

William Woodin Rowe uses this passage to illustrate his contention that in Nabokov's works "the reader is often subtly induced to draw premature, erroneous conclusions about *what* is taking place."[7] In "Signs and Symbols" the parents at first seem innocent.

Then they appear to be implicated in their son's condition and perhaps his death; finally, we sense the hoax: the story is a fiction, and nobody is responsible. Yet the joke is a serious one. Nabokov is not simply playing an empty game at our expense. He is affirming art as sacred play. In calling our attention to the artifice of his story, he reminds us of the superior vision of the artist. As a private world of the imagination the story shares something with the son's mania. But unlike the latter it is redeemed by an act of freedom— the artistic expression that consciously creates the fictive world of the story and the playful configuration of its language. Nabokov succeeds in capturing both our belief and our disbelief. We relish the irony after the terror of momentary belief. And in so doing we are rescued from the foul air of mortality by the pleasure and vivifying force of art.

Decoding "Signs and Symbols"

John V. Hagopian

Displaced persons and madmen are recurrent themes in Nabokov's fiction, and both are central to his early—and best—short story, "Signs and Symbols." The nameless family, probably Russian Jews, have shuttled from "Minsk, the Revolution, Leipzig, Berlin, Leipzig" to America where the father, "who in the old country had been a fairly successful business man, was now wholly dependent on his brother Isaac, a real American of almost forty years standing" (A10: 18). The geographic and socio-political displacement, however, is subsumed in a larger, cosmic displacement; these people have no place in life or in the universe.

The straightforward, declarative style ("That Friday everything went wrong") barely mutes the somber tone. Unlike the larger, grander treatments of this theme in *Pnin*, *Bend Sinister* and *Pale Fire*, there is no wit or levity here to relieve the intense sadness of the human experience. That somber tone is most appropriate to the mother, of whom—or *for* whom—the narrator says, "all living did mean accepting the loss of one joy after another, not even joys in her case—mere possibilities of improvement" (A13: 133).

Tone and point of view are closely related, because the external, objective narrator effaces himself, and, though he tells the story in the third person, presents only the thoughts and perceptions in her mind. The only factor that prevents a conversion of the story into an I-narrative simply by changing the third-person pronouns into the first person (i.e. "she waited for her husband ..." to "I waited for my husband ...") is that the mother, a poor émigré, cannot realistically have such a magnificent command of the English language. But even though the language is Nabokov's, the mind it manifests is the mother's. Hence, it cannot be as William Carroll maintains that "Nabokov has ensured, through his rhetorical strategy, that the reader will succumb to the same mania."[1] And that perspective is not at all, as W. W. Rowe maintains, "an almost paranoiac mode of perception."[2] On the contrary, the narrative technique serves as an implicit endorsement of her perspective on things. Indeed, the central thematic question of the story is:

Is it necessarily paranoid to feel that nature and the universe are enemies of man? To want to "tear a hole in [the] world and escape"? To put it another way, does the story depict a context for human experience so benign that it is obviously madness to want to escape? What do the "signs and symbols" indicate? Dr Herman Brink, presumably a Freudian psychiatrist and forerunner of John Ray, Jr., in *Lolita* (a breed that Nabokov detested), had diagnosed the boy's condition as "referential mania," a form of paranoia which the *Psychiatric Dictionary* defines as a delusion in which a patient misinterprets everything around him as having "a personal reference of a derogatory character toward him."[3] Dr Brink used the boy as a subject of a professional paper in which he gave a vivid description of his symptoms and drew the conclusion that to him "everything is a cipher and of everything he is the theme ... [that is] the ultimate truth of his being" (A11: 72). But is it a fact that the boy's interpretation is a delusion, an aberration inconsistent with the "real" world depicted in the story?

William Carroll endorses Dr Brink with the comment, "The boy lives in a closed system of signs all of which point, malevolently, toward him."[4] It may be that anyone who seeks to interpret the meaning of the signs and symbols betrays himself as one of another breed that Nabokov detested. In a reply to W. W. Rowe's book he expressed indignation at

> the symbolism racket in schools [that] computerizes minds but destroys plain intelligence as well as poetical sense ... The various words planted by an idiotically sly novelist to keep schoolmen busy are not labels, not pointers, and certainly not the garbage cans of a Viennese tenement, but live fragments of specific description, rudiments of metaphor, and echoes of creative emotion.[5]

But the story is entitled "Signs and Symbols" and clearly depicts characters who are intensely aware of them. The signs are not, as Carroll maintains, merely a "closed system" of the deranged son; nor is it true that "his parents are dull, sad people who are merely oblivious where he is paranoid."[6] The world presented by the narrator and observed by the parents is fully consistent with the boy's vision of it. The parents have suffered much and their greatest suffering issues from their compassion for their unfortunate son. They make great sacrifices for him, go to a great deal of trouble to visit him regularly in the sanatorium, worry about getting him an appropriate present for his birthday, and have poignant reminiscences about his childhood. Upon learning of his renewed attempt to commit suicide, they determine to bring him home and care for him themselves in their cramped two-room flat. Such concerns gainsay Douglas Fowler's bizarre observation that the parents "are allowed to come before us as without genius, beauty, comic vulgarity, or monstrousness because they are marked for extinction, too."[7] To be sure, they lack comic vulgarity and monstrousness, but they have a genius for survival and a beautiful capacity for family love. If they are "marked for extinction," it is only because they are old and have suffered much, and not because they are to be classed with the losers in Nabokov's world.

With respect to the significance of the signs and symbols of the story, it is important to keep in mind that everything is presented from the point of view of the mother. She is fully aware that, unlike Mrs Sol, "whose face was all pink and mauve with paint and whose hat was a cluster of brookside flowers" (i.e. she cosmeticizes the malevolence of nature), she "presented a naked white countenance to the fault-finding light of spring days." It is a fact and not a paranoid fantasy that the world she lives in is not at all friendly or succoring: "the Underground train lost its life current between two stations," "a tiny half-dead unfledged bird was helplessly twitching in a puddle," another passenger, a girl, was weeping on the shoulder of an older woman, the sanatorium was "miserably understaffed and things got mislaid or mixed up so easily," the husband's "clasped and twitchy hands had swollen veins and brown spotted skin," the son's "poor face was blotched with acne." These are not the insane imaginings of the boy, but a hard-fact reality that undermines Dr Brink's diagnosis. They depict a world from which the urge to escape is not at all a symptom of madness.

Carroll argues that

> Nabokov has insured, through his rhetorical strategy, that the reader will succumb to the same mania that afflicts the boy. The story is studded with apparent signs and symbols that the gullible reader—that is, any reader—will attempt to link together in a meaningful pattern. (A245)

Carroll is clearly a postmodernist who believes that the story does not have a closed form that crystallizes a specific meaning determined by the author and that a reader who feels a "need to see a completed pattern ... will have, in effect, participated with Nabokov in killing the boy."[8] But Nabokov once said to Alfred Appel, "the design of my novel is fixed in my imagination and every character follows the course I imagine for him. I am a perfect dictator in that private world."[9] It would seem to follow that a reader is obliged to discover the author's fixed design and follow the course he has imagined for his characters. But Carroll would have it that a reader who sees the design as leading inexorably to the death of the boy is guilty of murder! That raises the most crucial plot question: does the boy in fact die in the end?

The story has three parts. Part I depicts the abortive attempt of the parents to deliver a birthday gift, abortive because the boy had attempted to commit suicide. Part II focuses on the mother's meditations after their return to the flat, and Part III on the post-midnight decision to bring the boy home, followed by the ringing of the telephone. In effect, these are 1) the immediate context of the boy's suicide attempt, already examined above; 2) the family's history of pain and death, obviously modeled on Nabokov's own family history; 3) the successful suicide. The principal signs and symbols of Part II are the photographs and playing cards. Apart from the boy, the figures in the photo album include Aunt Rosa, exterminated by the Germans; a famous chess player cousin (readers familiar with Nabokov's sly practice of using principal characters in some works as background figures in others will recognize Luzhin, another suicide); and some "ugly vicious, backward children he was with in that special school" (like those in the school where Adam Krug's own son was killed in *Bend Sinister*) —all symbols of death and violence. At four, the boy looked away from an eager squirrel like Pnin, he did not consider nature friendly even then); at six, he drew birds with human hands and feet; later, an envious fellow patient thought he was learning to fly-and stopped him from committing suicide); and as a teenager he developed "those little phobias ... the eccentricities of a prodigiously gifted child hardened as it were into a dense tangle of logically inter-acting illusions, making him totally inaccessible to normal minds" (perfect description of Nabokov's own fiction). These images evoke in the mother thoughts of "endless waves of pain ... of individual giants hurting her boy ...

of beautiful weeds that cannot hide from the farmer and helplessly have to watch the shadow of his simian stoop leave mangled flowers in its wake as the monstrous darkness approaches" (A13: 136). That last image in which human perceptions and emotions are projected upon helpless weeds suggests that the mother, too, suffers from what Herman Brink called "referential mania." But the family's history fully justifies the feeling that they live in a malevolent universe. All this brooding on pain and death leads to Part III, which occurs in a period of "monstrous darkness." The father who cries, "I can't sleep because I am dying," insists that they bring the boy home. The mother readily agrees, stooping to pick up some photos and cards, including the ace of spades (a symbol of death). It is then that they are frightened by the ring of the telephone, a wrong number. When the telephone rings a second time, the mother (who obviously has acute perceptions and intelligence) patiently explains, "I will tell you what you are doing: you are turning the letter O instead of the zero." Carroll says of this, "while it is a plausible explanation of the wrong number, the fact remains that there is no hieroglyphic difference between the letter and the number."[10] He is so determined to keep the story from having a necessary closure that he cites the irrelevant hieroglyphic similarity of O and zero. But in fact on a telephone dial there is a significant hieroglyphic difference: the letter O is a perfect circle, whereas the number zero is a vertical oval. Even more important is the fact that the O appears in the sixth hole on the dial and the zero appears in the tenth! These significant details and the lapse of time between the second and third rings of the telephone make it highly unlikely that the third call is simply another wrong number. Nabokov said, "I like composing riddles with elegant solutions" (see the ending of "The Vane Sisters"). The signs and symbols of the story inexorably accumulate to make that third ring a portent of death. The fears of the parents come true, and the reader experiences the chilling shock of recognition that the sanatorium is calling to report that the boy has at last torn a hole in his world and escaped. Carroll is clearly wrong in asserting that

> it is just as plausible to argue, though, that the signs and symbols of death have no logically inherent and inescapable conclusion, that they point to nothing finally, and are as "meaning"-less as a sequence of random numbers. It is this ambiguity that makes

the story so profoundly eerie. The "cipher" is constructed so that we have to supply the key, constitutionally unable to admit that there is none.[11]

But no legitimate artist produces randomness. Such a reading assumes that the story does not have implicit lines of force shaping a gestalt and leading to the closure of a specific design. The post-modernists must not be allowed to kidnap Nabokov. He may revel in intricacies and labyrinthine complexities and he may relish topsi-turvical coincidences, but John Shade in *Pale Fire* nicely articulates Nabokov's aesthetic:

> Not flimsy nonsense, but a web of sense.
> Yes! It sufficed that I in life could find
> Some kind of link-and-bobolink, some kind
> Of correlated pattern in the game.[12]

As Hagopian observes,

> One might say of Nabokov that the more a particular novel engages his own passions, the more he controls and conceals them by converting them into games, puzzles, and various intricate patterns; clear and obvious plots emerge from his pen only when he contemplates the experience with a cool, dispassionate objectivity.[13]

In the final analysis, "Signs and Symbols," despite its pessimistic world-view, emerges as one of Nabokov's most beautifully made and poignant short stories.

The referential mania: an attempt of the deconstructivist reading

Álvaro Garrido Moreno

Life is a message scribbled in the dark.

Anonymous
Vladimir Nabokov, *Pale Fire*

I

Vladimir Nabokov often expressed his feeling of intense confinement within the Cell of artistic imagination:

> The type of the artist who is always in exile even though he may never have left the ancestral hall or the paternal parish is a well-known biographical figure with whom I feel some affinity.[1]

This remark engages with a whole gallery of characters and narrative developments in Nabokov's fiction which write and rewrite the same claustrophobic obsession of the individuals who experience intense isolation of consciousness: either the mad artist like Cincinnatus, Fyodor, Sineosov, Van and Ada, Hugh Person, or Krug, or else the criminal artist like Alex, Rex, Hermann, Humbert Humbert, or Van Veen. Consciousness and subjectivity are for Nabokov the fundamental dimensions of existence, the greatest and ultimate mystery, at the same time the scenario for both freedom and exile.[2] Nabokov's fiction writes and rewrites the solipsistic struggle for liberation from the constraints of consciousness through imagination, through art as the only means of catching a glimpse of transcendence. His belief in the primacy and universality of subjective experience involves, in turn, a concomitant belief in the individual imagination (especially through art) as a primal source of truth; in an interview he declared: "Average reality begins to rot and stink as soon as the act of individual creation ceases to animate a subjectively perceived texture."[3]

The metaphors underpinning this statement are extremely revealing of Nabokov's conception, or rather fiction, of the artistic performance. Such fiction, as I read it, presupposes a double division of experience. The objects of average reality are separated from the transcendental purifying realities they signify, and the individual consciousness is separated both from average reality and from the transcendental realm of uncorrupted truth. The act of individual creation based on these assumptions is an act that brings about a change in man's relation to the world of average reality. It animates an otherwise inanimate texture, as it were, without *anima*, without life, that incurably rots and stinks—these words posit the need for a healing and purifying creation as an ethical imperative. Thus the subjective process of creation animates, gives true life to a reality doomed otherwise to inertia and putrefaction in virtue of its averageness, its standardness, a coinage debased in the daily exchange. Such a perception of reality results from the enactment of a struggle which may take the artist to the very brink of truth. The individual creator must avoid at all costs a perception which is average and must become sensitive to a texture that is not commonly accepted or standardized—but which in fact is more real or true than average reality:

I have often noticed that after I had bestowed on the characters of my novels some treasured item of my past, it would pine away in the artificial world where I had so abruptly placed it. Although it lingered on my mind, its personal warmth, its retrospective appeal had gone and, presently, it became more closely identified with my novel than with my former self, where it had seemed to be safe from the intrusion of the artist. Houses have crumbled in my memory as soundlessly as they did in the mute films of yore, and the portrait of my old French governess, whom I once lent to a boy in one of my books, is fading fast, now that it is engulfed in the description of a childhood entirely unrelated to my own. The man in me revolts against the fictionist, and here is my desperate attempt to save what is left of poor Mademoiselle.[4]

The figure of the artist who partakes of some aristocratic disdain for the masses laboring heavily in more constricted and straitened versions of reality matches the solipsistic consciousness in the

works of Pound, Eliot, Woolf, Joyce, or Faulkner. Nabokov's
characters have their peculiar features and inscribe peculiar sets of
assumptions in his work, but if any background is needed for or
against them, it is within this tradition that they fall. In fact, "Signs
and Symbols"—signed "Boston 1948"—is permeated by some
features of the non-totalizable topography of classical modernism.[5]
This short narrative presents a decadent family; they are a sterile
old couple of Chekhovian exiles whose son is "incurably deranged
in his mind"; their economical situation has brought about his
internment in a sanatorium which is "miserably understaffed";
this damaged family make ends meet thanks to the charity of a
rich relative, the husband's brother, presumably another Jewish
emigrant who has been able to buy his way into the American
society and become a "real American." However, the situation
of this family has not always been so distressing and arduous:
in the old country, in Leipzig, he had been a "fairly successful
businessman" and they enjoyed a comfortable life, for they even
had a "German maid." If I were to qualify this depiction of a family
with one word—something which, of course, is unpermissible—an
apt epithet might be "Faulknerian," or "Chekhovian": an elderly
couple (the "silvery" bearded husband needs a dental plate, suffers
from a stomach disease and eats "pale victuals," his wife's "old
tired heart" "trudges heavily upstairs"), too old to be able to
procreate any longer, whose phobic only son is driven to suicide by
the claustrophobia of his obsession, present a landscape of hopeless
sterility; they cling haggardly to their golden past: the husband has
not been able to learn to speak fluently the language of his new
country; he has created a defense, as it were, against the corruption
of his relief-giving memory: he reads "his Russian language
newspaper" and wears over his nightgown "the old overcoat with
astrakhan collar" which he much prefers to his new bathrobe;
the wife unsleeps the night examining old photographs. There is
something Eliotic, I feel, about the celebration of a life-returning
spring in a world already enjoying death and avoiding natural
regeneration: the mother does not wear any makeup, unlike her
neighbor, who rebels against the poignancy of the "fault-finding
light of spring days" with an awkward pink and mauve embalment
and artificial flowers. The narrative sequentiality of "Signs and
Symbols" is also inhabited by the structures of Faulkner's, Woolf's
or Joyce's novels: the narrator, the open ending, the topography

of narrative "clues." I will return to this when discussing the assumptions about the reading process which sustain "Signs and Symbols."

However, the critical readings of Nabokov do not seem to agree as to the presence of Anglo-Saxon modernist writing in Nabokov's text: it seems there is an uncanny tension in the pathos of his solipsistic characters. The writing of solipsism and of its transcendence through artistic imagination, through the animation of a subjectively perceived texture, is divided in "Signs and Symbols"—into signs and symbols. Nabokov's story inscribes the affirmation of artistic "creative" language in a general economy that prevents its affirmation.

II

The pathos of "Signs and Symbols" depends on and is constituted by the dramatization of the clash between different modes of perception and interpretation of reality and their hierarchization, that is, between two ways of reading: the "average" reading and the "subjective" reading.[6]

The exiled couple's son is secluded in a sanatorium because of his strange "system of delusions"; "referential mania":

> "Referential mania," Herman Brink had called it. In these very rare cases the patient *imagines* that everything happening around him is a *veiled reference* to his personality and existence. (A11: 62, emphasis added)

This boy is trapped in "a dense tangle of logically interacting illusions" whereby he considers the movement of trees, the sounds of the mountain, the surfaces of still pools and store windows to be the activity of an awful conspiracy threatening his personality and existence. For him, "everything is a cipher and of everything he is the theme"; for him, "phenomenal nature" is a huge coded message which, within the folds of its coding, carries information regarding him; natural phenomena such as clouds, firs, rivers, pools, are veiled references, they are relational objects intertwined through a strange hidden logic which withdraws them from their literality in the realm of phenomenality in order to name what does not belong to this realm, to name this boy's ultimate truth. They are ciphers, that is, messages whose referent is another message; they are figures of his personality and existence. His reading of the world around him is—as I read it—*figural*, as opposed to the average literal one, the one shared by, among others, his mother, scholars like Herman Brink who write papers "in a scientific monthly," and us, that is, the people who are not incurably deranged in their minds. But we shall soon realize how these assumptions or illusions are immediately outplayed *by* this narrative—particularly the latter.

The dramatization of the binary opposition real/fictional is to be found at all levels: the son is caught by means of a dense tangle of illusions, of fictional objects imagined *by* figural language; he inhabits a fictional realm he has brought about around him by subjectively animating average reality. Such dramatization leads logically to a consideration of figural language and fiction as derivative activities that depend for their existence on the literal and real ones. Moreover, their beauty and existence is threatened by literality, in much the same way that beautiful weeds are menaced and mangled by the farmer:

> She thought of the endless waves of pain that for some reason or other she and her husband had to endure; of the invisible giants hurting her boy in some unimaginable fashion; of the incalculable amount of tenderness contained in the world; of the fate of this tenderness, which is either crushed, or wasted, or transformed into madness; of neglected children humming to themselves in unswept corners; of beautiful weeds that cannot hide from the farmer and helplessly have to watch the shadow of his simian stoop leave mangled flowers in its wake as the monstrous darkness approaches. (A13: 135)

Creative imagination, fiction, figurality, are thought of by average minds as beautiful weeds, parasitical, suspect, pernicious, secondary.

Nabokov, then, has been often read as privileging—in the aristocratic hierarchy-producing fashion referred to above—the second term in these oppositions (figural and fictional), identifying them with the special gifts of creative imagination whereby the human mind may catch a glimpse of the ultimate truth of his being, of transcendence. However, the pathos of "Signs and Symbols," as I read it, is somehow distanced, biased, is the echo of the pathos of the romantic isolation of a young imaginative mind bent on self-destruction—a recurrent theme in Nabokov's short stories.[7] Some statements produce a quaint weaving of meanings in the sorrowful portrayal of the son: he *is* a "prodigiously gifted child" who "considers himself to be so much more intelligent than other men." The hierarchization of this character, isolated, creative, pathetic, the type of the Chekhovian decadent romantic artist, physically weak (he had suffered from pneumonia and insomnia), is disrupted at source, not only by those mocking (remarkable) remarks, but by the pointing out of, and obedience to, a linguistic necessity: "Signs and Symbols" displaces and undoes the oppositions literal/figural and real/fictional which sustain the given order of priorities of logocentrism. The deviations of the son's deranged consciousness are repeated by his mother: her son painfully elaborates fictional patterns derived from the real ones around him—*outside him, outside* language—and whose theme is his own personality and existence. But she is already trapped in the overwhelming law of the *veiled reference*:

[I]t gave her a kind of soft shock, a mixture of compassion and wonder, to notice that one of the passengers, a girl with dark hair and grubby red toenails, was weeping on the shoulder of an older woman. *Whom did that woman resemble? She resembled Rebecca Borisovna, whose daughter had married one of the Soloveichiks—in Minsk, years ago.* (A10: 48, emphasis added)

The mother's perception of the features of the woman who is sitting in front of her in the bus leads her mind to "hook on" to a presence that is not part of her immediate environment "[d]uring the long ride": the presence of Rebecca Borisovna, of her daughter, of a marriage, of the Soloveichiks, of long-gone Minsk. It is the presence of an absence, it is a fictional presence; it is a story unleashed by the veiled reference to the physical appearance of a woman within a bus.

The same logic which relates physical objects to a narrative account—to her past, to the clues of the existence to which her husband stubbornly clings—of "incredibly detailed information regarding" her, is at work when she is examining the photographs from her old albums in a situation of longed-for isolation at night, alone in the living-room where she has pulled the blinds down. The coordination of the two activities in the sentence, "She pulled the blind down and examined the photographs," creates an intimate link between these two modes of action, isolating herself from outside activity to interpret the messages coded in and by her photographs; in Nabokov's tale, isolation is somehow the condition of introspection, which much resembles her son's mania:

> From a fold in the album, a German maid they had had in Leipzig and her fat-faced fiancé fell out. Minsk, the Revolution, Leipzig, Berlin, Leipzig, a slanting house badly out of focus. Four years old, in a park: moodily, shyly, with puckered forehead, looking away from an eager squirrel as he would from any other stranger. Aunt Rosa, a fussy, angular, wild-eyed old lady, who had lived in a tremulous world of bad news, bankruptcies, (rain accidents, cancerous growths—until the Germans put her to death, together with all the people she had worried about. Aged six—that was when he drew wonderful birds with human hands and feet, and suffered from insomnia like a grown-up man. His cousin, now a famous chess player. He again, aged about eight, already difficult to understand, afraid of the wallpaper in the passage, afraid of a certain picture in a book which merely showed an idyllic landscape with rocks on a hillside and an old cart wheel hanging from the branch of a leafless tree. Aged ten: the year they left Europe. The shame, the pity, the humiliating difficulties, the ugly, vicious, backward children he was with in that special school. (A12: 110)

The echoes, "silhouettes," or rather—to extend Nabokov in a Nabokovian way—the ghosts of modernist experimental stream (extreme?) of consciousness narrative devices, "flip over" within this quote. The grammatical structure of this paragraph creates but also, by this very same move, destroys—immediacy of experience by obliterating the terms usually sustaining the rendering of experience, by this detour of language called *zeugma*. There are no verbs designating the physical activity of this woman while she examines each photo, her movements, nor is there any (literal) mention of the objects, of each fold in the album, each photo. Instead, the narrator's omnipresent words overlap, blur, embody the old woman's language—almost completely, for there is still the ironic distance marked by "they"—trying to efface the presence of outside reality in order to release the contents of this mother's consciousness—by now, a setup familiar to us: the obliteration of phenomenality as a condition for introspection and imagination— the activity of this special form of imagination called memory. The law of the referential mania spreads its implications at every moment in this paragraph. The photographs, physical objects, "man-made" objects which copy—and distort dimensionally— physical objects reveal incredibly detailed information regarding her. Moreover, she does not name these man-made objects by means of (supposedly) literal terms: she does not design them using the terms "a photograph of ..." Instead, she names them directing her language backwards to the resources of memory, of imagination. It is not a photograph of a woman and a man that falls out of the album: it is a "German maid they had had in Leipzig and her fat-faced fiancé"; such a reading repeats the features of her son's mania, for the woman in the photograph (later we know her literal name, Elsa) is read only in terms of her past relationship to the family: a German *maid they had had in* Leipzig; a maid, in Leipzig, terms like any others which designate and depend on a relation, the professional engagement of that woman with the family, with the past of the family. Furthermore, the man who appears in the photograph is read only in relation to the family, for he is *her fiancé*, another relational term: this man is the boyfriend of a German maid of the family when they lived in Leipzig. Moreover, the qualifier "fat-faced" (later "bestial") testifies to the inevitability of a subjective "slanting" in any reading or interpretation of the world: probably we could not properly locate these words within Elsa's mind—if we were allowed to do so, which we are not.

The dictatorial partiality of subjectivity describes a picture of "rocks on a hillside and *an old cart wheel hanging from the branch of a leafless tree*" as an "*idyllic* landscape" [my emphasis]. The imprisoning and devouring nature of subjectivity inhabits the following sequence: "The shame, the pity, the humiliating diffi- culties, the ugly vicious backward children he was with in that special school." This loving mother's words for the sanatorium— "special school"—are euphemisms for (and used by) institutions that treat mental deviation, and have the effect of creating an opaque screen over what would otherwise be dangerously unset- tling definitions. She applies to her son's former fellow-patients a group of terms which easily apply to her own beloved child: his son's "poor face" is "ill shaven," "blotched with acne," words the reader readily relates to terms like ugly or vicious; besides, the other children are depicted as "backward," a word which is at odds with the description of her son as being "totally inaccessible to normal minds," falling in the region of the institutional euphemistic strategy above mentioned.

The (non)logic of the veiled reference is also at work when the photograph of the "wild-eyed old lady" directs the mother's consciousness to a narrative of "bad news, bankruptcies, train accidents, cancerous growths," the German invasion and the Shoah. This woman is called *Aunt* Rosa. The photograph of a boy, "*his* cousin" (my emphasis)—again relational terms—reveals a glimpse of a brilliant career as chess player. A photograph of her six-year-old son brings about—and around—the story of his quaint drawings and his distressing insomnia.

The overwhelming pointing-to-something-else of both readings problematizes the ontological status of reality. In the first section of "Signs and Symbols" referential mania was named in—by—a non-manic reading, in a reading that denominated natural phenomena by their literal average name. The link between an object and his name was safe there, stable, this stability being (institutionally) guaranteed by the capacity to detect deviations from literal reading, from the perception of things as they really are, the capacity to perceive and name, or rather, to both name and perceive a fir as a fir, a mountain as a mountain, a store window as a store window, and not "sullenly confuse" them with anything else. Her son's behavior is "a very rare case," which sets him apart from average models of conduct. It is a "system of delusions," "a dense tangle of logically interacting illusions." The words *illusion* and *delusion* de-nominate difficulties, mistakes, deviations from average perception which, nevertheless, by their relational and derived (and derivative) nature, involve average straightforward perception. They are produced, according to literal reading, by the impossibility of reading literally, that is, they are produced by figural reading. Literal terms are disfigured, drawn away from their realm and thrown aside—de-ranged—into a different realm: the objects of phenomenal nature are displaced from their natural location in the ordered system of average reality to designate such things as giants, conspiracies or spies. This displacement, which feeds on the firm ground of literality, is nothing but a momentary—as the semantic play field suggested by "illusion" and "delusion" indicates—swoon of language, a fainting fit, a sudden malaise which feeds on the texture of literality and deranges this healthy system. The illusions and delusions of figurality and fictionality are (I am echoing J. Hillis Miller)[8] something of a parasite, like "beautiful weeds" that uncomfortably appear in the tidy rows of crops within the economy of the farm. However, these weeds are sometimes indistinguishable from the flowers of crops. Weeds and crops grow entwined in a mutual invasion because both have the same natural drive, to the same beating energy which fights bravely to emerge everywhere, menacing and squeezing in the stability of the farmer's caring selection or animation of a specific vegetal texture within the manifold realm of nature. Literality and figurality somehow blur the frontiers of their opposition, and even reverse its terms, when objects of phenomenal nature, such as photographs, are thrown beyond their realm to designate the objects of this peculiar form of fiction we call memory—in Nabokov's works, memory requires the animation of creative imagination.[9] Thus, reality and fiction subjectively intermingle in the dense tangle of levels of meaning deployed by the term "imagination." There is no way out of figurality, nor is there a way out of fiction. We—I, the reader, Nabokov, the mother, the son—are plotting beings (proleptically and analeptically), and also plotted beings, for we inhabit the plots of other beings. In "Signs and Symbols" the metaphorical denomination "the Prince," which carries with it the seed of the fictional milieu inhabited by the now depending husband, becomes later the usual name for his brother: "We will have the doctor see him at least twice a week. It does not matter what the Prince says. He won't have to say much anyway because it will come out cheaper" (A14: 169).

Yet there is a contradiction—one among many—in what I have said so far about Nabokov's emphasis and aristocratic affirmation of imagination as the only means to prevent reality from rotting away, since imagination, figurality, fictionality, appear to be not the means but the condition of any reading of reality, that is, of reality. The inscription and reversal of the logocentric hierarchization literal/figural and real/fictional in "Signs and Symbols" produce a double, paradoxical logic: if average reality, the reality of normal minds is also the product of imagination, resulting from the animation of a subjectively perceived texture, governed

314 ANATOMY OF A SHORT STORY

by the deferring strategy of the veiled reference, then any attempt to (pathetically) favor subjectivity and imagination over normal reality is smashed, "crushed." The pathos of this story urges the reader to grant a privilege to solipisistic imagination while the possibility of such granting is eliminated.

III

The animation of a subjectively perceived texture is for Nabokov a matter of finding unexpected relationships and patterns between and within unnoticed details. In one of his first poems the Apostles are disgusted by the vision of worms leaking from the swollen corpse of a dog, but Christ is the only one who marvels about the pure whiteness of the corpse's teeth.[10] The narrators of *Transparent Things* recognize in a pencil the presence of the tree and, furthermore, the moment of its falling. Nabokov luxuriated in the perception of the unforeseen qualities and coincidences in the geometry of snow, in a pothook, in the wing of a butterfly, in the chink between the inner shutters:

> On a summer morning, in the legendary Russia of my boyhood, my first glance upon awakening was for the chink between the inner shutters. If it disclosed a watery pallor, one had better not open them at all, and so be spared the sight of a sullen day sitting for its picture in a puddle. How resentfully one would deduce, from a line of dull light, the leaden sky, the sodden sand, the gruel-like mess of broken blossoms under the lilacs—and that flat, fallow leaf (the first casualty of the season) pasted upon a wet garden bench.
>
> But if the chink was a long glint of dewy brilliancy, then I made haste to have the window yield its treasure. With one blow, the room would be cleft into light and shade. The foliage of birches moving in the sun had the translucent green of tone grapes, and in contrast to this was the dark velvet of trees against a blue of extraordinary intensity, the like of which I rediscovered only many years later, in the mountain zone of Colorado.
>
> From the age of seven, everything I felt in connection with a rectangle of framed sunlight was dominated by a single passion.

If my first glance of the morning was for the sun, my first thought was for the butterflies it would engender.[11]

The watery pallor of a line of light is also a veiled reference to a "sullen" future. The brilliancy of the glinting chink is the embryo of myriads of butterflies. A choir of sounds becomes related backwards over a past time span to some paragraphs within a book, and forward to a future delightful experience:

After making my way to some pine groves and alder scrub I came to the bog. No sooner had my ear caught the hum of diptera around me, the guttural cry of a snipe overhead, the gulping sound of the morass under my foot, than I knew I would find here quite special Arctic butterflies, whose pictures, or, still better, nonillustrated descriptions I had worshipped for several seasons.[12]

Patterns that relate elements from different regions of experience are inherent in, and created by, figurality as a mode of perceiving relationships, of finding parallels, of sending alternatives. The experiencing of patterns cannot escape from figural language.

The perception of patterns of Nabokov's characters is also displayed by the narrator of "Signs and Symbols." This narrator, whose consciousness is almost always married to the consciousness of the character of the mother and speaks for it without ever using "I," also uses figures to render the existence of unexpected patterns. The modernist new sense of the spatial dimension, which was a reading of the New Science and of Bergsonian relativism, is thematized in "the last dregs of the day were mixed with the street lights" or "he removed his hopelessly uncomfortable dental plate and severed the long tusks of saliva connecting him to it." The characterization of the father as a pathetically decadent figure is powerfully inscribed in the following figural (metaphorical and metonymical) sequence:

A few feet away, under a swaying and dipping tree, a tiny half dead unfledged bird was *helplessly twitching* in a puddle.

During the long ride to the Underground station, she and her husband did not exchange a word; and every time she glanced at his old hands (swollen veins, brown-spotted skin), clasped and *twitching* upon the handle of his umbrella, she felt the pressure of mounting tears. (A10: 40, emphasis mine)

For Nabokov—if we allow ourselves another (the same) swoon into generalization—the perception of patterns is not just a ludic investigation. It is not a merely hedonistic practice, but the way to avoid putrefaction:

> I confess I do not believe in time. I like to fold my magic carpet, after use, in such a way as to superimpose one part of the pattern upon another. Let visitors trip. And the highest enjoyment of timelessness—in a landscape selected at random—is when I stand among rare butterflies and their food plants. This is ecstasy, and behind the ecstasy is something else, which is hard to explain. It is like a momentary vacuum into which rushes all that I love. A sense of oneness with sun and stone. A thrill of gratitude to whom it may concern—to the contrapuntal genius of human fate or to tender ghosts humouring a lucky mortal.[13]

This densely figural fragment has something of the account of a mystical experience. The observation of patterns is the "hard to explain" interpretation of the veiled reference to this "something else" which stands behind aesthetic joy and ecstasy, which secures a contact with either "the contrapuntal genius of human fate" or with "tender ghosts humouring a lucky mortal," that is, a glimpse of transcendence, of true reality. As my epigraph puts it, "Life is a message scribbled in the dark."[14] The attempt to transcend solipsism is one of Nabokov's major themes and constantly writes the beating existence of *something else*, of transcendental existence. The narrator in *The Gift* asserts:

> The unfortunate image of a "road," to which the human mind has become accustomed (life as a kind of journey) is a stupid illusion: we are not going anywhere, we are sitting at home. The other world surrounds us always and is not at all the end of some pilgrimage. In our earthly house, windows are replaced by mirrors; the door, until a given time, is closed; but air comes in through the cracks.[15]

This quote metaphorizes the possibility of transcendence. Transcendence both permeates and tautens the texture of reality and the fabric of fancy. This possibility is in fact the *logos* which organizes and hierarchizes the whole network of presuppositions sustaining Nabokov's assumptions about language and existence. The affirmation of ontological transcendence is so involved with the basic concepts of logocentrism that it is very difficult for me to get rid of even if I wish to. The tradition of writers such as Woolf, Faulkner, Joyce, or Eliot explores and inscribes the epistemological possibility of transcendental truth in an *intolerable wrestle with words and meanings*—although other possibilities are reworked and redramatized in Nabokov's fiction against and within the modernist pathos of frustration, like the failure through sexual union of Ada and Van in *Ada* or Humbert and Lolita in *Lolita*, or through friendship, as thematized in the narrative of Kinbote and Shade's experience in *Pale Fire*, or even through liaison with ghosts, as Fyodor and his father in *The Gift* or Krug and his wife in *Bend Sinister*. The interpretation of the texture of reality thus becomes a vital—transcendental—experience. "Signs and Symbols" provides us with a family obsessively devoted to this task. The son is constantly absorbed in the deciphering of the dense tangle of references to the patterns he perceives. The mother "examines" the photographs of the album and interprets their hidden messages; she compulsively asks herself for patterns ("Whom did that woman resemble?") dwelling on the resemblance of phenomenal nature with her past experience. "[S]he and her husband" sadly "puzzled out" the eccentric behavior of their "prodigiously gifted child." The silvery-bristled father "re-examined with pleasure" the little jars, reading aloud, "his clumsy moist lips spelled out their eloquent labels" (which in fact do not name, again, the jelly they actually contain, but the fruit it is made of). Reading is the only true life:

> This, and much more she accepted—for after all living did mean accepting the loss of one joy after another, not even joys in her case—mere possibilities of improvement. (A13: 133)

In "Signs and Symbols" living does have a meaning, that is, it is the veiled reference to something else. But its meaning is precisely the intolerable search for this meaning which always surrounds us and, paradoxically, is always deferred. The acceptance of the constant frustration of the meaning envisaged in mere possibilities of improvement joins Nabokov's thematization of the reading process. He assures that the novelist, like the chess player, poses "problems," and a great part of a problem's value is due to the number of tries—*delusive* or punning moves, *false* scents, specious lines of play, astutely and lovingly prepared to lead the would-be solver *astray*.[16]

The accumulation of punning moves, false scents, specious lines of play, in other words, of interpretive clues (false or not), problematizes, twists, rugates, sublimates, and at once affirms the texture of classical modernist texts. In this tradition, whereby texts were conceived of as epistemological quests for truth, according to certain conventions, readers faced enormous difficulties in their attempt to understand those writings by determining their thematical and rhetorical modes. Those works—like much post-modern production—were (are) offered structurally (and institutionally) both as problems for interpretation and as epistemological speculations on the truth of human existence. The unveiling of meaning thus inscribes the possibility of the transcendence of solipsism.

However, the *story* of such an eager reading process is by no means simple. The complexity of modernist texts derives to a great extent from their exhausting intertextuality. They encapsulate echoes of and references to long series of texts which may belong to Western and even to Eastern tradition. In a sense, classical modernist texts postulate a very *learned* type of reader, either a reader already familiar with the intricate textual inscriptions and evasions through integrative mythical patterns, through religious patterns and symbology, through the so-called experimental techniques feeding on the New Science and Bergsonian epistemology, through Freudian and Jungian psychoanalytical structures, or else a reader forced, by the above mentioned difficulty, to read and *learn by* heart the texts of Jessie Weston, Jung, Freud, or Bergson, and to constantly check out her or his knowledge of previous major texts from both Western and Eastern traditions, in order to discover truth-revealing verbal treasures within the texture of the work. T. S. Eliot's notes to *The Waste Land* ironically played on both types of reader.

Nabokov's fictions abound in imaginative games, patterns of suggestion, allusion, reflection, and wordplay, which problematizes the very act of reading learned in a modernist context. His texts exploit the compulsive tendency we have as human beings to look at phenomena and try to discern meaningful patterns which seem to exist (according to the terms of his own formulation, since they can be "false"" or "delusive"). The reader is inveigled into a difficult quest for gradually emerging patterns and interlocking clues. Nabokov designates the reader with the term "solver": he or she must not only solve verbal puzzles and pursue cryptogrammic paper chases, but also recognize parodies and unravel the complex existence of reality and fiction through a series of interpretive attempts, which are "metaphoric approximations of the shifting kaleidoscope" in Nabokov's work.[17]

Nabokov's "Signs and Symbols" presents itself ironically eager for analysis. Its very title overtly declares what this story is about. This narrative is not a devoted account of the illness of an artistically gifted imaginative young boy and his parents, but a game of signs and symbols—or rather, signs or symbols[18] —which turns out to be the illness of any imaginative mind, including the reader's. "Signs and Symbols" is also a message scribbled in the dark by some transcendental law of signification, by a true meaning, by a *logos*. The assumption of the existence of a true meaning governs Nabokov's statements about the reading experience as a game of possibilities. If the reader is to discover that her or his assumption is just a "delusive" or "false" one leading her or him "astray," there must be a move or scent which is not delusive or false, a true meaning which permeates and gives sense to all the texture, which sustains and redirects the game of "moves" and of "tries" towards itself.

Thus the reader is inveigled into mimicking Nabokov's characters, isolated by their pattern-governed epistemological quest for true patterns, for a true meaning which always surrounds us and comes in through the cracks of our earthly door. One possible way of crossing the frontiers of solipsism is through death. The ironic distancing of the narrator's simple past tense powerfully inscribes the presence of death in Nabokov's short story: the open ending of the phone call which inevitably directs the reader's attention to the son's suicide, where this narrative unfolds backwards, is also the moment of the narrating act. The narrator uncannily speaks its existence beyond death (the simple past generates the irony of this privileged information from beyond). The presence of death is assured also in the disturbing presence of the zero: the girl's confusion is produced by the contingent typographical or material connection (though the number is given here its name "zero," playing again on the inevitability of figuration in fiction which depends on haphazard relational features of the signifier); this confusion also plays figurally on the son's tearing open a hole to escape from his isolation. Depending on the narrator's irony, the zero (nought, but also the origin of the endless series of numbers, the knot where both coordinate and ordinate axes intersect, the note—like the notes framing this paper— where the text acknowledges the presence of absence) is the possibility of communication, though at the same time the girl's dialing of the zero opens the ending and the possibility of suicide. The threat of the son's death permeates and tautens, so to speak, the pathetic texture of "Signs and Symbols":

> The last time their son had tried to take his life, his method had been, in the doctor's words, a masterpiece of inventiveness; he would have succeeded, had not an envious fellow patient thought he was learning to fly—and stopped him. What he really wanted to do was to tear a hole in his world and escape. (A10: 54)

The metaphor of the hole engages Nabokov's autobiographical depiction of a moment of transcendental, almost mystical experience of a "vacuum into which rushes all I love." Both, death or suicide and combinational or pattern perceiving joy, are sustained by the above mentioned confidence in a founding *logos*.

IV

"Signs and Symbols" offers itself as a veiled reference for the learned reader engaged suspiciously in a quest for signs and symbols which refer to a hidden and true meaning. This short story abounds in what this would-be solver, me, is entitled to consider to be scents or clues—including the narrator's metaphors mentioned above— punning names, such as Herman Brink; the *mise en abyme* echoes of the three phone calls and the three sections of the narrative; the enigmatic figurative possibilities of such different elements as the birthday present consisting of a basket with ten different fruit jellies in ten different jars, the sequence of labels, the underground train, the bus crammed with garrulous school children, the letter O, the zero; the open ended structure which redirects the whole narrative backwards, eager for a rereading that assigns a huge question mark, so to speak, which coincides with the upper edge of the text. The ending or lower edge of this narrative was already contained in the very title, in the upper edge. An open ending always sets itself up as a veiled reference to a meaning only attained after a rereading of the narrative; yet in "Signs and Symbols," this constant inquisitive rereading is the condition of any reading of the narrative—in fact, the condition of life. This vacuum-like title inveigles the reader into a constant searching for and checking of patterns, a constant attempt to decide whether they are *signs* or *symbols*.

The word *signs* is mentioned in the narrative:

> Clouds in the staring sky transmit to one another, by means of slow signs, incredibly detailed information regarding him. His inmost thoughts are discussed at nightfall, in manual alphabet, by darkly gesticulating trees. (A11: 67)

These gestures or motions of the clouds are figurally read by the deranged boy as signs. Through a staring prosopopoeia, they are the veiled references to signs which in turn are veiled references to himself. Still, to mention the word "signs" is, so to speak, to unveil this hidden meaning, to read this message scribbled in the sky. In addition to this, the word "symbols" is not mentioned by the text (with the exception of the title, which inveigles the reader into a quest for symbols), maybe—I seek support for my reading and thereby run the risk of becoming a referential maniac—because they cannot be mentioned *as symbols*, they need to remain as *veiled, hidden, unmentioned* references to the meaning that governs the text, of the *logos* of which the old couple, the maniac son, the jars, the zero, the echoes *en abyme*, the ending, and therefore the whole narrative, are veiled references.

Nevertheless, the confidence in the existence of a founding meaning which tautens the figural texture of the story and validates true readings has no solid ontological grounds. This *logos* is nothing other than the product of figuration and combinational creation of meaning. The writing of the groundlessness of such a foundation is deployed by the ambiguity inherent in the "puzzling out" of the referential mania, squeezing into the figural system like weeds in a farm:

> Pebbles or stains or sun flecks represent in some awful way messages which he must intercept. Everything is a cipher and of everything he is the theme. Some of the spies are detached observers, such as glass surfaces and still pools; others, such as coats in store windows, are prejudiced witnesses, lynchers at heart; others again (running water, storms) are hysterical to the point of insanity, have a distorted opinion of him and grotesquely misinterpret his actions ... The very air he exhales is indexed and filed away. If the only interest he provokes were limited to his immediate surroundings—but alas, it is not! With distance the torrents of wild scandal increase—in volume and volubility. The silhouettes of his blood corpuscles, magnified a million times, flit over vast plains; and still farther, great mountains of unbearable solidity and height sum up in terms of granite and groaning firs the ultimate truth of his being. (A11: 70)

Everything in phenomenal nature, stains, pebbles, sun flecks, is a veiled reference or cipher of himself. However, this veiled reference reveals (rather reveils) that he is a cipher himself for phenomenal nature, that he is the veiled reference to a meaning which nature distortedly and grotesquely misinterprets. Clear surfaces such as still pools and glasses are detached observers: they do not misinterpret him because they offer a true and clear reflection of himself, a bi-dimensional figure in which he recognizes the ultimate truth of his being, which is always already a cipher. Problems begin for him when these surfaces offer a figure where he cannot recognize himself: the shadowing presence of coats behind and within his clear reflection in a store window, distorting it, is read as the menacing presence of lynchers; objects in which he cannot find an image in which he can recognize himself are hysterical to the point of insanity. Store windows are distorted images of himself, they are veiled references to himself; but this *himself*, the true undistorted one, is another image, the one reflected on a still pool, another cipher. Moreover, still pools, glasses, are already ciphers, for they are read *as* spies, observers, readers belonging to some staring conspiracy. Readers become the reading of other readers who, in turn, are already some reader's reading. Everything is a cipher of something else: there are nothing but references and references to references, everywhere.

The weeds of referential mania invade any reading so that the inescapable moment of literality is postponed by granting this moment a figural essence. The narrator's puzzling out of the boy's referential mania, in what seems to be something of an elaborate paper in a scientific monthly, is also affected by the blight of these beautiful weeds. In this paragraph, the narrator completely marries the consciousness of the mother abolishing any ironic distance; it mimics, word by word, it *is* word by word, the language of the mother: there is no use of the word "she" and the verbs are in the present tense (suspending the distance of the more frequent simple past tense). The abolition of the narrating irony presents the paragraph as the literal reading of the son's behavior. However, this literality is illusory since we have no evidence of verbal activity in the son's conduct capable of explaining such a system of delusions. This paragraph is nothing but the figural reading of a wordless performance: the boy's movements, gestures, glances, phobias, are nothing but veiled references to this system of figural delusions.

In addition to this, the narrator never mentions the characters literally. The narrator does not use their proper names, but purely relational terms: "mother," "wife," "husband," "son"; even the pronouns "he" and "she" sanction the ironic distance and relation of narrator and characters. The narrator presents the figural extensions of such subjects, being itself a figural construct, a grammatical subject whose properties are transferred from contiguous predicates.

"Signs and Symbols" wonderfully inscribes by means of metonymy the vacuum of the deferring and differential essence of the referential mania:

> Bending with difficulty, she retrieved some playing cards and a photograph or two that had slipped from the couch to the floor: knave of hearts, nine of spades, ace of spades. Elsa and her bestial beau. (A13: 163)

Cards are purely relational elements, whose meaning in the game depends solely on their relation to the rest of the pack. And it is here, among sheer relational elements, that the German maid they had had in Leipzig is given a literal name: Elsa.

Yet there is still another weed in "Signs and Symbols." My reading of this last quote as metonymy is the figural expression of my referential mania. It narrates my de Manian (or rather demonic) failure to read modernist reading conventions. Any attempt within my reading to generate meaningful patterns by random relational patterning of signifiers rather than by the constraints of meaning is forbidden by the constraint of my attempt. My essay narrates the impossibility of affirming the non-existence of a founding meaning without affirming the existence of the founding meaning of this affirmation. It also narrates the impossibility of my writing out the distinction between naming and reading, between perceiving and creating patterns, between Eliot's two learned readers, which is already inherent in the textual game of signs and symbols, and therefore of "Signs and Symbols."

My reading of the way we have meaning in "Signs and Symbols," that is, my reading of signs *or* symbols, also tells the short story of an impossible historical sequence: London, 1971; London, 1982; New Haven, 1979; Yale, 10 November 1977; Boston, 1948. My reading cannot avoid the compulsion of a reference to an unquestioned meaning that it denounces. I cannot do otherwise, which leaves me with something of a de Manian "suspended ignorance."[19]

A referential reading of Nabokov's "Signs and Symbols"

Charles W. Mignon

Vladimir Nabokov's story "Signs and Symbols" has a plot that is a succession, not a sequence of events. There is a faint line of causality in the effect of a son's behavior on his parents, but the events are presented with little sense of an underlying meaning. There are two contrasting critical views of this story: John V. Hagopian finds "meaning," and Paul J. Rosenzweig sees significance in the difficulty of finding "meaning." Hagopian sees the family's geographical and socio-political displacement subsumed in a larger cosmic displacement: the family together and as individuals "have no place in life or in the universe."[3] Rosenzweig, focusing on reader-response, proposes that the reader of the story resembles the son in the sense that both have referential mania. The correspondence between the son's illness and the reader's state of mind begins with "an insistence on pattern and meaning [that is] followed by the frustration of that desire."[4] Hagopian sees the central thematic question in whether the boy and his parents are deluded in thinking that nature and the universe are hostile to them: is the boy's paranoid interpretation in fact a delusion? Hagopian believes that pain, suffering, and the sadness of human experience is real. Rosenzweig, on the other hand, wants us to see "the relativity of apparent absolutes, the provisional nature of all labels, categories, and conventions."[5] Hagopian still believes in the referential function of language, but Rosenzweig is skeptical of it in readers of fiction because it seems to duplicate the boy's mania. Between these views a referential position may be fashioned that yet recognizes the provisional nature of language.

The critical positions I have summarized briefly above are set out in response to what many critics see as a basic problem of interpretation in the story, namely the meaning of the third phone call. David Field in fact believes that the underlying question is "Are there any principles for determining reality?"[6] I will begin with this question, then move on to the question of "referencing" in the story. On the theoretical level I agree with Piaget that humans do "know" things, and they do so in at least two ways: by "assimilation," the integration of anything into current intellectual structures, and by "accommodation," the alteration of structures to deal with new or problematical thoughts or realities that do not fit into existing mental structures. Ginsburg and Opper describe Piaget's idea of intellectual adaptation, involving both assimilation and accommodation, as complementary processes: "Assimilation involves the person's dealing with the environment in terms of his structures, while accommodation involves the transformation of his structures in response to the environment."[7] For Piaget intellectual development is but another expression of biological adaptation.

The problems in the story are related to the boy's inability to "accommodate," to create a new cognitive structure to account for an apparently hostile world, to the parents' inability to assimilate the pain and suffering of their environment with the cognitive structures they have, and to the reader's difficulty in "reading" the meaning of the story. The factors Piaget called upon to explain the development of these structures were (1) maturation, (2) experience, (3) social transmission, and (4) equilibration, or self-regulation.[8] Piaget describes equilibration as an act of knowing in which

the subject is active, and consequently, faced with an external disturbance, he will act in order to compensate and consequently he will tend toward equilibrium. Equilibrium, defined by active compensation, leads to reversibility.[9]

I will be arguing that both the mother and the father in Nabokov's story have reached some form of self-regulation by at least partial reversibilities, and that their son has not.

With this beginning, I wish to work toward a statement of meaning related to Nabokov's intentions in this story. I begin with the observation that all three major characters have adopted referential assumptions. Language ("signs"), or the power to interpret "symbols," is central to the characters' sense of reality and to our understanding of the characters. The mother, in examining her photographs, places the shots of her son in their historical contexts, and many of the contexts are emotionally set "in a tremulous world of bad news" (A12: 116). Some contexts reveal character: "Age six—that was when he drew wonderful birds with human hands and feet, and suffered from insomnia like a grown-up man" (A12: 118). But the contexts extend to thought: even when the boy's phobias "hardened … into a dense tangle of logically interacting illusions, making him totally inaccessible to normal minds" (A12: 131), the mother is able to "accommodate"—the language of her description reveals a hypothesis that allows her to explain to herself her son's condition. As a result of her experience she applies this new cognitive structure to aspects of external reality. "This, and much more, she accepted …" (A13: 133). Her way of describing the effect of the boy's mania on her is revealing as a sign of her own potential mania: the images are of invisible giants; incalculable tenderness crushed, wasted, or transformed into madness; neglected children; and, of most striking relevance, the beautiful weeds destroyed as a "monstrous darkness approaches." She believes that language does refer to reality, but the reality that she describes is a blending of external objects and the larger forces that seem to her to rule them—it is an imaginative referencing. It is distorted, but by no means non-human, for many humans do try to find "meaning" in their worlds. Nonetheless, these distortions themselves have consequences, for the construction of a new mental scheme is an act of moral perception that expresses itself in language.

We know the father believes, probably naively, in the referential nature of language—of its power to refer to both objective and subjective realities. We have the basket of fruit jellies that he spells out laboriously, and, wishing to get the boy out of the hospital, he shows his feeling of responsibility for the boy in the language he uses. He fears for the boy's life; his posture of rending himself on the head is an outward sign of his concern. There is in fact a terrible discrepancy in his mind between the way things are and the way they should be. But he is more optimistic in his attribution of meaning: he believes that his plans to bring the boy home have a reality about them that they do not actually have. He is excited, smiling as he puts forward his plan; the mood is almost happy: "They sat down to their unexpected festive midnight tea" (A14: 190). This is a feeble "accommodation" to alleviate his anxiety about his son, and may be a displacement of his mood of unacknowledged guilt.

The boy's system of meaning also assumes references from external reality, complicated in his case by a failure to actively compensate for the effects of external events, and by the succeeding projection onto nature of a cosmic hostility. Paranoia, as Hagopian has reminded us, is a delusion in which the patient misinterprets everything external as having "a personal reference of a derogatory character toward him."[10] But the necessity to interpret is built into the boy's cognitive structure: the reference from things to thoughts is beyond his power to control: he must constantly attempt to interpret things, and he can only interpret them in one fashion. The only central coherence in his mind able to order the multiple impressions of external reality is his own massive projection of hostility. Assimilation overpowers accommodation: he cannot change his existing structures and thus he has no new structure capable of successfully mediating external reality. He not only cannot understand this flood of messages, but, needing somehow to account for them, he attributes hostility to them. He projects his failure outward on to the natural universe: "Everything is a cipher and of everything he is the theme" (A11: 72). The theme is the unknown shadow, the hostile side of the self that is often identified with unfriendly features of the external world (*Moby Dick*, sharks, etc.).

So, all three characters assume the referential nature of language and of symbols: the mother uses language along with her snapshots to confirm the painful reality of her life; the father uses language to affirm a hope that contrasts to his wife's deeper view of life; and the son is actually used by an unregulated and unchanging scheme—obsession with reference rules his reality. So there is a sense in which a deconstructionist approach (i.e. seeing the relativity of absolutes and the consequent provisional nature of language in expressing these absolutes) is not useful to the interpretation of the story because it does not completely account for the way the characters in the story seem to be using language. Yet, it is useful in the sense that it underlines the relativity of human attributions and the final difficulty of describing the indescribable.

The statement of meaning I propose now is derived from and assumes the referential framework I have suggested above: Nabokov's purpose is to show characters affected by forces beyond their control, beyond their comprehension and thus beyond their powers of expression. The characters do, nonetheless, in their own ways, attempt to explain their experience in the common-sense way we know that people use language for these purposes. One question that emerges from a consideration of the family's versions of reality is: which version is closest to a position of equilibrium in the assimilation and accommodation of external reality? The son is farthest away from attaining equilibrium—in fact, he is lost in a hostile and labyrinthine inner world; he desires nothing more than to "tear a hole in his world and escape." The word "his" is most significant because it signals to us the projective nature of his mania. A successful ending to his attempts at suicide would, in his lights, be most desirable. In his case, the process of assimilating impressions of the external world with existing structures has completely overcome any disposition on his part to accommodate these impressions into a new cognitive structure with which he could adapt to the vicissitudes of human life. His father, on the other hand, is closer to equilibrium than his son, but he seems to have interpolated a scheme of naive hope between the painful facts of his life and a full acknowledgment of these facts. This scheme, paradoxically, allows him to continue living in a world that cannot really be accommodated by the thin structure of this hope; in fact it is ironic that this hopeful scheme leaves him in a world where continued suffering will be his only reality. His suffering may be compounded because of his imperfect "accommodation."

The mother seems to hold a position somewhere between her husband and her son. The suffering her husband is able to moderate somewhat with his scheme of naive hope she has come to accept. "This, and much more, she accepted—for after all living did mean accepting the loss of one joy after another ..." (A13: 133). So we can say that she has assimilated the painful facts of their experience—the Russian Revolution, family pain, the shame and humiliation of dislocation, the hopelessness of their son's condition—and has come to an accommodation with a scheme that gives her some measure of consolation. Even so, she finds it necessary to posit behind these painful events unseen powers that she reifies in her language. These reifications take the form of personifications: the "invisible giants" that cause indescribable pain to her son; the tenderness that exists in the world only to be crushed and destroyed; the ominous figure of the simian farmer (Eastern European anti-Semitic peasant? or Cavafy's "barbarian"?) whose sickle destroys the weeds, flowers, and all. She attributes some "monstrous darkness" that approaches, threatening to envelop all. Her experience of suffering has taught her that what tenderness there is in human life seems invariably to be crushed, and this to her confirms the presence of some hostile—if not malevolent—force, inhospitable to human aspirations.

All of these characters assume, in one way or another, a metaphysical reference in the ways they use language and see reality: the son, "decoding of the undulation of things" (A11: 79), sees a hostility in nature directed specifically toward himself; the father, relying on hopeful illusion, plans action motivated to ease his own suffering; the mother, accepting their suffering, finds ominous hostility in invisible forces that seem to control their lives. But each of these efforts to give meaningful shape to their worlds is insufficient to account for the continued suffering they must endure. And this is why the third telephone call, in these contexts, seems so laden with ominous significance.

Nabokov's intention may be to show characters affected by forces beyond their control and beyond their comprehension, who attempt nonetheless in their use of thought and language to deal with the pain and suffering these forces create for them. The unique cognitive structures they devise for themselves in this process have in common a referential basis: each assumes that there is "meaning" somewhere. The story is not as much about "the relativity of apparent absolutes, the provisional nature of all labels, categories, and conventions" as Rosenzweig suggests[11] as it is about the failure of human thought and language to comprehend the powerful forces working beyond its ken.

If we take this view of the story, the meaning of the third telephone call is richly imbued with what Rosenzweig attributes to the whole story: "the symbolism of impotence and doom."[12] There are three equally active forces at work in the story: the powerful, indifferent, and invisible forces at work on human nature; the emotional effects of these forces on human beings—pain and suffering; and the inability of human thought and language to grasp the inaccessible causes of this woe in human experience. In the context of these three realities, the so-called "meaning" of the third phone call cannot therefore be described beyond its ominous quality. Wrong numbers or right numbers cannot, finally, affect human life; one simply must accept the conditions under which life is lived even if it means creating cognitive structures that we know are flawed and rendered ineffective by our own desires and obsessions. The signs and symbols we use in the analysis of invisible causes are rendered ineffective by the very limitations of our own human consciousness.

The recession of absolutes, the awareness of the provisional nature of our attributions, and the profound uncertainty that emerges from these realities seem to be balanced in the story by the unequivocal presence of outside forces hostile to human life and the manifest reality of human pain and suffering caused by these "invisible" forces. The father's "hope," flawed as it is in its incomplete acceptance of suffering, may be as serviceable as his wife's darker and more adaptable attitude in providing a guide to living life. The son's insanity is Nabokov's concession that the forces of chaos and uncertainty are present to human experience not only in the outer world but also in the inner world of the boy's shattered mind. Neither a reliance on the flawed referential instruments of language and symbol nor on the thin structures of attributed meaning designed to face reality—neither of these strategies seem to be intellectually fashionable these days, but they do seem to be a means of Nabokov's "decoding of the undulation of things" (A11: 79).

AN AFTERWORD

The saddest story
John Banville

Sings and Symbols is surely the saddest story that Vladimir Nabokov ever wrote. There is sadness in all of his stories, throbbing underneath everything, like a chronic toothache that will not be assuaged. For instance, *Spring in Fialta*, perhaps his greatest masterpiece in the form, is heartbreaking in the feather-light way in which it conveys the contingency and evanescence of our lives and loves, while *Mademoiselle O* catches the particular quality of yearning in an exile's memories—"something, in short, that I could appreciate only after the things and beings that I had most loved in the security of my childhood had been turned to ashes or shot through the heart"—but this little vignette of a mother and father's failed visit to their deranged and incarcerated son somehow manages to distill out of drabbest materials the most precious, purest drop, the quintessence, of anguish itself.

Nabokov knew a great deal about sadness. The Russian Revolution deprived him of his childhood, his family, his home, and homeland, and, perhaps the sorest loss of all, his language— "my untrammeled, rich, and infinitely docile Russian tongue," as he wrote in an afterword to *Lolita*—and sent him wandering through the world, a stateless and impoverished exile. He knew, with awful intimacy, the milieu he so skillfully sketches in his portrait of the old Jewish couple: her "cheap black dresses," his "swollen veins, brown-spotted skin," their two-roomed flat up three flights of stairs where we are presented with her "pack of soiled cards and her old albums," and bade take note of his "hopelessly uncomfortable dental plate" and his bald head where "a large birthmark stood out conspicuously."

Perhaps it was his biographical and therefore emotional closeness to the material of the story—for instance, in the deftly limned figure of the mother here it is hard not to see something of Nabokov's portrait, in *Speak, Memory*, of his own mother in her sad exile— that drew from the author one or two uncharacteristic wrong notes. We could have done without the dying fledgling twitching in that puddle, and those 'beautiful weeds' that are unable to hide from the grim reaper, a clear case of pathetic fallacy that Katharine White, Nabokov's editor at *The New Yorker*, rightly pounced on. Nabokov might have claimed, as Mrs White assumed he would, that in these instances he was speaking as if through the character, but if so he was making particularly free with free indirect style.

One of the most striking aspects of the story is the muted tone adopted by this usually most incandescent of stylists. True, there are a number of passages that could have been written by no one else but Nabokov, in particular the marvelous long central paragraph describing the son's mental derangement, that takes off from the dry lowlands of medicalese—"the subject of an elaborate paper in a scientific monthly"—and ends up soaring above those "great mountains of unbearable solidity" with their "granite and groaning firs." Elsewhere, however, the voice is a carefully calli- brated murmur, and the colouring is the shabby brown of old overcoats and piled-up shoes and shorn hanks of hair.

It had to be this way, for the story to achieve its strongest yet most subtle effects. All of Nabokov's work, from start to finish, is a business of signs and symbols. For all that he claimed to despise the "Viennese quack," it is Freud's notion of the *Unheimlich*, the uncanny, as the bringing back, the re-presenting, of the familiar in unfamiliar guise, that most closely characterizes Nabokov's artistic method. In John Updike's lovely prescription, Nabokov gives the ordinary its beautiful due, but in the process the ordinary is trans- figured. Not since Ovid have such changes been rung, and rung over, over and again.

Always in Nabokov's fiction we have the unsettling sense that behind the crystal-clear surfaces that he presents to our admiring gaze *something else is going on*, something we are to be aware of but not to know. A quality of the numinous pervades his pages. The gods are here, invisible, mischievous, and meddling. The most disturbing implication of "Signs and Symbols" is that perhaps the son is not deranged at all; that perhaps he alone, in his seeming insanity, has discerned the simple fact that "everything is a cipher and of everything he is the theme," and that the same is true for all of us, and that instead of breezing through the world as if none of it is really our business, we should be "always on guard and devote every minute and module of life to the decoding of the undulation of things." Or as Rilke, in the Duino Elegies, less imperiously put it:

> ... *Hiersein viel ist, und weil uns scheinbar*
> *alles das Hiesige braucht, dieses Schwindende, das*
> *seltsam uns angeht. Uns, die Schwindensten.*

> ... truly being here is so much; because everything here
> apparently needs us, this fleeting world, which in some strange
> way keeps calling to us. Us, the most fleeting of all.
>
> (trans. Stephen Mitchell)

ENDNOTES

Breaking the code: Nabokov and the art of short fiction

1 B. Boyd, *Vladimir Nabokov: The American Years* (Princeton, New Jersey: Princeton University Press, 1991): 117.

2 *Selected Letters*, 117.

3 Private communication with the Editor (July 6, 2011).

4 *A Book of Things about Vladimir Nabokov*, ed. Carl R. Proffer (Ann Arbor: Ardis, 1974).

5 Martin Amis, "The Problem with Nabokov," *The Guardian*, November 14, 2009.

6 Each month, the journal's fiction podcast features a story from the *New Yorker* archives chosen by a current fiction writer. The podcast, aired on June 9, 2008, is available here: http://www.newyorker.com/online/2008/06/09/080609on_audio_gaitskill (accessed October 19, 2011).

7 T. N. Tobias, "Anatomy of a Short Story," *T.N.T. Reviews Blog.* October 18, 2010; http://tnt-tek.com/writing/anatomy-of-a-short-story/ (accessed October 19, 2011).

8 From W. H. Auden's "Paysage Moralisé" (*cf.* the line: "Hearing of harvests rotting in the valleys ..." with Nabokov's "beautiful weeds that cannot hide from the farmer and helplessly have to watch the shadow of his simian stoop leave mangled flowers in its wake, as the monstrous darkness approaches"; A13: 142). *The Collected Poetry of W. H. Auden* (New York: Random House, 1945), 47–8.

9 See his *The Implied Reader: Patterns of Communication in Prose Fiction from Bunyan to Beckett* (Baltimore, Maryland: Johns Hopkins University Press, 1974); *The Act of Reading: A Theory of Aesthetic*

Response (Baltimore, Maryland: Johns Hopkins University Press, 1980).

10 Posting on NABOKV-L, an electronic Listserv, March 28, 1995.

11 Subscribers willingly agreed to participate: "Of course, that last phone call (the third one) is ambiguous. It might be the girl wanting to talk to Charlie once more, though that is unlikely as her mistake in dialing had just been explained to her. It might be somebody else neither the old couple nor the reader is acquainted with ... But I believe everybody is led to expect the worst: that the clinic is calling at this unusual hour to inform them that their son had finally succeeded in tearing a hole in his world and had escaped to death. Destiny says one, two, three, and at three it hits. 'Signs and Symbols' is one of the most perfect short stories I know" (Dieter E. Zimmer; posting on NABOKV-L, 30 March 1995); "I'm willing to play the game: I think the son has escaped" (Allan McWilliams, posting on NABOKV-L, April 2, 1995).

12 Posting on NABOKV-L, December 17, 2004.

13 Ibid.

14 Posting on NABOKV-L, December 19, 2004.

15 Ibid.

16 Ibid.

17 *Selected Poems of Charles Baudelaire*, trans. Geoffrey Wagner (New York: Grove Press, 1974). Baudelaire's text was mentioned in the context of "Signs and Symbols" (*cf.*: "his inmost thoughts are discussed at nightfall, in manual alphabet, by darkly gesticulating trees"; noted by Jansy Berndt de Souza Mello in her posting on NABOKV-L, December 20, 2004). Another poem that could have served as a potential poetic subtext for Nabokov's short story is Eliot's "East Coker" (1943). Alexander Drescher suggests a possible link between the image of the underground train losing "its life current between two stations" (A10: 23) and the following image in Eliot: "an underground train, in the tube, [that] stops too long between stations." The same poem also contains the line: "Still, in spite of that, we call this Friday good."

18 "A 60th Anniversary Exploration," May 11, 2008. Participants included scholars Jacqueline Hamrit, Phyllis Roth, and Stadlen himself. The program is available online: http://anthonystadlen.blogspot.com/2010/01/vladimir-nabokov-signs-and-symbols.html

Psychosis, performance, schizophrenia, literature

1 For further comments see the very end of this section for these answers.

2 http://www.alcyone.com/arcana/oracle.html.

3 See e.g. http://www.learntarot.com/s9.htm.

4 John N. Crossley, *Growing Ideas of Number* (Camberwell, Australia: Australian Council for Educational Research, 2007).

5 A number is "perfect" if it is the sum of its divisors. The first two perfect numbers are $6 = 1 + 2 + 3$ and $28 = 1 + 2 + 4 + 7 + 14$. Finding larger and larger perfect numbers has long intrigued mathematicians.

6 J. Jacobi, *Complex, Archetype, Symbol in the Psychology of C. G. Jung* (Princeton, New Jersey: Princeton University Press, 1974), 168.

7 For more details see Barry Jeromson, *Jung and Mathematics in Dialogue: A Critical Study*, PhD thesis (University of South Australia 1999—School of Communication and Information Studies).

8 See the last chapter of Carl Gustav Jung et al., *Man and his Symbols*, 13th ed. (Zürich, Düsseldorf: Walter-Verlag, 1968; first edition, Garden City, New York: Doubleday, 1964). There is an unfortunate mistranslation on the last page where "*Primzahl*" is rendered as "primary number" but should be "prime number."

9 William Shakespeare, *Hamlet*, Act V, Scene II, Hamlet's last four words.

Vladimir Nabokov's correspondence with *The New Yorker* regarding "Signs and Symbols," 1946–8

Olga Voronina

1 Although some of the letters from Vladimir Nabokov to Katharine White are published in Vladimir Nabokov, *Selected Letters, 1940–77* (Houghton Mifflin Harcourt, 1989), the correspondence presented on these pages is quoted from the original manuscripts, currently preserved in The Nabokov Archive at the Berg Collection, at the New York Public Library. See Correspondence with *The New Yorker*, Folders 1–24. The letters pertaining to the publication

of "Signs and Symbols" are on hold in Folders 6–13. The correspondence was partly published in Russian in Olga Voronina, "Vladimir Nabokov v zhurnale New Yorker," *Zvezda* 4 (2005): 126–42.

2 "Student Days."

3 *Bend Sinister.*

4 E. B. White's *Stuart Little* was published in 1945.

5 "He had first read E. B. White in 1940, as he sailed to America on the Champlain. Picking up a magazine in the ship's library, he came across White's definition of a miracle, "blue snow on a red barn" – which to him was a stab or Russia." Boyd, *Vladimir Nabokov: The American Years*, 86.

6 Edmund Wilson.

7 The folder contains a typeset draft of this letter, dated July 5, 1947: "As to the 'referential mania,' I really fail to see your point. The whole story is built around my invention of it. Had it been different, it would have simply consisted of an enumeration of medical symptoms in an individual case of an established sickness. Can you see this story built around, say, a case of scarlet fever or diabetes? It would have belonged in a medical journal, not in the New Yorker. I would not object, of course, to a footnote about the fictitious character of the sickness in question,—if you do not think that this would destroy the effectiveness of the story, as I cannot help thinking."

8 On the back of this letter, VN drafted his response to KW: "In regard to the proofs of 'Signs and Symbols' I am afraid I cannot accept most of the alterations and omissions. In fact I am completely against the whole idea of my stories being edited. Among the alterations inflicted upon this story, there is not a simply really necessary one and many are murderous. Frankly, I would prefer not to have you publish the story at all if it must be so carefully mutilated. I add a list of the things I really want restored [from my script]."

9 Typeset notes to galley proofs, on one page, are enclosed.

Lost in revision: The editing of "Signs and Symbols" for *The New Yorker*
J. Morris

1 Boyd, *Vladimir Nabokov: The American Years*, 117.

2 Cited in ibid., 126–7.

3 My italics; ibid., 124.

4 Doubleday, 1958.

5 See Boyd, *Vladimir Nabokov: The American Years*, 86, 121, 147.

6 *Selected Letters*, 156–7.

7 Charles Nicol's coda: "The original author of *The Elements of Style* was Will Strunk, E. B. White's teacher at Cornell in 1919. White got involved with revising a new edition of the little book after writing an essay on Strunk for the *New Yorker* datelined 15 July 1957. White's immediate impulse to write about Strunk was the arrival in the mail of 'a gift from a friend in Ithaca,' a copy of the original 'forty-three-page summation of the case for cleanliness, accuracy, and brevity in the use of English.' It would be curious indeed if that friend were Nabokov, but then, it has some of his handmarks: 'The Cornell University Library has one copy. It had two, but my friend pried one loose and mailed it to me.'"

Consulting the oracle
Michael Wood

1 F. W. Bateson Memorial Lecture given in Oxford on February 17, 1993.

2 Joseph Fontenrose, *The Delphic Oracle* (Berkeley: University of California Press, 1978), 236, 239.

3 Plutarque, *Oeuvres morales*, tome VI (Paris, 1974), 12–13.

4 Pierre Amandry, *La Mantique apollonienne a Delphes* (Paris, 1950), 164; Roland Crahay, *La Litterature oraculaire chez Hirodote* (Paris, 1956), 22.

5 H. W. Parke and D. E. W. Wormell, *The Delphic Oracle* (Oxford: Blackwell, 1956), vol. n, xxvi.

6 Herodotus, *The Histories*, trans. Aubrey de Se'lincourt (Harmondsworth: Penguin, 1954), 84.

7 Parke and Wormell, "Apollo tended to speak idiomatic Greek."

8 Herodotus, *The Histories*, trans. Aubrey de Sélincourt (Harmondsworth: Penguin, 1954), 112.

9 Ibid., 66.

10 Ibid., 58, 60–1, 75, 78–9.

11 Crahay, *La Litterature oraculaire chez Hirodote*, 21.

12 What Kafka actually said, according to Max Brod, after the remark about God's bad moods and bad days, was "Plenty of hope—for God—a limitless amount of hope—only not for us."

13 Quoted in Keith Graham. *J. L. Austin: A Critique of Ordinary Language Philosophy* (New York: Harvester Press, 1977), 172.

14 Walter Benjamin, *Walter Benjamin: Selected Writings, Volume 3; Volumes 1935–8.* Eds. Michael W. Jennings and Howard Eiland (Harvard: Harvard University Press, 2002), 145–6.

15 J. L. Austin, *Sense and Sensibilia* (Oxford: Clarendon, 1962), 73.

Arbitrary signs and symbols
Alexander N. Drescher

1 Vladimir Nabokov, "Symbols and Signs," in *The New Yorker* 24 (May 15, 1948): 31–3.

2 Vladimir Nabokov. *Pnin* (New York: Vintage International, 1989 [1957]). Between 1953 and 1955, Nabokov submitted six of the *Pnin* stories to *The New Yorker*: episodes (later chapters) 1, 3, 4, and 6 were accepted; 7 was not offered.

3 Boyd, *Vladimir Nabokov: The American Years*, 115.

4 On Nabokov's letters to Katharine A. White, see: Alexander Dolinin, "The Signs and Symbols in Nabokov's 'Signs and Symbols,'" (A259); Vladimir Nabokov, *Selected Letters 1940–77*, eds. Dmitri Nabokov and Matthew J. Bruccoli (San Diego: Harcourt Brace Jovanovich, 1989), 117; and Olga Voronina's publication in this volume (A42–60).

5 Leona Toker, "'Signs and Symbols' in and out of Contexts," (A203). The present study follows much of Prof. Toker's thinking and is indebted to her for her comments on an early draft.

6 Because the words interpreting "Signs and Symbols" exceed those of the story by several orders of magnitude, the general literature is not reviewed here: readers are referred to the bibliographies of Dolinin, "The Signs and Symbols in Nabokov's 'Signs and Symbols,'" (A257), and Joanna Trzeciak, "The Last Jar"; "'Breaking the News' and 'Signs and Symbols': Silentology," (A143; 216).

7 Leland de la Durantaye, "The Pattern of Cruelty and the Cruelty of Pattern in Vladimir Nabokov," *Cambridge Quarterly*, 35 (4) (2006): 301–26.

8 Nabokov's own dictionary: *Webster's New International Dictionary*,

Second Edition, Unabridged (Springfield, Massachusetts: C. G. Merriam, 1944).

9 J. Morris, "Signs and Symbols and Signs," *The Nabokovian* 32 (Spring 1994): 24-28.

10 Toker and Dolinin discuss the fatidic implications of triads; *The New Yorker* divided the sections by ellipses.

11 Anthony Stadlen (private communication) kindly offered this acute observation and questioned whether the calculated date would have been an official school holiday. If the numbered sections of the story are tallied like the floors of an apartment building: first landing = ground floor, second landing = first floor, etc., thus 0, 1, 2 and then are treated as exponents, the sum of the paragraphs would be: $[7 \times 10^0] + [4 \times 10^1] + [19 \times 10^2] = 7 + 40 + 1900 = 1947$.

12 Vladimir Nabokov, "Pnin's Day" (the third *Pnin* episode), *The New Yorker* 31 (April 23, 1955); see: Nabokov, *Pnin*, 74–5.

13 Pnin's birthday is given as May 18 in "Pnin" (the first *Pnin* episode), *The New Yorker* 29 (November 28, 1953), and then, having served its purpose, becomes February 5 in the novel. See Gennady Barabtarlo, *Aerial View: Essays on Nabokov's Art and Metaphysics*, (New York: Peter Lang, 1993).

14 Nabokov finds this process interesting. Pnin, explicating the chronology of *Anna Karenina*, says, "I can tell you the exact day …" and gives both the exact date and day of the week on which that novel begins: February 23, 1872, coincidently a Friday (p. 122; see also pp. 129–30 in *Pnin*).

15 John B. Lane, "A Funny Thing about 'Signs and Symbols,'" (A114). Lane notes narrative usages as "immigrant," "scientific," and the heightened diction of privileged passages. The emphatic *already* is a Yiddishism, derived from the German interjection *schon*, via the Yiddish *schoin*.

16 Vladimir Nabokov. *The Defense* (New York: Vintage International, 1990 [1964]) (Russian 1929).

17 I have suggested that Nabokov used this painting as an emblem of the Holocaust in "'That in Aleppo, Once …'" (see http://www.libraries.psu.edu/nabokov/dresch1.htm). The allusion to Peter Breughel's painting was also mentioned earlier in Terry J. Martin's article (A101).

18 "Vasily Shishkov" and "Spring in Fialta" in Vladimir Nabokov, *The Stories of Vladimir Nabokov*.

19 *A real American* is another Yiddishism, *a emesdike Americanishe*.

20 The hospital was likely Four Winds in Westchester County, a

compound of converted homes and cottages. Three other "Winds" appear in *Pnin*.

21 John V. Hagopian, "Decoding 'Signs and Symbols,'" (A298). Hagopian, Lane, and Toker note Nabokov's identification with the Wife in addition to her contribution to the narrative voice. Hagopian rejects (correctly in my view) the possibility that Nabokov would create an unsolvable problem.

22 Ten times itself, repeated six times, is 10^6. The word *million* is associated with the Holocaust in the patient's disturbed thinking, as is the *cipher*, the Arabic invention (*sifr*, *0*), which permits representation of vast orders of magnitude. See *cipher* in Appendix.

23 de la Durantaye, "The Pattern of Cruelty."

24 Good Friday was a public school holiday in New York City and Westchester County; *between stations* recalls "stations of the Cross."

25 The repetitions (*Mrs Sol*; *Dr Solov*) mark the importance of Rebecca's son-in-law, *one of the Soloveichik*, where *one of the* indicates not a family name but a follower of Rabbi Chaim Soloveichik of Brisk, the prominent anti-Zionist, at the time strongly opposed to emigration.

26 i.e. beyond the brink.

27 Dolinin notes that the ace of spades is traditionally associated with death, but in the game of faro the suit is ignored. See also John B Lane, "A Funny Thing About 'Signs and Symbols,'" (A114). The games:

Game no.	Player loses	Pushkin's Herman	Nabokov's Fate	Player wins
1	9	3	J	3
2	J	7	9	7
3	Q	A-->Q	A	A

28 The spelling in *The New Yorker* text is horticulturally correct: *beach plum* (*Prunus maritima*); Nabokov "re-corrected" to *beech plum*. The fruit of the European (*Fagus sylvatica*) and American (*Fagus grandiflora*) beech trees are, of course, nuts not suitable for jellies. Thanks are due Mary Bellino for help with this paper and the comment (NABOKV-L, November 12, 2004): "There is a very similar crux in the text of *Pnin*, where, at croquet, Pnin 'teemed' with Madam Bolotov." The passage is from the fifth episode of *Pnin*, which was rejected by *The New Yorker*. The spelling becomes "teamed" in the Vintage edition (p. 130).

29 *Buchen* as noun or verb translates alternatively as *book*, particularly in the sense of accounting, another aspect of the concentration camps.

30 This story, which conflates anniversaries, births, escapes, and restorations, was first published—either by design or Nabokov's "cosmic convergence" —on the day of birth of the State of Israel.

The patterns of doom
Brian Quinn

1 Roy Johnson, *Nabokov Tutorials—"Signs and Symbols."* Online Publication: http://www.mantex.co.uk/2009/09/26/signs-and-symbols/, 1.

2 Nabokov, *Nikolai Gogol*, 137.

3 Johnson, *Nabokov Tutorials*, 2.

4 Stephan Jan Parker, *Understanding Vladimir Nabokov* (Columbia: University of South Carolina Press, 1987), 133.

5 A. Field, *The Life and Art of Vladimir Nabokov* (New York: Crown Publishers, 1986), 29–30.

6 Boyd, *Vladimir Nabokov: The American Years*, 119.

7 Ibid., 118.

8 Johnson, *Nabokov Tutorials*, 2.

Ways of knowing in "Signs and Symbols"
Terry J. Martin

1 Critics who see the third phone call as a clear portent of the boy's death include John V. Hagopian and Pekka Tammi. At the other extreme is Larry R. Andrews, who concludes that all of the clues pointing to the boy's death are falsified by the author's irony. Between them are a variety of positions. For instance, William Carroll argues that, in completing the esthetic design, the interpreter "participate[s] with Nabokov in killing the boy" (A247). David H. Richter seconds Carroll's thesis. On the other band, John B. Lane calls the third telephone call a "genre gimmick" and argues that "the overwhelming impression of the signs and symbols in Nabokov's story is that the young man will die," but that nevertheless "the call cannot be interpreted with certainty" (A122). David Field agrees that we cannot know what the final telephone call means, but concludes that

"focusing on the boy's suicide is a false trail that has misled critics" (A187). Finally, in a brief discussion of the story, Carol T. Williams states that the identity of the next caller "is irrelevant, for alive or dead, the young man cannot live in this world" (A187).

2 Although Lane recognizes the difference, he both applies it to the story in a different way and sees in it a different set of implications than I do. I agree with the premise that "when the reader tries to interpret one of the images in Nabokov's story (or any sign or symbol), he or she quickly discovers that it is not obviously one or the other, but seems to be a muddy mixture of the two" (A127). However, this leads him or her to the conclusion that "the more scientific, exact, and concrete a sign or symbol, the less meaning it can contain, and therefore with perfect exactness comes perfect meaninglessness. The corollary is also true. The more meaning something carries, the less exact it must become, hence a thing which encompasses all meaning is also perfectly inexact" (A128). By translating the terms into the polarity of exactness and inexactness, Lane effectively annuls the significance of the difference between signs and symbols altogether, for their meaning thereby comes to be a function of their degree of exactness rather than their nature as indicative or representative of other things (which is the way that Lane initially distinguishes them). Indeed, in the passage cited above, the terms are used almost interchangeably. I seek instead to show that such terms are indicative of a different kind of epistemological conflict.

3 William Carroll, "*Prin* and 'Signs and Symbols': Narrative Strategies".

4 See, for instance, the use of such images in Breughel's "The Triumph of Death" in Walter S. Gibson, *Breughel* (New York: Oxford University Press, 1977), 80.

5 David Field, "Sacred Dangers: Nabokov's Distorted Reflection".

6 Although Nabokov frequently disclaimed any didactic intent in his literary works (e.g., "I have no social purpose, no moral message; I've no general ideas to exploit" (*Strong Opinions* [New York, St. Louis, San Francisco, and Toronto: McGraw-Hill, 1973], 16), his literary works contain numerous didactic elements. Indeed, Nabokov seems rather inconsistent on this point, or he elsewhere admits to what looks surprisingly like a "social purpose," a "moral message," and a "general idea ... to exploit" in his literary treatment of totalitarianism: "I have bridged the 'esthetic distance' in my own way by means of such absolutely final indictments of Russian and German totalitarianism as my novels *Invitation to a Beheading* and *Bend Sinister*" (ibid., 156).

7 *Speak, Memory* (London: Weidenfeld and Nicolson, 1967), 49.

8 Ibid., 291.

9 Nabokov, *Strong Opinions*, 66, 304–5.

10 Compare, for instance, the similarity between her view and one which Nabokov expressed in an interview published in *The Sunday Times* in London on June 22, 1969: "Thus if I hear or read the words 'Alp Grum, Engadine' the normal observer within me may force me to imagine the belvedere of a tiny hotel on its 2000-meter-tall perch and mowers working along a path that winds down to a toy railway; but what I see first of all and above all is the Yellow-banded Ringlet settled with folded wings on the flower that those damned scythes are about to behead."

11 Hagopian, "Decoding 'Signs and Symbols.'"

12 Ibid., (A299); is *that* what they were trying to do?

13 "The Art of Literature and Commonsense," in *Lectures on Literature*, 374.

14 Angus J. S. Fletcher, *Allegory, the Theory of a Symbolic Mode* (Ithaca, New York: Cornell University Press, 1964), 277.

15 Nabokov, *Strong Opinions*, 155.

16 "The Art of Literature and Commonsense," in *Lectures on Literature*, 373.

17 Ibid., 374.

18 Ibid., 373.

19 Ibid.

20 Ibid., 377.

21 Ibid., 374.

A funny thing about "Signs and Symbols"
John B. Lane

1 Nabokov, *Speak, Memory*, 290.

2 One deviation from literary transparency is the "Elsa and her bestial beau" reference, which obtrudes from the rest of the text because of its ambiguity. The purpose is almost certainly to give extra emphasis to this important allusion. The other deviation in this section is "Having more English than he did," which is a syntactically structural link to the "married already" and "anyhow" of the first section. Both this and the "bestial beau" allusion are discussed elsewhere in this paper.

3 William Carroll (A247).

4 Actually, there may be an implied fourth use of the root "sol" in the name Aunt Rosa. There is a small plant of wide distribution—now known as *drosera rotundifolia*—whose old European name was *rosa solis*, which means "flower of the sun," suggesting "Mrs Sol ... whose face was all pink and mauve with paint and whose hat was a cluster of brookside flowers." The plant lives in moist sunny areas and perhaps seems obscure, but in an earlier time when botanizing was a popular pastime, this plant was well known because it is insectivorous, and thus especially interesting. A naturalist of Nabokov's standing would almost certainly have known it well. The "Aunt" of "Aunt Rosa" suggests the homonym "ant" and thus the small insects it traps. The leaves are covered with long hairs, which each have a single drop of sticky liquid on the end. A single plant will often have numerous victims adhering to it, which suggest Aunt Rosa and "all the people she had worried about" trapped and killed by the Nazis. It is a difficult plant to describe, but the colors "pink and mauve" connected with Mrs Sol, and the adjectives "fussy," "wildeyed," "angular," and "tremulous" associated with Aunt Rosa all suit it. The fact that it would break the pattern of threes for the root Sol may seem a disadvantage, but as I attempt to demonstrate in this paper, this hidden deviation might actually suit Nabokov's larger purpose.

5 Carroll (A245–6).

6 Nabokov, *Speak, Memory*, 20.

7 Ibid.

8 Ibid., 48–9.

9 One might also claim a biographical reference here, since Nabokov had prodigious mathematical abilities as a child, which disappeared following a long illness involving a high fever.

10 It is interesting that Nabokov chooses the name "Brink" for his psychiatrist. It may be that he combined his disdain for Freudian psychology with another object of his scorn-detailed literary analysis (particularly of his own work) in this choice. Bernhard ten Brink (1841–92) was a well-known literary scholar around the turn of the century whose most famous work was an extremely detailed analysis of the language and structure of Chaucer's writing. The distinctive "ten" in his name also echoes the ten fruit jellies in ten little jars.

11 Alexander Pushkin, *The Complete Prose Tales of Alexander Sergeyevitch Pushkin*, trans. Gillon R. Aitken (New York: Norton, 1966), 301–2.

12 Alfred Appel, Jr., "An Interview with Vladimir Nabokov," *Nabokov: The Man and His Work* ed. L. S. Dembo (Madison, Wisconsin: University of Wisconsin Press, 1967), 22–3.

13 John V. Hagopian, "Vladimir Nabokov," in ed. L. S. Dembo, *American Authors Since World War II, Dictionary of Literary Biography* Vol. 2 (Michigan: Bruccoli Clark, 1978), 356.

14 Nabokov, *Speak, Memory*, 20.

15 Paul J. Rosenzweig calls attention to this transformation of a "tusked boar-like man" in his paper (A164).

16 In light of the prominence of the image of the basket of jellies, it is interesting that a now-obsolete definition of "symbol" is "a contribution (properly to a feast or picnic)" (*O.E.D.* Vol. 10, 1933, 362).

17 Pushkin, *Complete Prose Tales of Alexander Sergeyevitch Pushkin*, 305.

Names
Yuri Leving

1 Vladimir Nabokov, *Nikolai Gogol* (New York: New Directions Publishing, 1961), 1–2.

2 On S. Rozov and V. Nabokov, see Y. Leving, *Keys to The Gift* (Boston: Academic Studies Press, 2011), 487–502.

3 Cf.: "The American is more confused than other societies, and the American Jew is even more confused than the American gentile ... Man becomes aware of the Finite only when he is confronted with death" (Rav Soloveichik, Notes: Vol. 1. Source: http://www.613.org/rav/notes1.html).

4 "And even vastness here to Tatar arrows" (1922): "Not as a dazed Kursk nightingale."

5 "Stallions, stomp, monk": "Call dazed, cart hair."

6 Quoted from the original version of A. Dolinin's article ("The Signs and Symbols in Nabokov's 'Signs and Symbols'").

7 Ibid.

Five known jars
Carol M. Dole

1 Hagopian (A298); also see Geoffrey Green (A169).

2 Carroll (A236). Critics who take a similar approach are Paul Rosenzweig (A158); David H. Richter (A224); and Larry R. Andrews (A144).

3 Andrews argues unconvincingly that because the jellies are linked to the "feeling of self assurance" that makes the parents "ripe for disaster," they become, in a sense, a cause of the son's supposed death. Other critics have generally gone no further than to observe that the jelly jars and the order in which the old man lists their labels "seem to have some hidden meaning" (Rosenzweig, A161).

Five missing jars
Gennady Barabtarlo

1 See especially William Carroll; Rosenzweig; Richter; Leona Toker (all in this volume); also, Boyd, *Vladimir Nabokov: The American Years*, 117–19.

2 Boyd, *Vladimir Nabokov: The American Years*, 117.

3 See Toker (A203).

4 See Meyer, 1988, 184. The fact that the old lady patiently explains to the girl her exact error makes the third ring much less likely to be the third misdial in a row—see more on this line of reasoning in Toker (A203).

5 Nabokov, *Selected Letters*, 117.

6 Boyd, *Vladimir Nabokov: The American Years*, 119.

The last jar
Joanna Trzeciak

1 See Dole, "Five Known Jars" (A137).

Photographs
Maria-Ruxanda Bontila

1 R. Barthes, *Camera Lucida*, trans. Richard Howard (London: Flamingo, 1980/1984), 113.

2 Ibid., 4.

3 Barbara Harrison, "Photographic Visions and Narrative Inquiry," in eds. Michael Bamberg and Molly Andrews, *Considering Counter-Narratives: Narrating, Resisting, Making Sense* (Amsterdam: John Benjamin Publishing Company, 2004), 119.

4 Susan Buck-Morss, *The Dialectics of Seeing: Walter Benjamin and the Arcades Project* (Cambridge, Massachusetts and London: MIT Press, 1991), 259.

5 Alasdair MacIntyre, *After Virtue*, trans. Catrinel Plesu (Bucuresti: Humanitas, 1981/1998), 232–48.

6 Nabokov, *Speak, Memory*, part 1, 1. I thank Priscilla Meyer for helpful advice and graceful discussions on this article.

Cards
Pekka Tammi

1 For Nabokov's own remarks on "The Queen of Spades," *cf.* his commentary to Pushkin's *Eugene Onegin*, II, 258–9; for comments on Tchaikovsky, *cf.* 333–4.

2 I have tried to place this system into a more general theoretical network in my *Kerronnallisista paradokseista ja itsensä tiedostavista fiktioista* ("Narrative Paradoxes and Self-Consciousness in Fiction"), published in *Taiteen mont a tasoa* (*Festschrift for Professor Maija Lehtonen*) (Mantta: SKS, 1983), 121–37. The same volume contains an excellent discussion by my colleague Jyrki Nummi on Nabokov's (and Pushkin's) uses of the authorial persona as a textual device. Finnish-reading Nabokovians are hereby notified.

Telephone
Andrés Romero Jódar

1 Joseph Tabbi and Michael Wutz, eds., *Reading Matters: Narratives in*

the New Media Ecology (Ithaca, New York: Cornell University Press, 1997), 174–5.

2 Beverly Lyon Clark, *Reflections of Fantasy* (New York: Peter Lang Publishing, 1986), 53.

3 Patricia Waugh, *Metafiction: The Theory and Practice of Self-Conscious Fiction* (New York: Routledge, 1990), 34.

4 Nabokov, *Pnin*, 26.

5 Tabbi and Wutz, eds., *Reading Matters*, 75.

6 Nabokov, *Pnin*, 26.

7 Vladimir Nabokov, *Laughter in the Dark*, 66.

8 Vladimir Nabokov, *The Real Life of Sebastian Knight* (New York: Vintage International, 1992), 33.

9 Ibid., 96.

10 Ibid., 166.

11 Nabokov, *Pnin*, 158.

12 Ronell, Avital, *The Telephone Book* (Lincoln, Nebraska and London: University of Nebraska Press, 1989), 31.

13 Vladimir Nabokov, *Bend Sinister* (London: Penguin Classics, 2001), 55.

14 Ibid., 124–5.

15 Ibid., 180.

16 Nabokov, *The Real Life of Sebastian Knight*, 166.

The importance of reader response
Paul J. Rosenzweig

1 *A Midsummer Night's Dream*, Act V Scene I: 7–8.

The Jewish quest
Yuri Leving

1 Amis, "The Problem with Nabokov."

2 Toker, A211.

3 Ibid.

4 Trzeciak, A143.

5 Ibid.

6 Posting on NABOKV-L, 23 December 2004.

7 Ibid.

8 In Kabbalistic Gematria the number 18 means "life," due to the numeric values (based on the correspondences between the letters and the digits, or "signs" and "symbols," again) of the letters "chet" [= 8] + "yud" [=10]).

9 Posting on NABOKV-L, December 23, 2004.

10 Posting on NABOKV-L, December 2, 2004.

11 Vladimir Dmitrievich Nabokov. "Bol'noi Vopros" ["A Painful Question"], *Evreiiskaia tribuna* [*Jewish Tribune*] 1 (1920). In Russian, "*Strashny, beschelovechny i nevynosimy dlia normal'* nogo chelovecheskogo chuvstva eti proiavleniia zverstva, beskonechno zhalki ikh neschastnye i nevinnye zhertvy*" (translated by Y. Leving). Republished in the journal *LeChaim* 9 (September 2005): 161, http:// www.lechaim.ru/ARHIV/161/nabokov.htm. Accessed on 18 October 2011.

Signs of reference, symbols of design
Geoffrey Green

1 Herbert Gold and George Plimpton, "Interview: Vladimir Nabokov," *The Paris Review* (October 1967); rpt. Vladimir Nabokov, *Strong Opinions* (New York: McGraw-Hill, 1973), 106.

2 Israel Shenker, "Interview with Vladimir Nabokov," *New York Times Book Review*, January 9, 1972; rpt. Nabokov, *Strong Opinions*, 181.

3 Nabokov, *Strong Opinions*, 193.

4 My source for this is Edmund Wilson's letter of 12 November 1947, to Katharine White, a *New Yorker* editor, when she requested his opinion of "Signs and Symbols." See *New York Review of Books* 24 (4) (March 17, 1977): 16.

5 After five years of adjustment to America, during which he deliberately solicited criticism of his work, Nabokov wrote to Edmund Wilson on 17 June 1945: "I am always quite willing to have my grammar corrected but have *now* made it quite clear to the *New Yorker* that there will be no 'revising' and 'editing' of my stories *dorénavant*" (my emphasis on "now"). See Vladimir Nabokov, *The Nabokov-Wilson Letters, 1940–71*, ed. Simon Karlinsky (New York: Harper and Row, 1979), 154.

6 Nabokov, *Strong Opinions*, 302.

7 Nabokov, *Bend Sinister* (New York, 1947; rpt. with an introduction by the author, New York: Time, Inc., 1964), xiii.

8 Ibid., xiii.

9 Ibid., xv.

10 Ibid., xiv.

11 Translations of both stories are included in Vladimir Nabokov, *A Russian Beauty and Other Stories* (New York: McGraw-Hill, 1973), 183–218.

12 Vladimir Nabokov, *Pale Fire* (New York, 1962; rpt. New York: Berkley, 1969), 169.

13 Ibid., 192.

Sacred dangers: Nabokov's distorted reflection
David Field

1 Vladimir Nabokov, *Lectures on Literature* (New York: Harcourt Brace Jovanovich, 1980), 2.

2 Vladislav Khodasevich may have been the first to recognize the way that Nabokov's insane narrators stood for artists; he even implied a comparison between the narrators and Nabokov himself. Writing in 1937, he said, "The life of the artist and the life of a device in the consciousness of the artist—this is [Nabokov's] theme, revealing itself to some degree or other in almost every one of his writings, beginning with *The Defense*. However, the artist (and more concretely speaking, the writer) is never shown by him directly, but always behind a mask …" (quoted in Alfred Appel and Charles Newman, eds., *Nabokov: Criticism, Reminiscences, Translations and Tributes* [Evanston: Northwestern University Press, 1970], 100). John V. Hagopian, referring to "Signs and Symbols," has called the boy's "dense tangle of logically interacting illusions" a "perfect description of Nabokov's own fiction" (A301).

3 Nabokov, *Lectures on Literature*, 372.

4 Nabokov, *Strong Opinions*, 112.

5 William Carroll (A237).

6 David H. Richter (A235).

7 Larry R. Andrews (A296).

8 Paul J. Rosenzweig (A158). Although he does not engage in a reading that derives from reader-response theory, Geoffrey Greene has a subtle and carefully wrought interpretation of the ways that "Signs and Symbols" gathers meaning from its details: see his "Signs of Reference, Symbols of Design" (A169).

9 Hagopian (A303).

10 Thomas Pynchon, *V* (New York: Bantam Books, 1963), 300.

11 Carol Williams, "Nabokov's Dozen Short Stories: His World in Microcosm," *Studies in Short Fiction* 12 (Summer 1975), 219.

12 Nabokov, *Speak, Memory: An Autobiography Revisited* (New York: G. P. Putnam's Sons, 1966), 217–18.

13 Nabokov, *Pale Fire* (New York: G. P. Putnam's Sons, 1962), 265.

14 Nabokov, *The Gift* (New York: Capricorn Books, 1963), 255. Fyodor is not an insane narrator and his own story comes close to Nabokov's in many significant ways. In his recent biography, Andrew Field claims that "Nabokov is a closer analogue to Fyodor than to any other fictional character created by him in his mature prose" (Andrew Field, *VN: The Life and Art of Vladimir Nabokov* [New York: Crown Publishers, 1986], 171).

15 Nabokov, *Speak, Memory*, 212.

16 Nabokov, *Strong Opinions*, 168.

17 Ibid., 32.

18 Ibid., 330.

19 Ibid., 142.

20 Nabokov, *Lectures on Literature*, 377.

21 Ibid.

22 Hagopian's sensitive and intelligent reading recognizes that there are genuine reasons for the boy's "referential mania" and desire to escape the world. He says that "The world presented by the narrator and observed by the parents is fully consistent with the boy's vision of it" and recognizes that the horrors the story depicts "are not the insane imaginings of the boy, but a hard-fact reality that undermines Dr Brink's diagnosis. They depict a world from which the urge to escape is not at all a symptom of madness" ("Decoding 'Signs and Symbols'" [A298]). Hagopian is certainly correct, and Nabokov, like the boy in "Signs and Symbols," did suffer from the evils of the world: he saw the violence of the revolution from his bedroom window, his father was assassinated by a bullet intended for another, his mother lived in penury, his brother was exterminated in a concentration camp,

and his wife endured the indignities and threats of a Jew in Hitler's Germany. Nevertheless, Nabokov made clear that the powers of imagination must transcend such "hard-fact realities" and promote life in the face of such horrors. In his lecture on commonsense, Nabokov says that one result of the demolishing of commonsense is that "the irrational belief in the goodness of man (to which those farcical and fraudulent characters called Facts are so solemnly opposed) becomes something much more than the wobbly basis of idealistic philosophies. It becomes a solid and iridescent truth." The consequence is that "goodness becomes a central and tangible part of one's world" (Nabokov, *Lectures on Literature*, 373). Despite the horrors he suffered, Nabokov endured. He lived to write "Signs and Symbols." He did not commit suicide.

23 Nabokov, *Strong Opinions*, 12.

24 Nabokov, *Speak, Memory*, 296.

The mysticism of circle
Mary Tookey

1 William Carroll (A243).

2 Ibid., 213.

3 Hagopian, "Decoding 'Signs and Symbols,'" A298.

4 Ibid., A302.

5 H. M. Raphaelian, *Signs of Life* (New York: Anatol Sivas, 1957), 13–14.

6 George Ferguson, *Signs and Symbols in Christian Art* (New York: Oxford University Press, 1961), 153.

7 Martin Heidegger, *Nietzsche: Volume IV—Nihilism*, trans. Frank A. Capuzzi (Verlag Gunther Neske, Pfullingen, 1962, rpt. San Francisco: Harper and Row, 1982), 4.

The semiotics of zero
Meghan Vicks

1 Victor Turner, "Betwixt and Between: The Liminal Period in Rites de Passage," in *The Forest of Symbols: Aspects of Ndembu Ritual* (Ithaca, New York: Cornell University Press, 1976): 96.

2 Ibid.

3 For instance, Larry R. Andrews reads zero as both a "death omen," and as a "'veiled reference' to the 'cipher' of the referential mania" (A293). But for Andrews, it is no more than one of many parts of the son's mania, and no more significant than any of the other facets of his psychosis: "The zero is thus a part of the son's mania, and all the numbers seem to be a part of the code used by the hostile forces" (ibid). William Carroll also takes note of the zero, but does not know what to make of it: "Nabokov has placed us in the position of the boy here – is the O a letter or a number? Does it matter? Is this confusion a cipher – a clue to a hidden meaning? Or is it just null, a zero, without substance? It could be either" (A247).

4 Carroll writes, "The story is studded with apparent signs and symbols that the gullible reader—that is, any reader—will attempt to link together in a 'meaningful' pattern. Most of these signs point to the probably successful suicide of the boy" (A245).

5 Andrews rigorously analyzes the story's tree and bird imagery, numerological symbolism, and doubling patterns, thereby showing how the fictive world of "Signs and Symbols" very much embodies the boy's maniacal perspective. However, he ultimately concludes that the patterns of signs and symbols are meaningless, as the story and the boy are fictions: "As soon as we appreciate that the story is a fiction and that all its clues are therefore false, the "reality" of the boy and his mania is shattered, and it is no longer possible to speak of our participation in his 'world'" (A296). I find Andrews' ultimate conclusion to be unsatisfactory, as it delineates clear-cut borders between fiction and reality Nabokov's work.

6 See Barabtarlo's *Aerial View*, 90–3; also Carol M. Dole (A137)

7 See Dole (A137).

8 Carroll writes, "'Referential mania' is a critical disease all readers of fiction suffer from ... Over-reading is another, milder form of referential mania, and Nabokov has insured, through his rhetorical strategy, that the reader will succumb to the same mania that afflicts the boy" (A245). This idea is further enlarged upon in an essay by Paul J. Rosenzweig (1980): "At some time during the reader's floundering attempt to find meaning, he may notice as her rereads the description of the son's condition, that he is reading a description of his very own state" (A161).

9 Robert Kaplan, *The Nothing That Is: A Natural History of Zero* (Oxford: Oxford University Press, 1999), 46.

10 See ibid. and Charles Seife's *Zero: The Biography of a Dangerous Idea* (New York: Penguin Books, 2000) for full discussions of zero's mathematical properties and conundrums.

11 Michel Serres, *The Birth of Physics*, trans. Jack Hawkes, ed. David Webb (Manchester: Clinamen Press, 2000), 6.

12 Ibid., 21.

13 I would also argue that Martin Heidegger's notions concerning the ontological relationship between nothing and being are relevant in this context, but this exploration deserves more time and space than can be provided here. See his lecture, "What is Metaphysics?"

14 Nabokov, *The Defense*, 227.

15 Nabokov, *Ada, or Ardor*, 27.

16 Ibid., 24.

17 Ibid., 74.

18 Nabokov, *Transparent Things*, 13.

19 Ibid., 1.

20 Nabokov, *Look at the Harlequins!*, 8–9.

21 Ibid., 15.

22 Ibid., 42.

23 "Reality," wrote Nabokov in his "Afterword" to *Lolita*, is "one of the few words which mean nothing without quotes" (312); in *Transparent Things* (as well as elsewhere in his novels), the idea is reiterated: "We have shown our need for quotation marks ('reality,' 'dream')" (93).

24 Nabokov, *Speak, Memory*, 298 (italics mine).

"Signs and Symbols" in and out of contexts
Leona Toker

1 Richter (A233). Richter goes on to say that such expectations are a trap into which the reader falls; he discusses the story as an example of the works that activize the reader and then "punish" him or her for slipping into excessive cooperation with the text.

2 Rosenzweig (A164). Rosenzweig points out that this story demands a self-consciousness of its reader, a consciousness of the conventions of the writing and reading of fiction.

3 Rosenzweig and Richter concur with this view but John V. Hagopian rejects it; see "Decoding 'Signs and Symbols'" (A298).

4 In "The Tragedy of Tragedy" Nabokov expresses his preference for the "dream-logic" or "nightmare-logic" of Shakespeare, Gogol, or

Flaubert over the convention of "wide-awake causality" which he calls the "iron bars of determinism" (326–7).

5 Jorge Luis Borges, "Narrative Art and Magic," *Triquarterly* 25 (Fall 1972): 209–15.

6 Nabokov, *Bend Sinister*, 174.

7 Nabokov, *Strong Opinions*, 95. As Ellen Pifer has noted, the word "galley" here means both "the printer's proof of a manuscript" and "an ancient rowing vessel" (*Nabokov and the Novel*, 11).

8 "Decoding 'Signs and Symbols,'" (A298).

9 *Webster's New Collegiate Dictionary*.

10 Carroll, "*Pnin* and 'Signs and Symbols,'" A236.

11 Søren Kierkegaard, *On Authority and Revelation*, trans. Walter Lowrie (Princeton: Princeton University Press, 1955), 4. Nabokov, "The Tragedy of Tragedy," 330.

12 See his remarks on "something about bells, balls, and bulls," *Strong Opinions*, 80.

13 Friedrich Wilhelm Nietzsche, "The Birth of Tragedy," in *Basic Writings of Nietzsche*, trans. Walter Kaufmann (New York: Random House, 1968, 104 and 108.

14 Kierkegaard, *On Authority and Revelation*, liii.

15 For the distinction between the inner and the outer agenda of culture I am indebted to Stanley Cavell, *Pursuits of Happiness: The Hollywood Comedy of Remarriage* (Cambridge, Massachusetts: Harvard University Press, 1981), 16–17.

16 Nabokov, *The Defense*, 25.

17 Ibid., 22.

18 Ibid., 29.

19 Nabokov was shaken by the information about what had happened in Nazi-occupied Europe. "Much as one might want to hide in one's little ivory tower," he wrote to his sister in June 1946, "there are things that torment too deeply, e.g., the German vilenesses, the burning of children in ovens—children as funny and as strongly loved as our children" (*Perepiska s sestroi*, 41; my translation).

20 Nabokov, *The Gift* (New York: Vintage International, 1991), 176.

21 Nabokov, *Bend Sinister*, 173–4: "what is more important to solve: the 'outer' problem (space, time, matter, the unknown without) or the 'inner' one (life, thought, love, the unknown within) or again their point of contact (death)?"

22 "The Vane Sisters," 219.

23 Cf. note 13 above and the invocation of "nameless existence, intangible substance," *Invitation to a Beheading*, 26. "Something" is one of the most frequently repeated words in *Invitation to a Beheading*.

"Breaking the News" and "Signs and Symbols": silentology
Joanna Trzeciak

1 For example, see Andrews, "Deciphering" (A144).

2 The term "referential mania" comes from the psychiatrist in the story, Hermann Brink.

3 See Toker, 'Contexts,' (A203) and Hagopian, 'Decoding' (A298).

4 Michael Wood, *The Magician's Doubts: Nabokov and the Risks of Fiction* (London: Chatto and Windus, 1994), 66.

5 Vladimir Nabokov, "Opoveshchenie," in *Soglyadatay* (Paris: Russkie Zapiski, 1938).

6 In the notes to "Breaking the News" in *A Russian Beauty and Other Stories,* Nabokov wrote: "'Breaking the News' appeared under the title 'Opoveshchenie' (*Notification*) in an émigré periodical around 1935 and was included in my collection *Soglyadatay* (1938). The milieu and the theme both correspond to those of 'Signs and Symbols,' written ten years later in English." "Breaking the News" was published in the collections *A Russian Beauty and Other Stories* and *The Stories of Vladimir Nabokov* (New York: Vintage International, 1997).

7 Hers is a world populated by "rubbery pedestrians, cotton-wool dogs, mute tram-cars": Nabokov, "Breaking the News," 392.

8 Ibid., 391.

9 The Russian original does not state the year in which the story is set. Vladimir Nabokov added the year in his translation: See Nabokov, *Russian Beauty and Other Stories.*

10 I was not able to ascertain the degree of Nabokov's familiarity with Jewish religious culture in America and, more specifically, with the distinguished Lithuanian rabbinical family Soloveichik, one of the most prominent rabbinical families in the United States. Literary output of the members of the Soloveichik clan has been exceptionally

meager, the result of a family tradition against publishing except under special circumstances: See *Encyclopedia Judaica* vol. 15 (New York: Macmillan, 1973), 127–8, s.v. "Soloveichik" (Mordechai Hacohen).

11 Toker closely engages the descriptive details of the story from a different point of view from that presented here (A203).

12 Carroll (A236).

13 A thought-provoking philosophical analysis of acknowledgment can be found in Stanley Cavell, "Knowing and Acknowledging," in *Must We Mean What We Say?* (Cambridge: Cambridge University Press, 1976), 238–66.

14 See, for example, Toker (A203).

15 Ibid.

16 Carroll (A246). David Richter lists the photo of Aunt Rosa among a series of narrative details that move from inert to ominous once the reader has succumbed to the narrative entrapment of concluding that the son has committed suicide: see Richter, "Narrative Entrapment" (A224).

17 Carroll interprets the mother's lyrical train of thought at the end of part 2 as indicative of her obliviousness in contrast to her son's hypersensitivity. Although this is true, it misses the point, as Carroll interprets even the images of the mother's own reveries as somehow on a par with the symbols elsewhere in the story: See Carroll (A236).

18 It is as if by entering discourse, the morally reprehensible begins to leave the realm of the unacceptable and enter the realm of the tenable. Michael Wood discusses the unspeakability of evil in Nabokov's work: See Wood, *Magician's Doubts*, esp. chapter 3.

19 The couple lives on the third floor in their third country; the story is divided into three sections; three playing cards fall to the floor; there are three phone calls; and so on. The figure of the triad echoes the pattern found in Pushkin's "The Queen of Spades," where the plot hangs on numerical references. Alexander Dolinin has pointed out in conversation that any reader who believes that he or she has correctly completed the pattern in "Signs and Symbols" should recall the fate of Hermann in "The Queen of Spades."

20 Cf. Richter, "Narrative Entrapment," A224.

21 Nabokov, "Breaking the News," 393.

22 Ibid., 394.

23 Norman Davies, *Europa*, trans. Elzbieta Tabakowska (Krakow: Wydawnictwo Znak, 1999), 1035.

Pnin and "Signs and Symbols": narrative entrapment
David H. Richter

1 "Lector in Fabula" in *The Role of the Reader* (Bloomington: Indiana University Press, 1979), 256.

2 Vladimir Nabokov, *Pnin* (New York: 1967), 13.

3 For this analysis of Sterne and other contemporary authors, which was based not upon Eco's semiotics but rather upon the theories of irony of W. C. Booth and D. C. Muecke, see "The Reader as Ironic Victim," *Novel* 14 (1981): 135–51.

4 G. M. Hyde, *Vladimir Nabokov* (London: Marion Boyars, 1977), 150–6, traces Nabokov's debts to Gogol, along with Gogol's resemblances to Laurence Sterne. In Appel, "An Interview with Vladimir Nabokov," 29, Nabokov says, in reply to a question about his influences, that he "loves Sterne," but claims not to have read him before leaving Russia.

5 Nabokov, *Lolita*, 316.

6 Nabokov, *Lectures on Literature*, 297–314; Nabokov, *The Gift*, 313–21.

7 Nabokov, Pnin, 25–6.

8 Some of Nabokov's critics clearly share this lust for disaster. For example, William W. Rowe uses much sleight of explication to "prove" that Pnin in fact did bring the wrong lecture to Cremona. The hypothesis rests, however, on the sole authority of a dim colleague of Pnin's who is obsessed with doing comic impersonations of the Russian exile and who is even more entrapped within the codes of comedy than the narrator. The direct presentation of Pnin's lecture tends (at pp. 15–16 and p. 26) to contradict this. See "The Honesty of Nabokovian Deception," in ed. Carl R. Proffer, *A Book of Things about Vladimir Nabokov* (Ann Arbor: Ardis, 1974), 173.

9 Nabokov, *Pnin*, 53.

10 Ibid., 83.

11 I am referring to *Lolita*, pt. 1, chs. 27–9, which lead the reader to anticipate a carnal scene between Humbert and Dolly on which, at the last moment, Humbert directly draws the curtain.

12 Nabokov, *Pnin*, 129.

13 Ibid., 172–3.

14 Ibid., 58.

15 See Paul Grams, "*Pnin*: The Biographer as Meddler," in ed. Proffer, *A Book of Things about Vladimir Nabokov*, 193–202.

16 Nabokov, *Pnin*, 191.

17 For a similar Nabokovian game that balances interest between the subject and the writer of a fictional biography, see *The Real Life of Sebastian Knight*, his first novel in English.

18 Ambrose Gordon, Jr., "The Double Pnin," in ed. Dembo, *Nabokov*, 144–56.

19 Nabokov, *Pnin*, 16.

20 Ibid., 185.

21 A number of critics have noted dubious details in the narrative. For example, L. L. Lee has pointed out that the "Bob Horn" who helps Pnin hitch a ride on a truck to his Cremona lecture suspiciously shares a name with the "Robert Karlovich Horn"—the narrator's aunt's steward—who helps Pnin on another occasion in 1915: see L. L. Lee, *Vladimir Nabokov* (Boston: Twayne Publishers, 1976), 127. My own contribution to the collection is not a similarity but an out-and-out contradiction. The narrator calls attention (73) to the precise date of chapter 3. It is a Tuesday, February 15, in a year which the reader can determine (from the fact that Pnin has been eight years at Waindell) must be 1953. The narrator arrives at Waindell to give his first public lecture there two years later to the day, on Tuesday, February 15, 1955 (186). Needless to say, February 15 cannot fall on a Tuesday in both years. In the real world, February 15 was a Tuesday in 1955, a Sunday in 1954. This discrepancy, though very minor, is undoubtedly intentional; it is thematically related to two other episodes. One is Pnin's lecture on Pushkin's obsession with the fatality of recurring dates (67–8)—paralleled later in the novel by Pnin's two evictions, from his home and from Waindell, on the two February 15ths. The other is Bolotov's discussion with Pnin (122) of whether it is on a Thursday or a Friday that Tolstoy's *Anna Karenina* begins (both days are mentioned) —which leads to the further conjecture that the book runs on a dual time scheme, one for Levin and another for Anna and Vronsky—a metafictional hypothesis that might help rationalize *Pnin* itself.

22 Page Stegner, *Escape into Aesthetics: The Art of Vladimir Nabokov* (New York, 1966), 96.

23 See Gordon, "The Double Pnin," in ed. Dembo, *Nabokov*, 144–56.

24 See also William Carroll, "*Pnin* and Signs and Symbols" (A224), for a fine interpretations, from a slightly different perspective, of both this story and *Pnin*.

25 According to Carroll, "we will have, in effect, participated with Nabokov in killing the boy. The overdose of meaning is our own" (A247).

26 See Booth and Muecke, "The Reader as Ironic Victim," 151. For Umberto Eco too, the issue here is as much political as ethical, about works of narrative entrapment. Eco claims that "these works tell stories about the ways stories are built up. In doing so, these texts are less innocuous than they seem; their deep theme is the functioning of that basic cultural machinery which, through the manipulation of our beliefs (which sublimate our wishes), produces ideologies, contradictory world visions, self-delusions." *The Role of the Reader*, 256.

27 Ed. Proffer, *A Book of Things about Vladimir Nabokov*, 215.

28 This is now being seen by contemporary literary theorists as a universal motive in the reception of art. For the history of the reader's participation in literature in the role of vicarious creator, see Hans Robert Jauss, *Aesthetic Experience and Literary Hermeneutics*, trans. Michael Shaw (Minneapolis: University of Minnesota Press, 1982), 46–61.

Pnin and "Signs and Symbols": narrative strategies
William Carroll

1 Vladimir Nabokov, "Vladimir Nabokov: An Interview," in *The Paris Review* 41 (Summer–Fall, 1967), 96.

2 Appel, "An Interview with Vladimir Nabokov," 25.

3 As, for instance, in Nabokov's *Bend Sinister*.

4 William H. Gass, *Fiction and the Figures of Life* (New York: Vintage Books, 1972), 116.

5 Vladimir Nabokov, *Pnin* (New York: Avon Books, 1959), 167.

6 Other puns in his name: "Pun-neen" (*Pnin*, 26); "Think of the French word for 'tire': *punoo*" (Nabokov, *Pale Fire*, 268).

7 Andrew Field, *VN: The Life and Art of Vladimir Nabokov* (New York: Crown Publishers, 1986), 139.

8 *Pnin*, 133.

9 A number of critics have recently examined this aspect of the novel in greater detail, among them: Charles Nicol, "Pnin's History," *Novel* IV (3) (Spring, 1971), 197–208; Paul Grams, "*Pnin:* The Biographer as Meddler," *Russian Literature Triquarterly* 3 (Spring, 1972), 360–9.

10 Nabokov, *Pnin*, 16.

11 Ibid., 45.

12 Ibid., 181–2.

13 Ibid., 116.

14 Ibid., 180–1.

15 Ibid., 138.

16 Ibid., 168.

17 Ibid.

18 Ibid., 175.

19 Ibid., 178.

20 Ibid., 183.

21 Ibid., 52.

22 Ibid., 47.

23 Ibid., 171.

24 Ibid.

25 Ibid., 189–90.

26 Field, *The Life and Art of Vladimir Nabokov*, 132.

27 It seems that a certain "Vladimir Vladimirovich," an entomologist whose knowledge may be "merely a pose," is the narrator (*Pnin*, 127).

28 Cf. the reading of this scene by Julia Bader in *Crystal Land: Artifice in Nabokov's English Novels* (Berkeley, California: University of California Press, 1972), 86–8.

29 Nabokov, *The Defense* (New York: G. P. Putnam's Sons, 1964), 256.

30 Ibid., 57.

31 "Spy" is one of the possible synonyms for the Russian word which Nabokov eventually translated as *The Eye* (New York: Phaedra, 1965). Another possibility was "watcher" ("Foreword").

32 Discretion forbids entering the controversy over whether Shade, Kinbote, or Prof. Botkin is the "primary" narrator of *Pale Fire*.

32 "One of the few words which mean nothing without quotes": "On a Book Entitled *Lolita*," in Nabokov, *Lolita*, 314.

33 Rene Descartes, *The Philosophical Works of Descartes*, trans. E. S. Haldane and G. R. T. Ross (Cambridge: Cambridge University Press, 1968), 148.

34 Nabokov, *Pnin*, 23.

35 Ibid., 23.

36 Nabokov, *Ada* (New York: McGraw-Hill, 1969), 510.

37 As pointed out in the articles and books by Andrew Field, Julia Bader, Charles Nicol, and Paul Grams.

38 Nabokov, *Speak, Memory* (New York: G. P. Putnam's Sons, 1966), 27.

39 Nabokov, *Pnin*, 158.

40 Nabokov, *Speak, Memory*, 290.

41 Gass, *Fiction and the Figures of Life*, 116.

42 Nabokov, *Ada*, 426.

Pale Fire and "Signs and Symbols"
Vladimir Mylnikov

1 See "Cards" by P. Tammi (A151).

The signs and symbols in Nabokov's "Signs and Symbols"
Alexander Dolinin

1 Nabokov, *Selected Letters 1940–77*, 117.

2 Ibid.

3 See, for example, Hagopian, "Decoding 'Signs and Symbols,'" A298; Barabtarlo, "Five Missing Jars," A140.

4 Carroll, A236.

5 Malin, "Reading Madly," A277. See also Rosenzweig (A158), Andrews (A144), Richter (A224), Trzeciak (A143).

6 Wood, "Consulting the Oracle," A65.

7 Boris Tomashevsky, "Thematics," in *Russian Formalist Criticism: Four Essays*, trans. Lee T. Lemon and Marion J. Reis (Lincoln, Nebraska: University of Nebraska Press, 1965), 68.

8 Nabokov, *Selected Letters 1940–77*, 116–17.

9 *The Stories of Vladimir Nabokov* (New York: Alfred A. Knopf, 1995), 622.

10 Ibid., 622.

11 Ibid., 625.

12 See my paper "O nekotorykh angarammakh v tvorchestve Nabokova" in *Kul'tura russkoi diaspory: Nabokov—100* (Tallinn: TPU KIRJASTUS, 2000).

13 Ibid., 595–6.

14 Nabokov, *The Defense*, 597.

15 Andrews, A289. See also Tammi Pekka, *Problems of Nabokov's Poetics: A Narratological Analysis* (Helsinki: Suomalainen Tiedeakatemia, 1985), 344–5.

16 Nabokov, *The Defense*, 254.

17 Cf. also Nabokov's self-portrait in his poem "Fame" that, to quote his note, contains an allusion "to the sirin, a fabulous fowl of Slavic mythology, and 'Sirin,' the author's penname": "To myself I appear as an idol, a wizard / bird-headed, emerald gloved, dressed in tights / made of bright-blue scales" (Vladimir Nabokov, *Poems and Problems* [New York: McGraw-Hill, 1970], 105, 113).

18 It is interesting that in Mlle. le Normande's fortune-telling system, popular in Western Europe, the meaning of these cards is entirely different: the ace of spades represents a female inquirer, the nine of spades a successful voyage, faithfulness or illusions, and the knave of hearts love and happiness. See Mrs John King Van Rensselaer, *Prophetical, Educational and Playing Cards* (London: Hurst & Blackett, 1912), 369–72.

19 According to *The Penguin Dictionary of Symbols*, ten "possesses a sense of totality, of fulfillment and that of a return to oneness after the evolution of the cycle of the first nine digits. The Pythagoreans regarded ten as the holiest of numbers. It was the symbol of universal creation ... If all springs from ten and all returns to it, it is therefore also an image of totality in motion" (Jean Chevalier and Alain Cheerbrant, *A Dictionary of Symbols*, trans. from the French by John Buchanan-Brown [London and New York: Penguin Books, 1996], 981).

20 See, for example, Larry R. Andrews's strange idea that the jellies are linked to the parents' feelings of self-assurance and hence "are in some mysterious way a cause of the supposed death" (Andrews, "Deciphering 'Signs and Symbols,'" A286).

21 Barabtarlo, A141.

22 The choice of the word here is rather suggestive. Nabokov seems to play on several meanings of "spell out"—to read slowly and with difficulty, to find out by investigation, and to comprehend.

23 The man's name also hints at decoding, because Charlie is a communication code word for the letter C, which, in its turn, signifies a cipher or the numerical value of a cipher letter (for example O = 6).

24 The list of five jellies by itself looks rather artificial and because of that requires serious examination. Curiously enough, in all editions of the story there is a misprint in the third letter of the third label—*beech plum* instead of the correct *beach plum*—but it is impossible to tell whether this was intended or not. As Carol M. Dole observes, "the last letters of the four jellies in the list (aprico*t*, grap*e*, beec*h* plu*m*, quinc*e*) form the word *theme*" (Dole, "Five Known Jars," A137), but again this could be a coincidence. If it is indeed an anagram, one should not overlook the fact that last letters of *crab apple* would form the beginning of a word in an unfinished phrase—most probably *to be* (as an answer to Hamlet's question), *being* (the last word of section two), or *beyond*. It is tempting to conjecture something like "[the] theme's a beyond" using the last letters of a plausible list such as cherry, mango, lemon, guava, mixed berries.

25 Henry Wadsworth Longfellow, *Poetical Works in Six Volumes* (Boston: Houghton Mifflin, 1904), vol. 1, 21. The poem was inspired by Henry Vaughan's elegy "They are all gone into the world of light!," a meditation on "beauteous death" and after-life that could be a source for Nabokov's image of an "unfledged bird" under a tree that, as we can guess, fell out of its nest. Cf.: "He that hath found some fledged bird's nest, may know / At first sight, if the bird be flown; / But what fair well, or grove he sings in now, / That is to him unknown. // And yet, as Angels in some brighter dreams / Call to the soul, when man doth sleep: / So some strange thoughts transcend our wonted themes, / And into glory peep" (Henry Vaughan, *The Complete Poems* [London: Penguin Classics, 1995], 247).

26 See Wood, *The Magician's Doubts*, 72.

27 "Signs and Symbols" is not the first text by Nabokov in which a wrong number is connected to the theme of communication with the dead. In chapter 5 of *The Gift*, such a call triggers Fyodor's fatidic dream of his father's return. The next morning Fyodor finds out that "the luckless person who was getting their number by mistake, had rung up the previous night: this time he had been tremendously agitated, something had happened—something which remained unknown" (*The Gift*, 355–6).

The castling problem in "Signs and Symbols"

Yuri Leving

1 See his note to the story in 1976 collection, reprinted in *Stories*. A *selfmate* is a chess problem in which white, moving first, must force black to deliver checkmate within a specified number of moves against a player's will.

2 James Pierce and W. T. Pierce. *Pierce Gambit, Chess Papers and Problems* (London, 1888), 64.

3 "The story is a self-conscious and brilliantly constructed trap for interpreters, much like the chess problems that Nabokov loved to create ... 'Signs and Symbols' especially resembles a chess problem in its final gambit." Cf. also in Leona Toker's "'Signs and Symbols' in and out of contexts": "One of these characters is the mad chess player Luzhin in *The Defense*. He is alluded to in 'Signs and Symbols': the insane young man's cousin is 'a famous chess player'" (A211). A highly informative summary of the subject can be found in Janet Gezari's "Chess and Chess Problems" in ed. V. Alexandrov, *Garland Companion* (1995), 44–54.

4 According to Brian Boyd, who tried to reconcile two existing schools of thought (the "Shadeans" and the "Kinboteans"), Hazel's spirit has influenced both the composition of the poem by her father and its commentary by Kinbote (see in his *Pale Fire: The Magic of Artistic Discovery*). René Alladaye discusses the "ghost theory" and proposes an alternative authorship theory involving Shade's wife, Sybille ("Through the Looking-Glass—Pale Fire as Anamorphosis: An Alternative Theory of Internal Authorship," *Nabokov Online Journal* 6, 2012).

5 A. Dolinin, "Kak sdelana 'Lolita'" ["How *Lolita* is Made"], in V. Nabokov, *Lolita* (St. Petersburg: Vita Nova, 2004), 516–18. See also his "What Happened to Sally Horner?: A Real-Life Source of Nabokov's Lolita," *Zembla* (http://www.libraries.psu.edu/nabokov/dolilol.htm), accessed 12 October 2011.

6 *Cf.*: "This move, usually made in order to place the King in place of safety, and at the same time to bring Rook into play, must be made only once during the game" (Charles Kenny. *The Manual of Chess: Containing the Elementary Principles of the Game* [New York: D. Appleton and Company, 1859], 4).

7 Braj Raj Kishore. *Chess for Pleasure* (Dehli: Adarsh Printers, 2006), 50.

8 While the FIDE Handbook, appendix C.13, uses the digit zero (0-0 and 0-0-0), PGN (Portable Game Notation, 1993) requires the uppercase letter O (O-O and O-O-O). The Standard Algebraic Notation (SAN) movetext describing the game also uses the capital letter "O"s instead of numeral "0."

9 Jose R. Capablanca. *A Primer of Chess*, first published in 1935 by Harcourt, Inc., here quoted from the later edition (Boston: Houghton Mifflin Harcourt, 2002), 17, 21.

10 On Nabokov and Capablanca, see Brian Boyd, *Vladimir Nabokov: The Russian Years* (Princeton: Princeton University Press, 1990), 275. The poem, in Russian, is printed in *Sobranie sochinenii*, vol. 2, p. 559, with Y. Leving's commentary to this poem in the same volume, 738–9.

11 Etymology of the word was discussed in an intriguing linguistic analysis of the Russian chess terminology, long before Nabokov's birth. Based on his interviews with the members of the St. Petersburg chess club, the author maintained: "Do we wish for a philological but sure proof that up to Peter the Great, they did not castle in Russia? How is castling called in Russia? *rokirowat*, a word which has neither a grammatical Russian form or root, and which is directly taken from the German *rochiren*. The Russians have besides borrowed their laws from the Germans, their masters also in the military art" (*cf*. De Jaenisch. "Nomenclature of the Russian Chess Men," in ed. Howard Staunton, Esq., *The Chess Player's Chronicle*, vol. 13 [London: 1852], 370).

12 Ibid.

13 The most famous Morse signal is, no doubt, SOS ("··· — — — ···"), known as "save our souls," and it also entails a transcendental experience.

14 These military alphabets were in use during Nabokov's lifetime (until 1956); *cf*., for example, the Royal Navy 1914–18 (WWI): Apples, Butter, Charlie, Duff, Edward, Freddy, George, etc.; and of the U.S. phonetic alphabet (1941–56): Able, Baker, Charlie, Dog, Easy, Fox, George, etc.

15 Alexander Dolinin was the first to mention, although in passing, that "[t]he man's name also hints at decoding, because Charlie is a communication code word for the letter *c*." (Dolinin, A265, note A23).

16 So far the scholars focused on the significance of the number 6 [6 + 6; 6 + 6 +6 = 666 or 18, which, has been suggested, depending

on the desired interpretation, can mean either the sign of Satan and approaching Doom, or, quite the opposite, as a sign of Redemption in the Jewish Kabbalistic tradition of Gemmatria, where 18 also means "hai"/"Life."

17 *Cf.*: "With respect to the significance of the signs and symbols of the story, it is important to keep in mind that everything is presented from the point of view of the mother" (Hagopian, A300).

18 "It has long been known that schizophrenia runs in families. People who have a close relative with schizophrenia are more likely to develop the disorder than are people who have no relatives with the illness. A child whose parent has schizophrenia has about a 10 percent chance. By comparison, the risk of schizophrenia in the general population is about 1 percent" (Quoted in Leonard Holmes's "Causes of Schizophrenia," based on National Institutes of Mental Health articles and brochures on Schizophrenia. June 1, 2010 [http://mentalhealth.about.com/od/schizophrenia/a/sz2.htm]).

19 Y. Vorst. *Why? Reflections on the Loss of a Loved One.* Trans. from the Dutch. (New York: Kehot – Merkos, 2007), 27–8.

20 Ibid., 30.

21 Curiously, when Nabokov was asked in the 1970 interview "what is the meaning of life?" he resorted to the same combination of three zeroes in the context of chess: "For solutions see p. 000 (thus says a MS note in the edited typescript of my *Poems and Problems* which I have just received). In other words: Let us wait for the page proof" (Nabokov, *Strong Opinions*, 176).

Deciphering "Signs and Symbols"
Larry R. Andrews

1 I agree with William Carroll ("*Pnin* and 'Signs and Symbols,'" A236) on the deceptive nature of the symbols and omens in the story though not entirely on the ultimate relation of the reader to the author and the work. Furthermore, I attempt to give a fuller analysis of the story's image patterns and false clues than does Carroll.

2 *Cf.* Lawrence L. Lee, "Duplexity in Vladimir Nabokov's Short Stories," in *Studies in Short Fiction*, vol. 2 (1965), 307–15.

3 As Douglas Fowler puts it, "The mad young fantasts of the stories 'Lance' and 'Signs and Symbols' and Luzhin in *The Defense* create complicated second worlds—wholly subjective, yet both terrible and wonderful in the completeness and energy with which they are

endowed"; and later, "In Nabokov's world, fact kills, fantasy gives life" (*Reading Nabokov* [Ithaca: Cornell University Press, 1974], 161, 172). We note that the son has brilliant mental powers and considers himself superior to all other people.

4 Carroll, "*Pnin* and 'Signs and Symbols,'" A247.

5 Ibid., A249.

6 Nabokov, *Laughter in the Dark*, 143.

7 William Woodin Rowe, *Nabokov's Deceptive World* (New York: New York University Press, 1971), 82.

Decoding "Signs and Symbols"
John V. Hagopian

1 Carroll, "*Pnin* and 'Signs and Symbols,'" A245.

2 Rowe, *Nabokov's Deceptive World*, 80.

3 L. E. Hinslie, and R. J. Campbell, (eds), *Psychiatric Dictionary*, 3rd ed. (New York: Oxford University Press, 1960), 635.

4 Carroll, 208.

5 Nabokov, *Strong Opinions*, 305.

6 Carroll, 208.

7 Fowler, *Reading Nabokov*, 197.

8 Carroll, A248.

9 Nabokov, *Strong Opinions*, 69.

10 Carroll, A247.

11 Carroll, A248.

12 Nabokov, *Pale Fire*, lines 811–13.

13 John V. Hagopian, "Vladimir Nabokov," in *Dictionary of Literary Biography*, ed. J. Helterman and R. Layman (Detroit: Gale Research, 1978), 355.

The referential mania: an attempt of the deconstructivist reading
Álvaro Garrido Moreno

1 Quoted in Tony Tanner, *City of Words: A Study of American Fiction*

in the Mid-Twentieth Century (London: Jonathan Cape, 1971),
35. This reference turns out to be highly suitable here, for Tanner's
book was my first contact with Nabokov's fiction. I had not read
anything either *by* or *on* Nabokov before my former *liaison* with
Thomas S. Pynchon's work—particularly with *The Crying of Lot
49* and *V.*—*City of Words* being then an invaluable procurer. Hence
it is that my reading of "Signs and Symbols" is essentially shaped
by my biased knowledge of the postmodern condition, since the
totality of the critical work devoted to Nabokov's long narratives
and short stories considers "him" to be highly and decisively
influential in the work of writers like Pynchon, Heller, Burroughs,
or Mailer. However, since this paper started as an attempt to read
"Signs and Symbols" *a la* Yale School—no longer in Yale and never
a school—for a postgraduate seminar in a Spanish university, I am
not at all sure that terms like "postmodern" or "influence" prove
to be "suitable here." Moreover, the very nature of the writings of
Derrida, de Man, Miller, or Hartman makes it impossible to write in
a deconstructive way without betraying the deconstructive skeptic pull
and thereby becoming impossibly deconstructive, therefore inscribing
my attempt within a general economy—even in the institutional
sense—that prevents its fulfillment, thus *making it* always impossible.
Nevertheless, I would like to write in a *deconstructivist fashion*, to try
and write without and within some of the borders of the postmodern
shaping of my (mis)reading of "Signs and Symbols" that dramatize
some of the oppositions governing deconstructive texts. Although the
odds are against, it may "work."

2 Since I started from—and eventually reached—a state of complete
ignorance in order to describe Nabokov's (non)concept of
the relationships of consciousness, reality, and fiction, I must
acknowledge the sources of my paper: Boyd's *Vladimir Nabokov:
The Russian Years*; Laurie Clancy's *The Novels of Vladimir Nabokov*
(London: Macmillan, 1986); Beverly Lyon Clark's *Reflections on
Fantasy* (New York: Peter Lang Publishing, 1986); Peter L. Cooper's
Signs and Symptoms: Thomas Pynchon and the Contemporary World
(Berkeley: University of California Press, 1983). Equally important
to my reading are the texts produced by the *soi-disant* Yale School:
Jacques Derrida's *Of Grammatology* (Baltimore: Johns Hopkins
University Press 1977); Geoffrey H. Hartman's (ed.) *Deconstruction
and Criticism* (London: Routledge, 1979) and *Lectura y creación*,
trans. Xurxo Leboiro Amaro (Madrid: Tecnos, 1992); Paul de Man's
Blindness and Insight (London: Methuen, 1983) and *Allegories of
Reading* (New Haven: Yale University Press, 1979); J. Hillis Miller's,
The Ethics of Reading; Kant, de Man. Eliot, Trollope. James and

Benjamin (New York: University of Columbia Press, 19861990). However, these misreadings are nothing but my precarious trying-to-find-and-simply-agreeing-to some of the notions and themes suggestively posited in, within and around Jonathan Culler's *On Deconstruction* (London: Routledge, 1983); Christopher Norris's *Deconstruction: Theory and Practice* (London: Routledge, 1982); and William Ray's *Literary Meaning: From Phenomenology to Deconstruction* (Oxford: Blackwell, 1984). In fact, these last three books cooperated with my assumptions about modernism and postmodernism and about Nabokov's fiction in my reading of "Signs and Symbols"; actually, these two "groups" of readings co-operated *on* me while I was reading.

3 Tanner, *City of Words*, 33.

4 Nabokov, *Speak, Memory*, 95.

5 The term usually applied to this intertextual activity by many critics concerned with postmodern theory and literature is Hutcheon's *parody* (Linda Hutcheon, *A Theory of Parody* [London: Methuen, 1985]). Nabokov's narratives have often been portrayed by critical papers—if we consciously permit our commitment to seeking some pervasive unity of tone or theme in the whole work of an author, which is unpermissible—as essentially *parodic*—see Gass's remarks on Nabokov's parody of romance (William H. Gass, *La ficción y los personajes de la vida* [Buenos Aires: Juan Goyanarte, 1974], 139–42, 144–6). Clancy's statements on *Dar* as parody of Chernyshevski's *What is to be done?* (*The Novels of Vladimir Nabokov*, 15) or Tanner's commentaries on Nabokov's factual accumulation as a parodic device upon realism and naturalism (Tanner, *City of Words*, 37–8). However, I am not sure whether the word *parody* finds any appropriate place in a deconstructivistic reading, because the borders or limits of any text are much more problematic for me since I misread Culler's profitable *account* of the Derridadaic *Glas* (Culler, *On Deconstruction*, 134–56) and Derrida's "Living On: Border Lines" (Hartman [ed.], *Deconstruction and Criticism*, 75–176).

6 The basis of this affirmation rests on the effects of the sustaining figural implications of the metaphors of light and eyesight which permeate the texts of Western culture (Norris, *Deconstruction: Theory and Practice*, 81–3). Reading and visual perception are figurally related in my reading—as well as in "Signs and Symbols"—and underpin any (illusory) liability exhibited by this paper.

My intention in this re-mark is to sincerely acknowledge one of the tautening holes of my reading. However, to put all my argument under this note (or knot, and even nought), or under Tanner's quotes, or under this paraphrase of J. Hillis Miller, as if my contradictions were to be acknowledged and somehow exonerated here, is so far from innocent that it involves my argument and me at once in a dense tangle of assumptions and complicities, whether I want them or not, which will require an interminable disentangling.

7 Nabokov overtly exposed the recurrence of these themes in his brief introduction to the short story "Breaking the News" (1975): "'Breaking the News' appeared under the title of 'Opoveshchenie' ('Notification') in an émigré periodical around 1935 and was included in my collection *Soglyadatay* (*Russkie Zapiski*, Paris, 1938). The milieu and the theme both correspond to those of 'Signs and Symbols,' written ten years later in English (see *The New Yorker*, 15 May 1948, and *Nabokov's Dozen*, Doubleday 1958)."

8 Hartman, *Deconstruction and Criticism*, 271–3.

9 Clark, *Reflections of Fantasy*, 108–9.

10 Boyd, *Vladimir Nabokov: The Russian Years*, 292.

11 Nabokov, *Speak, Memory*, 119–20. This autobiography is shot through by similar passages reworking the dramatization of Nabokov's delight in and compulsion for observation; the paragraphs which recount his passionate activity as an entomologist (123–39) are remarkable, particularly the ones *narrating* his fondness for the specificity and concrete detail of microscopic observation (166–7).

12 Ibid., 138.

13 Nabokov, *Speak, Memory*, 139.

14 Cooper, *Signs and Symptoms*, 17.

15 Nabokov, *The Gift*, 549.

16 Nabokov, *Speak, Memory*, 290; my emphasis.

17 Clark, *Reflections of Fantasy*, 83.

18 *The Oxford English Dictionary* offers—among others—the following meanings of these two nouns:

Sign
1a.—A gesture or motion of the hand, head, etc. serving to convey an intimation or to communicate some idea.
1b.—A show or pretence *of* something.
1c. —A signal.
2.—A mark or device having some special meaning or import specially attached to it, or serving to distinguish the thing on which it is put.
2b.—A bookmark.

2c.—A conventional mark, device, or symbol, used technically (as in music, algebra, botany, etc.) in place of words or names written in ordinary letters.

3.—A mark of attestation (or ownership) written or stamped upon a document, seal, etc.

4.—A figure or image; a statue or effigy, an imprint.

5a.—A device born on a banner, shield, etc.; a cognizance or badge.

5b.—Something displayed as an emblem token; *esp.* an ensign, banner, standard.

5c.—A pilgrim's token.

5d.—Insignia.

6.—A characteristic device attached to, or placed in front of, an inn or shop, as a means of distinguishing it from others or directing attention to it; in later use commonly a board bearing a name or other inscriptions, with or without some ornament or picture.

7.—A token or indication (visible or otherwise) *of* some fact, quality, etc.

7d.—Trail or trace of wild animals, etc.

8.—A trace or indication *of* something; a vestige (chiefly in negative phrases).

8b.—A mere resemblance *of* something.

9.—An indication of some coming event; *spec,* an omen or portent.

10a.—An act of a miraculous nature, serving to demonstrate the divine power or authority.

10b.—A marvel or wonder.

11a.—*Astr.* One or other of the twelve divisions of the zodiac.

11b.—A constellation.

Symbol

1.—A formal authoritative statement or summary of the Religious belief in the Christian Church, or of a particular church or sect; a creed or confession of faith, *spec,* the Apostles' creed.

1b.—A brief or sententious statement; a formula, a motto, a maxim; *occas.* a summary, synopsis.

2a.—Something that stands for, represents, or denotes something else (not by exact resemblance, but by vague suggestion, or by some accidental and conventional relation); *esp.* a material object representing or taken to represent something immaterial or abstract, as a being, ideal, quality or condition; a representation or typical figure, sign or token, *occas.* a type (of some quality).

2b.—An object representing something sacred, *spec, (absol.*) either of the elements in the Eucharist, as representing the body and blood of Christ. (*Letter to Father Patrick*: The symbols become changed into the body and blood of Christ, after a sacramental, spiritual and real manner).

2c.—*Numism.* A small device in a coin, additional to and usually independent of the main device or type.

2d.—Symbols collectively; symbolism.

3.—A written character or mark used to represent something; a letter, figure or sign conventionally standing for some object, process, etc. *e.g.* the figures denoting the plants, signs of the Zodiac, etc., in Astronomy; the letters and other characters denoting elements, etc., in chemistry; quantities, operations, etc., in mathematics, the faces of crystal in crystallography.

These definitions unfold a complex span of criss-crossing references. Each one is contained within the other, which is to say that none contains the others. A sign is defined as symbol in 2c, and a symbol as sign in 3. These definitions run really close together, since they define signs and symbols as *conventional* (that is, whose use is agreed upon and common among a group, but which has no other basis for its existence but this agreement and communal character) *marks,* that is, writing, "scribbling." However there is some disparity within this apparent coincidence. On the one hand, a sign is used technically (as in music, algebra, botany, etc.) in *place of words and names written in ordinary letters,* in place of other conventional marks. A sign is a symbol used specifically (and conventionally) to replace other ordinary or average marks that belong to the whole community by means of conventional marks which are specific to a group, that is ordinary or average within this group. This (un)definition—which is nothing *other* than the attempt to translate one word into a sequence formed of any terms other than itself—unfolds itself through a series of repetitions brought about by the tyranny of the term *conventional*: any conventional mark is always already a conventional mark which replaces conventional marks. In addition to this, symbol is equated by SIGN 2c with mark and device (this last term, as I read it, contains the narrative of the use of the mark). On the other hand, symbol in 3 is a written character or letter used to *represent* something; *a letter, figure or sign conventionally standing for some object, process, etc.* The referential scope is strikingly (even transcendentally) different there; symbols are signs (no longer signs; signs forced to an estrangement) or conventional marks standing for objects, processes, etc., and no longer in place of other ordinary conventional marks. The terms "represent" and "stand for" (*instead of* "used technically in place of") point to the basic disparate feature: symbols are, as it were, performers, delegates of some utterly different mode of existence—whereas signs were conventional replacements among equally conventional modes of existence. Signs were caught up in an endless process of self-reference, while symbols are veiled references to something other, something immaterial or abstract, as a being, idea, quality or condition. This sense is essential in all the meanings *The Oxford English Dictionary* offers for symbol: symbols usually refer religious dogma, *truths,* they are reflections or expressions of the *logos* (*vgr.,* l.la, 2a); on one occasion (2b), these symbols are intimately connected with transcendence, becoming changed into the body and blood of Christ.

There remain also, as I conceive it, some other basic (seemingly) distinctive features. All the meanings offered for the word *sign* share the notion of a mark attached for technical uses, as a result of a deliberate act of stamping, printing, or imprinting in order to distinguish the object or referent from the others, basically through the inscription of one's relation to this object. As for the word *symbol,* this relationship seems to be given (and not deliberately attached), dictated by some utterly different design, by the obedience to a founding *logos* which can only present itself through representation by symbols—which is definitely complicated by the fictional character pointed to by the sequences "formal authoritative statement or *summary*" and "a formula, a motto, a maxim; *occas.* a *summary,* a synopsis." This divergence vanishes, or rather becomes unreadable, when we read in SIGN 9, 10a and 10b, that the intimacy with some transcendental otherness also inhabits the nooks and noughts (and notes) of the word "sign," or when we read in SIGN 11 how this conventional mark, when born on a banner or a flag also stands for something immaterial or abstract, as a being, idea or quality, or else when we read in SYMBOL 3 that this conventional mark is also conventionally used among disciplines (including and included in SIGN 2c, 11a and 11b). The apparent disparity between these two terms appears to be groundless in "Signs and Symbols," though neither "Signs and Symbols" nor my reading can avoid its constant inscription. The words *sign* and *symbol* form (without forming) a dense tangle of allusions which is at once tangled and disentangled by their definitions in a dictionary, whose expression is, it may be, the odd relationship they maintain in the title "Signs and Symbols," where they are linked by "and," and at the same time separated by this "and" which abolishes any identity between the two.

19 Which, tempted by a "referential de Mania" for contingent riddling phonetic associations and considering who this "me" is—a Spanish student writing his essay for an English graduate seminar— foreshadows a rather gloomy future for me. This somehow affirms in "Signs and Symbols" the (un)definition of life as the constant loss of

mere possibilities of improvement, or as J. Hillis Miller reads this: "To live is to read, or rather to commit again and again the failure which is the human lot" (*The Ethics of Reading*, 67).

A referential reading of Nabokov's "Signs and Symbols"
Charles W. Mignon

1 *Vladimir Nabokov, Lectures on Literature* (New York: Harcourt Brace Jovanovich, 1980), 2.

2 Ibid.

3 Hagopian, "Decoding 'Signs and Symbols,'" A298.

4 Rosenzweig, "The Importance of Reader Response," A162.

5 Ibid, A162.

6 Field, A181.

7 Herbert Ginsburg and Sylvia Opper, *Piaget's Theory of Intellectual Development*, 2nd ed. (Englewood Cliffs, New Jersey: Prentice-Hall, 1979), 19.

8 Jean Piaget, "Development and Learning," *Journal of Research in Science Teaching* vol. 2 (1964), 178.

9 Ibid., 181.

10 Hagopian A299.

11 A162.

12 Ibid., A159.

ALTERNATIVE TABLES OF CONTENTS

Chronological key

Alphabetical key

CREDITS

BIBLIOGRAPHY

Alexandrov, Vladimir E. *Nabokov's Otherworld* (Princeton: Princeton University Press, 1991).

—*The Garland Companion to Vladimir Nabokov*, ed. V. Alexandrov (New York and London: Garland, 1995).

Alladaye, René. "Through the Looking-Glass—*Pale Fire* as Anamorphosis: An Alternative Theory of Internal Authorship," *Nabokov Online Journal* 6 (2012).

Alter, Robert. *Motives for Fiction* (Cambridge, Massachusetts and London: Harvard University Press, 1984).

Amandry, Pierre. *La Mantique apollonienne a Delphes* (Paris: 1950).

Appel, Jr., Alfred. "An Interview with Vladimir Nabokov," in ed. L. S. Dembo, *Nabokov: The Man and His Work* (Madison, Wisconsin: University of Wisconsin Press, 1967).

Appel, Jr., Alfred, and Charles Newman. *Nabokov: Criticism, Reminiscences, Translations and Tributes* (Evanston: Northwestern University Press, 1970).

Austin, J. L. *Sense and Sensibilia* (Oxford: Clarendon, 1962).

Barabtarlo, Gennady. "Nabokov's Little Tragedies (English Short Stories)," in *Aerial View: Essays on Nabokov's Art and Metaphysics* (New York: Peter Lang, 1993).

Barthes, R. *Camera Lucida*, trans. Richard Howard (London: Flamingo, 1980/1984).

Benjamin, Walter. *Walter Benjamin: Selected Writings, Volume 3; Volumes 1935–8* (Harvard: Harvard University Press, 2002).

Booth, Wayne C. *A Rhetoric of Irony* (Chicago: University of Chicago Press, 1974).

Booth, W. C. and D. C. Muecke. "The Reader as Ironic Victim," *Novel* 14 (1981), 135–51.

Borges, Jorge Luis. "Narrative Art and Magic," in *Triquarterly* 25 (Fall 1972), 209–15.

Boyd, Brian. *Vladimir Nabokov: The American Years* (Princeton: Princeton University Press, 1991).

—*Vladimir Nabokov: The Russian Years* (Princeton: Princeton University Press, 1990).

—*Nabokov's Pale Fire: The Magic of Artistic Discovery* (Princeton, NJ: Princeton University Press, 1999).

Buck-Morss, Susan. *The Dialectics of Seeing: Walter Benjamin and the Arcades Project* (Cambridge, Massachusetts and London: MIT Press, 1991).

Capablanca, Jose R. *A Primer of Chess* (Boston: Houghton Mifflin Harcourt, 2002).

Cavell, Stanley. "Knowing and Acknowledging," in *Must We Mean What We Say?* (Cambridge: Cambridge University Press, 1976), 238–66.

Chevalier, Jean and Alain Cheerbrant. *A Dictionary of Symbols*, trans. John Buchanan-Brown (London: Penguin Books, 1996).

Clancy, Laurie. *The Novels of Vladimir Nabokov* (London: Macmillan, 1986).

Clark, Beverly Lyon. *Reflections of Fantasy* (New York: Peter Lang Publishing, 1986).

Connolly, Julian W. *Nabokov's Early Fiction: Patterns of Self and Other* (Cambridge: Cambridge University Press, 1992).

Cooper, Peter L. *Signs and Symptoms: Thomas Pynchon and the Contemporary World* (Berkeley: University of California Press, 1983).

Crahay, Roland. *La Litterature oraculaire chez Hirodote* (Paris: 1956).

Crossley, John N. *Growing Ideas of Number* (Camberwell, Australia: Australian Council for Educational Research, 2007).

Culler, Jonathan. *On Deconstruction* (London: Routledge, 1983).

Davies, Norman. *Europa*, trans. Elzbieta Tabakowska (Krakow: Wydawnictwo Znak, 1999).

De Man, Paul. *Allegories of Reading* (New Haven: Yale University Press, 1979).

—*Blindness and Insight* (London: Methuen, 1983).

Derrida, Jacques. *Of Grammatology*, trans. Gayatry Chakravorty Spivak (Baltimore: Johns Hopkins University Press, 1977).

—"Structure, Sign, and Play in the Discourse of the Human Sciences" in (eds). Joseph Natoli and Linda Hutcheon, *A Postmodern Reader*, (Albany: State University of New York Press, 1993), 223–42.

Descartes, Rene. *The Philosophical Works of Descartes*, trans. E. S. Haldane and G. R. T. Ross (Cambridge: Cambridge University Press, 1968).

Dolinin, Alexander. "Kak sdelana 'Lolita'" ["How *Lolita* is Made"], in V. Nabokov. *Lolita* (St. Petersburg: Vita Nova, 2004), 516–18.

—"What Happened to Sally Horner?: A Real-Life Source of Nabokov's *Lolita*," *Zembla* (http://www.libraries.psu.edu/nabokov/dolilol.htm).

Durantaye, Leland de la. "The Pattern of Cruelty and the Cruelty of Pattern in Vladimir Nabokov," *Cambridge Quarterly* 35 (4) (2006), 301–26.

Eco, Umberto. *"Lector in Fabula" in The Role of the Reader* (Bloomington: Indiana University Press, 1979).

Ferguson, George. *Signs and Symbols in Christian Art* (New York: Oxford University Press, 1961).

Field, Andrew. *VN: The Life and Art of Vladimir Nabokov* (New York: Crown Publishers, 1986).

Fletcher, Angus J. S. *Allegory, the Theory of a Symbolic Mode* (Ithaca, New York: Cornell University Press, 1964).

Fontenrose, Joseph. *The Delphic Oracle* (Berkeley: University of California Press, 1978).

Fowler, Douglas. *Reading Nabokov* (Ithaca: Cornell University Press, 1974).

Gass, William H. *Fiction and the Figures of Life* (New York: Vintage Books, 1972).

—*La ficción y los personajes de la vida* (Buenos Aires: Juan Goyanarte, 1974).

Gezari, Janet. "Chess and Chess Problems" in *The Garland Companion to Vladimir Nabokov*, ed. V. Alexandrov (New York and London: Garland, 1995), 44–54.

Gibson, Walter S. *Breughel* (New York: Oxford University Press, 1977).

Ginsburg, Herbert and Sylvia Opper. *Piaget's Theory of Intellectual Development*, 2nd ed. (Englewood Cliffs, New Jersey: Prentice-Hall, 1979).

Graham, Keith. *J. L. Austin: A Critique of Ordinary Language Philosophy* (New York: Harvester Press, 1977).

Grayson, Jane. *Illustrated Lives: Vladimir Nabokov* (London: Penguin, 2001).

Gregory, Richard Langton and Oliver Louis Zangwill. *The Oxford Companion to The Mind* (Oxford: 1987).

Guetti, James. "Aggressive Reading: Detective Fiction and Realistic Narrative," *Raritan: A Quarterly Review* 2.1 (1982), 133–54.

—"Vladimir Nabokov," in (eds). J. Helterman and R. Layman, *Dictionary of Literary Biography* (Detroit: Gale Research, 1978).

Harrison, Barbara. "Photographic Visions and Narrative Inquiry" in (eds). Michael Bamberg and Molly Andrews, *Considering Counter-Narratives: Narrating, Resisting, Making Sense* (Amsterdam: John Benjamin Publishing Company, 2004), 113–36.

Hartman, Geoffrey H. *Lectura y creación*, trans. Xurxo Leboiro Amaro (Madrid: Tecnos, 1992).

—ed. *Deconstruction and Criticism* (London: Routledge, 1979).

Heidegger, Martin. *Nietzsche: Volume IV—Nihilism*, trans. Frank A. Capuzzi (Verlag Gunther Neske, Pfullingen, 1962, rpt. San Francisco: Harper and Row, 1982).

Herodotus. *The Histories*, trans. Aubrey de Sélincourt (Harmondsworth: Penguin, 1954).

Hinslie, L. E. and R. J. Campbell, eds. *Psychiatric Dictionary*, 3rd ed. (New York: Oxford University Press, 1960).

Hutcheon, Linda. *A Theory of Parody* (London: Methuen, 1985).

Hyde, G. M. *Vladimir Nabokov* (London: Marion Boyars, 1977).

Iser, Wolfgang. *The Implied Reader: Patterns of Communication in Prose Fiction from Bunyan to Beckett* (Baltimore, Maryland: Johns Hopkins University Press, 1974).

—*The Act of Reading: A Theory of Aesthetic Response* (Baltimore, Maryland: Johns Hopkins University Press, 1980).

Jacobi, J. *Complex, Archetype, Symbol in the Psychology of C. G. Jung* (Princeton, New Jersey: Princeton University Press, 1974).

Jaenisch, C. F. De. "Nomenclature of the Russian Chess Men" in ed. Howard Staunton, Esq., *The Chess Player's Chronicle* Vol. 13 (London: 1852).

Jauss, Hans Robert. *Aesthetic Experience and Literary Hermeneutics*, trans. Michael Shaw (Minneapolis: University of Minnesota Press, 1982).

Jeromson, Barry. *Jung and Mathematics in Dialogue: A Critical Study* (PhD diss., University of South Australia, 1999).

Johnson, D. Barton. *Worlds in Regression: Some Novels of Vladimir Nabokov* (Ann Arbor, Michigan: Ardis, 1985).

Johnson, Roy. *Nabokov Tutorials*—"Signs and Symbols" (Roy Johnson, 2009), http://www.mantex.co.uk/2009/09/26/signs-and-symbols/.

Jung, Carl Gustav, Joseph L. Henderson, Marie-Louise von Franz, Aniela Jaffé, and Jolande Jacobi. *Man and his Symbols*, 13th ed. (Zürich, Düsseldorf: Walter-Verlag, 1968).

Kaplan, Robert. *The Nothing That Is: A Natural History of Zero* (Oxford: Oxford University Press, 1999).

Kenny, Charles. *The Manual of Chess: Containing the Elementary Principles of the Game* (New York: D. Appleton and Company, 1859).

Kierkegaard, Søren. *On Authority and Revelation*, trans. Walter Lowrie (Princeton: Princeton University Press, 1955).

Kishore, Braj Raj. *Chess for Pleasure* (Dehli: Adarsh Printers, 2006).

Lee, Lawrence L. "Duplexity in Vladimir Nabokoy's Short Stories," in *Studies in Short Fiction*, Vol. 2 (1965).

—*Vladimir Nabokov* (Boston: Twayne Publishers, 1976).

Leving, Yuri. *Keys to The Gift* (Boston: Academic Studies Press, 2011).

Longfellow, Henry Wadsworth. *Poetical Works in Six Volumes*, Vol. I (Boston: Houghton Mifflin, 1904).

Maclntyre, Alasdair. *After Virtue*, trans. Catrinel Plesu (Bucuresti: Humanitas, 1981/1998), 232–48.

Meyer, Priscilla. *Find What the Sailor Has Hidden: Vladimir Nabokov's Pale Fire* (Middletown, Conn.: Wesleyan University Press, 1988).

Miller, J. Hillis. *The Ethics of Reading: Kant, de Man, Eliot, Trollope, James and Benjamin* (New York: University of Columbia Press, 1986).

Morton, Donald E. *Vladimir Nabokov* (New York: Frederick Ungar Publishing Company, 1973).

Nabokov, Vladimir. *Ada, or Ardor: A Family Chronicle* (New York: Vintage International, 1990).

—*A Russian Beauty and Other Stories* (New York: McGraw-Hill, 1973).

—*Bend Sinister* (London: Penguin Classics, 2001).

—"Conversation Piece," in *The Stories of Vladimir Nabokov* (London: Orion/Weidenfield & Nicholson, 1945).

—*The Defense* (New York: Vintage International, 1990).

—Aleksandr Sergeevich Pushkin. *Eugene Onegin: A Novel in Verse*, commentary and translation by Vladimir Nabokov. (Princeton: Princeton University Press, 1991).

—*The Gift* (New York: Vintage International, 1991).

—*Invitation to a Beheading* (New York: Vintage International, 1989).

—*Laughter in the Dark* (New York: Vintage International, 1989).

—*Lectures on Literature*. Introduction by John Updike. Ed. by Fredson Bowers (New York: Harcourt, 1980).

—*Lectures on Russian Literature*, ed. Fredson Bowers (New York, 1981).

—*Lolita* (New York: Vintage Books, 1991).

—*Look at the Harlequins!* (New York: Vintage International, 1990).

—*The Nabokov–Wilson Letters*, 1940–71, ed. Simon Karlinsky (New York: Harper and Row, 1979).

—*Nikolai Gogol* (New York: New Directions Publishing, 1961).

—"Opoveshchenie," in *Soglyadatay* (Paris: Russkie Zapiski, 1938).

—*Pale Fire* (New York: Vintage International, 1989).

—*Perepiska s sestroi.* [Correspondence with his sister, Elena Sikorskaya] (Ann Arbor: Ardis, 1985).

—*Pnin* (New York: Vintage International, 1989).

—*Poems and Problems* (New York: McGraw-Hill, 1970).

—*The Real Life of Sebastian Knight* (New York: Vintage International, 1992).

—"The Tragedy of Tragedy" in: *The man from the USSR and other plays*: with two essays on the drama. Introd. and trans. by Dmitri

Nabokov (New York, San Diego: Bruccoli Clark / Harcourt Brace
    Jovanovich Publishers, 1984).
—*Selected Letters 1940–77*, Ed. Dmitri Nabokov and Matthew J.
    Bruccoli (San Diego: Harcourt Brace Jovanovich, 1989).
—*Speak, Memory* (New York: Vintage International, 1989).
—*Speak, Memory* (London: Weidenfeld and Nicolson, 1967).
— "Spring in Fialta," in *The Stories of Vladimir Nabokov* (London:
    Orion/Weidenfeld & Nicholson, 1945).
—*The Stories of Vladimir Nabokov* (New York: Vintage International,
    1997).
—*Sobranie sochinenii russkogo perioda v 5 tt.* (St. Petersburg:
    Symposium, 1999–2001), Vol. 2.
—*Strong Opinions* (New York, St. Louis, San Francisco, and Toronto:
    McGraw-Hill, 1973).
— "Symbols and Signs," in *The New Yorker* 24 (May 15 1948),
    31–3.
—*Transparent Things* (New York: Vintage International, 1990).
— "Ultima Thule," in *The Stories of Vladimir Nabokov* (New York:
    Vintage International, 1995), 500–21.
— "The Vane Sisters," in *The Stories of Vladimir Nabokov* (New York:
    Vintage International, 1997).
— "Vasily Shishkov," in *The Stories of Vladimir Nabokov* (London:
    Orion/Weidenfield & Nicholson, 1945).
— "Vladimir Nabokov: An Interview," in *The Paris Review* 41 (Summer–
    Fall, 1967).
Nietzsche, Friedrich Wilhelm. "The Birth of Tragedy," in *Basic Writings
    of Nietzsche*, trans. Walter Kaufmann (New York: Random House,
    1968).
Norris, Christopher. *Deconstruction: Theory and Practice* (London:
    Routledge, 1982).
Parke, H. W. and D. E. W. Wormell. *The Delphic Oracle*, vol. n (Oxford:
    Blackwell, 1956).
Parker, Stephan Jan. *Understanding Vladimir Nabokov* (University of
    South Carolina Press, 1987).
Piaget, Jean. "Development and Learning," *Journal of Research in
    Science Teaching* vol. 2 (1964), 176–86.
Pierce, James and W. T. Pierce. *Pierce Gambit, Chess Papers and
    Problems* (London: 1888).
Pifer, Ellen. *Nabokov and the Novel* (Cambridge, Massachusetts:
    Harvard University Press, 1980).
Plutarque. *Oeuvres morales*, tome VI (Paris: 1974).
Proffer, Carl R., ed. *A Book of Things about Vladimir Nabokov* (Ann
    Arbor: Ardis, 1974).

Pushkin, Alexander. *The Complete Prose Tales of Alexander Sergeyevitch Pushkin*, trans. Gillon R. Aitken (New York: Norton, 1966).

Pynchon, Thomas. *V.* (New York: Bantam Books, 1963).

Raphaelian, H. M. *Signs of Life* (New York: Anatol Sivas, 1957).

Ray, William. *Literary Meaning: From Phenomenology to Deconstruction* (Oxford: Blackwell, 1984).

Rensselaer, John King Van. *Prophetical, Educational and Playing Cards* (London: Hurst & Blackett, 1912).

Ronell, Avital. *The Telephone Book* (Lincoln, Nebraska and London: University of Nebraska Press, 1989).

Rowe, W. W. *Nabokov's Deceptive World* (New York: New York University Press, 1971).

Seife, Charles. *Zero: The Biography of a Dangerous Idea* (New York: Penguin Books, 2000).

Serres, Michel. *The Birth of Physics*, trans. Jack Hawkes, ed. David Webb (Manchester: Clinamen Press, 2000).

Stegner, Page. *Escape into Aesthetics: The Art of Vladimir Nabokov* (New York: Dial Press, 1966).

Tabbi, Joseph and Michael Wutz, eds. *Reading Matters: Narratives in the New Media Ecology* (Ithaca, New York: Cornell University Press, 1997).

Tammi, Pekka. *Problems of Nabokov's Poetics: A Narratological Analysis* (Helsinki: Suomalainen Tiedeakatemia, 1985).

Tanner, Tony. *City of Words: A Study of American Fiction in the Mid-Twentieth Century* (London: Jonathan Cape, 1971).

Tomashevsky, Boris. "Thematics," in *Russian Formalist Criticism: Four Essays*, trans. Lee T. Lemon and Marion J. Reis (Lincoln, Nebraska: University of Nebraska Press, 1965).

Trzeciak, Joanna. "Signs and Symbols and Silentology" in ed. Gavriel Shapiro, *Nabokov at Cornell* (Ithaca, New York: Cornell University Press, 2003).

Turner, Victor. "Betwixt and Between: The Liminal Period in Rites de Passage," in *The Forest of Symbols: Aspects of Ndembu Ritual* (Ithaca, New York: Cornell University Press, 1976), 93–111.

Voronina, Olga. "Vladimir Nabokov v zhurnale New Yorker," in *Zvezda*, vol. 4 (2005), 126–42.

Vorst, Yitzchak. *Why? Reflections on the Loss of a Loved One* (New York: Kehot – Merkos, 2007).

Waugh, Patricia. *Metafiction: The Theory and Practice of Self-Conscious Fiction* (New York: Routledge, 1990).

Webster's New International Dictionary, 2nd ed., unabridged (Springfield, Massachusetts: A: C. G. Merriam, 1944).

Williams, Carol T. "Nabokov's Dozen Short Stories: His World in
Microcosm," *Studies in Short Fiction* 12 (Summer 1975), 213–22.
Wood, Michael. *The Magician's Doubts: Nabokov and the Risks of
Fiction* (London: Chatto and Windus, 1994).

INDEX

7256243